ANDES
TO THE
AMAZON

ANDES TO THE AMAZON

Seven Journeys in Mexico, Central and South America

BRUCE B. JUNEK

Photographs by
Tass Thacker

An
Images of the World
Book

www.imagesoftheworld.com

Images of the World was created by the husband and wife team of Bruce Junek and Tass Thacker to promote awareness of the world's cultures, respect for the earth's environment, and to encourage individual achievement and growth in all people.

To order additional **Images of the World** books see page 333.

For **Images of the World** slide programs see page 332.

Images of the World
PO Box 2103
Rapid City, SD 57709-2103

www.imagesoftheworld.com

Printed in Boulder, Colorado on recycled paper

Copyright © 1999 by Bruce B. Junek

All photographs © by Tass Thacker, except pages 6, 26, 105, 120, 135, 149, 155, 159, 166, 179, 189, 197, 203, 222, 256, 270, 282, 318, 320, 323 © by Bruce Junek.

PHOTOS ON COVER (Clockwise from center): Bruce with friends in the Andes, Ecuador; Fuego volcano, Guatemala; Scarlet Macaw, Costa Rica; Humpback Whale, Baja; Mayan statue, Palenque, Mexico. Background plant: Saw Palmetto, Mexico. Spine photo: Tree Frog, Peru.

Library of Congress: 99-94596

ISBN 0-9630448-2-6

For Tass, who is my jokester, best friend, soulmate, and One True Love.

Contents

Introduction

Traveling in Latin America has always had romantic appeal: warm climates, tropical beaches, the mystique of ancient cultures—Mayan and Incan ruins—along with the thrill of banditos, guerrillas, and military dictatorships.

Tass and I first traveled in Central America in 1977. We hitch-hiked from South Dakota to Mexico and took third class trains and buses through the Yucatan and into Guatemala. We traveled over six months on less that $1200. Since then we have gone south of the border seven times, although never again quite so cheaply.

Each trip was a unique adventure. Each trip planted the idea and inevitability for later journeys. This then is a journal of beginnings. A tale of unfinished business.

This book covers a period of more than twenty years. Although the first sections were written strictly from memory, the entire book is formatted, like my later journals, in the present tense, placing the reader (and the author) in the same time period as the action. **Andes to the Amazon** is not a reflective memoir, but an adventure, which unfolds step by step.

I would like to thank all the people who read **The Road of Dreams** and continually urged me to keep writing. A special thanks to Dugan and my sister, Bobbi Looney, who edited and proof-read the manuscript—both have encouraged and respected my writing, even when I chose to occasionally follow my own rules of grammar. Michelle Vallery at GVS helped with the cover layout. Les Heiserman did the maps. Thanks also to our sponsors: Trek Bicycles, Patagonia clothing, Walrus tents, Madden panniers, MSR stoves and water filters, EagleCreek travel luggage, and Powerbars energy food.

Part I
1976-77

NOGALES

TEXAS

MEXICO

SAN FELIPE

ISLA MUJERES
CANCUN

MERIDA   CHICHEN ITZA

UXMAL
KABAH   TULUM

MEXICO

PALENQUE
SAN CRISTOBAL de
LAS CASAS

GUATEMALA
HUEHUETENANGO

SOLOLA
LAKE DE PANAJACHEL
ATITLAN

HONDURAS

EL
SALVADOR

1

The Way of a Pilgrim

I meet Tass Thacker in Jackson, Wyoming. Like me, she grew up in the Black Hills of South Dakota and moved to Jackson Hole for skiing and adventuring. Tass has been a ski bum in Jackson for four years, living variously in a trailer, a garage, and now sharing a cabin with three roommates. She had been a waitress, a laborer, a maid, and even tied fishing flies for a local outfitter. Now she is a baker at Bru's Buns and Breads.

I am twenty-two, two years younger, and have been in Jackson only a year. It is the spring of 1975 and I am learning to kayak. I launch a brief and lucrative business making fiberglass whitewater kayaks with my friend Chuck Auchterlonie in a backyard garage. Whenever possible we take breaks from resin madness, escape the noxious fumes from the curing kayaks, and head to the bakery to consume mass quantities of baked delights. During the summer we make twenty-six kayaks and become regulars at the bakery.

One late August afternoon between mouthfuls of Sweety Buns, I invite Tass on a two-day climb of the South Teton. The night of the climb we camp near the summit. We cuddle up to each other in our sleeping bags. The stars shine brightly in the sky. The temperature is too cold for romance—we don't even kiss—but the night is romantic nonetheless. By the end of the climb we feel a mutual respect, and a strong chemistry. Within a week we are inseparable, living between Tass's cabin near the bakery and my tipi on the Snake River.

Tass traveled the previous winter with her friend Suzanne Martell in South America, and two years before, I traveled overland across Africa with my sister, Bobbi. Amazingly, Tass and I have both separately been planning and saving for a trip to Central America after Christmas. Now everything seems pre-ordained that we will do the trip together. Our plan is to drive back to South Dakota to spend Christmas with our families, then store all our belongings, hitchhike to Mexico, and travel on trains and buses through the Yucatan and Guatemala.

In mid-December we take down my double-walled tipi. The ground is frozen solid around the tent stakes at the bottom of the tipi. We use a hatchet to chip away the ice to remove the stakes. We load the wood stove that kept us warm into the home-made plywood camper I built on the back of Jenny, my 1949 Jeep truck. All our belongings fit in the back of the camper, with the stiff, frozen tipi folded and stuffed inside. Our kayaks, skis, and tipi poles are lashed on top.

Our winterized tipi on the bank of the Snake river,
Jackson, Wyoming.

The normal nine hour drive from Jackson to the Black Hills takes us eighteen hours. Jenny usually has a top speed of fifty-five miles per hour. Overloaded with everything we own, she has trouble hitting forty, and slows to twenty and even fifteen on the steep pass leaving Jackson and crossing the Big Horn mountains. A ground blizzard sends swirling snow across the road. The temperature hovers around zero.

Jenny doesn't have a heater, or a defroster. We huddle inside the cab wearing long underwear, wool pants, heavy sweaters, down coats, and felt-lined Sorel boots, with down sleeping bags pulled over us like blankets. We do the work of the defroster by constantly using the scraper to remove the ice from both the inside and outside of the windows. The eight-track tape deck is so frozen the music plays at quarter speed. The radio has power to pick up only an occasional rural channel. We chat and listen to the howling wind blowing snow through the cracks in the floor and around the doors.

We spend Christmas with our families, store Jenny with everything loaded inside, and catch a lift from a friend to the highway leaving town. We carry enough food to hitch-hike to the Mexican border, and plan to camp hidden beside the road each night. We each have six hundred dollars in travelers checks, and hope to travel six months.

In our previous travels we learned that a shortage of funds isn't an insurmountable obstacle to going anywhere. We simply adjust our style of travel to the reality of our pocketbooks. Far from being a drag, we find extreme budget travel ultimately makes the journey a much more interesting adventure.

Both of us have hitched extensively in the past, Tass from Florida to Wyoming and throughout the Rocky Mountains, and I twice roundtrip from South Dakota to the east coast. Together we have hitching down to a science. We always try to stand where the cars aren't going too fast and can safely pull over to the side of the road. Tass stands in front with me smiling behind, our backpacks at our feet to show we are travelers, yet stacked so they don't appear too big.

Still, we sometimes wait for hours for a ride. During slow periods we develop a number of goofy routines out on desolate highways, trying to get cars driving seventy-five miles an hour to slow down and pick us up. Our most comical attempt starts in a low, forward crouch, thumb hand forward with the universal hitchhike signal. As the car comes down the road we dramatically shake and draw the thumb hand back, past our now standing bodies, and then beyond, until the thumb hand is way over our heads, up in the air behind us, at the end of a ten-foot arc. People don't always stop, but many honk and smile in enthusiasm.

After three days we arrive in Tucson, where my aunt and uncle, Pat and Arch Cosgrove, run a hotel. They treat us like royalty and give us a complimentary room. We enjoy a few restful days by the pool.

We hitch the last sixty miles to Mexico, cross the border, and catch a city bus to the train station. Mexican trains have first- and second-class coaches. We can't afford either, even though they are very cheap compared to U.S. rates. A separate third-class train runs at rock bottom prices, stopping at every little station, taking any load, and often sitting on the side tracks when faster trains pass through.

The first leg of the third-class journey, from Nogales to Guadalajara, is supposed to take thirty-six hours. The initial challenge is getting a seat. We find ourselves squeezed with three other people on a bench designed for two. The seats are wooden slats. No armrests, no padding. Those who board after us stand in the crowded aisles.

At every stop hawkers jump aboard the train and somehow make their way up and down the crowded isles selling tasty *empanadas,** *tortas, quesadillas,* and sodas. Once they learn we are vegetarians our fellow passengers point out which foods we can eat, and recommend various dishes. Although we have brought bread, cheese and fruit, we can't help trying the food. We each get a tasty meal for less than ten cents. Despite the low prices of the food, the *campesinos,* the poor farmers all around us, buy little. They have their own food, which they also offer to share.

Everyone is interested in what we are doing and where we are going. We chat amiably. They ask in Spanish, if this is our first time in Mexico? Do we like the scenery? Do we like Mexican food? Tass, who spent the previous winter in South America, translates everything while I practice repeating what she says.

After eating, everyone throws litter on the floor, or out the train window. We carefully keep all our trash in a plastic bag between our feet. The windows require a Herculean effort to open or close, so whichever they are, open or closed, they seem to stay that way. Most windows are open, which is best, as it is very hot with everyone packed together. An assortment of chickens, pigs, and goats also ride along. The smaller animals ride in boxes in peoples laps, the larger ones are kept tied up in the aisles or at the end of each coach.

Each of the train cars has just one bathroom. The toilet has no tank or water. I look into it and see a hole straight to the tracks below. Signs ask passengers not to use the toilet while the train is at the station, but only in the countryside. None of the sinks has running water. Luckily we thought to bring enough water for drinking and washing up.

The train station bathrooms are even worse. Before going inside men roll up their pant legs, and women hoist their skirts. Some have broken toilets literally overflowing with turds. People just keep on using them and the poop piles higher.

---

* Frequently used Spanish words in italics are defined in the glossary on page 330.

Tass on our first trip to Central America, age twenty-five.

Clackety-clack-clack. The train rocks rhythmically back and forth as we roll southward. The scenery, dry sandy hills and wide-open sky, passes as if in the view finder of a slow panning camera, looking across the horizon.

I stare out the window and think about the spiritual side of the budget traveler's journey. Throughout history seekers have left home, friends, and family to help clarify personal and spiritual issues. Most religions have a tradition of travel as a spiritual quest. Aboriginal Australians went on walkabouts. Native Americans did vision quests. Early Jewish and Christian mystics went into the desert. Russian Orthodox mystics embraced a spiritual path by embarking on a physical journey. Hindu sadhus renounced their possessions to live as wandering mendicants and seekers of spiritual truth.

I view our trip as a sort of pilgrimage, an opportunity for introspection about life goals and beliefs—a chance to clarify what is important, what is central to a life well-lived. I like the archetype of the pilgrim traveler: one who realizes how miraculous the natural world is, and how little of life we really understand. The pilgrim watches and learns, contemplating with compassion the lives of those he or she meets. A pilgrim's journey does not require a specific destination. In fact the destination can be secondary to the overall purpose of the experience. The journey itself, the act of mindful travel, is the purpose.

When the destination is not the emphasis of the journey, indeed, when you hardly even know where you are going, day-to-day interactions become the focus. Here and Now. A three-day train ride is not something to be endured to get to a specific destination; the train ride becomes the primary event. I **want** to spend three days riding funky third-class trains across Mexico. The fact that we will end up in the rainforests of Chiapas when finished is a bonus. I would ride the train, just for the experience, even if it went straight back to Nogales. I want adventure, and I want to be challenged, not only physically, but mentally and spiritually.

At night we use our sleeping bags as blankets, our extra clothes as pillows, and we try to sleep. Everyone is again packed together, leaning against each other sleeping. Luckily, both Tass and I are adept at sleeping in unusual circumstances and places.

Around one a.m., just about the time we are finally falling into a deeper sleep, we pull into a large station and the entire coach is filled with a mob of new passengers crowding onto the train so fast that the people inside the train are pushed back from the doors and have to fight through a wall of bodies and luggage to get off. What meager space we had to stretch our legs is now claimed by someone else's feet. At two A.M. things calm down enough for us to fall back asleep.

Bruce on our first trip to Central America,
age twenty-two.

We sleep off and on until dawn's first light, then rouse up to check out the scenery. We follow our progress on our Mexico map, which is shaped like a horn-of-plenty. Before leaving home I cut the oceans off our maps. In our campaign to travel as light as possible we weighed everything from silverware to socks. Since we would never be traveling far off the coast, I figured oceans were just extra weight we didn't need. Now we laugh each time we use the map. Okay, maybe I got a little carried away.

The train is climbing into the Sierra Madre. I ride kneeling on the seat so I can stick my head out the window with the wind in my face and hair. On the sharp turns I look out both ahead and behind as the train rounds the corners, working its way higher into the mountains. Approaching a tunnel I pull my head inside at the last second and we roar through. The car has no lights, everything is pitch black for a few seconds. The moment we are on the other side, I poke my head back out and watch the rest of the train come out of the mountainside.

As the train climbs higher, we pass through countless tunnels and across high, arched trestles. I ride outside, standing in the little alcove porch where the railroad cars connect with each other. Holding on to the railing, I lean out over the tracks and watch the line of train cars bob and sway as the earth flashes by under the train. The conductor walks past and doesn't give me a second look. He is totally unconcerned about me hanging out over the edge of the train.

This is what I love about travelling in third-world countries—the relaxed attitude of people. No one worries about lawsuits. Nor should they. I alone am responsible for taking care of myself, which gives me an incredible feeling of freedom. I don't want the government or any lawyer to threaten others with lawsuits on my behalf, trying to protect me from myself. I am twenty-three years old. By my reckoning, I have been an adult for seven years! I should be responsible for my own decisions.

At an early-morning stop the conductor finally takes up a broom and sweeps the trash from the floor of the coach. We toss in our garbage with what he has swept, convinced we have done our duty to keep down the litter. But after the conductor has all the garbage piled up at the end of the car he sweeps the whole pile out the door onto the ground! So our trash ends up like everyone else's, blowing across the railroad tracks in the wind.

We arrive in Guadalajara late, around four o'clock in the morning on our second night. It takes only an hour to buy our tickets and switch trains, but then we sit for almost three hours at the station until our train finally leaves town. The train to Mexico City is supposed to take just twelve hours, but we arrive eighteen hours later, at one a.m.

The next third class train doesn't leave until morning. Finding a nearby budget hotel will take at least thirty minutes, and doesn't seem worth the effort or cost for less than five hours of sleep. We could nap in the chairs in the train station lobby, but after two days and two nights on the train bench from

Nogales we want to stretch out. We shuffle off with the *campesinos* to a quiet, back part of the station to sleep on the cement floor. Hooking our backpacks together next to us to make them harder to steal, we lay out our small ensolite sleeping pads on the floor. As we pull out our sleeping bags, we joke to remind ourselves that sleeping on the floor is one of those adventures that adds to the flavor of our travel.

Beside us some *campesinos* have scrounged pieces of cardboard to lie on. Others lie right on the floor without even a pillow for their heads. As I lie down it feels right, deep in my soul, to travel like this. To experience this. Even if we are only "playing poor" it gives us an idea of the kind of life millions are born into with no choice, and no way out. It is humbling to remember that for those around us, this type of life is not a grand adventure, but day-to-day reality. We are not ashamed when other passengers wander past and look askance at us with the *campesinos*. Who we are, what we believe and stand for, is not altered by our present situation. Yet society often forgets that economic standing, whether it be wealth or poverty, has little bearing on a person's character.

We leave Mexico City early the next day, standing in the crowded train aisles. Our destination in Chiapas is a thirty-hour train ride away. By mid-morning, as short-distance passengers depart, we finally get window seats, facing across from each other so we can stretch out our legs. I like knowing the train ride is more than one day and night, and that we'll wake up tomorrow in a whole new part of the country.

But in the evening I sleep fitfully. I am moderately thin, and my bony rear end feels like it is grinding into the hard wooden seat. In the middle of the night, with my butt numb from the train bench, I decide I absolutely have to stretch out. I put my sleeping pad on the floor under our seat, then squeeze and crawl under the seat to try to sleep. My head is up against the wall, my legs out across the aisle, my feet under the seat on the other side.

I am hot and uncomfortable. I thrash and roll on the floor in the tight spot, and wake a few times feeling all sweaty. But in the morning I discover my "sweat" is something else. Few of the people riding third-class can afford diapers. The family behind us has a little baby that slept on the seat above me. During the night the baby peed all over itself, the seat, and me. I don't say anything to the family. How can I blame them for not having money for diapers, and besides, what was I doing sleeping under the seat anyway? I grab a couple of our water bottles and charge to the train bathroom to clean up. I strip down, my bare feet balanced on top of my shoes on the grungy, stinky, bathroom floor, and give myself a sponge bath. We have just enough water. I change clothes and put the soiled clothes in a plastic bag to hand wash when we get off the train.

A sense of humor is helpful in being a pilgrim.

2

Rainforests and Mayan Ruins

We get off the train in the southern Mexican state of Chiapas at a small town near the Mayan ruins of Palenque. Close to the ruins is the quiet Mayabell campground with bathrooms, showers, and a place to pitch tents. The campground also has two small *palapas*, little pole structures with thatched roofs, but no walls. The camping fee, whether we stay in our tent or in the *palapa*, is less than a dollar a day. We move into the *palapa* on a little hill at the back of the campground, at the very edge of the rainforest. This area has one of the highest rainfalls in all of Mexico, over 110 inches per year. The humidity is about eighty percent.

The first morning we are awakened before dawn by a deep, rumbling growl that sounds like a very close, and angry, jaguar. The roaring continues until we wonder if a family of lions has been let loose. The noise is deafening, and rather unnerving as we lie in our hammocks under the *palapa* with no walls, wondering what is going on. When the booming roars draw closer, we realize the noise comes from a group of black howler monkeys in the trees above us. Howler monkeys seldom fight physically; they determine social hierarchy by who can make the most noise. Individual howlers roar at each other to establish leadership within each group. Territorial boundaries are established by two or more groups of howlers who fill neighboring trees, and then boom out roars and growls at each other.

We eat an early breakfast and head out on a small trail to the ruins. As the sun comes up the morning rainforest mist rises from the jungle floor. The ruins appear to be floating on clouds. We have the place to ourselves.

Archeologists believe the golden age of Palenque was from 600-800 A.D. About thirty buildings have been excavated, including a number of pyramids and a large building with a tall observation or ceremonial tower. Many of the buildings have ornate stone roofs, stucco sculptures on the walls, and hieroglyphic monuments. Estimates put the number of stone buildings in the city at

10

five hundred, with perhaps many more smaller, wooden buildings that have long since disappeared.

The main pyramid, the Temple of Inscriptions, has eight levels. Hieroglyphics on the pyramid date the dedication of the building to 692 A.D. Sixtynine steps rise up the front of the pyramid to the top, capped by a small ceremonial room with stone walls and ceiling. The rear wall of the room has three panels with hieroglyphic inscriptions that tell the history of Palenque and the building of the temple. In 1952 archaeologist Alberto Ruz found a sealed stone passageway at the back of the room. Behind a stone wall were two skeletons guarding a passageway, along with clay pots full of jewelry and tools for the journey into the world after death. A steep staircase was discovered, leading back down, into the heart of the pyramid.

We descend down this dark, narrow passage. The air, quiet and still, has a strong, damp smell that feels very old, from another time. Deep inside the pyramid is an ancient crypt, a small, dimly lit chamber with a large, stone sarcophagus. The coffin has an elaborately carved lid with a stylized picture of Pakal, who ruled the city from 615-683 A.D., a remarkable sixty-eight years. Pakal built many of the buildings and plazas in the city. Some archeologists believe he may have been crowned at the age of twelve, and lived to be nearly one hundred years old.

Circling Pakal on the carving are serpents and mystical monsters. Carved on the walls surrounding the sarcophagus are the nine Lords of the Underworld. When Ruz and his team of workers lifted the heavy stone lid off the sarcophagus, they found Pakal inside, buried with beautiful jewels and a jade mask. Pakal is represented in the pyramid hieroglyphics by the sun and a shield. Hieroglyphics also reveal that Pakal's reign was predicted thousands of years prior to his ascension, and that his reign would be celebrated far into the future, which, in one sense, has certainly proven true, since we know about him today. Pakal's son, Chan-Balum, who is represented in hieroglyphics by the jaguar and the serpent, built the pyramid in memory of his father and also continued to enlarge the city.

Across from the Temple of Inscriptions is the Palace, a large block of buildings with a tall tower believed to have been used as an astronomical observatory. On December twenty-second, the winter solstice, priests and royalty would view the sun setting directly into the Temple of Inscriptions from the tower. At the base of the tower is an area thought to have been used for steam baths, with toilet drains, which means the building had some type of indoor plumbing. A maze of underground corridors and small rooms are thought to have been ceremonial chambers for meditation and prayer; they are certainly well-suited for such use, as they are both quiet and very cool compared to the hot and humid air outside.

Throughout Palenque superb stucco reliefs are sculpted on building walls. Using a mixture of clay and tree bark to keep the stucco from drying too quickly,

Less than half of the Mayan Hieroglyphics have been
deciphered by archeologists.

Mayan sculptors created beautiful artwork. Some archeologists believe the images of people were first sculpted nude, and then as the artwork dried, clothing was added layer upon layer, as if the persons were being dressed.

I love sitting on top of the pyramids, or up in the observation tower, imagining what the city was like full of people over a thousand years ago. Many archeologists believe that during the two hundred year cultural peak of the city, all the stone buildings were painted a bright vermilion red.

The entire city of Palenque was completely abandoned not long after Chan-Balum's death. No one knows exactly why. Palenque was unknown to Europeans until a Spanish priest, Father Ordonnez y Aguiar, was shown the ruins by Mayan hunters in 1773. By then the verdant rainforest had completely overgrown the city. The shapes and forms of the buildings were hardly recognizable in the thick, lush growth. Aguiar wrote a book about his discovery, which he claimed was the capital of a vast civilization.

In 1787 Captain Antonio del Rio explored the ruins and wrote a report, which was basically lost in government archives. It wasn't until thirty-five years later that the report was read, translated into English, and published in England in 1822. The book quickly encouraged others to mount expeditions to see and study the ruins. One of the more unusual early visitors, Count de Waldeck, lived on top of one of the pyramids from 1831-1833. He also wrote a book, which was totally inaccurate in its description of the buildings and features of the site.

In 1837 the American archaeologist John L. Stephens, along with artist Frederick Catherwood, excavated six pyramids and a section of the city's aqueduct system. For the first time, factual knowledge about the site was available to serious scholars. A steady stream of archeologists, scholars, and interested tourists has been visiting ever since.

Now daily tour buses arrive at nine a.m., bringing crowds of camera toting tourists to the site. Most people have just a few hours to explore the ruins. By three o'clock the last of the tour buses has gone and the ruins are again quiet and peaceful.

We quickly adapt our schedule around the crowds, to insure we are alone at the ruins as much as possible. We arrive early when it is quiet and the light is good for photographs. During the heat of the day when the temperature is sweltering and the ruins are crawling with people, we slip away to a nearby jungle stream for a refreshing dip and a hike along the rainforest paths. After the crowds have left, we head back to the ruins until sunset.

During her previous winter traveling in South America, Tass, along with her friend Suzanne, became an accomplished birder. Now Tass is eager to head out into the rainforest and share her excitement for birdwatching. The first bird we spot is a barred antshrike, a little flitty bird with a jaunty crest, and wild black-and-white stripes similar to a zebra, or a prison uniform.

We bird for an hour, walking slowly down a narrow jungle path, and quickly see a dozen colorful species. I am amazed how quickly Tass spots the birds, and then notices every slight variation not only in color, but body shape, wing shape, tail size, and bill length and shape. She even observes the way they perch their feet! Birding is surprisingly fast and exciting.

We stand quietly ten feet apart, peering into the thick jungle growth. Suddenly Tass gasps.

"It's a trogon!" she whisper-screams, hardly able to contain herself. Luckily, the bird doesn't spook and fly away, but sits proudly, fifteen feet away. The perfect light showcases its wonderful, shimmering, iridescent green head and bright red stomach.

We each have small travel binoculars, which when used in conjunction with prescription glasses have a minimal viewing width. In other words, trying to quickly find the bird with the binoculars can be tricky. Tass is whispering out field marks and all I see is a blur of foliage as I scan with the binoculars, still trying to locate the bird.

"Black tail, white stripes!" Tass notes. "White band across the chest!"

Finally the fire-engine-red stomach and chest pop into view in my binoculars.

"Yellow bill!" I chime in at last. The bird flies deep into the trees and disappears.

In excitement Tass dances me around in the rainforest. She pulls out our Peterson guide to Mexican birds, which shows a full page of trogans—eight species, with both males and females shown, plus one subspecies, for a total of seventeen birds. The tail of one of the birds, the resplendant quetzal, is over two feet long, and in the picture takes up the entire length of the page. We try to identify the trogon we have seen through the process of elimination. Obviously it wasn't the quetzal, nor was it a citreoline or violaceous trogon, which have yellow breasts.

"It had a yellow beak!" I remember excitedly. Out goes the eared trogon, and a number of the other females. Only five remaining birds have a yellow beak. One of them, the female elegant trogon doesn't have a green head. She is out. Four possible birds left. Tass smiles. She already knows the answer.

"Which bird was it?" she asks. I stare at the page, back and forth between the four birds. When looking at the bird in the binoculars I was positive I could easily pick it out of any line-up. Now I am not sure.

"Remember the thin band of white across the chest between the red and the green?" Tass hints, eliminating the male slaty-tailed trogon. Three birds left. Still, I am stumped.

"Remember the distinct tail?" Tass quizzes. I remember the tail as very long, kind of square on the end, with black and white stripes. Unfortunately the mountain, collared, and elegant trogan all have similar shaped tails, with black and white stripes of varying widths.

"I don't think the elegant trogon has enough black in the tail," I guess hesitantly.

"Good!" Tass smiles. Now I am down to two birds, the mountain and the collared trogon. Again I am stumped.

"If you are uncertain check the range," Tass helps me out. "Maybe one of them is not found in this area or habitat." I turn to the text.

"*Mountain trogon. Lets see...similar species: collared and elegant trogons have differing and distinctive tail patterns.* No kidding!" I add sarcastically at the end, unsure which one I saw. I continue to scan the page.

"*Voice.*" We didn't hear any call. No help there.

"*Range: Highlands of Mexico, Guatemala, and Honduras. Mexico: Mountains from Chihuahua, Tamaulipas to Chiapas (4,000-10,000 feet).*" Well, it is certainly found here.

"*Habitat: Pine or pine-oak woodlands, cloud forest.*" Cloud forest, we are in the right habitat.

"Okay, check the collared trogon," Tass reminds me. I look across the page.

"*Range: East Mexico to northern Bolivia, Brazil. Mexico: Eastern slope from east San Luis Potosi, south Tamaulipas south through Oaxaca, Chiapas, Yucatan Peninsula. Habitat: Forest edges, clearings, plantations; lowlands, foothills to 5000+ feet.*" Again we are at the right elevation, and in humid forests. The ranges of the two birds overlap. I am stumped.

"I can't believe you don't remember the tail!" Tass teases. "It was so distinctive!" she laughs, pointedly using the word from the field guide. I turn back to the color plate showing trogans. I shrug my shoulders. I don't have a clue.

"The collared trogon!" Tass points dramatically at the center of the page. Again she dances on the rainforest path.

Each day we have a favorite bird sighting. Birds are grouped by species into families. The tropical family of cotingas varies widely in size, shape and color, including such unusual South American birds as bellbirds, umbrellabirds and cock-of-the-rocks. Only one member of the cotinga family is found in Mexico, and that is our favorite bird the next day: the lovely cotinga. Seven inches long, it is a vibrant, shimmering blue with large splotches of deep purple on the stomach and throat.

The following day our favorite is the red-capped manakin, a squat "chubby" bird with hardly a tail, basically black except for a bright red head. The yellow feathers on the top of its legs are called "trousers" in our field-guide, and it does look like the bird is wearing little yellow knickers. The book also says males of many species indulge in unusual group dance displays, wing snapping, etc. Although we don't get to hear it, the voice during display is described as a rough, flat buzz or "Bronx cheer."

Despite our U.S. army surplus Vietnam mosquito repellent, which we joke is probably like slathering our bodies with Agent Orange, we are slowly being covered in a variety of bites. We make frequent trips to the small pools of the jungle stream to ease the itching in the cool water. The rainforest is like our own little Garden of Eden, with bugs. By the end of the week we have spotted more than one hundred birds and have repeatedly explored the Mayan ruins.

One night, near the small jungle stream, Tass and I have a ceremony to show and express our dedication to one another. From the beginning of our

Our *palapa* at the Mayan ruins of Palenque, Chiapas, Mexico.

relationship we have taken our commitment to each other very seriously. We pledged at the start to always be sincere, honest, and truthful.

Now, under a half-moon sky, we stand in the jungle stillness of dew-kissed foliage, holding hands, with faces bathed in nightlight, and whisper further pledges to each other. To love unconditionally. To be strong when the other is weak. To be better people through the guidance of each other. To work toward an enlightened life together. To always love and support the other, even if someday we should live apart. Although no one else is there to hear our words, we speak aloud, and seal the vows within our hearts.

We leave Palenque on the third-class train to Merida, which is supposed to come through around midnight, but arrives after three A.M. The cars are so loaded we can't even squeeze inside. We ride the first few hours in the alcove outside between the cars, which is also standing room only. As the sun comes up we are able to move inside the coach and stand packed in the aisle. After a few more hours we get a seat.

In the evening we arrive in Merida, the capital of the state of Yucatan. Since we will be in Merida a few days, we get a cheap room in an old hotel near the train station. Many budget hotels have cramped, box-like rooms with no windows. However, this hotel at one time was quite grand, with stately colonial architecture, marble colonnades, beautiful large black and white tiles on the floor, and double French doors into all the rooms. The ceilings are very high, which helps keep the rooms cool at night. But time and deterioration of the building, and the neighborhood, has left the hotel in serious disrepair. Built long before electric lights, or inside bathrooms, these later amenities were added haphazardly with new wires and plumbing pipes now running criss-cross every which way along the ceiling, walls and floor. Regardless of the upkeep, we love the feel of the hotel, the large rocking chairs in our room, and the shuttered balcony next to our bed that overlooks the crowded street below. Best of all, it is in our price range.

We stay in Merida a few days and find the city wonderfully vibrant and interesting. However, getting around is hot, muggy, and exhausting. All the main streets are congested with snarled traffic. Clouds of diesel smoke pour out of the noisy, rickety old buses. In places we can hardly make our way down the obstacle-laden sidewalks. Still the narrow streets have a wonderful charm, bordered by four-hundred year old colonial buildings, beautiful aging mansions, cathedrals, and churches. We also find a number of small side streets with little traffic, and quiet, shady parks, flower gardens, and statues.

We visit the *Mercado Municipal*, the main market, where vendors sell vegetables, fruits, prepared foods, and every inexpensive household item imaginable. We also explore the textile market, famous for the hand-woven blouses called *huipils* that the Indian women wear in this part of Mexico. The Yucatan *huipils* are made of lightweight white cotton with colorful embroidery along the tops of the shoulders and the upper part of the front and back of the blouse. Tass bargains for a few different styles while I buy an embroidered all-white shirt commonly worn by *Latino* business men, along with a loose cotton shirt with an open collar worn by the *campesinos*.

We spend an entire day learning all about Yucatan hammocks. Because of the air circulation, hammocks are the coolest way to sleep if you don't have air conditioning. All the budget hotels have hooks on the walls for hammocks. And hammocks are a great way to sleep when staying in dirt-floored *palapas* and *cabanas*, up off the ground from insects and snakes. In the old days the best hammocks were woven from silk. Today the hammocks are hand-woven from brightly-colored cotton string. Several different widths are available: singles, doubles, *matrimonials* and *familias*. Most novices lie in a hammock straight from end to end, their bodies curved like a banana. But the best way to sleep in a hammock is to lie at a forty-five degree angle to the hammock ends, putting the body in a flat, uncurved position, which is much more comfortable for the whole night.

We buy another necessity of life in the tropics, straw hats. Although Panama-style hats are made throughout Latin America, the true Panama hat actually comes from Ecuador. Because this highest quality straw hat was first imported through Panama, it was given the title of the wrong country right from the beginning, and the name stuck. Panama-style hats are tightly woven from pliable palm fronds, and can be rolled up for storage or travel and then unrolled, without any noticeable crease or damage to the hat. We are told the locally made hats of this style are woven in humid caves and workshops to keep the fibers pliable, although it is hard to see how any cave or workshop could be more humid than the already stifling air of the Yucatan. It is fascinating to examine and feel the soft texture of the very best made hats, which even here can cost over one hundred dollars. When the time comes for us to buy, we settle for a much cheaper variety, which we are quite pleased with nonetheless.

On every street in Merida are wonderful *panaderias*, where we get tasty baked goods and sweet breads. Because of the oppressive heat and humidity, Merida also seems to be the fresh fruit juice capital of Mexico. Every fifth shop is a *jugoria* where lengthy menus offer every conceivable mixture of fresh fruit juice. Our favorites: *jugo de narranja*, fresh squeezed orange juice; *banana con leche*, a wonderful banana smoothie; *sandia licuados*, watermelon juice on ice; and *fresas con leche*, strawberries blended with milk.

Next to each juice shop are vendors pushing little ice coolers on wheels selling *paletas*, fruit juices frozen with water or milk and served like a popsi-

Future *banana con leches*, Merida, Mexico.

cle on a stick. Again we try every variety available. My favorite is *coco con leche*, coconut frozen with milk. The *paletas* cost only a penny each, and we quickly find we can eat an enormous number of them each day. We follow the shock therapy technique of adjusting our bodies to the local food, and try almost everything.

The Mayan ruins of Uxmal are about fifty miles south of Merida. Traveling on third-class buses, with numerous stops and a bus change along the way, takes us half a day.

Uxmal in Mayan means "thrice built," but its largest pyramid, the Temple of the Magician, has actually been rebuilt five times, each time being buried and covered by a larger successor. Built on an unusual oval base, the final version of the pyramid stands 128 feet high. Archeologists have installed a thick chain up the center of the temple steps to serve as a handrail for nervous tourists unaccustomed to such steep, narrow and exposed staircases.

Across from the Temple of the Magician lies the Nunnery complex, a large building with seventy-four rooms. Archeologists are unsure of the building's use; the name comes from a Spanish priest, the first European to visit the site, who thought the building was designed like a convent. The outside of the building is covered with strange carvings of Chac, the Mayan god of rain.

We visit all the sites at Uxmal: the Governors Palace, the House of Pigeons, the House of the Turtles, the ball court, along with a number of huge mounds covered with grass—ruins of older buildings yet unrestored. We find the ruins interesting but rather sanitized. Large colored spotlights have been cemented into the base of many of the buildings for evening light shows. Uxmal seems more like a Hollywood set than an ancient city. One long afternoon is plenty of time to see everything we want.

The next day we catch a rickety local bus to the ruins of Kabah, which is only about twelve miles south of Uxmal yet is nearly empty of visitors. The appropriately named Palace of Masks has over three hundred carvings of the rain god Chac. The masks are not carved out of single stones, but made of ten to twenty stones which are sculpted and then cemented together to form a bizarre, comical caricature—bulging eyes, almost buck teeth, and a giant hook nose that looks like the end of a shepherd crook. The masks cover the entire building, from the ground to the top, even on all the corners. Replicas of Chac loom over the doors and on the side of the doors. In a few doorways the masks actually form part of the steps, allowing us to stand on Chac's big, hooked nose to enter some of the rooms. The tiny bare rooms inside are typical of Mayan architecture. Without a true arch with a keystone, the walls had to be very close to support the weight of the massive ceilings.

Looking out from the palace, which like most buildings is set high on a terrace mound, we are surrounded by dry tropical forest. The entire area is devoid of rivers and lakes. It is amazing that such large cities could ever have existed here. No wonder the rain god played such an important role in the beliefs of the people. Like Uxmal, the Maya here built reservoirs in the ground, which they sealed with lime to hold the precious rainwater. Archeologists have long speculated that prolonged drought may have forced the Maya to abandon their cities. While that seems quite plausible here, why would they have abandoned Palenque, which gets almost ten feet of rain each year?

The Maya never had use of the wheel, so they never had wagons, carts, or even wheelbarrows. They also never had draught animals. No horses, donkeys, mules, or oxen. Still, they built huge elevated cobblestone roads called *sacbes*, which ran from city to city. The *sacbe* here, as in most Mayan cities, has all but completely vanished over the centuries. Only a very small section has been restored by archeologists.

To visit the Mayan ruins of Sayil we hike back to the highway. The once-a-day local bus that brought us here won't return until tomorrow. We begin walking further south along the road, hoping to catch a ride. But there is little traffic. The heat is sweltering; each mile we hike seems to take hours. We walk all the way to the Sayil turnoff without a ride.

The road to the ruins is simply a rutted track through the dry tropical forest. We see just one four-wheel-drive vehicle on our trek to the ruins, going the opposite direction. At least we get some relief hiking in the shade of trees hanging over the road. As we hike the last three miles, we begin to ration the water we brought, and wonder if we are carrying enough to visit all three sites found in this area. When we finally get to the ruins, we have the place completely to ourselves, and the hike seems worth the effort.

The Palacio at Sayil looks like an ancient Greek temple. Stately columns grace the entire front of the building. Perhaps because we are completely alone, the ruins seem particularly interesting to us. We feel as if we are the first people to visit the site in hundreds of years. Although the tiny rooms inside the building provide us some cool moments, we find scampering through the forest around the ruins hot, exhausting work. Despite our attempts to ration, we find ourselves guzzling more and more of our meager water supply. After a day at Sayil, we decide hiking further into the forest to Xlapak and Labna might not be a good idea without a few more gallons of water. The next day we hike back to the road and catch a series of buses back through Merida and then eastward.

The main highway across the Yucatan runs from Merida to Cancun, right through the middle of the ruins of Chichen Itza. Despite the highway, and the bus loads of tourists who daily visit the site, Chichen Itza has a fascinating aura. Near the ruins the Piramide Inn has a grassy camping area under the trees in a secluded corner of the well-kept grounds, close to the swimming pool, the shower house, and the shaded patio tables. Perfect.

Again most of the visitors make day trips to the ruins, arriving late morning and leaving mid-afternoon. During the congested hours of mid-day we visit isolated outer buildings in the forest, relax at the pool, or rest in hammocks at the hotel.

Unlike most Mayan ruins, which were mysteriously abandoned after their classical period, Chichen Itza was abandoned twice. The Maya built most of the city between 550-900 A.D., and then over a short period of years suddenly left not only the city, but the entire area. Almost two-hundred years later, in about 1100 A.D., Toltecs from the central highlands near present day Mexico City moved to Chichen Itza. The civilization they created was a mixture of both Mayan and Toltec beliefs. The Toltecs brought the religion of Quetzalcoatl, the plumed serpent, embodied in a blonde king with great powers, who was forced out of central Mexico and traveled east across the sea.

The Toltecs were obsessed with human sacrifice and blood offerings. They occupied Chichen Itza for another two-hundred years, and then like their Mayan predecessors, mysteriously abandoned the city. However, they left behind throughout the Yucatan their beliefs and legends surrounding Quetzalcoatl, which foretold that he would someday reappear across the sea from the east. Two hundred years later, this legend led many Maya to believe it was their fate to be subjugated by the blonde Spanish conqueror Cortez, whom they identified as an embodiment of Quetzalcoatl.

Chichen Itza has many interesting structures, but the most famous is the pyramid the Spanish named El Castillo, the castle, which doesn't look like a castle at all. The huge, four-sided pyramid is eighty-two feet tall with nine levels, designed to symbolize the Mayan calendar. Stairs run down the center of each side of the pyramid, making eighteen terraces per side, which corresponds to the eighteen 20-day months of the Mayan Vague Year. Each of the four stairs has ninety-one steps, which added together with the top platform equals 365, the number of days in a year. On each facade of the temple are fifty-two panels signifying the fifty-two years in the Round Calendar. The Toltecs added sculptures of giant serpents along the sides of the pyramid staircases. During the spring and autumnal equinoxes, the shadows made from the serpents create an illusion, which lasts over three hours, of the snake ascending the stairs in the spring and descending the stairs in the fall.

The Observatory at Chichen Itza was built and rebuilt over several centuries. Inside, a giant spiral staircase gives the building its Spanish name, *El Caracol*, the conch, a marine gastropod. Windows in the walls are aligned to view specific stars on auspicious dates. The top of the building, which has not been restored, is thought to have been where priests announced appropriate days and times for celebrations, and the planting and harvesting of food.

Like civilizations around the world all through time, the Maya loved sports. Chichen Itza has the largest and best-preserved ball court in Mexico,

El Castillo, the largest pyramid at Chichen Itza, Mexico.

along with at least seven other ball courts spread through the town. Just how the game was played is open to some interpretation. Carvings show players with padding on their knees and elbows. Other carvings show players with bats. Some believe the first team or individual player to hit or kick a rubber ball through one of two stone hoops placed high up on a wall, won. During the Toltec period the game was played with great seriousness. Carvings along the walls of the ball court show some players, presumably the losers, having their heads lopped off. Living in Chichen Itza during Toltec times must have been frightful. Numerous carvings show sacrificial events—skulls and eagles ripping open the chests of victims to eat their hearts.

Chichen Itza is located in the center of the Yucatan peninsula. The only water available is in *cenotes*, huge natural caverns in the limestone with collapsed roofs, leaving them open to the sky and to people and animals. During the rainy season, May through October, rain water percolates through the limestone and collects in the *cenotes*. The Sacred *Cenote* at Chichen Itza is 197 feet in diameter and 115 feet deep. Archeologists have recovered all kinds of offerings: gold, jade jewelry, along with the remains of a few men, women, and children who were sacrificed.

As we hike back from the *cenote* we continually spot motmots, one of the more peculiar families of birds in the area. Of the eight motmot species in the world, six are found in Mexico. Motmots are solitary birds, green and brown colored with a black spot in the center of their breasts. Most motmots have an unusual racket-shaped tip at the ends of their tails. The birds create the distinct tail designs by plucking sections of their tail feathers clear of webbing, but leaving the ends intact. To further dramatize their tails, motmots often perch, swinging their tails back and forth below them like pendulums. Our favorite is the blue-crowned motmot, sixteen inches in length, the largest of the species.

On the east coast of the Yucatan, sitting on a limestone cliff overlooking the turquoise Caribbean ocean, lies the small Mayan ruins of Tulum, Mayan for "City of the Dawn." Tulum is one of the few Mayan cities that may still have been occupied upon the arrival of the Spanish. In 1518 a Spanish expedition that sailed past the city reported the buildings were painted red, blue, and white, and that a ceremonial fire was burning from the top of one of the buildings. Further evidence of the late date of the city's occupation can be found in a stone carving showing the rain god Chac riding a four-legged animal, which the Maya never saw until the arrival of the horse-riding Spanish. Even before the Spanish arrived, warfare and strife was bad enough that Tulum had to be heavily fortified to survive. Huge ramparts were built around the city from which defenders could throw spears and rocks down on their attackers.

In the Temple of the Frescoes, which may have been built as late as 1450 A.D., paintings with reds, blues, and greens give an idea of the extraordinary colors that at one point covered all the buildings. Murals show the Mayan Universe with three levels or realms. A dark underworld of the deceased is at the bottom, the middle level is for the living, and above is the home of the creator and the rain god.

I am taken with one carving, which has been described in a number of ways in archeological books. Some interpret the carving of the god to have wings and a tail, making it a diving or descending god. Others see in the carving links with Venus, the morning star, which is also a symbol associated with Quetzalcoatl. Some have even suggested the carving represents the Mayan god of the bee.

I look at the carving and think of the descending god theory, which is found in the beliefs of so many people and cultures throughout history. God reaches out to interact with humanity, moving from an ethereal, spiritual level of creation into the physical levels. The belief resonates strongly within me.

3

Isla Mujeres

After traipsing around a month in the sweltering heat of the Yucatan, we are ready for a break from exploring Mayan sites. We head for coastal Xel Ha (pronounced Shell Ha), where there are a fascinating collection of salt water and fresh water pools eroded out of limestone. We snorkel in the pools, which vary in size from small backyard swimming pools to large Olympic-size. In some of the pools are huge submerged boulders and underwater caves. But best of all are the tropical fish and rays. We see parrotfish, three feet long, with thick bodies; they are different shades of blue, with bright colored lines drawn across their faces. Grazing for algae, they gnaw on the coral with their huge front teeth. As we swim past we can hear the steady grinding and chewing noise as they feed, breaking down the hard coral into fine sand in the process.

Yellow and blue angel fish and even thinner butterfly fish swim past in small groups. Fresh water percolates out from the sandy floors of many of the pools and caves; as it mixes with the salt water it creates weird, blurred vision for snorkeling, which adds to the surreal feeling of the area.

The best part about Xel Ha is the rays. Huge southern stingrays, some five feet wide and even longer if you include the thick serrated tail, hide down in the bottom of the pools, with only their bulbous eyes sticking out of the sand like periscopes, watching and waiting. A stab from the spine of a ray tail causes extreme pain. But unless stepped on, or grabbed, they are harmless to snorkelers. When I spot them I usually swim past giving the rays enough room that I don't disturb them, more out of respect for their space than fear. But sometimes they are so hidden I don't even know they are there. Then, as I am following other fish, I inadvertently swim over the hidden rays. Spooked, the rays erupt out of the sand in swirling clouds of sediment. With great dramatic flaps of their enormous wings, the rays rocket off and away to another part of the pool. On one of these unexpected encounters, I am only a few feet away when an enormous stingray with a five-foot wingspan explodes out of the sand below me. Startled, I swallow and choke on a great quantity of lagoon water.

Also living along the bottom of the pools are flounder, one of the strangest of fish. Flounder skim along sideways, pressed down against the sandy floor. Since they spend their whole lives with the same side hugging the bottom of the ocean, both of their eyes are located on the opposite, upper side of their bodies. The real oddity is that they are born with symmetrical bodies, with eyes on both sides of the head. Within days of hatching one eye migrates from the side that faces down, to the side of the body that faces up.

I dive repeatedly into the caves and swim as far as the light and my breath will allow. The backs of the caves are dark and mysterious. Just as my eyes begin to adjust to the low light, my lungs run out of air and I bolt back out of the caves for the surface.

Xel Ha is wonderful, but small. We want more Caribbean experiences, so we head for a small island just off the Yucatan coast. Isla Mujeres, the Island of Women, is named after a small Mayan temple found on the island. Long ago Mayan women who were pregnant, or wanted to become pregnant, would come to the island as a pilgrimage to pray for a safe childbirth. Today all that is left of the temple of Ixchel, goddess of the moon and fertility, is a few unimpressive stone blocks. Although there is not much to see for archeology, the charm of the island quickly captures our hearts.

Isla Mujeres is five miles long and just half a mile wide. Construction on a luxury tourist hotel was once started at one end of the island, but the work was stopped when it was only half finished, and now the skeletal shell of the building is deserted. With no big hotels and hardly any place to stay, the majority of tourists in the area visit nearby Cancun, a resort complex recently built by the Mexican government on a sand spit off the mainland coast. In the few years since its inception, Cancun has already become a major destination, leaving sleepy Isla Mujeres pretty much abandoned.

On the north end of Isla Mujeres is a small town with some *tiendas* and a little *supermercado* selling food, a few quiet restaurants, and a couple of decrepit and half-empty budget hotels. We stay at a campground, Los Cocos, right on the beach. The campground has two communal, tin-roofed *palapas* sleeping 10 *gringos* per building, sardine-like, in a row of hammocks. We opt for a little more space and privacy and pitch our tent in the sand and hang our hammocks under the shade of a coconut palm.

The owner, Ruben, is a sly, weasel-like fellow with slick-backed hair who spends all his time chasing after *gringa* women, offering free massages and bottles of hand-pressed coconut oil lotion. Ruben's partner is an old, bent-over fellow named Francisco, who shuffles around the campground, whistling, carrying an old, weathered razor. Whenever he has an audience he

Tass relaxing at Los Cocos, Isla Mujeres, Mexico.

acts in mime as if he is standing in front of a mirror, pulling the razor against his dry neck, shaving in the sunlight of mid-day under the coconut palms, laughing and giggling. Francisco rolls his eyes and whispers conspiratorially to us that Ruben is "*loco para las mujeres*," crazy over the girls. Personally we think both of them have been standing too long in the sun.

The beach in front of Los Cocos is picture-perfect, with white sand that slopes gradually down to transparent water, gently lapping at the shore. One hundred yards from shore the water is only knee deep, another hundred yards and it is waist deep—still bathtub-warm—and turning the most exquisite turquoise color. We immediately fall in love with the island and decide this would be a great place for two South Dakotans to learn about the rhythms of the ocean and the tides, snorkel, and learn about tropical fish.

We start each day beachcombing, finding colorful shells. We lie on the beach reading in total luxury until we are good and hot. Only then do we take the two-minute walk up the beach to snorkel off the northern point of the is-land. The snorkeling is exciting, with small waves and a slight current that scoots us along. When the tide is low we have to time the waves perfectly to swim over parts of the reef without scraping our stomachs or legs across the sharp coral just below the surface. The surge is moderately strong; we rock back and forth, along with all the other fish, sea grass, and sea fans, with each rhythmic movement of the water around us.

Porkfish, a type of grunt, named for the odd sounds they make, noisily swim past. We hear a cacophony of sharp popping noises, moans, groans, and grunts as they feed. They are a foot long with thin horizontal blue and yellow strips across their bodies and two big black bars running vertically across their faces.

A three-foot-long blue parrotfish swims under us. The stocky fish has a rounded blue body, distinct white lips, and buck teeth, which give the fish its name. The smaller stoplight parrotfish is bright green with pink stripes across its face and gills, pink along the edge of its long dorsal fin, a yellow circle at the base of its tail, and both a yellow and blue half moon at the end of its tail. We can't get within five feet of the parrotfish without spooking them, but we have fun trying.

I follow a pair of enormous gray angelfish, two feet long, toward an underwater cave full of smaller tropical fish. When I dive back down for a closer look I am surprised to see the cave is actually an underwater tunnel. The tunnel is just long enough that I pause for a few moments, questioning my ability. But the challenge is irresistible. I take a few slow, deep breaths and dive down into the tunnel as fast as I can. Half-way through the tunnel I start to run out of air. I begin to doubt my strategy, but my momentum carries me further forward. I am now in too far to back out, so I go for it. Just when I think I can't hold my breath another second, I shoot out the far end of the tunnel. Mentally it is a big relief, but I still have twenty feet to the surface to breathe. I rocket toward the surface and break through into the sunshine, gasping for air. Once is enough—for today. Tomorrow I'll try again.

The best snorkeling is on the south end of the island at Playa Garrafon. Although it is rumored that a bus goes half-way down the island, we never see it. The island also has a taxi, but it is out of our budget. So we simply walk the five miles each way.

Garrafon is a small reef tucked into a little sheltered cove. Although the coral itself is rather sickly, the water is calm, clear, and full of tropical fish. As we swim out the short, narrow channel through the reef, damsel fish called sergeant majors dart quickly toward us and then away again. They are about hand-sized, and hand thickness; like many tropical fish they have a very thin profile from the front or back, but when viewed sideways they suddenly quadruple in size. Sergeant majors get their names from the five distinct black stripes running vertically along their bodies, which I think look more like prison bars than army insignias. Extremely territorial, they occasionally nip at us if we stop too long near their little domain in the reef. From the way they behave, like hoodlums, I would call them convict fish.

At the mouth of the channel a large school of silvery jacks swims close to the shimmering, mirrored surface of the ocean, out of sight of predatory fish living below. A beautiful group of blue tangs with bright yellow tails swims together in fluid motion beside us. Below, two brown-and-white spotted trumpetfish, three feet long yet only as big around as a wrist, patrol the sandy bottom. Their long snouts are like suction tubes, which they use to vacuum in tiny fish and shrimp like we suck through a straw.

A school of tropical fish, Mexico.

We snorkel slowly along the reef watching the dazzling array of life before us. Tiny fairy basslets, only a few inches long, have the most exquisite colors: dark blue heads, blending into a purple midsection which fades into a bright yellow tail. They shyly skitter about the coral and zip into the nearest hole whenever we get too close. We playfully chase after many fish, holding our breath and diving deeper to peer under ledges and into cracks to spot red squirrelfish, with enormous eyes, peering back out at us from dark crevasses in the coral.

During midday a boat from Cancun sometimes shows up, bringing a group of tourists who generally snorkel once and then eat lunch on their boat. A few of them briefly snorkel again before boating back to the mainland. They seldom come ashore. Usually only a few other people are on the tiny beach; sometimes we have the whole beach to ourselves.

The road from Garrafon to town passes right through the middle of a small military base on the island. One day as we are walking back from snorkeling, we pass through the military compound just as I am suddenly stricken with severe stomach cramps. There is no place within half a mile for me to go to the bathroom. A wave of nausea comes over me, and I stand, swaying on the sidewalk, doubled up in pain from the cramps. Things don't look good. The pain passes after a few moments, leaving me weak and wobbly. I walk only one hundred feet and again my stomach churns violently. I have just a few seconds to decide what to do. I look around wildly. It appears I have three choices.

One. I can just stand here and let it rip. If I had on long pants, I might consider it, and then simply shuffle awkwardly back to our campground to clean up. Gross, and unpleasant, it might have worked—but I am wearing shorts. From the severe pain and rumbling in my stomach I can expect big volume, more than my shorts can hold. That would make leakage down my leg inevitable, and that is a bit more than I can deal with.

Two. I can simply drop my shorts and go in the gutter. Again gross, and rather risky, as the road in the compound has occasional traffic. I don't embarrass easily but that definitely sounds like something I would just as soon avoid.

Third. I can jump over a waist-high iron fence on the military compound and squat behind a bush in front of a building that has just one window off to the side and a door that is shut.

My stomach rumbles. Without another thought I opt for the third option and vault over the fence. I barely hold everything in for the two seconds it takes to squat behind the bush. As I am yanking down my shorts the diarrhea explodes out of me. Hardly a second later a guard suddenly appears out of nowhere to stand over me, pointing a rifle in my face. He yells at me in Spanish, demanding that I stop what I am doing and leave immediately.

While I contritely jabber "*Pardon, pardon!*" I'm sorry, I'm sorry!, Tass shouts from the sidewalk, "*Mucho inferma! Mucho inferma!*" Very Sick! Very Sick!

Even with a rifle in my face I can't stop nature from its course. I have absolutely no control over what is happening. I continue to squat for about five seconds, which seem like five minutes, before I can pull up my shorts and stand up again. The guard is absolutely flipped out. He yells and waves his gun wildly in the air. I take this as a sign that he doesn't want to shoot me, or arrest me, but simply wants me to disappear—fast. Repeating "*Pardon, pardon!*" I jump back over the fence, and Tass and I high tail it down the street and out of the compound.

The snorkeling and wonderful luxury of reading on the beach lulls us into continually postponing our departure. Each evening we watch the sunset over the ocean, and put off leaving our island paradise. We came to Isla Mujeres thinking we would stay four days. When we finally board the ferry back to the mainland we have been on the island six weeks.

4

Flamingos and the Mexican Circus

In the sweltering village of San Felipe, we walk down the dusty, wind-blown street in search of a cheap hotel. A couple of people give us directions to "the only hotel," but when we arrive we find the building half built. Construction was stopped a year ago. Back we walk through town, stopping at little *tiendas*, asking if anything else is available for lodging. Finally an elderly woman offers to rent us a large empty house with enormous rooms for four dollars a week. The windows in the giant kitchen let in wonderful light, but the stove has no gas, and salt water flows from the faucet. The bathroom toilet almost flushes. We take it.

We sit in the living room in two giant rocking chairs looking at maps and discussing plans for the next week. We have come to this isolated town at the north end of the Yucatan peninsula in search of American flamingos. Each winter a flock of the beautiful pink birds comes to breed in the vast shallow waters off the coast.

As we discuss our birding strategies, I am slowly overcome by a fever. Before long I am prone on a straw beach mat spread on the concrete floor, delirious, sweating from fever and then shivering from sudden bouts of freezing chills. Tass also begins feeling ill. She is spared the fever and chills but gets a rather serious case of diarrhea. Things would be so much easier if the toilet worked properly.

In the evening a loud, distorted sound rocks the house. The reverberations continue. Tass bolts out the door to find out the source. In my delirious state I slip in and out of the fog, trying to get some grip on reality and what is happening. Horrendous screeches and howls fill the house, accompanied by gleeful laughter. Tass returns to inform me that the back of our house is connected to a movie theater on the other side of the block. Through the paper thin wall of the house we are hearing, at full volume, an animated Spanish version of *Puss and Boots*.

After a few days our illnesses pass, and we head out in search of flamingos. A local fisherman offers to take us through the channels and waterways to see the birds. Along the way flocks of beautiful snowy egrets roost in the trees overhanging the water. Herons and roseate spoonbills wade in the shallow water hunting for food. The day is still early, yet the stifling humidity and oppressive heat make the air feel like a sauna.

As we leave the mangrove channels and head for the vast tidal flats, we see the flamingos. The flock is enormous. A pink sea of birds stretches across the horizon. Our boatman wisely keeps his distance from the skittish birds; still, a small section of the flock takes to the air in a dramatic flutter of wings and a chorus of calls. As the pink birds fly and turn across the blue sky, they appear as if they are a reflection of the flock in the water.

Since our house is rented by the week, we hang around enjoying the quiet town. One afternoon on a stroll we find the *zocalo*, the town square, covered with a large orange canvas. A man sits in the middle of this giant tarp, repairing a tear with a needle and thread. He uses a broken shard of glass to cut the thread after tying a quick knot, then moves to another section of the tarp and patches again. We watch him work for a few minutes. He looks up, smiles at us, and continues with his work. We hear laughing, as a group of teenagers comes out of an orange bus parked nearby. They are all carrying ropes and begin straightening the canvas in different places. As they work we realize the canvas is a tent they are going to erect. Two of the boys begin pounding huge metal stakes made from old car axles into the ground. Incredibly, one of them uses just one arm for this task; the other arm dangles uselessly at his side, shriveled from a birth defect. As they work we chat with them and discover they are part of a circus that will be in town for three days. They invite us to come to the first performance tomorrow night.

The next day we return to the *zocalo* and find the tent is up and looks quite professional. Small bleachers have been erected inside, along with ropes for a trapeze and high wire act. One of the boys, Alexander, stops his work to give us a tour of the grounds, and again encourages us to come back that evening for the performance.

As the sun goes down, we join an excited crowd of children and adults funneling into the Big Top. The show starts with a slapstick clown routine that is a big hit with the audience. Next, acrobatics and juggling. There are only half a dozen members of the troupe, so everyone performs a variety of routines. The kids are all extremely talented and do quick costume changes between each act. We had expected something a little more amateurish.

A small box, hardly fifteen inches high and twenty-four inches long, is brought out and set on a table. The lid is opened and a hand pops out, followed by an arm. Next comes one foot, then a leg. Another hand and arm emerge from the box followed by the smiling face of Alexander. How he managed to squeeze his body into the box is a wonder. Alexander extracts the rest of his body and stands before the crowd. He begins to unhinge the joints in his shoulders and moves his arms behind his back in the most amazing ways imaginable. After a series of unbelievable contortions, he returns to the box and folds his body back into the tiny compartment. The lid is closed, and the box is carried away to much applause.

After another slapstick clown routine, the circus finale is a daredevil trapeze act. Four members of the troupe—the older man who had been sewing the canvas tent and three teenagers—climb the center poles in star-spangled costumes and swing above the audience on two trapeze bars. The man swings upside down on the far trapeze, holding on with just his legs, while the two girls and a boy swing out on the first trapeze, let go, and do somersaults in the air. At the last second the man swings in on his trapeze and catches them before they fall to earth. Big thrills, no spills.

We are so impressed we hang around after the show to congratulate the performers. Suddenly everyone gets shy as we exclaim how much we enjoyed the show. Alexander tells us that tomorrow the show will feature different acts, and he invites us back.

Early the next afternoon we return to watch everyone working on routines. We are invited into the troupe's "home," a bus that has been set up with a kitchen, a living area, and curtained bedrooms in the back. Nine people make up the circus, one big extended family. The father, Leon, has performed in circuses all over the world. He shows us a scrapbook with photos of himself as a young man in a number of trapeze troupes. His wife, Manuella, also has a circus background. She no longer performs, but keeps everything running smoothly, from making the Big Top tent and sewing costumes to cooking, bookkeeping, and selling tickets. They have five kids, Rafi, Alberto, Francesca, Juanita and Jorge, ages eight through seventeen. All the kids are trained in numerous disciplines, including acrobatics, juggling, and trapeze. The boys also work as clowns while the girls train dogs. Alexander is their cousin. He juggles, does acrobatics and the contortionist routine, and is the main clown. The other cousin, Juan, is the boy with the disfigured arm. He is not in the show but helps set up and take down the Big Top and does other odd jobs.

That evening we help sell tickets, but Manuella refuses to let us pay for our own tickets. Again we are amazed at the quality of the performances. We spend much of the next day with the family. The following evening after the last show in town, Leon invites us to come with them to the next town. Alexander and Juan chime in and tell us there is plenty of room for us to sleep in the second bedroom/storage bus where they sleep. Tass and I look at each other and smile. How often is a person invited to travel with a Mexican circus? The offer is too good to refuse.

I'm not sure which is more work, pounding the huge metal stakes into the ground for the Big Top, or trying to get the stakes back out when the tent comes down. Using both arms to wield the sledgehammer and drive the stakes is exhausting after just three or four stakes. I am astonished to watch Juan pound in stake after stake after stake, using just one arm to swing the heavy sledgehammer. In big, smooth arcs he lifts then drops the hammer, keeping a slow but steady rhythm. He never stops to rest, and soon is far ahead of me in the number of stakes solidly in the ground.

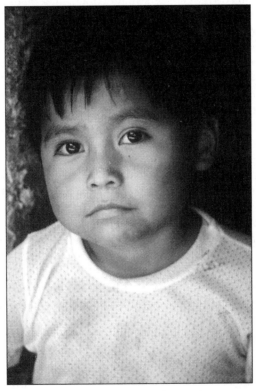

A young Mexican boy.

Although the circus has just one show each night, the work of the troupe never ends. Yet like Juan's stake pounding, the tasks get completed at a steady, stress-free pace, with numerous jokes and lots of laughter accompanying each chore.

While I am in the Big Top, helping Leon set up bleachers, Rafi and Alberto, ages eight and ten, run into the tent, chasing each other playing tag. Alberto grabs a rope hanging down from the trapeze platform and climbs hand-over-hand into the air. Rafi instantly grabs a second rope, and climbs hand over hand after his brother. Within seconds both are thirty feet in the air. Although the safety net is up, half the time the boys dangle to the side beyond the net, swatting and swinging at each other as each tries to get onto the trapeze platform without being touched by the other.

Manuella and another woman who has come to visit sit chatting below, mending costumes, completely oblivious to the shenanigans going on above them. Leon likewise goes about his work. I can't help but imagine this same scenario elsewhere. The two kids wouldn't get five feet off the ground before all the adults would panic, yelling for them to come back down. I find it interesting that the parents trust the two kids to watch out for themselves, and are willing to let the boys suffer the consequences if they make a mistake. Perhaps the most important thing for a circus performer is confidence in one's abilities. The two boys certainly have that!

After a few minutes the boys come back down the ropes. Leon gives me a little smile, and then stoops down to put one hand on the ground, palm up. Instantly Alberto runs toward his dad. At the last second Alberto does a hand stand, and then, still upside down, puts both his hands on his dad's single hand. With hardly any discernible effort, Leon lifts his son, still balanced upside down, into the air and up above his head. Next Alberto lets go with one hand and balances with just the other above his dad. Leon walks in a small circle with his eyes on his son above him, then bends his elbow and tosses Alberto lightly into the air. Alberto does half a somersault, lands on his feet, and runs out of the tent after Rafi.

Another day Leon, Francesca, Juanita and Jorge practice their trapeze act. When they finish they all do big, slow, laid-out somersaults into the safety net. On the ground Jorge talks me into giving the trapeze a try. He climbs up the rope ladder to the trapeze platform and I follow. Climbing the rope ladder is in itself quite a challenge, as it bends and sways with every tug. I am exhausted by the time I reach the top. There hardly seems enough room for the two of us on the tiny, narrow stand. I am impressed as I think back to the performances when three and even four people were up here, balancing on the little ledge, smiling and waving at the crowd. This seems exciting enough, and I haven't even tried the trapeze yet.

The safety net is strung out below us, but from above, the net looks very small and narrow. Jorge unhooks the trapeze bar and gives me directions. The plan is for me to simply swing out, swing back, and land on the ledge. Sounds easy, but actually it is quite tricky. I have to lean out away from the center pole just to reach the trapeze bar. To get enough momentum to make the return swing to the tiny ledge, I must start by leaping up into the air above the platform, making sure that I have enough speed. I'm not too sure how I am supposed to jump and get this thing going right.

I have always been nervous around heights. Now I am terrified. What have I gotten myself into? If I think too long I will never be able to do it, so before I talk myself out of it, I jump, very lamely as it turns out, into the air.

Immediately I go in a surprisingly quick arc across the top of the tent. I am so nervous that I don't dangle, relaxed from the trapeze bar, but rather hold my arms completely bent with a sweaty, death grip on the bar. At the end of the arc, I try to kick my legs up slightly as Jorge instructed to increase my momentum, but my effort is not enough. On the back swing toward the trapeze platform, which to me seems at rocketing speed in reverse, I don't have enough velocity. Instead of swinging up high next to Jorge, where he planned to grab me around the waist and help get me back on the tiny platform, I stall out about three feet away from him. Now I swing back toward the center of the tent. With each successive swing the arc lessens, and soon I am hanging, stopped, in the middle of space, dangling over the net. My hands and arms are exhausted from clenching so tightly to the trapeze bar. The thought of dropping into the net far below makes me sick to my stomach, but I have no choice. I can't hold on much longer.

Jorge tells me to stick my legs out in front of me when I drop, so the entire length of my legs hits the net, which will help to lessen the impact of my fall. I don't consciously let go; instead my arms give out and I drop like a rock. I manage to get my legs out, but I also tumble slightly backward and basically land on my bottom with my feet sticking up into the air. I sink deep into the net. Unfortunately I have not quite spread the weight of my fall out along my body. The net dips under my weight and my butt smacks the ground. For a moment I wonder if I have broken my tailbone. I lie in the net in pain, and then roll out to the side of the net doing a pitiful crab-like move to drop from the net back onto the ground, six feet below.

My arm muscles are completely seized up from the trauma of my death-grip on the trapeze bar. For the next three days the little-used muscles across my chest are so sore it hurts to take a big breath. My stomach muscles hurt when I sit. Despite Jorge's laughter and assurances that the next time I will do better, I never make another swing across the Big Top. For some things, once is enough.

Each morning everyone gathers for breakfast in the kitchen built inside one of the buses. Breakfast is beans, eggs, and tortillas, a meal I find delicious and could easily eat every day for months. A large bowl of tiny green peppers, a particularly hot variety, sits in the center of the table. When Tass and I first came to Mexico we put just one of the peppers in a large bowl of lentil soup we were cooking; the soup was so spicy hot we could hardly eat it.

But that was months ago, and I have been steadily increasing my tolerance, and enjoyment, for hot peppers. Now Alexander and Jorge encourage me to eat like they do: one bite of egg, one whole pepper, another bite of egg, another whole pepper. With about six bites of egg left, I am determined to finish off the bowl of peppers. My tongue, mouth, and the back of my throat are on fire. I am careful not to lick my lips with my tongue, as I am sure it would put me over the edge.

"*Macho, macho!*" Alexander chants with approval as I finish off the last of the peppers. "Now you are becoming a real Mexican!"

5

In the Land of the Maya

After three months in the Yucatan peninsula we return to Palenque, our favorite of all the ruins. We spend another week exploring the area. When we leave we head south-east, over the mountains toward Guatemala. We take a pitiful, broken-down bus, with huge holes in the floor that suck in a steady stream of exhaust fumes. Within five minutes we are both nauseous.

We stumble off the bus at the turnoff to Agua Azul, Blue Water, and welcome the fresh air, even though the temperature is sweltering. We hike three miles down to the river and find a sea of litter, where locals have had numerous weekend picnics and parties. Luckily it is mid-week and we have the place to ourselves. We pass through the wasteland picnic area to find the river flowing over a beautiful series of limestone rock formations with dazzling turquoise pools and waterfalls, all surrounded by tropical rainforest. We hike upriver, away from the litter, and camp beside a quiet pool of exquisitely colored tourmaline water. We stay three days.

Our next bus ride takes us to the wonderful Mexican city of San Cristobal de las Casas. In cities we always stay in the cheapest of the budget hotels. Some of the hotels are in old colonial buildings and have wonderful character despite their quirks. Others are cobbled-together shanties with wood-scrap walls, doors, and shutters, with everything hanging by a single nail, a single hinge, or a broken latch. Since some don't even have locks, we carry our own small padlock for the doors. The plumbing works only half the time; the electricity, even less. Almost all have courtyards, a great place to meet locals or other travelers.

Our first night in San Cristobal we arrive late and exhausted. The third class bus station is in a bleak part of town. After half an hour of searching, we get the only room within walking distance. The handmade bed sways decrepitly. The mattress is so disgusting, we remove the single bedsheet, cover the mattress with our tent ground cloth, put the bedsheet back on, and climb

37

into bed. The walls around us are all light blue. One wall is made of a flimsy pressed wallboard with a couple of small holes broken out in the corners.

"Do you think a mouse could come through there?" I ask Tass, eyeing the corners.

"Probably," Tass shrugs.

"I don't know," I reply, "It looks kind of small."

No sooner do the words leave my mouth, than a large white rat sticks its pink head out of the corner, and with no concern or fear of us, dashes through the hole, runs straight up the corner of the wall, and disappears into another hole in the corner of the ceiling. It happens so quickly that neither of us even has time to throw something at the brazen intruder. I jump up, run to the corner, and bang on the wall a few times, a belated warning to discourage return visits during the night.

The next morning we eat breakfast and move to Casa de Huespedes Margarita, a different hotel in a more pleasant area of town. The amazing paradox of budget travel is that for the same price we get a wonderful room located off a delightful courtyard filled with plants, all potted in colorful, handmade, clay pots.

San Cristobal is over six thousand feet in elevation, in a temperate, pine-filled valley. The town has long been one of Mexico's most popular tourist destinations, with a college, an established artistic community, and a number of Spanish-language schools. The town is very well kept, with massive old colonial buildings and wonderful architecture.

San Cristobal is a cultural crossroads. Tzotzil and Tzeltal Indian villages dot the surrounding countryside. San Cristobal's vibrant market is open six days a week, bringing Indians into town to buy and sell their wares. Early each morning the narrow streets of San Cristobal fill with barefoot Indians shuffling heavy loads on their backs to the market. They all wear handwoven clothes and, depending on their village, the colors range from pink and turquoise cotton *huipiles* to rougher-textured black-and-white homespun wool. Despite their frequent visits to the city, the Indians living near San Cristobal are some of Mexico's most traditional, not only in dress, but also in their beliefs. Although they are mostly Catholic, the Indians still maintain strong pre-Hispanic elements in their religious practices.

We get up at dawn each morning and head straight to the food and vegetable market. The air is crisp and cool. Sometimes small clouds of mist hang over the streets. The market bustles with activity as the vendors chat amiably with their neighbors while laying out their wares. Although numerous food stalls line the plaza, my favorite breakfast spot is in the middle of the market, where a woman, surrounded by vegetable sellers, has simply two little wooden stools, and a big pot of the most delicious red beans I have ever eaten. She ladles a serving of beans into a small red plastic bowl, and places a bundle of fresh, warm corn *tortillas* in a cloth napkin to keep them soft and moist. She doesn't offer any silverware. I use a chunk of *tortilla* to scoop up each mouthful of beans. My breakfast, all I can eat, costs about eight cents. I eat breakfast here every morning we are in San Cristobal. Sometimes Tass joins me; other times she tries neighboring food stalls.

A man carrying three tables to set up in the market.

Near the central plaza in town are a number of tourist shops selling Indian weavings, pottery and other handicrafts. Many of the women's *huipiles* have stylized people, animals, birds and even snakes woven into the fabric. Some of the designs are hundreds of years old. Shelves and tables are covered with pottery figures of people and animals in all sorts of fantastic shapes and sizes. When shopping we have to remind ourselves we are supposedly traveling light. We buy a couple of smaller pieces, then break down and purchase a cabbage-sized figure—a man lying on his stomach, impossibly contorted in a backbend with his feet pulled around up next to his ears, his mouth open and cheeks puffed in a most curious expression. We dub him Yoga Man. Despite his size, I make room for him in my backpack.

I spend a number of days in the library at Na Bolom, the home of a husband and wife, archaeologist and anthropologist respectively, who have worked in southern Mexico for much of this century. After Frans Bolom died, his wife Trudy opened their home to aspiring anthropologists working in the area, and made their enormous library available to anyone interested in learning more about the many indigenous Indians in southern Mexico and Guatemala. I spend hours reading obscure books about the Maya and copying by hand detailed maps of many Mayan sites.

For most of history, the area that is now the southern Mexican states of Yucatan and Chiapas have been more closely connected culturally and politically with Guatemala than Mexico. This was true in Mayan times as well as early colonial times, when the area was governed from Guatemala City. Being here has made us excited to see Guatemala, which is still the cultural center for the Maya today. Even though the numerous Indian villages up in the mountains around San Cristobal would be fascinating to visit, we suddenly have a urgent desire to get to Guatemala itself.

We take a bus from San Cristobal to Ciudad Cuauhtemoc on the Mexican border, then walk the two miles across the frontier to arrive at the Guatemala police and customs post. A small group of buildings sit isolated along the road, far from any town. The custom agent's only job is to stamp our passport and fill out a couple of lines on a document page. Still, he acts totally put out, as though our showing up has ruined his day. At eleven o'-clock our passports are taken into a back room. We sit and wait in the building lobby. At noon a different official comes to inform us that our paperwork is not finished. The customs office closes from noon until two o'-clock. Would we please leave the building and wait outside until customs reopens? At 2:30 a bored and grumpy official unlocks and reopens the door and somewhat reluctantly returns our passports to us. We pass into Guatemala.

The pine covered Sierra Madre mountains of Chiapas continue on into northwestern Guatemala. Many of the mountains are volcanic in origin, a number of them six to eight thousand feet above sea level.

We spend a day in Huehuetenango, visiting the local market. Like many city markets, much of the activity is crowded into a large open pavilion where hundreds of vendors are packed together, each claiming a small bit of floor space, selling vegetables, fruit, handicrafts, weavings, cloth, and clothes. The handwoven clothing of the Indians from the mountains creates a sea of wonderful colors in the market. Many of the mountain towns are more than a thousand years old, having been settled long before the arrival of the Spanish. The traditional lifestyles and beliefs of the Mayan Indians remain strongest in these mountain towns. The first language for many of the indigenous people is one of the thirty-five different Mayan dialects spoken today. Many speak Spanish only when confronted by officials, or when selling or bargaining with *mestizos*, people of mixed Spanish and Indian ancestry, or *gringos* in the markets.

Under Spanish rule much of the highlands of Guatemala was administered by friars who came to convert the Maya to Christianity. Many friars worked tirelessly to protect the people from exploitation, and in some cases even helped preserve aspects of traditional Mayan society. Today the highlands of western Guatemala are a magnet for travelers who want to learn more about the present Mayan Indians, as well as to see some of the most scenic countryside in Guatemala. The rainy season is May through October, when the hills are lush and verdant. Now in the dry season, the grass is golden brown, as are the fields of harvested corn, with only the stalks left standing dried in the sun. The only green is the pine trees high in the mountains and on the steep hillsides between corn fields.

The Mayan culture has long been influenced by the ubiquitous cultivation of corn or maize. Traditionally the Indians have farmed by hand on small plots of land. Everywhere we look we see small cottages surrounded by *milpa*, fields of maize. The houses have mud walls with thatched or red-tiled roofs and no chimneys; the smoke from the cooking fires simply wafts through the ceiling. People shuffle along the mountain roads carrying enormous loads on their backs using a tumpline, a band across the forehead tied to the loads. Tumplines shift the weight of the load from the lower back, but it looks to me like it simply takes the stress from the back and places it on the neck. I can't imagine carrying such a load.

Our destination is Lake Atitlan, surrounded by mountains and volcanoes in the western highlands. As the bus pulls into the small village of Solola, we get a spectacular view of the lake two thousand feet below surrounded by mountains and volcanos.The road drops in huge, dramatic switchbacks through steep pine forest. The lake itself is a caldera, a collapsed volcanic cone, one thousand feet deep and fifteen miles long with no outlet. Eleven villages are located along the shores of the lake, and seven more in the mountains overlook the area.

The little town of Panajachel on the edge of Lake Atitlan has long been a popular tourist destination for a small group of wealthy Guatemalans, who generally stay a mile from town in a high-priced hotel. In the last few years, Panajachel has also become a destination for the growing ranks of backpackers and budget travelers, who congregate in a few cheap hotels along the city streets. But we have heard there are also some small, unadvertised "guest houses" away from the town center. We hike down a side street and stop in a little *tienda* to ask for directions or suggestions where we might find lodging. The store owner looks at us blankly, unsure what we are asking. Another customer, a short Indian man, wearing a suit coat and a felt hat, overhears our questions. He offers to rent us a room at his house. Outside he jumps on a huge one-speed bicycle and rides across town while we follow, as fast as we can, on foot with our backpacks.

His house is a stucco building with a tin roof, built like a small duplex, with a covered walkway down the middle separating the two sides. He shows us a small, square cinderblock room with a cement floor and a single, bare lightbulb hanging from the ceiling. There is no furniture. Attached to the room is another, smaller room with a thatched roof and a dirt floor—the kitchen. In the corner is a three-foot high hearth where a cooking fire can be built. In the front yard is a water spigot and a basin to wash dishes or clothes. The yard is filled with flowering plants, a lemon tree, and an avocado tree, dripping with ripe fruit. In back is an outhouse and a shower in a wooden shanty we can share with the family. He tells us he will rent us the house for five *quetzales*, five dollars per week. We take it.

On the street in front of the house men shuffle past with enormous loads of chopped firewood carried down from the mountains on their backs. We buy a load of wood for one *quetzal*, one dollar, which will provide us approximately one month of cooking fires, the length of time we plan on staying. We borrow a homemade wooden bench with a back rest from the family for a couch, lay our sleeping pads out on the cement floor for a bed, and settle into our new home.

Tuesday and Friday is market day in Solola, the largest market in the area. Brightly-dressed Mayans from the surrounding villages and towns pack the plaza selling fresh produce, fruit, vegetables, and flowers. We see piles of tiny,

Women in market, Solola, Guatemala.

bright pink potatoes, oblong tomatoes, onions, fresh garlic, oranges, plus a variety of prepared food dishes: *tamales, tortas, frijoles* and *tortillas*. One walkway of stalls displays brightly-colored textiles, piles of yarn, and weaving and sewing supplies.

This area has one of the largest populations of traditionally-dressed Indians in all of Guatemala. The women around Solola wear striped red clothing, while the men have black-and-white embroidered high-water pants with calf-length hems, embroidered "cowboy style" shirts, wool jackets with distinctive embroidered patterns, and small black-and-white checkered blankets worn around their waists like skirts. The Indians from each village around the lake wear a different style of clothing, different colors, different embroidery. Most of the clothing is woven on a backstrap loom, with each weaving being about fifteen inches wide and three or four feet long. Two weavings are then sewn together with colorful thread and a hole is cut in the center for the head to make a *huipil* blouse. Although each village has distinct weaving styles, the women don't use set patterns. Each piece is unique, the design created as it is woven. The clothing is so colorful and festive we can't resist going native and buying a few *huipils* to wear, along with woven bracelets and colorful waist sashes. By creating a demand for different types of hand-woven textiles and crafts, the growing tourist industry helps revitalize the indigenous economy and encourages pride in the native culture.

We meet Marcos, a traveler from Lake Tahoe, who is also staying in Panajachel. After wandering the market most of the morning, we all buy bean *tamales* from an old woman, then walk around to the side of the cathedral to eat in the shade and watch the activity of the market. The *tamales* are hot and moist, wrapped in steamed corn husks. We each eat a *tamale*; Marcos' has meat inside, while Tass and I, being vegetarian, each have one with just beans. I unwrap another *tamale* and take a bite. Something about the second *tamale* tastes peculiar. I suspect it might have meat instead of beans inside, so I break it open to have a look. In the middle of the *tamale* is part of a small jaw, complete with a row of molar teeth. Marcos, who is not even a vegetarian, completely loses it.

"What is it?" he shrieks, spitting the last of his own *tamale* onto the street in disgust.

"Probably a jaw bone from a dog," I guess, unsure. Marcos is about to throw up.

"I can't believe I ate the first *tamale*!" he shudders in horror.

"What difference does it make whether it is a cow, a pig or a dog!" we tease him. "Meat is meat!" Marcos is unconvinced.

We visit a number of villages in the area on their market days. We also spend time hanging out, talking, and reading voraciously on a variety of subjects, especially Central America, then sharing and discussing the books together.

Bruce's "vegetarian" bean tamale, complete with the
jawbone of a dog, Solola, Guatemala.

Before we came here we read of the violent history of the Spanish conquest and the subjugation of the Mayan people. Traveling through the countryside we realize how brutal life continues to be. The Maya, along with other local indigenous people, are still on the fringe of the economic system.

The Guatemalan government warns travelers to stay out of specific regions of the countryside. We meet Peace Corp workers, church social workers, and other relief agency workers who talk of entire villages in the mountains where men, women and children have been murdered by government forces. The government controlled newspapers don't even mention it, or when they do, they say it is isolated guerilla fighting.

The history of the region shows how brutal actions can negatively affect people not just for one generation, but for hundreds of years. The Spanish conquistadores simply divided the Mayan lands into large estates. The Maya obviously had no legal title registered in the Spanish court system, so they lost all rights to their land. The new owners viewed the Maya simply as a vast labor force to exploit.

The harshness of Spanish rule resulted in frequent revolts by the subjugated people throughout Latin America, all of which were ruthlessly crushed. It wasn't until Napolean's conquest of Europe in the early 1800s and the deposition of Spain's King Ferdinand VII that the Spanish colonies in the New World were able to fight and win their independence from a weakened Spain.

Unfortunately for the Maya, the Spanish government throughout the area was replaced by extremely conservative and militaristic local governments, whose only concern was furthering the wealth of the Spanish ancestory upper class. In fact, the oppression of the Maya actually became worse. Again Mayan claims to ancestral lands were ignored, and huge plantations were created to grow sugar cane, tobacco, henequen for rope, and later coffee and bananas.

Although they were legally declared as free, the Maya were held in bondage through debt peonage, an exploitative system where peasants were forced to work to pay exorbitant "rent" on land where they lived and were refused legal title. In the early 1900's two Guatemalan presidents continued this tradition by ceding vast tracts of Mayan lands to the United Fruit Company.

In 1945, in one of the first truly free elections in the country, Guatemalans elected Juan Jose Arevalo, a philosopher, as president. Arevalo established a social security system, a health care system, liberal labor laws, and even a government department to monitor Mayan civil rights and concerns. During his six-year rule an astonishing twenty-five coups were attempted by the disgruntled right-wing military leaders. Arevalo managed to survive all the coups and stay in power, an obvious sign of his popular support with the people.

In 1951 Guatemalans elected Colonel Jacob Arbenz Guzman president. Although a former military officer, Arbenz surprisingly continued the reforms started by Arevalo. Then he went a step further and expropriated large areas of unused land held fallow by the United Fruit Company. His plan was to distribute the land to peasants and put it into cultivation for food. The United Fruit Company was paid for the land that was taken, but the company didn't feel it was enough, and United Fruit began engineering the downfall of Arbenz.

The Secretary of State for the U.S. government at the time was John Foster Dulles, who, along with his brother, owned a large share in the United Fruit Company. Dulles quickly rallied communist paranoia in Washington, and soon the CIA organized an invasion of Guatemala from neighboring Honduras, led by two disgruntled former Guatemalan military officers. Arbenz was forcefully removed from his elected office and many of his reforms, as well as Arevalo's reforms, were reversed.

Since then violent right-wing dictatorial governments have ruled Guatemala. Opponents of those in power are generally murdered by the ever present death squads.

Part II
1978

MEXICO

Palenque.
San Cristobal
Belize
Guatemala
Honduras

TIKAL.

IXIL TRIANGLE
GUATEMALA

Huehuetenango
★

Santa Cruz del Quiche
Chichicastenango
Quetzaltenango
Solola
Lake Atitlan
Panajachel

6

Volcanoes

After six months in Mexico and Guatemala we take a train back to the U.S. border, hitch-hike to South Dakota, and drive our Jeep truck back to Wyoming. Tass returns to work at the bakery. I help our friends Bob and Anna Dennis enlarge and remodel their log cabin in Jackson. We move into a little garage on their property with no running water, so we share the bathroom in the house. I work without pay, just for room and board. Then comes an opportunity for me to take one short break from cabin building to get my travelling finances together.

To raise travel and ski bum money in the past I have worked in the eastern Wyoming oilfields as a roughneck and roustabout, and I have also built coal silos. Now Dave Snyder, a friend and former workmate, hires me for a ten-day job near Decker, Montana, building a pair of two-hundred-foot high coal silos.

Cement coal silos are built using slip-form construction. Once the slip starts, the silos are built in one continuous, non-stop effort. Concrete is poured into a six-foot high form the circumference of the silo, and every few minutes the form is jacked half an inch into the air. A huge, wooden deck attached to the form rises with the slip. From this platform iron workers assemble rebar as the slip rises, and concrete pourers keep a steady stream of fresh concrete going into the mold.

I am hired as a cement finisher. Twelve of us work dangling below the slip form on a narrow and wiggly, wooden scaffolding that circles the outside of each silo. As the slip moves up, we smooth and gloss over the cement emerging from the form to insure the silos have no surface cracks or tiny air pockets that could be a potential weak spot for weathering. Since a large work force is needed for the slip, the company must pay well enough to attract experienced workers for a job that lasts only ten days. Two crews work twelve-hour shifts to keep the project going around the clock. Our contract gives us daily overtime pay after eight hours and double time for Saturday and Sunday. Plus, as a cement finisher, I get an additional danger pay because I work from a hanging scaffold and not up on the deck.

Despite being hard workers, our finishing crew is not exactly a legitimate union staff. So we are given the night shift, from seven p.m to seven a.m., which we actually prefer to the day shift. Shortly after we go to work each evening, we see a beautiful sunset over the prairie. We don't have to deal with the intense summer daytime heat; instead we work under the pleasantly cool starry sky. During the last few hours of our shift the eastern sky grows light and then turns dramatically pink with the coming sunrise. Each day the slip rises about twenty feet into the air. By the end of the project we are two hundred feet above the prairie, with spectacular views of the countryside, and I make real progress overcoming my fear of heights. In ten days I earn eighteen hundred dollars, which even after taxes is more than enough for another winter south of the border.

After Christmas Tass and I hitch-hike back to Mexico. Our plan is to spend a month revisiting some of our favorite spots and then to take up where we left off in Guatemala. Tass's South America travel partner, Suzanne Martell, meets us in Tucson and together we head for the border. Suza plans to travel a month or so with us; then we will meet again later in Guatemala. When we finish our trip and go home Suza will travel on to South America and the Galapagos.

Again we take third-class trains south, but this time we stop in Mexico City for a day to visit the Archaeology Museum. And we can't help but get off the train at Palenque. We have fun sharing the ruins with Suza, and we appreciate her expertise while birding on the trails.

One day we find a dead barred antshrike along a trail. The neck of the bird is still limp; it has just died. The black-and-white zebra pattern of the feathers is even more beautiful up close. We were recently talking about Mayan priests who wore cloaks made of hummingbird feathers, and wondering how the cloaks were made. Now we decide to skin the antshrike to see if we can remove the pelt from the bird with the feathers intact. Armed with our only tools, a Swiss army knife, a small pocket scissor, and a pair of tweezers, the three of us perform the delicate operation as best we can. We tack the finished product out on cardboard and salt the tiny hide. As it is drying I whittle an antshrike-size mold out of wood to see if we can make a mount like taxidermists do. But the pelt shrinks as it dries. A few days later we have a hysterical time trying to fit the pelt on the carving. The finished product is terribly mottled, and even with the distinct black-and-white feathers it is hard to tell what the bird might once have been.

We move on through Chichen Itza to the Caribbean coast. Numerous small changes have taken place in the last year. Nowhere are the changes more apparent than Isla Mujeres. The ferry taking us to the island is almost full. Most of the travelers are still young people carrying backpacks, but now most are from Europe. Los Cocos, the little beach campground, is packed. Unfortunately the aging sewer system is not up to the increase in volume, and a nasty odor occasionally wafts through the palm trees. In town various construction projects that were haphazardly going on last year have miraculously taken a giant leap forward. The sandy main street has been covered with stone tiles. Newly planted palm trees border the walkway. Garrafon reef has a dramatic increase in boats bringing day visitors from Cancun, which we hear is growing at a phenomenal rate. After a week we are ready to move on. We say goodbye to Suza with plans to meet later in Tikal.

After a month in the Yucatan we return to the shores of Lake Atitlan in Guatemala. Panajachel has also sprouted numerous new businesses catering to *gringos*. Instead of one restaurant selling granola and yogurt, there are three, two of which also list *Hamberguesas*, hamburgers, on the menu. A family of Guatemalans who work in a new souvenir shop is renting the little house we stayed in before. We rent a little *cabana* in the growing *gringo* part of town.

We make friends with a number of other travelers, including Doug and Mark from Wisconsin, whom we meet at a highland market. After a couple of market trips together we all decide to climb 11,600-foot Atitlan volcano, the largest of the three extinct volcanoes surrounding the lake. We start early in the morning from the village of San Lucas Toliman. Pressed up against Atitlan volcano is just slightly smaller Toliman volcano. As we hike, the morning mist turns to cold rain. Route-finding is tricky. We have a considerable ongoing debate to make sure the trail we are on is going to the top of Atitlan, not Toliman.

The rain stops halfway up the volcano and the mists clear for spectacular views of Lake Atitlan below us. Toliman is beside us. Good, at least we are on the right volcano. Across an inlet in the lake stands majestic 9,824-foot San Pedro volcano.

Although the sun has come back out, we all arrive on top chilled. The volcano doesn't have much of a crater, just crumbling piles of broken rock. In a few places steam hisses out of cracks in the ground. The wind picks up, and clouds swirl around us as we search for a campsite in the jagged volcanic rock. We scramble all over the top of the volcano until we find two small, tent-size spots where someone has moved the rock and cleared the ground to camp.

We set up the tents and eat a cold supper, watching the steam hiss out of a nearby vent. By the time we finish eating we have convinced ourselves we have studied the fissure long enough to know its every nuance—and that it would make a perfect sauna. The crack is four feet wide at the top and twelve feet deep. We cover the top of the fissure with our nylon ground cloth, strip down to our underwear, and shinny down into our own private steam room.

Although the mist pouring out the top of the fissure felt wonderfully warm while we were making our plans, now that we have hardly any clothes on the air is chilly. Even with the nylon roof to catch and hold the steam, we are not exactly basking in comfort. Icy drafts keep blowing in from above. We find ourselves descending deeper into the crack for warmth. I get all the way to the bottom of the fissure, trying to avoid scalding my feet where the steam pours directly out of the crack. Tass, Doug, and Mark are crowded on top, trying to squeeze closer to the heat. Suddenly I hear a change in sound, like a low-toned teapot ready to boil. Earlier we had observed that the noise preceded an enormous belch of steam.

"It's gonna blow" I yell. "Hurry and get out!"

We frantically scramble out of the crack and huddle, exposed to the biting wind, as we wait for the blast of steam to go back down. After the steam stabilizes we crawl back in, jokingly piling once again on top of one another. We repeat the scenario a few times. Finally we get the tarp sealed well enough to actually break a sweat. When we are finished we stand out in the wind and use our T-shirts to dry off—and quickly lose all our warmth.

But as we crawl into our sleeping bags, we have a great surprise. Whoever cleared the sleeping areas picked the sites well. The ground is just warm enough under us that our beds are wonderfully toasty. We sleep on a thermal area, in luxurious comfort.

The next morning the sun comes up behind three more volcanoes on the distant horizon. One of the volcanoes, Fuego, has an enormous plume of smoke rising from its summit. Next to Fuego stands the double-coned summit of Acatenango volcano. As the sun strikes our faces we all decide we must climb Acatenango, where we hope to be rewarded with spectacular, close-up views of active Fuego.

Route-finding and getting directions from locals is the hardest part of climbing volcanoes. The most obvious trail at the bottom doesn't necessarily go to the top, but rather to the most used fields higher on the mountain. As we hike along the lower slopes of Acatenango, we occasionally meet farmers going to and from the fields. We quickly learn not to ask, "Is this the trail to the top?" because no matter which trail we are on, the answer is always an automatic, and enthusiastic, "*Si!*," Yes! Many of the Indians have a hard time disagreeing or saying no to anything a foreigner says. They feel they are being rude.

We phrase our questions so a yes or no answer is not an option: "Which trail goes to the top?" We try to act disinterested as we ask, like we really don't care if it is the trail we are on or not. Hopefully we will encourage a little more candor in the reply. But still the answer always seems to be an automatic affirmation of the trail we are on. We are even told we are on the right trail when we are coming back down from an obvious dead-end. After much backtracking up and down through the fields we finally find a trail, we think, that will take us all the way up the mountain.

Above the cleared fields we hike into lush, tropical forest. Again the mist settles in and soon it is raining. We hike in the rain for a time but, as it gets colder, we are soon chilled and miserable. We have no choice but to find a place to set up our tents. Moments after making this decision, we miraculously arrive at a little cleared ridge, the first spot since we started climbing that is flat enough for two tents. We put up our tent in lightning speed, strip off our leaking rain gear, and dive inside.

In the tent our mood quickly improves. Inclement weather is not necessarily a bad thing when you are warm and dry in a tent. This is the reason we brought a pile of books and plenty of snacks! We relax in cozy comfort under our sleeping bags, and wile away the hours reading. There is no need to even get up to look outside and check the weather, as the constant drumming of rain against the tent fly tells us the storm continues unabated. As darkness falls we light candles, which supplies not only reading light, but a comforting glow and a pleasant warmth to the air in the tent.

In the middle of the night we are jolted awake by a violent movement in the earth.

"The volcano is erupting!" Tass shouts in terror, leaping out of her sleeping bag. We hear a large tree, or trees, crashing to the ground in the forest nearby. Tass scrambles for our tiny flashlight. If we are going to die at least we want to be able to see. We stare at each other wide-eyed, frozen in place, unsure if we should bolt from the tent or just sit where we are. The continual sound of falling branches and trees reverberates through the forest. After five or ten seconds, which seems more like minutes, the ground stops moving. We don't hear any deep rumble or sound coming from the volcano.

"It was an earthquake!" I offer hesitatingly, still listening for the sounds of a volcanic explosion. The noise of the crashing trees has stopped and the air now seems remarkably still.

"Yahoo!!" I shout at the top of my lungs, like an emotional survivor of an accident, the joy and thrill of being alive rushing through my veins.

"Yahoo!" echoes an exuberant reply from Doug and Mark in the neighboring tent. We peer out our tent door into the darkness and talk with each other, reliving the experience. The rain has stopped and the clouds are breaking slightly as a few scattered stars twinkle in the sky. After a few minutes we grow silent. Finally, with nothing else to do, we go back to sleep.

The next morning we find we are in an ideal spot to see the sunrise and also bask in the warmth of the morning sun. We string up a number of clotheslines to take advantage of the sunshine and try to dry out some of our gear. We bird and eat a leisurely breakfast. All too soon the clouds build and obscure the sun. We repack our partially dried gear and resume climbing the volcano.

Unlike the top of Atitlan volcano, which was covered with broken shards of lava, the lower summit of Acatenango is a giant scree cone of ash and lapilli. Vulcanologists define volcanic ash by size. Lapilli is formed when a volcano erupts under tremendous pressure and blows lava high into the air. The lava separates into droplets, and as they fall back to earth they cool off enough to solidify back into rock. Droplets ranging from one to three inches in size are called lapilli.

Climbing a hill of lapilli is like climbing a hill of marbles. We take one step forward, and then slide back half a step. Plus, with each step our feet sink six inches into the pulverized rock. Hiking in lightweight boots, without gaiters, our shoes quickly fill with the loose rock. But it is useless to stop and empty our boots of the annoying sharp pebbles grinding into our feet; they would simply fill up again within five steps. In one day we put two years of wear and tear on our boots, and our feet.

We arrive at the top of the first cone to find a grand view of the saddle linking with the highest cone. Two deep craters, both about 150-feet in diameter, lie side by side between us, gaping holes where the volcano last erupted. Despite our high viewpoint, we are unable to look down inside the craters enough to see the bottom. We descend the first cone, and drop down to the saddle. The rock directly around each of the craters is no longer loose ash and lapilli, but superhardened rock with fractured cliffs. Try as we might, without ropes we are unable to peer over the edge to see into the craters, the very throat of the volcano.

Above us rises the dramatic main cone of Acatenango. Unlike the first cone, where we could discern no trail and simply blazed our own way to the top, here we can see the faint line of a trail above us. But once we start hiking it is questionable whether the trail offers any easier climbing. The footsteps that made the trail didn't pack down or in any way clear the scree and ash away, but simply pulverized the lappili into a finer ash. We climb sections of the trail until we tire of the futility of our struggle, then head off onto untracked scree to try a different approach. There is simply no way to get up the volcano without an inordinate amount of sweat and exertion.

The summit of Acatenango is an enormous caldera, a half-mile wide depression where the top of the volcano has caved back in on itself, creating a bowl-shaped dip in the top of the mountain that is also covered with ash and lapilli. In the center of the caldera are a group of incongruous white rocks in a sea of black scree, rocks someone has obviously hauled up from the lower slopes of the volcano to anchor down tents. We gratefully use the campsite and then climb the far rim of the caldera to check out the views of active Fuego volcano, which during our entire climb has remained unseen off the back side of Acatenango.

The view of Fuego is even better than we had hoped. We are perched about one thousand vertical feet above the volcano, and just over a mile

Our campsite in the caldera of Acatenango volcano, Guatemala.

away. A small black plume of dark ash wafts up from the crater of Fuego, while grey rain clouds swirl high up and down the mountain and also around our volcano. Above us, high in the air, an immense cloud of black ash hangs over both volcanoes.

A large black plume of smoke begins to rise out of the crater of Fuego. A few moments later we hear a rumbling explosion. The distance of the volcano has delayed the sound from reaching our ears. The sound continues to grow. We are astonished as the cloud of ash also grows and grows up into the air, a rolling, churning mass of superheated gas. Only when the top of the ash pillar is far above us does the summit of the cloud expand and billow outward into the classic, top heavy shape of a tree or mushroom. A few minutes go by, and, like clockwork, Fuego belts out another gigantic plume of smoke and ash. Watching the volcano is so captivating, we can hardly tear ourselves away to get warmer clothing when the sun sets on the far horizon.

As the sky darkens, Fuego's eruptions become even more dramatic. With each belch of smoke and ash, lava comes out that we could not see during the day. Now every twenty minutes the summit of the volcano glows bright orange and red as lava blasts into the sky and rolls down the side of the volcano. As it grows colder and the wind picks up, we return to our tent just long enough to grab our sleeping bags, and any extra clothing we can find to try to keep warm. We literally wear every item of clothing we brought. After our

Fuego volcano viewed from the summit of Acatenango, Guatemala.

sauna in the steam vent on Atitlan volcano, Tass brought her bikini swimsuit on the climb, which she now wraps around her neck like a scarf. We huddle together and stay up most of the night watching the show. Only when the clouds roll in and obscure the volcano do we reluctantly go to bed. In the morning a quarter-inch coating of black ash covers our tents.

We brought enough food for three days. We enjoy watching Fuego so much we stay four days. Our last night on top, Tass and I share a squished and blackened banana and a single avocado for supper. We are also running out of water. Reluctantly we take our tent down the next morning, and hike back down the mountain.

7

Tikal

In Panjachel we meet Jim, a longtime traveler in his early fifties who has just finished a two-year Peace Corps project in Africa. When he finds we are leaving for Tikal, he offers to split gas expenses and give us a ride. He has a four-wheel drive truck with a small camper. Jim wants to take a seldom traveled route. Instead of going east through Guatemala City, we will drive north through the Quiche highlands. Our route will take us near the infamous Ixil triangle, the towns of Nebaj, Chajul, and Cotzal, an area long plagued by poverty and war.

In the eleventh century large bands of Toltec Maya left central Mexico and conquered the western highlands of Guatemala. The most powerful of these armies was the Quiche. In the 1400s the Quiche empire stretched over an enormous area with perhaps one million inhabitants. Empires built by charismatic, powerful Kings often decline upon the death of the warrior King. When the Quiche king, Quicab, died in 1475, his domain split into groups. Some of the tribes fought so fiercely among themselves the region began tumbling into chaos. The entire area was also overpopulated. Food became scarce. Cities turned into fortified strongholds built on inaccessible hilltops. Siege living. When the people thought things couldn't get any worse, the Spanish arrived.

In the first big battle the Spanish quickly overpowered a large force of Quiche warriors. The defeated Quiche leaders brought the Spanish to their capital, hoping to negotiate. The Spanish responded by burning the city, along with many of the inhabitants—such was 16th century Spanish diplomacy. Another Indian tribe briefly joined forces with the Spanish, hoping to get rid of rivals. But that partnership dissolved quickly when the Indians lost their usefulness to the Spanish. The Mayan cities were further wracked by warfare. Epidemics of smallpox, typhus, and plague descended upon the Maya. In some areas nearly ninety per cent of the people died. The population of the Quiche highlands didn't return to the pre-conquest levels until the twentieth century, four hundred years later.

The Spanish used the highland Maya basically as slaves to grow cacao and indigo, relocating many of the Maya to huge plantations along the Pacific coast. With Guatemalan independence, Spanish authority was replaced by *Latino* governments, catering to urban constituents and powerful landholders of Spanish descent. Indians were still often forced to work the plantations along the coast and denied title to ancestral lands in the mountains. Since that time the fighting has never stopped for long. The dead are still mostly unarmed and defenseless Indians.

In the last decade the villagers in the Ixil area have tried to start cooperatives and unions. But the military government believes such efforts are all socialism—i.e. communism in disguise—and has fought violently to stomp it out. In response guerilla activity draws support in the mountains. In the last few years tensions have erupted into violent battles where the army has burned and wiped out entire villages, in some cases shooting everybody in sight—men, women, and children.

The Quiche highlands road heading north out of Santa Cruz del Quiche has little traffic. Because of the continuing military violence, soldiers at various army checkpoints tell us not to stop or veer from the road ahead. The sky is covered with haze and dust. We gaze out the truck window, watching the winding dirt and gravel road twist through dry pine forest, up one hill, down another. The town of Sacapulas seems deserted. The only gas station is closed. Jim wisely has extra gas. Leaving the Rio Negro valley, the Cuchumatanes mountains are hidden from view in the haze.

We drive eastward, through the highlands into Alta Verapaz state. At the time of the Spanish conquest this area was home to the Rabinal Maya, feared for their warrior habits and merciless conquests. The Quiche were never able to conquer the Rabinal Maya. The Spanish had similar difficulty trying to defeat the Rabinal in their mountain hideouts. In disgust, the Spanish leader Alvarado named the area, *Tierra de Guerra*, the Land of War.

Finally the monk Fray Bartolome de las Casas convinced the Spanish authorities to try another, less blunt, technique. In 1537 de las Casas and three other Dominican friars set off into the highlands. For five years Spanish soldiers were not allowed into the region. Bartolome befriended the Rabinal chiefs, learned their dialects, translated hymns and scripture into their language, and succeeded in pacifying and converting the Rabinals. Within the first year large numbers of Indians converted to Christianity. Incredibly, at the end of five years the area was renamed Verapaz, True Peace.

Verapaz remained isolated and thereby in many ways independent. The people continued to farm small plots on ancestral lands. Life remained unchanged until the coffee boom of the early 1900s. Suddenly German immigrants swelled into the region to buy and run *fincas*, small coffee plantations. Since the Maya were never given a way to legalize the title to their land and didn't have claims filed in government offices, they lost everything. The government sold the land to whomever would pay. In the 1930s many wealthy German *finca* owners openly supported Hitler. When World War II began, the U.S. government pressured Guatemala to deport most of the Germans, along with all their descendents. The large *fincas* remained, under new owners. Coffee is still the region's main crop.

The mountains here are much greener. Even though it is the dry season, a wet mist fills the air. To the north is the rainiest region in all of Guatemala. We spend a night in a small, cheap hotel and in the morning turn northeast and drop into the enormous tropical lowlands.

El Peten is a vast, featureless expanse of tropical rainforest, swamps, dry tropical forest, and dry savannahs covering the northeastern third of Guatemala. Like the central Yucatan further north, El Peten has two seasons: hot and humid, and hot and dry.

Now, late March, is the hottest and driest time of the year. The road is covered with a two-inch layer of fine, powdery dust that billows into an enormous cloud behind our truck. We drive all day to reach Tikal, the largest and the greatest of the Mayan cities. Because of the terrible condition of the road and the length of time to travel overland to the ruins, only hard-core budget travelers arrive by bus. Most people fly into the ruins. Near the small airstrip are a couple of lodges. The cheapest rooms are five dollars per night—way out of our budget. Jim sleeps in his truck camper. We find a spot to hang our hammocks under a nearby communal *palapa*. Because of the lack of water in March and April, we will not be able to buy showers at the hotel. Bathing water is saved for higher paying guests. However, we can get drinking water at the Jungle Lodge, and do sponge baths.

Tikal sits by itself surrounded by tropical rainforest. When the Spanish arrived Tikal had already lain abandoned for six hundred years. Toltec-Maya from the Yucatan were living around Lake Peten Itza, barely thirty miles away. The forest was so impenetrable that the Spanish didn't gain complete control of the area until 1697, over one hundred and fifty years after conquering the rest of Mexico and Central America.

The Spanish had little interest in the vast area of rainforest around Tikal. Missionaries traveling through the area heard rumors of an ancient Mayan city, but were unable to locate it. Finally in 1848 the Guatemalan government financed an expedition into the rainforests of El Peten and found the ruins. As word of the fabulous city spread through the scientific community, various museums and universities began financing expeditions to the site. The ongoing work of studying and restoring the impressive temples and buildings continues to this day.

From our *palapa* to the Great Plaza of Tikal is a twenty-minute walk. The trail runs under ancient, towering ceiba and mahogany trees more than one hundred and fifty feet high. The air is filled with the sound of tropical birds. Two-foot long Montezuma oropendolas with huge conical bills swoop past like giant orioles.

Temple group on the Great Plaza, Tikal, Guatemala.

The Great Plaza once had a floor of hard finished stone. Today it is a flat, grassy plain surrounded on all sides by pyramids and temple groups. In a number of areas *stelae*, carved statues, and stone monuments mark dates of important historical events. In front of us stands Temple I, the Temple of the Grand Jaguar. The pyramid is 174 feet high, not the highest in Tikal, but the most impressive and certainly the steepest. The pyramid was built in the mid 700s in memory of Ah-Cacau, Lord Chocolate, who was buried in a tomb with no entrance, along with beautiful jade carvings, jewelry, and pearls. Hundreds of tons of rock were piled on the finished tomb, and the pyramid was built around the core of stone.

The pyramid has nine steep, sloping terraces, a sacred number to the Maya. The top platform has a small three-room temple; three being another sacred number. Built above the roof is an elaborate roofcomb, a towering, decorative crown with badly worn carvings. Archaeologists believe the roofcomb was originally painted red. Some believe it shows an enthroned ruler surrounded by scrolls or snakes. Others claim it depicts the thirteen levels of the Mayan heaven.

The stairway leading up the pyramid, which was built by the Maya during the temple construction, seems nearly vertical. The finished stairway, made of huge tenoned blocks of rock, has not been rebuilt by archaeologists. The steps of the workers stairs are so narrow I have to put my feet at an angle to get my entire foot on stone, or my heel sticks out into the air. Archaeologists have anchored a large chain at the top of the pyramid and draped the length of the chain down the middle of the stairs like a handrail. The first thirty feet of climbing I ridicule the chain, believing it ruins the ambiance and feel of the monument to have a thick, rusty chain running up the middle of the stairs. Halfway up many of the steps are badly rounded and worn, making it even harder to get secure footing. I stoop forward more and more as I climb, and soon use my hands on the stairs above as if climbing a ladder. Near the top I use the chain with each step.

At the top of the pyramid are three small, simple rooms with corbelled arches. They are empty, with the strong smell of cool, moist limestone. It is strange to think that few inhabitants of the city ever stood here, inside the sacred rooms, atop the pyramid.

Across the Great Plaza is Temple II, slightly shorter and not nearly as steep as Temple I. To our right is the North Acropolis where during a period of more than one thousand years the Maya built over one hundred buildings. Often one temple or building was used for a period of time, then torn down and another more impressive building was built in its place. Archeologists have reconstructed the area to how it looked around 800 A.D., with more than a dozen temples on a large platform. To our left are the Central Acropolis, Temple V, the South Acropolis, and the Plaza of the Seven Temples.

In the distance is Temple III, whose very top has never been cleared of rainforest. Both the ceremonial building and roof comb have giant tropical trees growing out of the sides and top, seemingly right out of the rock, their roots entangled in stone blocks and carvings. It gives an idea of how the entire city must have looked when first rediscovered in the rainforest. Further back we see the top of Temple IV, Tikal's highest pyramid, sticking out above the rainforest canopy. Everywhere in between lie vast ruins of other buildings, all part of the central portion of the huge Mayan city.

Evidence from arrowheads, knives, and pottery suggests the Maya first arrived in the area about 700 B.C., and began erecting stone buildings around two hundred years later. Within a short time Tikal became an important cultural and religious center with a large population. As the city grew, so did rivalry with other Mayan centers, which often led to warfare. Most wars were highly ritualistic, with the focus on taking captives alive for sacrifice. Around 350 A.D. the leader of Tikal, King Great Jaguar Paw, began using a new fighting strategy. Rather than meeting opposing armies straight on in hand-to-hand combat, he deployed groups of soldiers to flank and surprise the enemy with simultaneous attacks on all sides. Instead of using hand-held clubs and wooden stabbing swords embedded with razor sharp pieces of chipped jade or shark teeth, his army used spear-throwers with light obsidian-tipped spears and darts, enabling them to defeat the opposition without putting themselves in danger. Using such tactics, the Tikal general, Smoking Frog, decimated the army from neighboring Uaxactun, and took control of the city. Tikal became the dominate military force in the region. Tikal continued to grow until the city had one hundred thousand people, one of the largest cities in the world at the time.

In 553 A.D. Lord Water was enthroned in the neighboring Maya city of Caracol, in present day Belize. His armies used the same military tactics Smoking Frog had perfected two hundred years earlier and soon turned the tables on Tikal. In victory Lord Water sacrificed the king of Tikal, and for almost one hundred and fifty years Tikal languished under the rule of Caracol.

Around 700 A.D. Lord Chocolate was crowned ruler of Tikal, and the city finally broke free from Caracol's domination. Tikal experienced a renaissance and was again the most magnificent city in the Mayan world. This golden age lasted almost two hundred years. The last *stela* erected in the city dates 889 A.D.

The Maya abruptly left Tikal by 900 A.D., over a thousand years ago. Many of the inhabitants went northwest into the Yucatan. Only a few small groups stayed in the area. Within one hundred years the last remaining Maya moved out. Occasionally a few small groups returned to certain temples for brief rituals. But soon the abandoned city disappeared into the rainforest.

On top of the Temple of the Grand Jaguar we walk on a small ledge around the ceremonial rooms to the back side of the pyramid. We are just above the top of the forest canopy. All around us colorful tropical birds flit through the branches in the trees. The dry season is a great time for birding, as some rainforest trees drop their leaves, making it easier to see into the forest. Also, numerous trees fruit this time of year, attracting huge flocks of hungry birds. Macaws and parrots fly above us, honeycreepers and euphonias flit through the trees around us, and hummingbirds chitter as they buzz past.

Collared aracaris, a medium-sized member of the toucan family, noisily play follow-the-leader in a disorganized flock as they feed through the trees. They have yellow breasts with a black spot, red and black belly band, and bright red rumps. Moments later the much larger keel-billed toucans fly past. Their bill is neon green, orange, red, and blue. Like all toucans the bill is structurally porous, mostly hollow, and astonishingly light. Toucans mainly eat fruit, but will also eat eggs and young from the nests of other birds, which I assume makes them less than desirable neighbors.

Maya carving in stucco relief.

A couple of two-foot long Montezumas oropendolas begin displaying in the cleared branches beside us. The male bird throws itself forward until it is almost upside down, hanging from its feet. This alone is rather startling to watch, but then it inverts and flares its wings backward around its body. At the same time the male sings a very unusual song. One of our bird books describes it as "*a most melodious, long-drawn-out, rapidly ascending liquid gurgle, sounding like the lively flow of water bubbling over a stony brook.*" Another book says it "*sounds like water pouring out of a bottle: 5-7 liquid glubs or gloob's, getting higher and faster.*" The world master of birds, Roger Tory Petterson, notes the sound as "*Khruk, khruk, glug, glug, glug-glug-gluglooglookacheer.*" We agree with RTP.

We carefully descend the first pyramid and walk across the flat, grassy plaza to Temple II, the Temple of the Masks. The pyramid is shorter, built with three terraces, 125 feet high without its original fifteen foot roof comb. On each side of the main stairs are two large, eroded, grotesque masks with contorted and freakish grimaces. We then climb Temple III, 180 feet high, called the Temple of the Jaguar Priest after a carving on a doorway lintel in the top room.

Late in the day we hike through the rainforest to reach Temple IV, sitting by itself to the west of the central part of the city. At 212 feet high it is not only the highest pyramid in Tikal, but the highest structure built by indigenous people in the New World. We climb the stairs then scramble over rocks and roots and up a metal ladder to reach the top. We have a great view of the pyramids around the Great Plaza sticking out through the rainforest canopy.

A second ladder around the back of Temple IV takes us up to the base of the enormous roof comb, offering a view to the west of undisturbed rainforest as far as we can see. Flocks of parakeets race through the air, wheeling around the temple, squawking excitedly. We sit exhausted after a full day of exploration in the incredible heat, enjoying a refreshing breeze, and watch the sunset over the treetops. We have made a good start in seeing the main pyramids; tomorrow we'll begin exploring the rest of the city.

To avoid the oppressive heat of mid-day, we return early to the ruins. With the detailed hand-drawn maps I previously copied at Na Balum, we begin learning the layout of the ruins, including little-known side trails and hideaways. We arrived the week before the full moon to insure bright, moon lit nights during our ten-day stay. As the full moon nears, I spend more and more time in the ruins at night.

Each evening I watch the sunset from the top of Temple IV, looking west over the rainforest. Then I skirt back around the ledge to the front of the temple, facing east, to watch the moon rising into the sky. The soft and luminous glow of moonlight reveals the ruins and the surrounding rainforest in an enchanting mystique.

Unfortunately thieves stole some of the rock glyphs and artwork from the ruins a few years ago. Now guards with rifles patrol the ruins in protection. Not wanting to be confused for a thief, I keep plenty of distance between me and the guards. They are easy to keep track of, as they all chain smoke cigarettes, making bright orange glows on each inhalation—which I monitor with my binoculars. The key rings on their belts jingle as they walk, and can be heard a remarkable distance in the clear jungle night. The guards climb each of the main pyramids once each night. By nine p.m. the guards are at Temple III. I descend Temple IV, sneak behind the Bat Palace, through the Plaza of the Seven Temples, and climb Temple V. I usually stay on top of Temple V until one p.m., then climb Temple II or Temple I.

As I sit in quiet contemplation alone on top of the pyramids, I feel empathy for the generations of people who lived, dreamed, hoped, and loved here. Sometimes I sense a brief glimpse into the immensity of history and time. The pyramids will sit here long after I am gone, slowly eroding until nothing is left but dust. Viewing my life and the culture in the immensity of time is humbling. The entire civilization in which I live will pass away just like the Maya.

Yet that time is nothing compared to the age of the earth. Or to the age of the sun, which will also die and pass from the universe. A baffling thought. The reality of that ending, for everything around me, not just my body, but the world and even the universe, is a startling reminder of the transient nature of created life. In moments like this, when I have glimpses of life's ending, I feel most alive and aware of everything around me.

The ruins are bathed in the surreal light of the full moon, which dramatically illuminates the white limestone buildings against the darker shadowed rainforest trees. The ancient city seems like a glowing white dream floating above gray clouds. Sitting on the pyramid I feel a deep joy in the celebration and marvel of life. How dramatically life is being played out in nature and humanity! Each day a unique blessing. A miracle. I feel a burning awareness of the gift of life; and an overwhelming drive not to waste time, but to follow what is important deep inside myself, to have purpose in my life.

Bruce chasing butterflies, Tikal, Guatemala.

Sometimes I stay awake all night, and watch the colors of the morning sky grow bright. But usually I slip out of the ruins at two or three a.m. for a quick catnap before dawn. Either way, I am usually up by six o'clock. The best birding is always in the early morning. The air is still relatively cool from the night, and the birds are all frisky with the new dawn. During mid-day when the heat is oppressive, I catch up on my sleep. We nap listlessly, swinging gently in our hammocks under the shade of the *palapa*, trying to create a breeze.

Suza arrives for our planned rendezvous four days late by bus from Belize, and moves into the hammock next door. She has a wonderful butterfly net. Between naps during the heat of the day, we take turns running out into the sun to chase especially beautiful specimens across the clearing. The brightly dancing colors are like flashes of quivering light as the wings open and close, appearing and disappearing in the air. Successfully caught, we carefully examine the exotic colors and shapes and then let each one fly away.

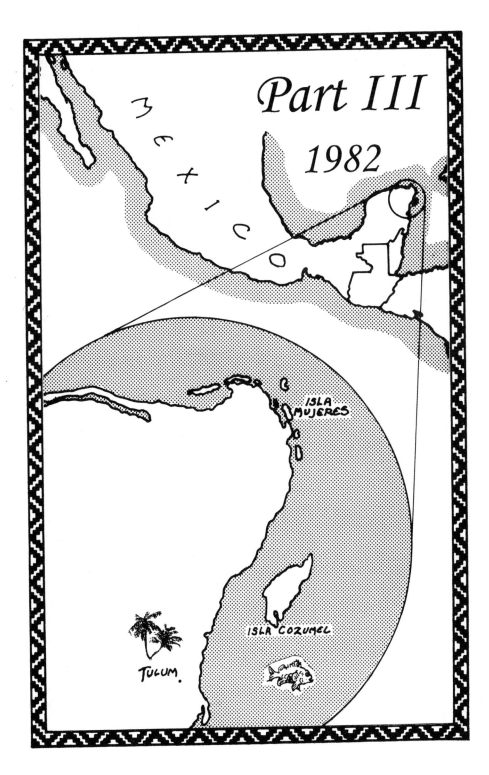

Part III
1982

MEXICO

ISLA MUJERES

ISLA COZUMEL

TULUM.

8

Return to the Caribbean

After our second winter in Central America, Tass and I exchange marriage vows officially in front of all our family and friends. Our plan is work for a long period to save money for a world bicycle trip. In the past we have had jobs that paid well, but the work wasn't what we wanted to do for long. Now we want something more meaningful. We consider the Peace Corps, but end up much closer to home.

We get jobs at Storm Mountain Center, a youth camp and adult retreat center owned by the United Methodist Church in the Black Hills of South Dakota. We are hired to teach environmental education to local school students. Tass also cooks and I do maintenance. After a year I am promoted to director/manager; Tass becomes the head cook. Our new positions come with free housing; we move out of the tiny, crowded staff cabins into a spacious, comfortable home. We are sent to a number of national training workshops, and are encouraged to continue a career in camp management. Suddenly, and unexpectedly, we find ourselves a few steps up a career ladder in a profession we both enjoy immensely. We wonder if our long-term goal of traveling is still the main priority in our life.

As the time for our world bike trip draws near, we decide before we abandon our jobs and spend our life savings that we need to take a "practice trip." After three years in a nice home with a fireplace and all the comforts, we want to make sure we still enjoy the challenges of life on the road. Our plan has always been to quit our jobs rather than take a leave of absence, since we don't know how long we will be gone, and don't want to feel pressured to return by a specific date.

Each year the camp closes from Thanksgiving to Christmas. We decide a little jaunt to the Caribbean will be the perfect practice trip. We plan to relax on the beach, do a lot of snorkeling, and see how it feels to be back out on the road.

With our tight schedule, overland travel from South Dakota to southern Mexico is not realistic. We fly directly into Cancun, spend a night, then take a ferry to Isla Mujeres. Four years have passed since our last visit. Los Cocos, the little beach campground we stayed at previously, is completely gone. Camping is no longer allowed on the northern beach. The small town bustles with activity, with numerous budget *pensiones*, little cheap hotels, which is fortunate as the first three we stop at are completely full. Everywhere sidewalk cafes are doing a booming business for breakfast, lunch and supper. Most of the travelers are from Germany.

Isla Mujeres is a different place, and a different experience. We try not to get caught up in the comparisons with previous visits. Places change. Quiet beaches become tourist havens. Travelers attract other travelers. Most of the people we meet are enjoying themselves immensely. In fact they would not come if they had to camp on the beach and cook their own food. Perhaps we can accept the changes easily because we too have changed. For this trip, the oceans have not been cut off the maps. In fact, I have a small portable type-writer in my backpack; I am working on a science fiction book about a post-nuclear world. I would like to be a writer.

Knowing we have only six weeks to travel, and a job to return to, has changed our financial status. Instead of staying in rock-bottom, one or two dollar per night hotels, we move up to mid-priced budget hotels at five or six dollars a night. We even treat ourselves to cold sodas and eat out in the little sidewalk cafes. And we take advantage of quicker transportation options—instead of walking the length of the island to snorkel, we get together with other travelers and split the taxi fare.

The small beach at Garrafon has been completely transformed, with rock walls and terraces built onto the hillside to make more room for sunbathers. The area is packed with people. We strike up a conversation with two plucky New Zealanders, Mark and Sue, who are on the final stages of a long journey through Asia, India, Europe, the U.S., and now Mexico.

Tass and I have new masks, fins, and snorkels—my mask is adjusted to the prescription of my glasses, so I can see perfectly underwater. We also have better guidebooks to tropical fish. Each time Mark and Sue come out of the water they ask to borrow our guidebook, as do a number of people next to us on the beach.

Seeing a distinctly-colored fish in the ocean and then trying to find it in the book is not easy. Many tropical fish change the colors of their bodies, some-times dramatically, to camouflage and match the background where they are swimming. Also many species are one color as juveniles, another color during an intermediate phase, and still a third color upon reaching adulthood.

The water is full of three-inch, bright yellow fish with black horizontal strips, but we can't find them in the book. Finally we realize they are juvenile blueheads, which as an adult are six inches long with a dark blue head, black and light-blue vertical strips in the center of the body, followed by green fading to blue again at the tail.

We enjoy studying all the unusual adaptations of different tropical fish. Triggerfish are beautiful swimmers. Brightly colored, they grow to almost two feet, yet use only their tiny undulating dorsal and anal fins to propel themselves quickly through the water. They have long, pointed snouts, powerful jaws, sharp teeth, and eyes located far back in their heads, which allows them to eat sharp spiny sea urchins without being poked in the face. Triggerfish are named for the way they can swim into a crack and lift their dorsal spine and lock it into place like a trigger, making them very difficult to remove, even when injured.

Surgeonfish have sharp, hinged spines on each side of the base of their tails, which are covered in a sheath like a concealed weapon. If threatened they lash their spine out like a dagger, which they use to slash the face of any fish that tries to eat them.

We see trunkfish, puffers and porcupinefish that are not only covered in sharp spines, but have an underlying armor of bony plates covering much of their bodies. Some of them can also inflate themselves up to three times normal size by drawing water into their abdomen. Under stress they secrete a toxic substance that can kill other fish. A type of puffer is eaten as a delicacy in Japan. As the fish is being prepared, the toxins must be removed properly or, even after being cooked, the puffer can kill the person eating it.

We join Mark and Sue and another couple from Germany and rent a boat to take us to nearby Isla Contoy, Bird Island. Contoy hosts an enormous population of sea birds, including one of our favorites, the magnificent frigate. Frigates have the longest wingspan of any bird in relation to the weight of their body. Mostly black, frigates are virtually all wing, with a long hooked beak and an even longer forked tail. They glide effortlessly in the steady sea breezes, seldom if ever flapping their wings, simply soaring in the air. In the breeding season the males puff up enormous red pouches under their chins and necks, and sit, ridiculous, in the thorny tree branches, trying to impress one another.

I find it fascinating that colorful male birds primp and parade in front of each other to stake territory and establish breeding status. While all the males strut their stuff, the plainly colored females hardly seem to pay attention. Yet the males act as if the world revolves around them, and often get so caught up in their displays, they will go days, even weeks, without resting or eating.

We stop repeatedly to snorkel in the reefs around the island. The water is crystal clear; the snorkeling, delightful. We spot a huge brown-and-white Nassau grouper, a stocky, heavyset fish that can grow to four feet in length. As we follow it, the grouper changes the colors and patterns on its body to perfectly match the surrounding coral and crevices in which it hides. One of our books says all groupers are born and then mature as females and even produce eggs. Only later, as they grow older, will some of the females change their sex to become males.

We have so much fun with the New Zealanders, Mark and Sue, that we all decide to travel together to Cozumel, the largest Mexican island in the Caribbean. The Mayan name, *Cutzmil*, means Place of Swallows. The Maya also came here in pilgrimage to Ixchel, the moon goddess of fertility. In 1519 Cortez stormed through the island on his way to conquering Mexico, and destroyed all the Mayan shrines. War and smallpox decimated the remaining Mayan population. A few hundred Spanish settlers lived on the island for the next two hundred years, until pirates like Jean Lafitte and Henry Morgan began sailing the waters of the Caribbean plundering Spanish ships. The pirates also attacked villages and towns, and forced those living on Cozumel to move to the mainland for safety. It wasn't until 1848 that the island was resettled by Indian refugees fleeing the War of the Castes in the Yucatan.

Cozumel was a busy port for the *chicle* gum trade in the early 1900s, and the U.S. Air Force built a base on the island during World War II. In 1961 Jacques Cousteau brought world attention to the extraordinary diving in the crystal-clear water along the reefs of Cozumel. Since then tourism has continued to grow, and today it remains the main economy.

In San Miguel, the island's only town, we check into a little hotel with Mark and Sue. To get oriented we rent mopeds for a day and cruise the island, which is twenty-eight miles long and ten miles wide. Most of Cozumel's larger reefs are fifty and even one hundred feet under water, too deep for snorkeling. Although we have relaxed our purse strings on this trip, SCUBA diving is still out of our budget. So most days we hang out along the shallower reefs along the northwest coast so we don't have to hire a boat every time we want to snorkel.

The water is crystal clear. Small, territorial damselfish dart out toward us, and even lightly nip at our legs trying to chase us off. They aggressively charge every fish that swims past their little spot on the reef. Below us, goatfish, like brightly-colored suckers, scrounge the sandy ocean floor using their chin barbels like little fingers under their mouths to probe and stir up sand and mud in search of food.

We see four-inch redlip blennys, a dark-red, flat-faced fish with bright red eyebrows and lips. The shape of their mouths, combined with the red lips, makes blennys look like they are smiling at everything. They use their pelvic fins like little feet to hold on and move about along the reef.

Between dives we lie on the beach and entertain each other by reading of the highly unusual mating habits of fish. Hamlets, a small, brightly-colored seabass, don't have male and female sexes. They are all hermaphrodites.

Boys diving for tourist coins, Mexico.

Each fish can produce both eggs and sperm, although not at the same time. Fish in the wrasse family are perhaps strangest of all. Like many tropical fish, most wrasses undergo changes in color and shape during their growth. At first glance the members of the wrasse family seem rather normal, with both males and females. But in many wrasse species there are also supermales, which are much larger than either the males or the females, and much more brightly colored. For a long time scientists considered the supermales to be a completely different fish, until they learned about their transformations. What makes the wrasse supermales so bizarre is that they are transformed males. Only certain females, who go through a little understood sex-reversal, can grow into the supermales.

Another species with supermales is the large, brightly-colored parrotfish. Females and males are often differently colored. In the few species that have the same coloration between sexes, larger supermales appear, with even brighter colors. In parrotfish the males are the ones that grow into supermales, or terminal-phase males. Each night parrotfish wrap themselves in a mucous cocoon to keep from being eaten by larger predators.

At La Ceiba beach we snorkel out to an airplane sunk off the coast of Cozumel in 1977 during the filming of a movie. The plane is just forty feet under, and one hundred yards off the coast. We dive down to find schools of fish hanging out beneath the wings, while others fill the inside, flitting in and out of broken windows and holes in the body of the plane.

We walk up and down the shoreline beachcombing and shelling. Using our seashell book we identify measled cowries, sunrise tellins, and zebra nerites, among other shells, and pass the time drilling holes in shells with a little awl we brought, creating beach jewelry. The days slip by much too quickly.

Mark and Sue, who by now have become grand friends, leave Cozumel with us. We spend our last week snorkeling together off the mainland coast at Aukumal, Xel-Ha, and Tulum. Finally we bid them a sad farewell.

At the end of our six week trip we are tan, healthy, and rejuvenated. Ahead of us we still have another eighteen months working at Storm Mountain before we will have the money together for our world bicycle trip. Any doubts we might have had about our future have been dispelled. Once the finances are together, we are committed to quitting our jobs, taking our life savings, and heading out on the road. We don't plan on returning until we have spent every last penny. There is nothing we want more than to continue traveling and exploring the world.

Part IV

1991-92

• Puerto Vallarta

MEXICO

El Rosario •
Zitacuaro • Mexico City
★
Cuetzalan •
Xaltipan •
Teziutlan
Veracruz •

Santiago Tuxtla

San Cristobal
de Las Casas

• Huehuetenango
Solola
Lake Atitlan & Panajachel
★ Guatemala
City •

★ Tegucigalpa
• Yuscaran
• Ocotal

• Leon

Masaya Volcano • Managua
Lake
Nicaragua

Tamarindo &
Monteverde Natl Park • △ Arenal Volcano
△ Poas Volcano
Manuel Antonio Natl Park ★ San Jose
• Col del Muerto

Corcovado
National Park

PACIFIC OCEAN

9

The Garden of Eden

In 1984 Tass and I leave South Dakota heading west on our bicycles. Our goal is to ride to California, island hop across the South Pacific to New Zealand and Australia, bicycle through southeast Asia to Nepal, and hike to the base of Mount Everest. We think the trip will take about eighteen months.

Eighteen months later we are cycling in Thailand. We are having so much fun that we don't want to end the trip after Nepal and India. Since the Russians are in Afghanistan, and Iran and Iraq are at war, all we have to do is cycle the mideast, cross Europe and half the United States, and we will ride all the way around the world.

We run out of money in Israel and use our credit card to finance our journey across Europe in just thirty-two days. After cycling through twenty-four countries, we fly from England back to the United States. We leave Vermont in early November, and endure numerous snowstorms our last month riding across the United States. But we are so close that, despite the freezing weather, we never once consider giving up. After twenty-six months we ride back into my parents' driveway in Spearfish, South Dakota. We view the two years as the most fascinating in our lives.

We need to work, so we begin by managing Black Hills Bicycles, a bike-hike-climb-ski-shop in Rapid City, South Dakota. The job immerses us in mountain biking. In addition to great riding in the Black Hills and yearly fun-ride trips to Moab and Colorado, we race throughout the U.S. Tass places second in her age group at the National Mountain Bike Championships in Mammoth, California, and we both race in the first World Championships in Durango, Colorado.

We create Images of the World, a series of slide programs about our travels, which we present in schools. After three years we quit the bike shop to travel the school year on a speaking circuit giving programs. I write **The Road of Dreams** about our world trip, and we begin saving for our next journey.

76

In 1991 we get ready to leave on a three-month bicycle trip through Central America. We'll spend a month in Costa Rica, take another month to ride through Nicaragua and Honduras, and spend our last month in Guatemala and Mexico.

The snow is falling heavily on the first day of December as we drive to the Rapid City airport. We nearly freeze in our lightweight traveling clothes as we ferry loads of gear from our van into the terminal. Inside, everything is piled onto the baggage scale: two large boxes containing bicycles, panniers, helmets, and tools, plus two enormous cargo bags stuffed full of gear. We discreetly put our overloaded carry-on bags, packed full of our heaviest gear, up against the counter and out of sight. The attendant shakes his head in amazement at the pile of gear on the scale, then shrugs and lets us pass through.

We have a bumpy, jarring flight through the snowstorm to Denver. In Houston we have heartstopping downdrafts seconds before we land. And in Managua, Nicaragua, the cracks in the concrete runway from earthquakes are so rough it feels like the plane is coming apart.

Despite the nerve-wracking flights we arrive safely in San Jose, Costa Rica. Our bicycles do not. We are stunned to find they were unloaded in Nicaragua to make room for other cargo. We are assured that this sometimes happens— and told not to worry—everything will certainly arrive on the next flight tomorrow night. Leaving the airport we meet a couple who flew from the U.S. with their bicycles four days ago. One of their bicycles is still missing.

Costa Rica is one of the most biologically diverse regions in the world, packed into a country one third the size of South Dakota. At the widest point Costa Rica is only 185 miles across. The country has a variety of tropical forests, rainforests, cloudforests, high mountains, numerous active volcanoes, and miles of beaches along both the Pacific and Caribbean coasts. Costa Rica is famous for its large national park system. Combined with various government and private forest reserves, refuges, and parks, nearly thirty percent of the land is protected in some way. The country is at the same latitude as southern India, so the temperature is pleasant with little seasonal changes. The temperature varies more according to altitude than to time of year, with numerous microclimates in the rugged mountains. Four different *cordilleras*, mountain ranges, divide the Pacific and Caribbean coast; the tallest peak is 12,529 feet.

When Christopher Columbus arrived in Costa Rica in 1502 on his fourth and last voyage, he thought he was dropping anchor off the southeast coast of Asia. His boat, badly beaten in a tropical storm, required seventeen days of repair. Columbus visited a few coastal villages and the Indians offered him gifts of gold, hence he called the land *Costa Rica*, "Rich Coast." He wrote that the Indians were gentle and friendly—and could easily be conquered.

Four years later in 1506 King Ferdinand of Spain sent Diego de Nicuesa as governor to colonize the new land. Diego's ship ran aground off Panama, and Diego's party had to walk up the Caribbean coast to their selected location. Tropical diseases and food shortages soon reduced the settlers by half. The "gentle" Indians burned their crops and disappeared into the forest where most died of diseases brought by the Spanish. Diego's group found neither gold, minerals nor any indigenous population to subjugate for forced labor. Spanish interests quickly focused on more lucrative areas to exploit.

The colonists who remained became small landowners, each family subsistence farming on its own little plot. During the reign of the Spanish empire, Costa Rica remained a poor and neglected outpost. This turned out to be a blessing, as the isolation encouraged strong individualism, self reliance, and a communal bond and spirit.

In 1820 the revolution in Spain brought about the independence of Mexico and Latin America. Not until a month after the documents were signed did isolated Costa Ricans finally learn Spain had relinquished all claims over their country. Costa Rica joined a federation of Central American states, then seventeen years later in 1838 declared itself an independent country. Costa Rica has been a democracy for over one hundred years, and has not had an army since 1948. It has one of the highest literacy rates in the world, and a national health care system that covers every citizen.

The next evening we anxiously return to the airport for our bicycles and sweat it out at the baggage claim area. The plane is late, of course. When it finally lands we peer through a window and watch the workers unload the luggage. The main cargo area is unloaded completely. No bicycles. The baggage workers go to a smaller luggage hold near the front of the plane. Halfway through the process I spot a large box marked TREK being unloaded. The last thing off the plane is our second box. Still, we don't relax until both boxes come up the conveyor belt and we can see up close that they are ours.

We take a mini-bus back to our hotel and stay up till midnight putting the bikes together—sporty Trek 520 touring bikes, set up cyclo-cross-style with drop bars, knobby 700 cc tires and a 24x30 low gear. Everything survived the flight intact.

We get up early the next morning, totally excited to be doing another bike trip.

"Well, I wonder what I'll wear today?" Tass smiles as she jumps out of bed and grabs her only pair of long pants. "I think I'll wear these black pants," she jokes. "And I wonder how this orange shirt will go with it?" she laughs, putting on her only T-shirt. Despite bringing very few clothes, our room is full of gear. We spent the last two months on slide show tour through the southwestern U.S., and were home only a few days before flying to Costa Rica.

Much of our gear was packed three months ago. At that time we simply threw everything we might need into stuff stacks and bags. Now everything needs further organization before packing onto the bicycles. We jump into the task. By evening we can't tell if we have made things better or created an even bigger mess.

We spend another two days getting visas and sorting gear before heading out into the countryside. We have outlined an ambitious and circuitous route through Costa Rica, traversing nearly every mountain range and more than a few National Parks, with frequent side trips down to the coast. The Cordillera Central, the Central Mountain Range, runs northeast of San José and contains numerous active volcanoes: Turrialba, Irazu, Barva, and Poas. Our first destination is to ride to the top of Poas.

The road up the volcano is a brutally steep, twenty-two percent grade. We carry a ton of gear: camping equipment, backpacking gear, cameras, lenses, binoculars, a library of field guides, natural history books, and more. On an improbably steep section of road, we ride so slowly that little old ladies pass us going uphill carrying big loads of vegetables on their backs.

But as we ride we limber up, and work our way through cultivated farmland into rainforest and then even higher into cool, cloudforest mist. Trees, ferns, and enormous plants hang shrouded in fog, dripping over the road. The temperature is perfect for the hard work of riding up the volcano. We ride at a

Bruce riding through Costa Rican cloudforest.

comfortable pace, relaxed enough to enjoy the lush growth around us. The mist turns to intermittent rain, but it hardly dampens our spirits.

Poas volcano is a National Park. At the top we meet the head ranger, who informs us no camping is allowed at the summit. When he finds out we are on bicycles, he offers to let us stay in a utility room behind a small museum. We have the trails to ourselves as we hike through the dense cloud forest growth. Because of the thick mist and clouds, visibility is never more than one hundred feet. The rain is cold and numbing as it grows dark.

The next morning we head for the crater rim but can see little through the thick mist, rain and wind. We return again and again throughout the morning until finally the mist clears for spectacular crater views.

We are excited to begin the long, paved downhill off Poas. On our world trip we had some stellar downhill rides. Now we want to try out our new bikes at speed. They feel solid and stable as we fly down the mountain, gaining confidence and speed with every corner and straightaway. We make only a few stops. When we do pull over, we begin whooping and laughing as we recall high-speed corners, passings, and spectacular views glimpsed on the way down.

Next we head south toward the Col de Muerte, the Pass of Death, the highest road in Central America. Although the road is part of the Pan American highway, the traffic is sporadic. As we climb out of the central valley, we leave towns and farms behind, and again ride up into lush tropical forest. Climbing steadily for a day, we see very few settlements or houses along the road. We spend a rainy and cold night in a little thatched hut in Tapanti National Wildlife Refuge. Not many tourists.

The next morning we continue riding up the pass. On sections of road with no traffic, we often ride side by side, occasionally chatting and joking, but mostly quietly enjoying the scenery, the lush growth of trees and foliage along the road. During one of these silent moments, we both happen to be looking up in the trees ahead when a bird suddenly flies rapidly across our line of vision, from the top of the trees on one side of the road to the other. Although we have never seen the bird in the wild, we know it immediately, having often gazed with admiration at its picture in books.

"A quetzal!" we triumphantly shout in unison. It has already disappeared into the forest canopy, but the stunning image of the bird in the air remains forever in our minds. The resplendent quetzal is the most beautiful of trogans. Our field guide describes it as the most spectacular bird in the New World. Fourteen inches in length. An intense emerald green with a small rounded crest. A bright red stomach. But the "tail" is what makes the quetzal famous: two, two-foot long green tail coverts—beautiful feathers that float behind like glorious, shimmering banners as the quetzal flies across the sky. The tail coverts have none of the barbules that 'zip' regular feathers together for rigidity. Instead, they have a wonderful flowing motion, a delicate softness, and because of this the feathers have long been used throughout Central America by Mayan and Aztec nobility for ornamentation and decoration on head-dresses and clothes.

At the top of the pass is a small restaurant where we stop for a lunch of tortillas, beans and eggs. The cafe is full of truck drivers who are all impressed by our ride over the pass. Out on the highway they honked and repeatedly gave us the thumbs-up sign. Now they give us friendly pats on the back and tell us about the road conditions ahead.

As we ride down the other side of the pass, the weight on our bikes is now an advantage. On downhills gravity is the friend of a fully-loaded bike. The road is banked and graded perfectly for high G-force corners. We fly down the mountains making power turns around tight hairpins, standing back up to accelerate out of each corner as we try to catch one another. As we drop lower the switchbacks end. Now the road cuts through thick rainforest foliage in steep, long, straight descents built on the side of a steep wall. The hillside on the upper side of the road is a solid wall covered with dripping ferns. The other side of the road hangs over precipitous dropoffs into mist-filled canyons. We really let it rip in one section, going so fast our eyes water. In other places we slow down just to look around for a few minutes, then race on down the mountain!

On the Pacific coast we visit the Osa peninsula, store our bikes, and set off on a four-day trip backpacking through Corcovado National Park. We spend the whole first day hiking down a narrow and seemingly endless stretch of beach, ocean on one side, impenetrable lowland rainforest on the other. The scenery is magnificent, but by mid-afternoon the continual hiking in soft sand along the slanted beach becomes a bizarre type of torture. The sand is loose and deep. We walk near the water's edge, along the high tide line, up next to the rainforest, vainly looking for hard-packed sand that will make hiking easier. The Achilles stress test.

As the sun drops toward the ocean, we find a wonderful spot to camp, our own private paradise between rainforest and ocean, without another soul in sight. We are serenaded by the soothing sound of the breaking waves. A refreshingly cool breeze blows off the ocean; a few scattered clouds move slowly across the horizon as the sun turns orange and sinks below the ocean, dramatically lighting up the clouds and the entire sky.

The next morning we leave the beach along a trail that heads inland, which will ultimately take us across the width of the peninsula. As we first enter into the rainforest, the shade from the trees is a wonderful respite from the hot, tropical sun. But we also leave behind the fresh breeze off the ocean. The air soon becomes muggy and then almost stifling with humidity.

We come across a group of white-nosed coati feeding noisily across the forest floor. They are members of the raccoon family, with a longer tail and

Camping on the beach of the rainforest covered Osa peninsula, Costa Rica.

more pointed nose. The dexterity in their hands is amazing as they grasp objects. They climb up into the trees as we draw near, and loudly scold us for disturbing their foraging. We try to make a few photos but the light is too low for a normal shutter speed, and they are moving too quickly for a longer exposure. So we simply watch them through our binoculars, and enjoy their antics in the trees.

As we continue hiking, the mosquito population builds. The buzzing around our ears soon becomes a constant presence. Recent heavy rains have turned the trail into a slippery quagmire; in places the sticky mud balls up and clings to our boots in heavy, enormous globs, adding pounds of weight to each shoe. Still, our spirits remain high—this is what we came for, or so we tell ourselves. We had no delusions that this would be an easy hike. We stop repeatedly to bird. We sweat off our insect repellent, and have to continually slather on more.

In the afternoon we arrive at Sirena station, a large wooden building built by the National Park for researchers and visitors. It resembles a rustic barn, with one large open room and a loft. A wide overhanging tin roof covers a porch on all sides, and open windows without glass or screening allow a constant flow of air and mosquitoes into the building. We set up our tent in the loft for protection against being eaten alive. The door, back wall, and entire top of our Walrus Archrival tent is made of mosquito netting—the perfect tropical shelter. We share the huge building with about a dozen other hikers, all of whom pitch tents and hang mosquito netting inside the building.

As we cook supper that night we chat with other hikers. Two men camped near us are from Australia.

"What part of Australia?" Tass asks, just making conversation. "Ohh, a little town near Dubbo," a fellow named Richard replies, convinced we won't know of the remote town in the outback of New South Wales.

"We've been to Dubbo!" Tass responds, "We spent three months bicycling in Australia. It is a great country. We would love to go back."

Richard gets a surprised look on his face. "When were you in Australia?" he asks.

"It was in the 80's," Tass says, and then looks toward me for confirmation. "Lets see...it must have been about the summer of 1985." I nod my head in agreement.

"Were you two bicycling around the world?" he suddenly asks. Now we are startled.

"Yes!" we reply in unison.

"I met you!" Richard says incredulously. "You spent a night at my friend's house!" Richard can hardly believe it!

The coincidence is amazing, yet hardly surprising to us. We continually run into people we know in many different corners of the world. The next morning Richard, like most visitors, hikes out the shortest route, back down the coast. Tass and I set out alone on a two-day hike across the penninsula. The rains come and go throughout the day. The trail passes through numerous swamps and bogs. Again thick mud clings to our boots like leaden weights.

In one particularly long stretch of heinous trail, Tass momentarily loses it. Both feet stuck in deep mud, surrounded by biting flies and mosquitoes, the straps of her backpack straining at her shoulders, she screams loudly into the air.

"Why does everything we do have to be an epic?" Kamikaze black flies buzz tangled in her hair. "Why can't we ever take just a normal vacation? Maybe I am getting too old for this!" Tass continues, arms flailing at the insects surrounding her head. She will turn forty during the trip. I don't say anything. This is a dangerous subject. She turns her frustrated gaze from the sky, and levels steely eyes my way.

"When we get home I'm going to get a boyfriend who is a couch potato!" she shouts in desperation. "Someone who only wants to lie around the house!"

"I can be a couch potato!" I reply, quickly side-stepping the age issue. "Don't blame this all on me! You helped plan this trip as much as I did!"

During the planning of our journey, we often felt smug about our high level of fitness from mountain bike racing. Plus, after our twenty-six-month world bicycle tour, a three-month trip seemed a flash in the pan. We jokingly called the trip the "Central America Training Camp," which we hoped would give us a solid fitness base for next year's bike racing season. On cycling days we planned an aggressive itinerary with numerous sixty-mile days, even in mountainous terrain. We thought we could pull off mega-miles, along with hiking and wilderness adventures on the side, and still have time for "rest" days to experience the culture.

Now, just two-weeks into the "Training Camp," we both question the pace of our schedule. That night in the tent we look over our maps and the calendar, trying to figure out where we can adjust our route through Central America to add in a little more relaxation during the next three months. The problem is, everything on our itinerary sounds appealing; we can't find anything we are willing to leave out. Finally we decide to simply move our departure from Costa Rica back a few days. We'll allow ourselves extra time here, and hopefully adjust our schedule somewhere further down the line.

Our relaxing does not start the following day. We get up before dawn and begin hiking after a quick breakfast. During the night it rained nearly four inches. Now the trail is an even worse quagmire of mud and slick roots. Suddenly rivers and streams are everywhere. Regardless, we are much more relaxed. The hike is greeted with more humor than frustration. After we both assure each other we aren't going to spend the whole trip having epics, we can more easily laugh at the craziness of the current epic. At least it is no longer thick mud, but moving water we are hiking through. Our feet shrivel into prunes in our soaked hiking boots. Our toes cover with blisters. By the end of the day we have made thirty-four creek crossings.

We bicycle a few days northward along the coast to Manuel Antonio, Costa Rica's most visited National Park, with a small, idyllic beach town nearby—a perfect place to finally get some of that relaxation. But despite our plans to be totally lazy, the area is too beautiful for us to sit still. We hike about four hours a day in the rainforest and along the coast. White-faced monkeys, sloths, parrots, and toucans make each hike an exciting outing. Still, we take time every afternoon to just relax on the beach, and each night we eat seafood in quaint, oceanside cafes. It would be easy to spend weeks, even months here. But Christmas is coming, and even the cheap hotels have all their rooms booked up long in advance. Besides, this is not where we want to spend Christmas. Up in the mountains near Monteverde National Park is a Quaker community where we plan to spend the holiday season.

We ride up the coast and camp near the Tarcoles River. We sit high above an eroded creek bank and watch through our binoculars as a fifteen-foot crocodile battles a five-foot rival. The splashing water calms, and for ten minutes the creek returns to normal. Finally the big croc resurfaces with the smaller croc halfway down his gullet. Only the tail of the smaller reptile,

The rainforest is full of insects and beetles.

thrashing frantically, sticks out of the big crocs mouth. After witnessing such a battle, neither of us want to walk down close to the river to get water. I tie a section of clothesline to one of our waterbottles and, standing high on the bank, toss the bottle down to the water. After it fills I carefully pull the water-bottle back toward me, trying not to spill the contents. That night we sleep restlessly, dreaming of marauding crocodiles; we are nervous when we have to go out into the darkness to go to the bathroom.

The next day we leave the lowlands and begin the climb into the mountains. Pointed cobblestones fill the road, anchored half into the earth and half sticking sharply up into the air.

"Turn your neck when you hit the bumps and your neck will crack!" Tass merrily informs me as we ride up the road. A bicycling chiropractic adjustment. The cycling is gruesome, relentless bike bashing. We bounce up the twisting trail into the mountains, stopping occasionally to admire the view and check the straps on our panniers. We slowly leave the heat and dust behind, and soon are swallowed up in the ever-present mist of the cloud forest.

Our first day in Costa Rica we met a man named Oss at the Peace and Justice Center in San Jose. He invited us to visit the home of his family when we came to Monteverde.

Now we arrive in time for a delicious vegetarian supper at the home of Oss's parents. Like the community around them, the family is Quaker, and their religious views have strongly influenced not only their spirituality but their day-to-day lifestyle.

In the early 1950's a large group of Quaker dairy farmers moved from Alabama to Costa Rica. The Quakers, who believe in a pacifist lifestyle, were unhappy with the growing military industrial complex in the U.S. after the end of World War II, the involvement in the Korean War, and the entire cold war mentality. They were attracted to Costa Rica for a number of reasons—the early abolition of slavery during the colonial period, free obligatory education guaranteed in the 1869 constitution, the elimination of the death penalty in 1882, and the disbanding of the army in 1948.

When our host, Oss Sr., was seventy years old he and his wife, Rebecca, briefly considered moving into a retirement community. Instead, they sold everything and moved to Costa Rica to homestead in the mountains. That was sixteen years ago. Today, at eighty-six, Oss and Rebecca still live a pioneer lifestyle. Although they have had electricity now for eight years, they only recently got a telephone. The challenge of such a life seems to have given them vigor and enthusiasm! Far from being lonely, they are surrounded by a small but dedicated community of like-minded individuals.

On Christmas day we join one hundred people for a community Quaker church service and potluck. The Quaker service is loosely structured with an emphasis on quiet time and personal meditation. After church, gifts are exchanged. People drew names some time before, as many of the handmade gifts have taken weeks to make.

The meal is a typical church potluck. The hungry group hardly makes a dent in the overflowing tables of delicious food. Halfway through the meal a loud cry hails the arrival of Santa—pedaling up a steep hill through the forest on a red Trek mountain bike, complete with a large white sack of handmade toys on the back rack! Despite all the celebrations, it is hard to believe it is actually Christmas, and because of this neither of us gets too home sick.

Between visits with people in the Quaker community, we hike into the cloudforest. Our guidebooks claim that December through March is the dry season in Costa Rica. Now we find that "dry season" is a misnomer in the mountains near Monteverde. In the rainy season daily afternoon cloudbursts are common, with two inches of rain. During these storms the rain simply washes down the trail in a flash flood. After the storm the sun often comes out and dries things up.

Now, in the "dry season," there is less volume of rain, but it comes in a slow and constant drizzle. Endless soaker rains. During this "dry season," when there is actually less total rainfall, the Monteverde trails are the muddiest. The sun seldom appears to dry the ground.

The ever-present mist and dark grey light adds an intense, almost overbearing energy to the cloudforest. The sky is too dark and misty to see clearly up in the top canopy. In the sub-canopy, trees, that anywhere else would be considered large, crowd each other, battling for the light and water that filters down through the taller trees. Around us down on the forest floor a thick tangled web of growth covers the ground, seven feet deep, with a snarled mass of vegetation impossible to negotiate without laboriously whacking a path with a sharp machete. Or chain saw. Everything is a tangled mess, a dark, dripping world, full of rich and rotting smells. We often hear little birds chirping just a few feet away, still we have difficulty seeing them. Even the tiniest birds do not fly through such growth, but hop from branch to branch, working their way through the forest underworld in search of insects.

The thick, lush growth surrounding us does not feel like an idyllic garden. The cloudforest here is a fierce battleground, where each plant fights for space and survival, twisting and choking each other in a quest for sunlight. Giant strangler figs throttle enormous trees, halting growth by wrapping tourniquet-like vines up and down the host tree. Bromeliads and airplants fill every nook and crook between each fork of each tree branch. A single bromeliad can hold over a gallon of water—adding eight pounds of weight for the host tree. Moss, as much as four inches thick, further coats every limb and branch, blocking out sunlight and absorbing hundreds of more pounds in water, adding even more weight and stress. It is a jungle out here.

Because of the thick growth and the difficulty of seeing birds and animals, we rely on our hearing to know which birds are in the area. Three-wattled bellbirds have a brown body, a white head, and three, black, worm-like wattles hanging from the base of their bill. They have one of the strangest calls. Our book describes it as *"BONK seee k'k' see K'berk; bonk see k'k' berk see see see BONK."* The black faced solitaire makes a sound like a violin being tuned, or a squeaky gate. We also hear the constant ping-ping of male tree frogs.

In the evenings we load up with flashlights and headlamps for nighthikes. The cool drizzle of the day is replaced by a much colder nighttime rain. But that does not stop our hike. If we waited for a clear night, we might have to wait until the rainy season, if that makes any sense. Now the moisture brings out little bugs, which bring out the bigger bugs that eat the little bugs, which bring out the frogs and lizards that eat bigger bugs and sometimes each other as well.

We spot countless leaf mimics, strange insects with bizarre bodies resembling twigs, green leaves, and brown leaves. Some species of leaf mimics

that feed and crawl in the leaf litter covering the ground are even camou-
flaged as dead and decaying leaves.

We continually lift up the larger leaves along the path, looking on their
undersides for lizards and frogs perched upside down. Many lizards have
splayed-out, spidery thin fingers and toes, with large suction cups rather than
claws or nails to hold onto the slippery, wet leaves. The lizards glisten with
water, then—faster than a blink—scamper across one leaf and hop to anther.
Abruptly they stop in a frozen pose, dangling on the underside of a dripping
leaf, waiting for us to shine our lights elsewhere, leaving them in their wet,
dark, predatory world.

As we hike we hear a variety of tree frogs—some sound like loud drops
of water echoing down a metal culvert. Many species of tree frogs live in the
small pools of water collected in bromiliad plants, often high up in the
branches of rainforest trees. Their calls fill the rainforest night. We find various
species of glass frogs with translucent skin and other cute little brown varieties, but none of the species with bright splashy colors.

Deep in the rainforest we turn off our flashlights. Almost immediately we
see little phosphorescent mushrooms growing in the mud along the side of
the trail. After our eyes adjust to the dark we begin to see phosphorescent
shapes all around us, glowing algaes and fungi spreading across various
leaves. We walk in the darkness very slowly, holding hands, using our feet to
guide us down the trail. The thick foliage makes it impossible to veer off the
trail, so we have no fear of becoming lost.

The rain continues without a break as we bicycle out of Monteverde
northward, across a seldom-used, high, muddy and wind-swept pass. The
next day we descend to the shore of Lake Arenal and finally drop down below cloud level, for a few hours at least. We rent a little hotel room and fill it
with a spider web of clotheslines to dry all our gear.

In 1968 an earthquake rocked this part of Costa Rica. Twelve hours later,
nearby Arenal volcano blew three new craters on the top and sides of the
mountain, killing seventy-eight people and destroying the town of Pueblo
Nuevo. Since then, Arenal is considered one of the most active volcanoes in
the world.

Arenal sits like a fiery, booming guardian on the eastern end of the lake.
As we ride toward the volcano we circle the western edge and then ride along
the northern shore the length of the lake. The vegetation thickens again, along
with rainforest clouds. The booming sound of howler monkeys in the trees is
soon overshadowed by the much deeper, powerful rumbling of the volcano.
The sound is like an ominous thunderhead, building on a hot August afternoon
over the South Dakota prairie. As we ride closer we catch just a few glimpses
of an immense steaming volcanic cone poking through the shrouds of mist.

Arenal volcano rising above the rainforest canopy, Costa Rica

We ride off onto a small rutted track leading up to the lower slopes of the active side of the mountain. Fresh lava flows cover the entire area, like crumbled, baked rivers of death. Mounds of twisted, convulsed rock, stirred by pressurized gasses and mixed with sharp, fragmented boulders, lie strewn across the countryside. The inside of the earth has spewed out in a fiery swath of scorched destruction, cutting through the lush, green rainforest.

We push our bikes over a hill of sharp, jutting volcanic debris and find what looks like a safe spot to put up our tent where the sharp rock is covered with volcanic sand. Clouds and mist roll up and down the volcano, intermittently showering us with rain, along with ash and soot. Camped in a sea of churned rock, surrounded by debris from countless explosions, we are reminded that no place near the volcano is ultimately safe. Sanctuary is only a moment in time. At this moment none of the rocks from each rumbling explosion is reaching where we are standing with our cameras and binoculars, hoping to see the power that shapes worlds. But sometime, a year, a month, a week from now, maybe even tomorrow, the volcano could explode and obliterate our campsite with huge lava bombs. We better do our viewing quickly.

We hike along the scree fields at the base of the mountain, watching the spectacle. Near the bottom of the mountain is an immense fissure. During the day all we can see is clouds of steam and gas smoking out of the hillside. But at night the entire hillside turns bright orange, oozing lava and molten rock.

The fiery, newly formed rocks bubble from the vent and then roll down the mountain sounding like shards of broken glass tumbling down a spinning metal culvert, cracking and fracturing, not thin and delicate, but heavy and razor sharp.

During our second night enormous, heart-stopping explosions rock the mountain every few hours, sending streamers of glowing boulders bashing down the mountainside, breaking apart like fiery comets as they roll off the side of the volcano. The night air is filled with the echoing sound of their impact, crashing down chutes and cliffs. Each eruption releases gigantic clouds of ash into the air. The wind takes about half an hour to carry the ash our direction. Then the ash rains down on us, covering everything with gritty, black dust. The fine particles have a slight prickly feeling when they hit our faces, and they tickle as they fill our hair.

Long distance bike tourers are often unique individuals, and sometimes a bit eccentric. A few are out on the fringe, not only financially, but socially. Near Lake Arenal we meet a Dutchman who travels very light: two small panniers, only half full, and a tiny torn handlebar bag. He sits under a store awning out of the rain, wolfing down an unappetizing lunch of cold wieners and canned corn.

"I often eat cold canned food," he tells us. "It is very high in salt." He pauses for a few mouthfuls of food.

"Yesterday I cycled all day without water. Since my food is so salty, I didn't eat anything. I knew it would only make me thirsty." He says this as though we will agree with his logic. Instead, we wonder why he would carry heavy canned food when there is good, fresh local food available.

He begins boasting of riding numerous one hundred and even one hundred and fifty-mile days. Feeling like we are in excellent shape ourselves, we are amazed he can go such enormous distances, even with his lightweight gear.

"I ride alot at night," he confides. "In fact, I didn't get here until 3:00 a.m. this morning!" Although he has cycled enormous distances, he has missed some of the finest scenery in all of Costa Rica. He asks about our route, and is dismayed to hear of the mountains we have traversed.

"I can't go that way," he shakes his head. "Mountains hurt my knees." Since he carries less than half our weight, we express surprise that his knees hurt.

"My front derailleur is broken. I can't use any of my low gears," he states emphatically, as if this is further proof of his nothing-can-slow-me-down strategy. I tell him I have tools and would be willing to see if the derailleur is fixable. But he declines the offer.

"I really hate to take time to work on my bike." He shakes his head then boastfully adds, "I haven't oiled my chain since Mexico!" We leave him to his lunch, and head down the road.

We also meet Marcos, a German on a mountain bike with an enormous load. He has been traveling alone for six months and is so eager for company he completely changes directions and rides with us for a few days just to chat. He tells us the only thing he could get to eat in Nicaragua was rice and chicken, and warns us to stock up with plenty of food before crossing the border.

As we bicycle west out of the mountains, we crest a hill where a car and a motorcycle have had a head-on collision. The driver of the car is uninjured. But the man on the motorcycle lies crumpled in a heap in the middle of the road. His head is bent, tucked down next to his chest. A group of four people stands fifteen feet away, talking nervously among themselves. They tell us someone has gone to get an ambulance. But we are far from the nearest town; an hour could easily pass before it arrives. I kneel beside the man on the road. He is unconscious. His head is twisted, the chin strap on his helmet is choking his neck, and he can hardly breath. Each labored breath is accompanied by a gurgling sound. Blood oozes from his nose and mouth. I don't want to move him, as he might have a spinal injury. But he can hardly breathe. I can't release his chin strap without moving his head, so I use my knife to cut the strap off his helmet, allowing him to breathe.

I look at him lying in the road, and think how easily it could be Tass or I lying there. One mistake, a little swerve in the road while chatting or watching the scenery. Or maybe just bad luck, cresting a hill to find a car in the wrong lane, barreling down on us—through no fault of our own, in the wrong place at the wrong time. Whether it comes from an unexpected volcanic eruption or an unexpected car, suddenly life is irrevocably changed, or perhaps ended altogether.

Oddly enough, seeing how fleeting life can be does not make me feel vulnerable and timid. It makes me want to fully embrace each moment, each hour, each day. I realize we have little control over such accidents, illnesses, and tragedies. The future is not always certain. No amount of planning or worrying can change that. I accept that as a fact of life. NOW is what is truly important. Seize the day! Not, seize tomorrow, or seize retirement after age sixty-five. I need to do something daily that gives my life meaning.

The rain, mist, and drizzle slowly seeps into our gear, despite wrapping everything in plastic bags, and putting rain covers on our panniers. During brief lulls in the rain we strap our wet clothes all over our panniers like moving clotheslines, but nothing seems to dry out. In the evenings we huddle over maps, constantly evaluating our itinerary and schedule. We want one last visit to the coast, one last break at the beach before riding into Nicaragua.

We drop out of the mountains and head west, across the scorching hot Guanacaste lowlands. In Liberia we leave the Pan American highway to head southwest across the Nicoya Peninsula. Our destination is Playa Tamarindo, a beautiful large beach with a small town and a wildlife sanctuary.

The roads on the peninsula are rough. The gravel doesn't slow our bikes much, but the dust is annoying. Luckily the road does not have many vehicles. A number of large resorts are spread out along the coast. Most people arrive via bus or fly into the small airports near the hotels. In 1940 almost half of the peninsula was covered with rainforest. Much of it was cut down by 1960 to make way for cattle, which along with tourism, is still the main industry.

Tamarindo is a sleepy little town, yet the hotel we want is full. We spend our first night in our tent. But the next morning we get a room. The beach scene at the Hotel Lucy is relaxed and quiet. Surfers from all over the world fill half the hotel—predominantly male, most but not all in their twenties, friendly, and full of energy. The best surfing is four miles south of our beach, so the surfers are usually not around during daylight hours. The other hotel guests are a variety of travelers and beach lovers, some on one-week vacations, others travelling for months or even years.

The great thing about our hotel is the wonderful balcony looking over the beach, with excellent sunset views. The rooms at the hotel are simple yet somehow very pleasing. The cement floors, polished rock hard and smooth from bare feet, sun lotion and sand, are cool and refreshing to the touch. I sit on the floor doing yoga stretches during the heat of the day. Our room is so quiet, I can meditate without using my ear plugs. I feel grounded and complete here.

Each morning we pamper ourselves with breakfast at Johann's Bakery: coffee and cream cheese croissants with raspberry topping.

We spend three days lying on the beach, reading and soaking up the sun. Total pamper mode. We treat ourselves to cold sodas during the day and fresh fish suppers with a beer each night.

We must, however, do at least one little adventure. Just north up the coast is the Tamarindo National Wildlife Refuge, a favorite nesting spot of huge leatherback sea turtles. After supper we walk the short way to Playa Grande for the ultimate night hike. The turtles come to the beach only on nights with a high tide. We quietly hike down the beach, using our ears more than our eyes to locate turtles. We listen for panting, laboring, gasps.

The leatherback turtles emerge from the ocean with a lumbering grace for an animal that can weigh over one thousand pounds and is totally unsuited for moving on land. Using their flippers like oars on a beached galley, they push their way up the beach, one lunge at a time, with hearty, sighing gasps between each heave of their flippers. Their struggle to cross the beach evokes a deep, sympathetic response in us. Once they are well above high tide line, about one hundred yards up the beach, the turtles scout for just the right place.

We select one to follow closely. Using all four flippers, our turtle disturbs a large area of the beach by aggressively throwing sand with her flippers in every direction. Then she begins to dig in earnest. Rather than a large shallow trough, she digs a single deep hole, only eighteen inches in diameter but three feet deep, using each end of her rear flippers to dexterously scoop out the sand.

When satisfied that the hole is complete, she lays her eggs. Leatherbacks normally lay sixty to eighty eggs. The last ten or fifteen are increasingly smaller in size, lightweight, and hollow; eggs that will add space to the top of the nest. When the other, fertile eggs hatch, the hollow eggs on top will give the newborn turtles a little breathing room to move around before digging their way back up to the surface.

After laying the eggs, the turtle fills in the hole, and carefully packs the sand firmly back over the nest. For good measure she uses her considerable body weight to again tamp everything back down. When she is finished, a great flapping commotion begins as she again throws sand in all directions. By spreading her smell up and down the beach, she hides the exact location of her nest. When this last effort to protect her brood is finished, the turtle turns back toward the ocean, and begins the laborious journey back to the water's edge.

The turtle's arrival at the ocean is greeted with soft cheers of encouragement from us. We wade into the surf to watch the huge animal swim out into the night. The experience is extremely moving. The cycle of life, the instinct

Leatherback sea turtles take several hours to lay sixty to eighty
eggs in the sand, Playa Tamarindo, Costa Rica.

toward creation of a new generation is universal. Life sustains itself not through personal immortality, but through a continuation of the species. We all want life to continue, even if we are not around to be a part of it.

At Tamarindo we meet up with a couple we first met on the beach at Manuel Antonio. Francois and Jaqueline from France are taking the winter to travel up the Pacific coast of Central America. They spend their days reading and building sand castles, staying about two weeks at each beach. Tass and I each claim that with a little encouragement from the other, we could do a similar, totally relaxed trip. A vacation.

Yet right now neither of us is willing to give up a section of our elaborate traveling schedule to allow for more time here. Despite our sadness in knowing this is our last beach stop until the end of the trip in Mexico, we pack up to leave. We are both totally committed to cycling through Central America, even if we must leave Costa Rica, the Garden of Eden, to do it.

10

Through a Dark Past

When the Spanish conquered Central America, they were most interested in Mexico, for its wealth and gold, and Panama, for its strategic location with trade routes across the Isthmus. The rest of Central America was felt to have little value. As Spanish settlers moved into the isolated regions, many married Indians. Today the population is predominantly mestizos, people of Spanish and Indian ancestry.

After being set free from the Spanish empire in 1821, Nicaragua, along with the rest of Central America, signed treaties to be a part of Mexico. Two years later the countries of Central America proclaimed their own independence as a single state with the seat of government in Guatemala City. The first President of The United Provinces of Central America immediately abolished slavery. The province of El Salvador claimed he had exceeded his authority, and revolted. Honduras, Nicaragua and Costa Rica, disgruntled for a variety of reasons, soon joined the revolt. After more than ten years of fighting it became obvious that unifying Central America under one government was unworkable, and each province declared itself independent. Nicaragua did so in 1838.

In 1855 William Walker, a lawyer and doctor from Tennessee, put together a small army of fifty-six followers equipped with the best rifles, and sailed to Nicaragua. Walker exploited existing political tensions, seized a steam ship on Lake Nicaragua, and used the boat to attack a rival political group in the lakeside colony of Granada. Walker won, formed a new government, which conveniently "elected" him President. Unbelievably, the United States legitimized Walker's exploits by recognizing the new government! Walker next took control of the assets of the Transit Company, including the ship he had stolen, owned by U.S. millionaire Cornelius Vanderbilt.

The other Central American governments, along with Vanderbilt, formed a coalition and overthrew Walker the following year. To avoid capture he es-

caped with the help of the U.S. Navy. Six months later he returned with another fighting force, but was arrested and again returned to the U.S. Three
years later Walker tried again. This time his party attempted to land in Honduras. He was taken prisoner, tried, and quickly executed. William Walker
was gone, but the problems for Nicaragua were not.

In 1909 the U.S. Marines helped the Conservative leaders overthrow the
elected Liberal government. In 1912 the Marines returned to help enforce new
laws. Except for a few brief periods, the Marines stayed until 1933, often battling nationalists and patriots under General Augusto Sandino. When President
Roosevelt announced his "Good Neighbor" policy of non-intervention in the
sovereignty of other countries, the Marines were sent home. All power in the
country shifted to the Nicaraguan National Guard, trained and financed by the
U.S., and commanded by Somoza Garcia. Within a year Somoza's men assassinated Sandino. In 1936 Somoza declared himself President.

Somoza remained dictator of Nicaragua until he was assassinated in
1956. His oldest son took over; then the youngest son began his iron-fisted
rule. The U.S. government continued training and arming various bands of
unsavory military units for the Somozas, some of which were used as death
squads against anyone who did not share the government's right-wing politics. The U.S. government justified supporting militaristic strong men throughout Latin American in the name of anti-communism. The dictators exploited
U.S. cold war paranoias by labeling all dissent as subversive and communis-
tic. By doing so they received a continuing supply of arms and money, which
further increased their hold on power.

In Nicaragua, disgust with the corrupt Somoza dynasty perpetuated constant guerilla activity and uprisings of people's armies. In 1978 war engulfed
the entire country. After a year of heavy fighting and the death of thousands of
people, Somoza was finally overthrown. A broad opposition movement
headed by the Sandinista guerrillas took power. Four years later, in the first
elections, the Sandinistas won two-thirds of the National Assembly. But a
right-wing group loyal to Somoza boycotted the elections, which caused the
U.S. government to condemn the whole process.

The U.S. began arming the remains of Somoza's army, and the *contra*
guerilla movement was formed. Despite official and private support from the
U.S., including Ollie North and the CIA, the *contras* never gained popular
support in Nicaragua. The contras terrorized cooperatives and blew up power
stations and bridges, which only postponed the rebuilding of the country. In
the late 1980s the President of Costa Rica, Oscar Arias, helped implement a
truce between the two sides. Despite mass desertions, a small group of *contras* continued fighting.

Last year, in 1990, another election was held. Violeta Chamorro, the
widow of a newspaper editor assassinated by the Somoza government, won

the election. More of the *contras* put down their weapons. But just months before our arrival, several bands of *contras* have resumed fighting in the north, near where we plan to enter Honduras.

The turmoil in Nicaragua is very much on our minds as we ride toward the Nicaraguan border. We are leaving Costa Rica, a country that has not had an army for nearly fifty years, and spends a large portion of its gross national product on health care, rural services, schools and national parks. Ahead of us lies Nicaragua, hopefully at the final chapter of a thirty-year civil war.

The smoke from countless farmers using slash-and-burn agriculture fills the hot and dry air. Grim cycling. At a small town near the frontier, I stop and get a haircut. The old-style barber shop has a red-and-white-striped pole out front, a huge ornate iron barber chair inside, and a straightforward, no-frills barber. Despite my directions I quickly find the barber has just one haircutting style: short on top and even shorter on the side, buzzed out with clippers and a comb in rapid succession. Tass is horrified at my new haircut. She calls me Ellsworth, implying I am a recruit from the Air Force base near our home. It is not a compliment. I don't get too excited; it will grow back.

The Nicaraguan border is simply a group of buildings lining the road, with a small crowd outside each of the doors, waiting for various officials to do their various official duties. We stop at the first building, which has no sign on it, and ask if we are supposed to go inside. The response is a bored nod. In the building are two custom officials and two lines. I queue up behind a group of four men and begin the waiting process. Three buildings and four lines later I am in the last line, getting a special permit to bring our bicycles into the country. I show our proof-of-purchase receipts and get the last document. We are waved on to the actual customs check.

When the German cyclist told us to stock up with plenty of food before crossing into Nicaragua, we took his warning seriously. At every stop during the last day and a half we have picked up more and more fruit, baked goods, peanuts, crackers, and snacks.

The first pannier the custom agent opens is half full of food. So is the second. We make a few jokes about cyclists always being hungry. The top of the third pannier is also crammed with food. This time the official laughs along with us.

Going through customs we meet a couple from Australia who are bicycling in the opposite direction. They left southern California five months ago. They thought it would take six months to ride all the way to Patagonia at the tip of South America. Ha-ha. They spent four months getting through Mexico alone, and have since rushed through Honduras and Nicaragua. They are almost out of money and are simply hoping to see Costa Rica before flying to England to resume work. South America will wait for another trip.

Because we meet right on the frontier there is no place we can stop to chat, which is unfortunate, because they seem to have a traveling philosophy similar to ours. We ask each other about the route ahead. They rode the Pan Am highway straight through Nicaragua and had no problems getting food, or toilet paper, as some have reported. Everyone was very friendly. They ask about our favorite rides and spots in Costa Rica. All too soon we are waved through customs.

The entire west coast of Nicaragua lies along a geographic fault which has created a string of volcanoes and hills called the Pacific lowlands. In a large basin east of the range is Lake Nicaragua, the largest lake in Central America or Mexico. Although it is a fresh-water lake it contains many salt-water fish, including sharks, which swim up the San Juan river all the way from the Caribbean. Cool. Lake Nicaragua is dominated by two giant volcanoes rising out of the center of the lake, filling the skyline. Very cool.

The main highway, full of ruts and enormous potholes, follows the western shore of Lake Nicaragua. The dry-season wind blows fiercely; luckily mostly a flanking tailwind. The landscape on our side of the lake is flat, rolling terrain. Along the road there are no trees, no traffic, no houses. We get spectacular views of the lake. One of the island volcanoes, Concepcion, is the

Cycling along the shore of Lake Nicaragua.

second highest volcano in Nicaragua. It is hard to ride past such perfect volcanoes and not take a boat out, spend a few nights, and climb to the top. But we are now a week behind on our former schedule and traveling in mileage mode; we'll climb other Nicaraguan volcanoes. By afternoon clouds form over the tops of the volcanoes. We console ourselves by joking that it is raining on top and not much of a view anyway.

Halfway up the shore of the lake is Riva, the first town. The city has little traffic, and the streets are a mess of rough pot-holes. We cycle past a few bombed and burned-up cars. Some have been sitting so long they are half-covered with flowering weeds and vines. A number of the buildings are completely demolished. Those that remain standing are badly dilapidated, many with pock marks from bullet holes. The walls are full of cracks and in need of mortar and paint. Instead, they are covered with political slogans and graffiti exhorting the need for social change—pictures of Che Guevera and condemnations of Yankee Imperialism.

At a small *pension* we get a clean but simple room with painted cement walls, no windows, and a thin mattress on a wooden bed. Thirty *Cordobas*, six dollars, nearly twice the cost of a similar low-budget hotel in Costa Rica. Because of terrible inflation, Nicaragua has the highest lodging and food prices in Central America. The *pension* is full of truck drivers who spend the night drinking beer and watching TV in the hotel restaurant.

With the U.S. government sponsoring the discredited *contras*, we wonder how the people of Nicaragua will react to us as U.S. citizens. We even joke about sewing little Canadian flags on our panniers. We need not have worried.

"My cousin lives in Orlando!" the first truck drivers tells us proudly upon learning we are from the U.S. We quickly find the U.S. is viewed as an almost mythical place, a fabled land of opportunity. The most common response is not a lecture on politics, but wide smiles and wistful looks.

We eat a typical meal of beans, eggs and rice. In the evening we go for a walk. The city is dark, with few street lights. Not many vehicles either, but a number of bicyclists. The *zocolo* is quiet and nearly deserted. A large monument in the central boulevard lists columns of martyrs who died fighting for freedom from the Somoza government.

The next morning we change money, buy food in the market and visit a few sites, including two large churches. Inside, more photos of people killed in the war. Yet on the street a tremendous enthusiasm is in the air. People want to look forward, not backward. Everyone is optimistic about building a future for the country and their families. Everywhere we see signs of the burgeoning economy, as people open businesses out of their homes, selling everything from home-made cheese to household supplies, clothes, shoes, freshly butchered meat, even medicine and pharmaceuticals.

The town has a number of elaborate horse-drawn carriages on the streets that serve as great taxis. Some have ornate scrolled iron work and polished wood frames. Others are painted bright white. They all have enormous wooden wheels, some with fancy handcarved spokes. The horses are groomed to perfection.

We resume riding north. The highway stays flat, and we begin turning away from the shoreline of the lake. The volcanoes slowly recede behind us into the haze and smoke of the dry season. A hot wind picks up. By mid-morning the winds have shifted direction and hit us sideways with ferocious gusts. Our speed slows to a crawl. Morale fades. Our mouths are full of dust. The road is rough; our bikes bounce along at an excruciatingly slow pace.

Bicycle riding is especially hard when it takes so long and requires so much energy to go such a short distance. Now is a good time to second guess leaving the beach in Costa Rica. What are we accomplishing here? We are working like slaves to ride through boring scenery at an absurdly slow speed. Is this adding anything important to our trip? We have less than two months left. With so much to see and do, why are we frittering away the hours, battling winds and pot holes?

In the late afternoon we ride into Jinotepeh. Tass has a fierce headache—probably from stress. I feel exhausted and defeated. The one hotel listed in our guide book has shut down. All the locals direct us to the Hotel Jinotepeh, which turns out to be totally beyond our budget at forty dollars per night.

We pedal to the market and ask some vendors about cheap lodging. They direct us down a back street to a small *hospadaje*. We ride around in circles, up one block and down another, asking and reasking for directions to the hotel. We ride up and down the same street three times. A man selling ice cream cones from a little push-cart freezer points to a doorway across the street. The building looks like every other house, with no sign on the door or wall.

We knock on the door. After a minute a woman opens the door.

"*Si, esta hotel Jinotepeh,*" she tells us with a nod. I follow her down a hall to an open courtyard, devoid of plants or even grass, surrounded by dingy, windowless rooms—dungeonesque cubicles. The place is filthy. The price is thirty *cordoba*, six dollars.

We search out another *hospadaje*, which is even harder to find. Inside a troupe of dirty, snot-nosed kids follow me to a room that is worse than the last place. The bed looks both soggy and lumpy, a breeding ground for bugs, fleas, and any number of organisms and fungi.

We return to the first place and take a room. The bed is a grungy mattress on a homemade frame with strips of old bicycle inner tubes woven together to make a "spring." I sit on the bed and instantly sink to the ground as the weathered tubes stretch to the floor. The bottomless bed. We slide the con-

A bombed car, covered in flowers, left abandoned after Nicaragua's civil war.

traption up on its side against the wall and sleep on our backpacking mattresses on the floor.

The communal bathroom down the hall is even worse. Dark. Windowless. Lightless. Moldy fungus covers the walls, which sweat from the dampness. A urinal made of cement leaches rust-colored water. The smell of urine and wet cement is a deadly combo. The floor is so gross it gives me the willies to cross it, even with thongs on my feet. The shower door is rotting wood; the lower half has decayed away to leave a two-foot gap between the bottom of the door and the floor. Inside a slick, slimy board has been placed as a pedestal to stand on while showering. Of course there is no place to hang a towel or clean clothes. Yet once the water is running it feels sooo good to wash off all the sweat and dust from the road. We both wrap our towels around ourselves and bolt from the bathroom to dry off in our room. We are too tired and it is too hot to cook. We search fruitlessly for a restaurant. There is none. We return to the Jinotepeh Hilton, as we call our hotel, and feast on huge peanut butter, honey and banana sandwiches.

Although we are on the Pan Am highway, traffic is sparse. We ride through rolling hills with small coffee farms. None of the intersections has highway signs, or numbers marking the roads. To find our route around the base of Santiago volcano, we try to figure directions off a map with a scale of 1:1,800,000. After exploring the town of Masaya, we finally ride up the eastern flank of Santiago and enter Masaya Volcano National Park.

We strike up a conversation with a friendly ranger. When he learns we do volcano programs in schools, he insists on taking us into a five-hundred year old lava tube on Santiago volcano. He drives his truck and we follow behind on the bikes.

At the entrance we light kerosene lanterns. The tube averages about fifteen feet in height and twenty feet in width, and is nearly half a mile in length. The sworling black lines of the old lava flows give the walls fascinating patterns. In places the ceiling is covered with stalagtite-like formations, suspended, hanging in space. Everywhere thick tendrils of tree roots weave through cracks in the rock, searching for water and nourishment.

We hike around the two large volcanic craters, then stand on a ledge and peer straight down into the abyss. Smoke and steam rolls out of the deepest crater. Something in the power of volcanoes evokes a deep fascination in us.

The last stretch of road into the capital of Managua is bustling with trucks and buses. The first large intersection into the city has no signs for directions. We shrug our shoulders and follow the flow of the traffic as best we can, to work our way into the capital. None of the street corners has any signs, so as we near the city center we continually stop for directions.

I get a little ahead of Tass, and stop pedaling for a moment to coast and look around. Suddenly, a large city bus appears over my left shoulder, a rushing blur of noise and metal, seemingly on top of me. My heart hammers in my chest and I totter on the bike as my reflexes jerk in surprise. I try to turn out of the way, away from the bus, but my balance is off, and I feel like I am veering the wrong way.

The bus keeps roaring past, inches from my elbow. It seems like the longest bus in the world. Just when I see a flash of space and think it has passed, another large rush of metal again towers over me. The bus is a tandem! I regain my balance and begin turning to the right, away from the bus. But the bus also turns right, and keeps coming closer! The towering wall of rushing metal stays just inches from my shoulder. Suddenly the back bumper zips by, almost catching my foot. The bus is past.

My hands tremble on the brakes as I slow to a stop. Tass stops beside me a few moments later, unaware of what even happened. I stand beside the road for a few minutes and let my confidence return before I remount my bike and rejoin the flow of traffic. We continue on to a small section of town dubbed "gringolandia," and check into a pleasant *Casa de Huespedes*.

An enormous area in the center of downtown Managua is a desolate, abandoned graveyard of dilapidated buildings. Hardly a single person is out on the streets. The center of the city was destroyed in an earthquake in 1972. After the quake, relief agencies from all over the world sent money and supplies to help in the rebuilding of the capitol. Somoza used his vast network of corrupt governmental agencies to funnel most of the money from relief agencies into his own pocket. This was the final outrage that started the civil war, in which the city was further damaged during the revolution of 1978-79. When Somoza finally left the country, the U.S. government granted him complete political asylum. He fled to Florida, taking everything that was left in the Nicaraguan treasury with him. He was later assassinated in South America.

The old central business district of Managua has still never been rebuilt. We walk through the abandoned buildings, stunned to think that all this damage was from an earthquake almost twenty years ago. The ruins stand as a monument to a brutal dictatorial government that never cared about the people it ruled.

A family has moved into one of the doorless, windowless buildings. Two hammocks hang from the walls, a few pots and a blackened circle of stones

A young girl plays on the streets of Managua, Nicaragua.

from a fire serve as the kitchen. Embarrassed that we have stumbled into the middle of their "home," we quickly back out into the street. Two little boys shyly follow us out into the street and stare quietly at us. We discreetly watch them in return. They cling to each other, standing side by side. Being raised in a safe and secure middle-class home in South Dakota, I can not imagine growing up in an abandoned building in a war-torn country. These two have just as much right to happiness and economic security as anyone else. Yet life has given us very different opportunities.

We leave the Pan American highway to bicycle up the western shore of Lake Managua, skirting the two volcanoes that rise from the shores of the lake. The largest, Momotombo, is active with a geothermal power station at its base. In a row behind Momotombo are three more volcanoes, including majestic, smoking San Cristobal, the highest in Nicaragua. Our destination, the city of Leon, lies at the base of the first two volcanoes.

Leon was founded in 1524 and has long been called the intellectual capital of Nicaragua with its large university and a number of religious colleges. Leon also has the largest cathedral in Central America. The city is picturesque with narrow streets, adobe houses, and red-tiled roofs. We also see a number of brightly colored houses, in neon pastels, bright turquoise, pink, yellow, and gold, all with dramatic trim. The colors are so striking Tass repeatedly stops to make photographs.

Leon sustained heavy damage during the revolution, especially during the final victorious battle against Somoza's national guard. We spend just one night and have a relaxed breakfast in a dilapidated but charming sidewalk restaurant overlooking the *zocalo*.

Our route leaving Leon climbs the pass between two of the volcanoes. On the left is Telica, a cinder volcano whose top is a beautiful pattern of rust and brown colored ash, outlined by the swirling patterns of deep, eroded gullys. Near the summit of the pass we allow ourselves a quick side trip at San Jacinto to see a field of hot bubbling mud, steaming up from the ground.

We cycle off the pass down into a wide valley and begin climbing into the central Nicaraguan highlands. The weather continues to be hot and dusty. The river beds are all dry, and there are no houses where we can stop to get water. The road has no traffic, and no road signs. We meet a couple of young boys on tired-looking horses. Yes, they assure us, we are still on the right road.

Throughout our time in Nicaragua we have read the daily newspapers to monitor the *contra* guerrilla activity on the road north of Esteli. Now when we ride into Esteli we talk with a number of truck drivers who say the region further north is probably okay during the day, but they advise us definitely not to get caught out on the road at night. We go to bed thinking we will ride across the area the following day. But when we wake up we change our

Tass with an escort of inquisitive kids, Nicaragua.

minds. We are running short of time anyway. Why take a chance? We hop on a bus to Ocotal which will take us through the worst region.

We leave Ocotal cautious yet optimistic that we can safely bicycle the last twenty-five miles to the border. The countryside is much more tropical and moist, richly verdant, and eerily quiet. After an hour we stop for a quick stretch and a drink. At the edge of the road where we pull over is a single, large caliber bullet casing. Suddenly we feel uneasy. The spent bullet feels like an omen. I hear the sound of a car motor.

"Lets get out of here!" I say suddenly, and jump up to better see the vehicle, a small blue pick-up truck. I stick out my thumb. Tass quickly stands up and does the same, no argument from her. The driver pulls over with a smile. We hoist our loaded bikes into the truck and jump in back beside them. The truck takes us safely the last few miles to the Honduran border.

11

Mayan Kings

Much of Honduras is mountainous. The Caribbean coast has high rainfall and is covered with tropical rainforest, while the central mountains are slightly drier with pine and oak. Our route will take us across the country through the central mountains and the capital, then to western Honduras and the ancient Mayan city of Copan.

From the border we descend into a large valley full of sugar cane fields. We resupply with food in Danli and ride back up into the mountains. Because of the prevailing winds, we have chosen to ride through Central America from south to north, to ensure tailwinds as often as possible. We see an average of three or four cyclists a week, mostly on the Pan Am highway, all riding north to south through Mexico and Central America, with a few having started in Alaska and going all the way to the southern tip of South America. Now we meet two male cyclists from the Netherlands who are riding to Panama. Like all the others, they tell us we are the first cyclists they have seen on their whole journey. When they ask why we are riding south to north we point out the wind direction.

"No kidding!" they shake their heads. "We have been battling headwinds since southern Mexico!" They are amazed to hear of other cyclists just a few days ahead, and probably more close behind.

About thirty miles before Tegucigalpa we leave the Pan Am highway to check out the area around Yuscaran, an old Spanish city. A rough gravel road takes us up through more pine-covered hills. As we climb, the mountains begin to cover in mist. Everything is a lush, vibrant green. The air is clear and rich with the smell of a giant garden.

Yuscaran is a picturesque colonial village, built on a hillside with narrow cobbled streets and large homes. We ask the woman who runs a small *comedor*, a little restaurant, if she knows of anyplace we can get a room. She directs us to a great stucco building, three stories high. A massive, ornately carved

106

double wooden door leads into a courtyard. The big doors are too difficult to open and close to let people go in and out, so smaller, normal-size doors are cut into the big doors for day to day traffic. The big doors are used only for driving vehicles in and out of the central courtyard, or sometimes opened wide during the day when the weather is pleasant.

The courtyard is wonderfully peaceful, a great place to relax and read. I love the architecture of an open courtyard in the center of the house, a completely private sanctuary away from the bustle and noise of the street and town. Staying in a building over four-hundred years old is interesting and thought-provoking. I lie in the bed and look at big hand-hewn log timber beams running across the ceiling. Craftsmanship built to last. Many generations of the same family have lived in the house. Imagine being born, living and dying, just like your parents and grandparents, in the same house! What a sense of history!

We spend a few days in the capital, Tegucigalpa. Unlike many Central America capitals, Tegucigalpa is not located on a fault line, and has never been destroyed by earthquake or fire. We visit local markets and relax at Cafe Allegro, a little beatnik coffee shop with black-and-white photographs on the wall and old men in berets having lively discussions, playing chess, and reading books. We browse the secondhand bookstores, restocking our supply of travel books, guide books, and novels.

Guards armed with rifles stand on most street corners. Others with machine guns stand in the shade and under awnings of stores. We stop at a travel agency to ask a question. A soldier with a rifle steps up, interested in our bikes. He smiles and offers to guard them for us while we step inside. When we leave he happily poses for a picture with our bikes. One of our books claims Honduras has had three hundred internal rebellions, civil wars and changes of government since its independence in 1821.

The Spanish had little interest in the area that is now Honduras, except for the silver mines near where they built Tegucigalpa, which in a local Indian dialect means "silver hill." After Honduras gained independence from Spain, U.S. companies imported black workers from Belize and the West Indies to create large banana plantations in the northern lowlands. Honduras earned the nickname "Banana Republic" in the early 1900s with the rise of Standard Fruit and United Fruit, two U.S. companies whose plantations made bananas the major export crop. United Fruit, known locally as *El Pulpo*, the octopus, had major influence politically not only in Honduras, but throughout Central America, with strong ties to a number of right wing dictators.

Most, but not all, of the wars have been fought over land rights. One of the stranger battles was the "Football War." In 1969 tensions arose as Honduras was inundated by migrant workers from war torn and heavily populated El Salvador, who were all seeking work in Honduras. A disputed decision during a World Cup soccer match between the two countries sparked a riot which escalated into a battle lasting thirteen days. More than two thousand people died. A cease fire was implemented by the Organization of American States, but the treaty was not actually signed by either side until eleven years later.

In the 1980s Honduras allowed the *contra* guerrilla armies to base and train their forces in Honduras, and attack across the border into Nicaragua. By playing off U.S. cold war fears of communism, the military government built the largest air force in Central America, further entrenching its power. Now the capital is run like an armed camp. According to the Central America Peace Plan, the *contras* were supposed to be demobilized and disarmed six months ago. They are still living in camps in Honduras near the Nicaraguan border. And the U.S. government is backing the entire mess, while encouraging the building of the huge Honduran forces in a country that is in constant turmoil politically, with no accountability whatsoever. And this is supposed to be making the region safer for democracy?!

From Tegucigalpa we ride northwest through the highlands. Since the prevailing winds are from the east we have tailwinds. Puma, jaguar, and bear all range in the quiet, pine-covered hills. Near Lake Yojoa we ride down into the Ulua river valley, the hot lowlands, an area famous for making Panama style hats of junco palm.

Copan is seven miles from the Guatemalan border at the south-eastern edge of the Mayan world. In the early days of Mesoamerica, the Copan Valley was a tranquil and fertile place to live. Archaeologists report that the quantities of jade found in tombs from the Middle Preclassic period far exceed the wealth of burials at other Mayan centers of the time.

Mysteriously, during the Late Preclassic period around 300 B.C., Copan saw a rapid decrease in population and had almost no building or activity. This was at a time when other Mayan cities were institutionalizing governments through the concept and development of kingdoms; already Tikal and Uaxactun were proclaiming their first kings.

Nearly five hundred years later, in 160 A.D., *stelae* resume recording activity in the city. Within a short time Copan rejoined the mainstream of Mayan life, with ritual and elaborate building projects becoming a main focus of the society. Farmers and craftspeople flocked to the growing center of power, building their homes as close as possible to the city. As the city grew, the best land which had been used for farming was slowly acquired for buildings, plazas, and causeways. Social standing was linked to the location of where one lived, and the new urban elite wanted to live in areas closest to the Acropolis. Farmers were forced to move up higher in the valleys.

Copan is famous for its intricately carved *stelae* depicting
former kings, Honduras.

On September 9, 426 A.D., Blue Quetzal Macaw was proclaimed King
of Copan, and founder of a new lineage of rulers. His twelfth successor,
Smoke Jaguar, reigned from 628-695 A.D., and presided over an extraordinary transformation of Copan. Suddenly the city became a major center of
power and commerce in the Mayan world. The next successor, Eighteen Rabbit, encouraged sculptors, architects, and artisans to create even more beautiful buildings, artwork, and *stelae*.

New temples were constantly being built upon foundations of older
temples, layer upon layer, each larger and grander than predecessors. Destruction of old monuments and *stelae* required special rituals to neutralize
and cancel the power of ceremonial objects. Older *stelae* were "terminated"
by carefully breaking the stone or smashing part of the face. Dates and in-

scriptions were also rubbed out, and then everything was buried in elaborate ceremonies.

The prosperity from the city gave rise to a growing group of elite aristocrats, who began building their own pyramids, *stelae* and monuments. The court of nobles who helped govern the city also increasingly managed regions in the growing kingdom. When Eighteen Rabbit was killed during a battle with the vassal city of Quirigua, Copan hardly seemed to suffer; the inhabitants continued to build and trade. The government now seemed to run itself.

The kingdom continued to grow. Within the one-kilometer radius of the Ballcourt were fifteen hundred structures. Three thousand people per square kilometer near the center, twenty thousand people in the valley, all trying to live off the small farms pushed up higher into the mountains. People had to walk great distances to find firewood, as all the nearby forests had been cut down long ago. In an effort to feed more people, farmers were not letting the land lie fallow, and the soil was being depleted. And then there was drought.

For the first time during the changing of a *katun*, an auspicious date, neither the king nor any nobles of Copan erected any monuments. A *stela* dated 820 A.D. commemorates King Yax Pac's death, and implies that the dynasty of Blue Quetzal Macaw had ended with the death of the sixteenth successor, Yax Pac.

Yet he was not the last. On February 10, 822 A.D., U Cit Tok was crowned King, but on the back side of the monument the carving is unfinished. Archaeologists have theorized that during the carving of the monument the central authority of Copan simply collapsed. The sculptor never came back to work. Still, the city was not totally abandoned. Many of the residential areas continued to be occupied for another century. But by the end of that one hundred years, nearly everybody was gone.

From the town of Copan it is a half-mile walk to the ruins through a cluster of trees and numerous old mounds, still uncovered by archaeologists. Upon entering the grounds, the first view of the ruins is much different from other Mayan cities. Copan is not as immediately impressive as Tikal, with its numerous giant pyramids sticking above the tropical forest canopy, nor does it have the mysterious aura of Palenque, tucked into thick, lush rainforest. Instead of building tall pyramids, the architects of Copan emphasized horizontal planes. Although the main ballcourt in Copan is the second largest in Central America, Copan is not famous for its buildings. Copan is famous for its monuments and sculptured *stelae* that have revealed so much of its history.

In the center of the ruins is the Great Plaza. Over a thousand years ago the ground was smoothly-finished plastered rock, probably painted bright colors. Today the Great Plaza is a flat green lawn, dotted with intricately-carved *stelae*, vertical stone monuments, ten feet high, carved with full-figure portraits of kings and nobles. The monuments have beautiful carved faces, elaborate costumes with intricate designs, and fanciful zoomorphic creatures along the top, bottom, and sides, along with deeply carved glyphs. A few still carry traces of red paint. Like the plaza and much of the city, all the *stelae* were painted. Many are royal portraits; we gaze up at statues commemorating Blue Quetzal Macaw, Eighteen Rabbit, and Yax Pac.

Across the Great Plaza is the Hieroglyphic Stairway, the longest surviving Maya text, with more than two thousand glyphs carved into sixty-three steps. The glyphs describe the long history of the royal house of Copan, the descendents and successors of Blue Quetzal Macaw.

We take a break in the shade. The ruins are quiet; no one is around. A couple of spider monkeys work their way through the nearby trees and drop onto the ruins. They scamper across the tops of a few stone walls, and descend into the grass. One of the monkeys stands up on his back legs to look around, then walks out into the grassy plaza. The monkey looks so comical standing on its back legs with its tail curled in the air behind its head, hands at its side. The other monkey does the same. They cross the grassy area and then scamper back into the trees.

A spider monkey takes a leisurely stroll through the Mayan ruins of Copan, Honduras.

12

Guatemalan Highlands

We leave Copan at dawn's first light, in the cool morning mist. The air is sharp and still, the streets of town mostly empty. The short ride to the border seems almost magical, through mountains with mist-filled valleys, brightly illuminated by the sun rising behind us.

The border crossing is effortless. The first official stamps our passport in sixty seconds. The next guy pokes at our panniers for a few moments, opens a couple of bags, and simply waves us through. We are in Guatemala.

The landscape changes quickly to drier pine hills interspersed with terraced croplands and fertile valleys. As we ride, the countryside becomes even more parched, the hills covered with haze, the road a dusty ribbon winding through the growing heat. Since we started at dawn, by mid-morning we have bicycled four hours. We stop at the town of Jocotan.

With just one month left in our journey, we want to split the time and spend two weeks in the western highlands of Guatemala and two weeks in Mexico. Rather than using precious time crossing eastern Guatemala on our bicycles, we head for the bus station. Although the bus ride will give us a break from cycling in the heat and dust, I don't look forward to it. Even when the scenery is only marginally interesting, I prefer the freedom of cycling, and the sensation that I am a participant, moving through the landscape, as opposed to being a spectator in the bus.

At the bus stop we bundle Tass's bicycle panniers together and hand them up to the attendant on top of the bus, followed by her bicycle, which frees her up to scramble aboard as quickly as possible to try and get a seat. I next hand up all my gear and bicycle and quickly climb up to help. The top rack is nearly full with sixty-pound bundles of produce. The bus attendant has set Tass's bike where everyone else will walk over the wheels to get their bundles. I reposition her bike, and make sure both bikes are tied securely. I watch the rest of the luggage being loaded, just to make sure there are no problems, and board the bus last.

In Chiquimula we unload our gear in the crowded and somewhat frantic terminal, and then load up again on a bus to Guatemala City. We drop further out of the mountains into the wide Motagua river valley. The road is moderately busy with truck traffic; the air is hazy, the visibility low. There is little to see. We nap and lazily gaze out the window. Arriving in Guatemala City at mid-afternoon, we change buses one more time. Our last bus takes us just a bit further west to Chimaltenango, where we resume bicycling.

Traffic on the Pan Am highway through the highlands is light, and the buses all give us plenty of room. Bicycling on paved roads feels great, like we are flying. At Los Encuentros we turn north to Chichicastenango. The road winds through beautiful pine forest with terraced hillsides of corn. Now, in February, it is the middle of the dry season. The rains won't come again until May. We race down huge switchbacked corners and drop into a steep canyon, which of course we have to ride back up on the other side.

Our route through the western highlands has us arriving at each town the day before the weekly market. This way we can find a place to stay, get a good night's sleep, and be ready to enjoy the market early the next morning. The area around Chichicastenango, or Chichi, as it is called, has had weekly markets for hundreds, if not thousands, of years. The markets are always a big social activity for everyone in the area. The market at Chichi is so big it is held twice a week, on Sunday and Thursday. Chichi is also a center for traditional Mayan religion and beliefs. As we approach town, we pass a religious procession on the road. A few men carrying religious items and shrines are accompanied by a small band playing flutes and drums.

Although we had visited the Chichi markets during previous trips to Guatemala, we never spent a night in the town and don't really remember much about the area. The village is fairly quiet; we cycle up and down the main streets to orient ourselves and check everything out. Chichi appears quaint, with cobbled streets and adobe houses with red tiled roofs. These materials don't seem the best choice in an area with frequent earthquakes, but since they are inexpensive, everyone uses them anyway.

The cyclists we met at the Nicaraguan border recommended a small *pension* guest house in Chichi whose owner, Pedro, is an avid cyclist. We soon find the El Arco, which luckily has a spare room. Pedro is a balding *mestizo* who is very proud of his Indian heritage. Although in his 60s, Pedro has a mountain bike which he frequently rides on the trails all around town. He offers to take us out on a ride through the countryside. We suggest doing so tomorrow after the market. Right now we are more interested in seeing if the shower really has hot water. It does, and it is wonderful.

The Chichi market brings in Indian weavers from throughout the highlands along with all the local farmers, plus tourists from all over the world. Many of the streets are packed with people and lined with stalls bursting with colorful textiles, pottery, wooden masks and other assorted crafts. In the center of the tourist market is the local market, where farmers buy and sell food and vegetables and catch up on the local gossip. Although we repeatedly foray out into the tourist market looking for a few gifts and souvenirs, we spend most of our time in the inner market and in front of the main Church.

Chichi has long been a center for Mayan tradition. Before the arrival of the Spanish this area was inhabited by the Cakchiquele Maya, rivals to the powerful Quiche. The present town was founded by the Spanish in 1524 to hold the Mayan refugees from Utatlan, a city the Spanish completely destroyed.

Over the next three centuries the Spanish tried to replace the power and influence of former Mayan centers with the church, often simply by changing the Mayan names and symbols used in various ceremonies into Christian terminology, customs, and beliefs. But a lack of clergy in the seventeenth and eighteenth centuries allowed many isolated villages to establish their own interpretations of church festivals. The Indians developed strong village allegiances, along with localized blendings of Catholicism and Mayan belief. Many of these beliefs are still the base for highland life today.

The Catholic church on the main square was built in 1540 on the site of a Mayan temple. Legend has it that most Indians didn't use the church until the early 1700s when a local priest began showing interest and respect in Mayan beliefs. The Maya must have had great trust in him for they showed him a priceless manuscript, a copy of the Popul Vuh, the Quiche Maya book of cosmology and history, one of the very few books to escape being destroyed by the Spanish. The priest began reading from parts of the manuscript during church. The Indians responded by bringing many of their altars down from the hills and into the church. Today the church continues in its acceptance of Mayan belief and custom. Outside on the steps Indians kneel, pray and burn incense before entering. Inside there are no pews. Instead grass has been spread out over most of the floor. Altars have been set up throughout the church. Statues of saints are grouped together, draped in satin and covered with offerings of flowers and more than a few bottles of *chicha*, home-made alcohol. Groups of candles placed before the altars flicker and burn, providing the only light in the building. Other altars commemorate ancestors, former priests and religious leaders. Despite the darkness, or perhaps because of it, the inside of the church has a unique mood and an unusual feel. The grass on the floor makes the building feel less formal and somber, spiritual but not in the normal religious sense, more of a natural mysticism. I sit in the corner. Although I am not Catholic, and I am certainly not a Maya, I find the darkened recesses of the church conducive to meditation and prayer.

In the late afternoon we strip the panniers from our bikes and have a great time mountain biking with Pedro. We cycle on narrow footpaths through

Surrounded by clouds of incense, a Maya woman kneels in
prayer outside the church at Chichicastenango, Guatemala.

cornfields, in and out of farmers' back yards, around houses and gardens and
back out into cornfields. We visit a few small villages surrounding Chichi.
Everyone smiles and waves at Pedro, who is totally enthusiastic about riding
with us and sharing his knowledge of the area. We have so much fun together,
we decide to stay another day and do more rides.

Up in the mountains are a number of old Mayan religious sites. One of the
shrines, Pascual Abaj, is only a mile from town. We leave our bikes and hike up
the ridgetop to the site. We arrive as a shaman performs a ceremony involving the
sacrifice of a chicken, and repeated offerings of alcohol and flower petals. The
shrine is an ancient black stone carved with a primitive face. The entire grounds
are covered with flower petals from earlier offerings. A ceremonial fire burns
nearby. In 1957 Catholic reformers smashed the altar, but Mayan traditionalists

patched and cemented everything back together. Although the ceremony is interesting to watch, I don't like the energy of the site. We don't stay long.

With some reluctance, we say goodbye to Pedro and ride out of Chichicastenango. On the ride back to the Pan Am highway, we stop and watch a group of women weaving beautiful *huipils* in the courtyard of a house along the road. After twenty minutes they invite us to sit in the shade of the courtyard. Like all Mayan weavers they use backstrap looms. They create their works of art freeform, without using a pattern. Still, certain design styles and images are common to each area, and once you learn the colors and styles it is easy to tell where a woman is from by the weaving on her *huipil*.

We ride through the rolling hills to Solola, the small town perched on a ridge almost two-thousand-feet above Lake Atitlan. Like Chichicastenango, the town of Solola actually has two governments, an official *Latino* government and a parallel Indian government made up of different clans, much as before the Spanish conquest. The people of Solola are mostly descendants of the Cakchiquele Maya.

Today is not market day, so the town plaza has only a few vendors selling vegetables and inexpensive household and kitchen items: plastic wash basins, cookpots, candles and batteries. We stop to browse, and a crowd quickly forms around our bicycles. Everyone pinches the tires, squeezes the padding on our handlebars, rings the bells and looks at themselves in our bicycle mirrors. We are definitely a big hit on a quiet afternoon.

A traditionally-dressed Indian man is especially interested in our bicycle gears. I explain how the shifter works and then ask if he would like to take my bike for a quick spin. His face lights up with a big smile. But when he gets on my bike it is much too big, especially with all the weight of the panniers. Tass offers her bike which is closer to his size. I show him how the brakes work, just to be safe, and he climbs aboard. The crowd parts just enough to let him through. He rides around the town plaza, accompanied by much cheering of the crowd. I am impressed how well he handles the bike, which is tricky to steer with the weight of our luggage. When he returns no one else steps forward to give it a try. Apparently one ride was excitement enough for the crowd.

The road from Solola drops at an extremely steep grade down to Panajachel on the shores of Lake Atitlan. The views of the lake as we fly high-speed down the road are spectacular. We stop at a few overlooks just to take in the scenery, and then jump on the bikes for more adrenaline-filled descending.

The change in Panajachel since we were here thirteen years ago is remarkable. The laid-back, hippie backpackers who flocked to Panajachel in the late 1970s have been replaced with a middle-class vacation crowd, both foreign and Guatemalan. Small craft shops and souvenir stands, open seven days a week, line the main streets of town. Almost as numerous as the tourist shops are the restaurants and hotels, all doing a booming business. We check into a cheap *pension*, and I immediately come down with stomach cramps and a fever. I spend the next three days in sweaty delirium, shuffling in agony from the bed to the bathroom with major diarrhea and vomiting.

Tass and I both take travel illness in stride. We often find it very difficult to pinpoint exactly where an illness has originated. Even when we both eat the same foods, one of us will often get ill, and the other will not. We eat from little sidewalk vendors because we can see first-hand how the food is prepared and cooked, and judge for ourselves whether the sanitation meets our standards. We religiously purify water, and simply hope for the best. Luckily we both have an ability to forget about an illness rather quickly after the symptoms disappear. We feel the fun and ease of eating local foods is worth the risk.

On the fourth day I have enough energy to leave the hotel room. It is Friday, so we catch a bus up to Solola for the market. We end up staying six hours. By the time we head back to Panajachel, I am exhausted. But now Tass is excited to take me to one of the new restaurants in town. Inside are a few other travelers Tass has been getting to know. A big topic of conversation is the news that a tourist from the U.S. was killed last night on the outskirts of Panajachel. Everybody in the restaurant is discussing it. Conflicting rumors abound. Some say he was simply a tourist; others claim he had lived in the area for months and was possibly involved in the local drug trade.

I find it interesting how everyone reacts to the news. A surprising number of people seem to be panicking. Convinced that travel in Guatemala is too dangerous, they seriously discuss changing travel plans and heading straight for home. Suddenly every story, fact or fiction, from the last twenty years involving travelers having problems in Guatemala is being recirculated. A couple of the stories, which supposedly happened recently, sound like variations of tales we heard thirteen years ago, and even at that time we questioned their validity.

Another smaller group is convinced the dead foreigner was hanging out with the wrong crowd. Classic blame-the-victim. This group shows little concern, feeling they are safe because they would not be so foolish as to put themselves in a dangerous position.

Chris, one of our new friends, wryly observes, "The city where I live in the U.S. has about four murders every night! If you ask me, Panajachel is safer than my hometown!"

Later in the evening the scant information we get seems to support the idea that something unusual was going on at the time of the murder, which happened at 2:30 a.m. in a place a "normal" tourist shouldn't be at that hour. Still I don't want to completely discount the incident. To me the death is a reminder that sometimes bad things happen, no matter where you are. Perhaps the *gringo* was courting trouble, but then again perhaps not. The truth is that even when we are being totally careful, we can all have bad luck. Through no fault of our own, we can simply be in the wrong place at the wrong time.

Life has risks. It is the nature of our world. I don't want to take foolish chances, but at the same time trying to eliminate all risk seems impossible. Besides, trying to protect one's self from risk would eliminate the challenges and excitement of life. I prefer to accept a little risk, and keep experiencing life! That is why I am in Guatemala.

My illness put a damper in our Lake Atitlan schedule. We had planned to take a few days and ride our bikes around the lake, exploring all the little towns. We consider delaying our Atitlan departure, so we can still do the ride. But then we reconsider. Already we have repeatedly pushed back our schedule. We really don't want to take any more time out of our Mexico itinerary and there is nothing we are willing to forgo from the rest of our time in Guatemala. The bike ride around the lake just won't happen on this trip.

Instead, we take a boat ride across the lake to the town of Santiago Atitlan, the largest village on the lake. The morning weather is beautiful, a great time to be on the water. The town is located between the immense, towering cones of Atitlan, the first volcano we climbed in Guatemala years ago, and Toliman and San Pedro volcanoes. Guerrillas have long based out of this area. In 1981, three years after we climbed Atitlan, the Guatemalan army occupied the town. The area experienced little direct fighting. But right-wing death squads, most likely supported by the army or at least tolerated by the military, carried out a number of political killings. Not surprisingly, almost all the dead were Indian farmers.

The Tzutujile Indians of Santiago wear their own distinctive dress. The women's *huipils*, along with the men's pants, which are cut off right below the knee, are white with thin purple stripes, heavily embroidered with colorful birds and flowers. Many of the older women also wear a band of embroidered cloth, sometimes fifteen or twenty feet long, wrapped and tied around their heads.

We slowly work our way from the docks, up past a number of shops and stalls selling native crafts, toward the center of town. At the main plaza we go into the large Catholic church, where one whole wall lists the names of the many people from the area who were killed or have simply disappeared in the fighting.

We visit *La Casa de San Simon*, a small religious shrine with a statue of a strange "saint" dressed in polyester western-style clothes and felt hat, smoking a big cigar. Saint Simon has many names, including Judas Iscariot, Pedro de Alvarado and Maximon. He is often portrayed as an enemy of the church and is scorned by reforming Catholics. Yet to Mayan traditionalists he is an important part of most religious celebrations. A sort of "sinner's saint." On

Monday before Easter his image is taken to the lake to be washed, on Tuesday he is dressed, on Wednesday he is moved to a small chapel on the town square. On Good Friday the statue of Christ is taken from the main church, paraded through town, then tied to a cross. In the afternoon the statue of Christ is brought down from the cross, put in a casket, and paraded through town along with the statues of the Virgin Mary and San Simon.

The shrine to San Simon is maintained by a *confradia*, a traditional Mayan social and religious body which oversees village activity. Most visitors to the shrine leave offerings of cigarettes and cheap alcohol. I don't know what to make of San Simon. Perhaps those who pray to him need a "saint"

The Guatemalan government's brutal repression of
Maya Indians has killed thousands and
forced many people to flee as refugees.

Tass wishing for lower gears on the steep climb leaving Lake Atitlan, Guatemala.

who is not judging them, someone who will not refuse them or turn from them, or condemn them for their vices.

In the evening we return to Panajachel. As we are walking from the docks to our hotel, we come upon a number of soldiers and military personnel, and then a small crowd. A man is working his way through the crowd, shaking hands. It is Jorge Serrano Elias, the new president of Guatemala, out doing a little politicking. We step in closer. He shakes our hands. I look in his eyes. He seems sincere and decent. The question is, does he have the political power to really control the military? Can he make a difference in the future of the country, or is he just a figurehead, while others wield the true power? We pose for a quick picture.

"*Buenas suerte!*" I tell him sincerely. Good Luck! Guatemala needs it.

Our next destination is the area around Quetzaltenango. Although it is not too far, we no longer have time to ride everywhere. Still, we really want to ride out of Lake Atitlan. So we cycle the hardest and most scenic part, the road leading from Panajachel all the way back up to Solola. The climb is about as steep as a highway can get. In places we have to zig-zag up the road to keep our momentum going. But the views are superb and it is a fun challenge to leave Lake Atitlan on our bicycles. At the top of the mountain we take one final view, and then grab a bus west on the Pan Am highway.

We get off at the town of San Cristobal Totonicapan and ride our bikes down into the enormous Quezaltenango basin. The ride is spectacular. The valley is filled with beautiful, towering storm clouds. The peaks of volcanoes poke out of the clouds, which churn and roll across the landscape. We race into the valley, chasing after the storm in the fresh, moist air of the recent rain.

Quetzaltenango lies at the base of Santa Maria volcano, surrounded by mountains. In 1902 the city was almost completely destroyed in an earthquake. The town was rebuilt with many buildings in the city center using a grand architecture heavy on Greek columns. But economically the city never attained its former glory. Today everything seems relaxed and easygoing.

The weather is cool during the day, and quite cold at night. We walk the streets, stopping to buy corn on the cob from sidewalk vendors. The corn is grilled over charcoal until almost blackened, then rubbed with fresh lime. The corn is an unusual variety with very hard and crunchy kernels, slow to chew but wonderfully delicious and surprisingly filling, even for hungry bicyclists.

In the morning chill we cycle to the nearby town of Almolonga for market day. The valley is incredibly fertile, the countryside full of vegetable gardens. The women wear *huipils* covered with a bright orange zig-zag pattern and bright woven headbands. The next day is market day in Zunil, where the preferred color for *huipils* is light purple, which happens to be Tass's favorite color. In the afternoon we bicycle to Totonicapan, so we will be ready for their market on the following day. We are on a market binge.

We cycle to Cuatro Caminos on the Pan Am highway and take a bus west to Huehuetenango. As usual, at each stop I get off the bus to make sure that everything is okay with our bicycles perched up top in the luggage rack. The bus ride is uneventful until we come into the city. The streets of Huehuetenango are quite narrow, and as we near the market the bus has to slow repeatedly to get past other vehicles, wagons, and carts in the road. Suddenly we hear a loud crashing noise above in the luggage rack. At the same time a huge mass of cables, electric wires and phone lines falls into the street. A policeman immediately blows his whistle and flags the bus to a stop.

The bus attendant jumps off the bus to talk with the policeman. They look at the top of the bus for a moment, and then call for the driver, who also gets off the bus. A big discussion ensues, with much shouting and hand waving. When we hear them arguing about *bicycletas*, bicycles, I get off the bus to see what is happening.

Apparently the last time the assistant unloaded a few sacks of vegetables from the roof, he moved Tass's bike so the handlebars were sticking up into the air above the rest of the luggage. When the bus drove under the mass of wires hanging over the street, her handlebar caught on the wires, and pulled everything down. I climb on top of the bus and find that one side of Tass's handlebar is now completely bent at a ninety degree angle!

The cop yells at the driver, saying he will have to pay for the wires to be fixed. The driver turns and yells at us, saying since Tass's bicycle hooked the wire we are at fault, and we must pay for the damage. We argue that the attendant moved Tass's bike too high on top of the luggage, and that the bus company owes us for the cost of fixing the handlebars.

We continue arguing for quite some time, until the entire street is jammed with honking vehicles. When the policeman realizes that no one is ever going to agree with anyone else, he angrily orders the driver to get the bus out of the way. At the bus station we continue to argue with the driver. Both of us demand money for damages. After awhile, we simply load up the bikes and ride out of the station.

We spend the afternoon at a blacksmith shop, where to our amazement the handlebars on Tass's Trek are heated and bent back without breaking or kinking. The next day as we leave town, a work crew is still trying to sort out and repair all the wires.

13

Sergio Hernandez Becarra

Mexico is huge, diverse, and continuously interesting. We could spend a year cycling here. Unfortunately we only have two and a half weeks. We plan five quick adventures: a short cultural tour in the mountains of Chiapas; a visit to the giant stone Olmec heads in lowland Veracruz and then the city of Veracruz; a bike ride into the mountains of Puebla to find a boy we sponsor through Christian Children's Fund; a hike to the winter migration site of Monarch butterflies in Michoacan; and a few days relaxing on a Pacific beach before flying back to work in the U.S. Whew!

The road we take out of Guatemala runs through San Cristobal de las Casas, one of our favorite cities in Mexico. We can't resist getting off the bus a few days to see the town again and explore some nearby villages we have never visited.

During the eighth and ninth centuries Maya leaving the collapsing lowland cities settled in small villages throughout the mountains of Chiapas. When the Spanish arrived in 1524 they quickly subjugated the three Tzotzil villages in the area and laid claim to the region. The town of San Cristobal was originally known locally as Villaviciosa, the evil city, for the ruthless oppression of Indians by the colonial inhabitants. Today the town is named after Bartolome de las Casas, the same man who brought peace to the Rabinald Maya in Verapaz, Guatemala.

Las Casas came to the New World as an ordinary colonist. But he soon joined the Dominican order and, like a number of monks, spent his life working with the Indians. He was appointed the first Catholic bishop of Chiapas in 1545. Las Casas is often called the "Apostle to the Indians" for his tireless efforts not only in converting them to Christianity, but in crusading for Indian rights, including banning Indian slavery in 1550.

Still the region has had a long history of Indian and peasant uprisings, and their violent defeats. A long succession of governors chosen by politicians in

Mexico City, along with a few powerful local landowners, has continued to this day to rule the Chiapas highlands almost as a feudal state. It is often said the Mexican revolution never came to Chiapas.**

Today the farmers in the mountains face contining problems with poverty and oppression. On top of everything else, Indian traditionalists are now clashing with evangelical protestants. Recently groups of Tzotzils from Chamula have been expelled from their village for being protestant.

From San Cristobal de las Casas we bicycle into the mountains to visit the Tzotzil village of Zinacantan. The road winds through pine forest—pleasant, relaxing cycling. We notice a number of crosses marking sacred spots, many associated with Mayan ancestor gods. The Indians here are among the most traditional in all of Mexico. Many of their beliefs originate with their Mayan ancestors, and take precedence over a sometimes thin veneer of Catholic terminology.

Community respect and leadership focuses not on acquiring wealth and possessions, but on taking responsibility for "cargo" posts. The cargo groups, which are men-only brotherhoods, overlook the upkeep and care of the saint's images in the churches. Becoming a *mayordomos*, a traditional cargo elder, is a serious financial commitment. Organizing and paying for elaborate festivals and ceremonies on sacred days is expensive. On many of these occasions large quantities of *posh*, locally brewed alcohol, is also consumed by the participants. This practice is frowned on by the reforming Catholics, and derisively condemned by evangelical protestants, which has further inflamed the disagreements between the groups.

The town is small and quiet, the streets virtually abandoned. Like most of the villages in the region, Zinacantan is simply a collection of religious and civic buildings and a few huts. Most of the population lives in the surrounding countryside.

On market day we cycle to Chamula. The small town plaza is a sea of women's cobalt and light blue *huipils* and shawls. The market has little to offer, only a few varieties of vegetables, corn, a couple of chickens and part of a butchered cow cut up into piles of bloody meat on a wooden table, in the sun, with flies.

Unlike the San Cristobal markets, we make very few photographs in the mountain villages. The Indians here expressly forbid taking pictures during religious ceremonies, and have a rather low tolerance for photography the rest

---

** In 1994 the Zapatista National Liberation Army led by Subcomandant Marcos took over San Cristobal, Ocosingo, and a number of smaller villages, destroying government offices and police stations, and demanding political reform. Popular sympathy toward the Zapatistas by many people in Mexico, and around the world, forced the Mexican government into dialogue with the so-called rebels. Whether any lasting reform will occur remains to be seen.

of the time. A commonly told story claims that in the 1970s two Germans, despite being warned, photographed a sacred ceremony in town. They were subsequently attacked by a mob and lynched. True or not, signs now posted outside the church warn against taking pictures of religious events.

Inside the brightly white-washed church a hazy, ethereal smoke from incense and candles fills the building. The pews have been moved out, the floor covered with pine branches. The walls shimmer with the wavering light of hundreds of lit candles. Small, scattered groups of people huddle on the floor in prayer.

The energy in the building feels sacred in a simple yet profound way. It is a sincere devotion. I may not agree with some of the theology, but I like being in the church. I spend the morning sitting in contemplation in a out-of-the-way corner.

We bus from San Cristobal to the gulf coast state of Veracruz. Much of southern Veracruz is a hot, flat, and humid coastal plain. Our bus ride ends at San Andres Tuxtla, the center of the Los Tuxtlas region with rolling hills, lakes, and waterfalls. We stretch our legs with a short ride to nearby Santiago Tuxtla. This area was once the western end of the ancient Olmec empire.

Archeologists believe the first Americans came to the New World via a land bridge across the Bering Strait between Asia and Alaska 50,000 years ago. The earliest evidence of humans in Mexico—nomadic hunting camps—date around 20,000 B.C. Around 6500 B.C. people in Puebla state began planting squash and chile peppers. Over the next few thousand years the people slowly domesticated maize and beans, and began living in semi-permanent villages instead of nomadic hunting camps. Pottery developed by 2300 B.C.

The Olmec culture, Mexico's first official civilization, began in the tropical lowlands along the gulf coast of southern Veracruz. The Olmec center of San Lorenzo flourished from 1200 to 900 B.C. Nearby La Venta in Tabasco thrived from 800 B.C. to 400 B.C. The Olmecs left behind large carved basalt heads with unusual helmets, wide and flattened noses, and grim expressions. Olmec art features beings with a combination of human and jaguar features, called "were-jaguars." Olmec culture, art, and religious beliefs, including maize gods and the feathered serpent, influenced later civilizations of Teotihuacan, Mayan, Toltec, Aztec, and even traditional beliefs still held today.

In Santiago Tuxtla we visit the *zocalo*, the town square, to see the largest Olmec head ever found, and the only one with closed eyes. The head is ten feet tall and six feet wide, the expression on the face is stern and severe; the mouth is frowning, possibly representing anger or pain. Today is Monday, and we are sad to learn the nearby archeology museum is closed. Inside is another colossal head, plus a giant toad and a rabbit head we really wanted to see. Unfortunately, we don't have time to wait around another day to see the museum. Within an hour we are on a bus to the city of Veracruz.

Olmec head, Santiago Tuxtla, Mexico

Veracruz is a lively, tropical port city with great streetside cafes, and plenty of music at night, with wandering musicians and mariachi bands everywhere—a great place to enjoy some *Latino* culture. Although we will probably get little sleep from all the music, we check into a room right above a restaurant next to the *zocalo*. The building must be three-hundred years old. A giant stairway, forty feet long with a fifteen-foot ceiling, leads up to our room. We push/carry our loaded bikes up the stairs one at a time to our room. Inside the ceiling is at least twenty feet high. The paint on the walls is old, faded and musty. A small six-foot-high wooden cubicle in the corner is the bathroom, added nearly eighty years ago with indoor plumbing. The wooden shutters open to a balcony, criss-crossed with a few electric and phone wires. Half the view is taken up by the branches of a giant tree growing out of the sidewalk. The other direction overlooks the street and a quaint sidewalk cafe.

In 1519 Cortes established Veracruz as the main Mexican port for contact with Spain. For centuries the city remained small because of the unhealthy coastal climate with malaria and yellow fever. Throughout the sixteenth and seventeenth centuries English, Dutch, and French buccaneers terrorized the city with raids. In 1683, six-hundred pirates led by a Frenchman named Lorencillo attacked the city and held, by some accounts, virtually the entire population of five thousand people hostage in the church with little food or water. Lorencillo threatened to blow up the whole building if the people would not reveal where their money was hidden. After a few days 600,000 *pesos* was raised and the pirates sailed away.

In 1847 during the Spanish-American war, U.S. soldiers captured Veracruz in a week-long battle in which many civilians died. British, French, and Spanish forces have also occupied the city. In 1914 U.S. troops again took Veracruz to supposedly protect American interests during the Mexican revolution.

Today the foreign troops are finally gone, and malaria and yellow fever have been eradicated. Still, surprisingly few international tourists come to the region. The beaches are nice, but nothing like the Caribbean or the along the Pacific. Coastal Veracruz is one of the wettest regions in Mexico, although most of the rains come in brief torrential downpours, with the sun quickly reappearing.

The city is famous for its seafood specialty, Veracruz-style grilled red snapper with tomato sauce, garlic and spices. We have a wonderful supper at a sidewalk cafe, and then go to Cafe La Parroquia, a famous spot for coffee and dessert. Like everyone around us, when we want a refill we tap our empty glass with a spoon. The waiter soon appears with two giant kettles, one with coffee and the other with steaming milk. He quickly and impressively pours whatever mixture of the two we want into our cups from a height of two feet, without spilling a drop.

But our plan for a night on the town begins to fade around nine o'clock. We are feeling the effects of long distance bus travel. We return to our room and prepare to go to bed. An hour later a very loud band begins playing in the cafe below our room. We lie in bed listening to the music and the shouts of the crowd between songs. After half an hour, we realize we are never going to be able to sleep. We get up, get dressed and head downstairs to join the dancing. The town is full of musicians, marimba bands, mariachis, individual xylophone and trumpet players, singers and guitarists, along with tourists from all over Mexico who have come to enjoy the entertainment. Groups of sailors sit together, their tables brimming with empty beer bottles which the waiters never clear, instead leaving them as trophies to prove how much beer the patrons at the table have consumed. Our table looks rather empty. We wander the streets listening to the music, and stay out until the wee hours of the morning.

Veracruz is too much fun for just one night. We sleep in, and then have a wonderful, relaxed breakfast at a sidewalk cafe. We explore the docks and run a few errands, then return to the cafe district. At night we head back out to enjoy the continuing celebration.

The next day we begin a series of bus rides into the mountains of the Sierra Norte de Puebla, a remote northern region of Puebla state. We get off the bus at Teziutlan, the largest town in the region. The Indian women wear black wool *rebozos*, long scarves around their head and shoulders decorated with colorful flowers, birds and animals. We ride west from Teziutlan, looking for a small village named Xaltipan.

A little over a year ago, Tass and I began sponsoring a young boy through Christian Children's Fund. He lives in Xaltipan and his name is Sergio Hernandez Beccara. The money we send not only helps Sergio and his family, but also contributes to a broad range of community projects. Sponsor families work together with project coordinators on community issues such as running health clinics, building water reservoirs and bringing in electricity. Prior to our trip we sent a letter to Sergio's family telling them we would like to visit, and the approximate date of our arrival. But apparently the letter did not reach them in time, as we did not get a response before we left the U.S.

A hard-working *campesino* from the
mountains of central Mexico.

with exact directions to where they live. We know Xaltipan is much too small to be on any map, located somewhere near the towns of Zacapoaxtla or Cuetzalan in a remote area of highlands known for beautiful weavings, colorful markets, and religious festivals.

We bicycle west into the mountains under sunny skies, which is rather uncommon. Drizzle and mist is the normal weather. This area gets over 150 inches of rain each year. The countryside is pine forest, with beautiful mountains every direction around us.

By early afternoon clouds begin to form. Even when the fog descends, the warm temperature makes riding in the mist enjoyable. The clouds of mist, hanging in the valleys and rolling over the mountains, simply add to the great scenery. We stop to spend the night in the town of Tlatlauquitpec. In the *zocalo* we meet Jose, a young, local bicyclist. He says he would like to do a ride with us. We tell Jose we are looking for a village named Xaltipan. To our surprise he says it is nearby, and he will gladly show us the way tomorrow.

The next morning the sky is hazy but dry, perfect weather for cycling in the mountains. We leave our panniers at our hotel and ride behind Jose into the mountains on a narrow singletrack path. In the village of Xaltipan we go to the school and are soon introduced to the principal. We ask about Sergio, but the principal says there is no family by that name in the village. One of the teachers says she believes there is another village, also called Xaltipan, further north in the mountains, two or three days away by bicycle. Perhaps Sergio lives there.

We leave the first Xaltipan and continue our day tour of the area. We ride to the village of San Juan, where a number of old, eroded pyramids covered with vegetation are scattered through town. Many of the pyramids have Christian shrines and churches built on top. The Spanish commonly erected churches on top of ruined temples, just as people throughout Mesoamerica replaced older temples with new pyramids and buildings on top of their older shrines.

Back in Tlatlauquitpec we load up our luggage, say goodbye to Jose, and bicycle northwest to Zacapoaxtla. I love the tongue-twisting names in this area! Like most Indians names, x is pronounced ch, with a "scchh" sound under the front of the tongue. Many of the other accents are spoken more from the back of the throat. At intersections, signs point out other towns along the way: Tlatlauqui, Zapotitlan, Xochitlan.

Like many of the small towns in the mountains, Zacapoaxtla is an old colonial town, built on a hillside with whitewashed buildings and red tile roofs, centered around a plaza facing an enormous two-story church with five-story bell towers. In the center of the courtyard in front of the church is a sixty-foot-tall pole where four *voladore* dancers ascend to "fly," rotating in the air around the top of the pole, upside down, arms outstretched, held only by a single rope around their leg. Quite the bold ritual. The ceremony originated in old fertility rites, and is now incorporated into Christian celebrations. The pole seems incredibly high. I count sixty wooden rungs to the top. Unfortunately there won't be any flying while we are here; February is the wrong time of year for the *voladores*. We cross the plaza and check into a wonderful old hotel with a peaceful courtyard.

A somewhat tarred road leaves town twisting further north into the mountains. In places the highway is cut into steep hillsides with huge drop-offs; on corners the road hangs in the air. The dirt banks where the road was cut are now covered with ferns and tropical plants. High above us limestone cliffs crown the mountains, along with thick forest. Forest also covers all areas where the ground is too steep to clear. Shrines dot the highway: whitewashed monuments, crosses and little altars. One has cut-out paper decorations attached like prayer flags to string lines, radiating out from the building.

In the valleys and canyons where the mountains are not so steep, the countryside is a patchwork of farms and terraced hillsides with only a few scattered stands of forest. Despite the initial green appearance, the area looks overtaxed and overused. Scattered clouds of smoke rise from ongoing slash-and-burn agricultural practices. Numerous groups of firewood collectors walk along the road pulling carts in search of wood, which is ever further away in the higher hills.

As we ride we see more and more coffee farms. We climb up in elevation and the clouds thicken. We are soon blanketed with fog and a steady drizzling rain. The air takes on a quiet stillness as we round the last corner into Cuetzalan.

Cuetzalan is the most picturesque of all the towns in the region. The center of town is completely dominated by an enormous, beautiful church with tall bell towers and steeples. Surrounding the church are incredibly narrow cobblestone streets. Some of the streets and alleys are so steep they have occasional drop-offs like stairs, and are obviously pedestrian-only as the steps make the roads impassible for vehicles. A solid and imposing wall of two- and three-story colonial buildings towers over both sides of the narrow streets. In places the roofs overhang from the building four or five feet, overlapping the roofs from buildings across the road like a canopy over the street. As the mist rolls through town, the buildings take on an ethereal quality, poking in and out of the fog as if built on clouds.

The next day is the Sunday market. We take the day off from our search for Sergio and head early to the main square to browse and people-watch. The Indian women wear white blouses with colorful embroidery across the top and front, red and blue shawls called *quechquemitles*, and black wool *enredo* sashes. The men wear white baggy pants and shirts, natural-wool-colored *serapes* swung over their shoulders, and leather thong sandals with rubber bottoms cut from old car tires. The market is filled with locally grown vegetables and fruit. Although we don't see any tourists, we do see a few handicrafts including baskets and woodcarvings for sale.

Around mid-morning we begin seeing a few people in festive costumes making their way to the church. We follow behind and join a crowd that is forming around the main plaza. Before long a group of dancers comes out of the church dressed like *matadores* with huge felt *sombrero* hats embroidered with gold and silver designs. A couple of them wear mirrored highway patrol-style sunglasses. In the middle is another man carrying a six-foot long papier-mache bull on his shoulders. As the dancers weave back and forth in front of the church, the bull charges at the *matadores* at regular intervals, to the great enjoyment of the crowd.

The next group of dancers looks like gaudy gauchos. They wear cowboy boots, black chaps covered with sparkles and glitter, yellow waist sashes, blue satin long-sleeved shirts with pink sashes covering one shoulder and half the front and back of the shirt, and black felt cowboy hats covered with pink and green ribbons with a white lacy crown perched on top. In one hand they carry a collection of colorful silk scarves. A small band accompanies them as they dance together in front of the church.

When they finish, ten boys emerge from the church with huge head-dresses, only a few inches thick but four feet in diameter, like giant colorful disks perched on top of a cone hat. The boys dance to the accompaniment of a man playing both a flute and a small drum at the same time. While the first two groups of dancers are from more recent Spanish traditions, the group of boys now before us performs an older, pre-Hispanic ritual.

The Nahua Indians—the largest Indian ethnic group in all of Mexico—moved into this area in the fourteenth century. Their ancestors were probably of Chichimec origin, the so-called barbarians from the north that periodically invaded ancient cities throughout central Mexico. Amazingly, after their military wins, the Chichimecs often abandoned their nomadic warrior traditions to embrace the agriculture practices and urban lifestyle of those they had conquered. In the fifteenth century the region came under control of the Aztec empire. The dance with the colorful headdresses probably originates from that time.

When the dancers finish, a clothed statue of Saint Peter is brought out from the church and carried in procession around both the plaza and the church. The whole crowd follows the procession like a giant, slow-moving parade. The dancers repeat their performances in a courtyard and then the statue of Saint Peter is taken back into the church.

After the festival we take a walk through town. On a side street we pass a building that says Tosepan Titataniske Regional Cooperativa. The door is locked, and no one is around. A painted mural on the building depicts the cooperativa working with the Indian community on a variety of health and educational issues. We figure this will be the best place to resume our search for Sergio.

Early the next morning while Tass does some errands, I return to the cooperativa. I wait an hour on the front sidewalk until a man shows up to open the door. I explain that we sponsor a boy from Xaltipan named Sergio, and we would like to get directions to his village so we can visit him. The man tells me something about it being necessary that I meet or talk with another man, whom I assume will know more about Xaltipan, maybe even where Sergio lives. I don't understand everything he is saying, but one thing is clear. We are to return tomorrow when the other man will be at the cooperativa.

We spend the day further exploring town, and talking about what might happen when we finally meet Sergio. Now that the time draws near, we are a little nervous. As we were riding a few days ago we saw a man passed out drunk along the road in the grass. His two young children were sitting listlessly beside him with glazed and bewildered expressions, waiting for him to wake from his stupor. Suddenly we realized since this was near where Sergio lived, it was possible for anyone along the road to be related to Sergio. Unemployment and alcoholism are common, creating many dysfunctional homes. Sergio's family might suffer from problems even worse than poverty.

The next morning we return to the cooperativa and ask about the man we are to meet. There has been a slight delay, we are told, some problem with a truck. But he will be here shortly. An hour later, after nothing has happened, we ask again. We are assured the man will be here soon. We get the impression the truck might be going on to Xaltipan.

Thirty more minutes pass. We are motioned to a side room. Inside are four men and a young boy. We are introduced to the first man, whom we assume has the information about where Sergio's village is located.

"Sabe de puebla de Sergio Hernandez Beccarra?" We ask with a smile. Do you know Sergio's village?

"Esta es Sergio!" This is Sergio! He proudly points to the young boy and smiles. We are stunned.

"Esta es Sergio?" We ask twice before we are sure that indeed Sergio is standing before us! Sergio appears as bewildered as we are. We take a step forward and say *"Buenas dias!"* Good day! Sergio looks at his feet. One of the men tells him to say something to us in return. But Sergio is shy, and suddenly begins to cry from the pressure of everyone standing and staring at him.

We tell Sergio we are glad to meet him, and it is okay if he wants to wait a moment before talking with us. We are relieved to see one of the men stoop and give Sergio a kind, reassuring pat on the shoulder. It is Sergio's father, Maurilio Hernandez Gonzalez. We are introduced, and we express our surprise. We thought we were simply meeting someone who would give us directions to Xaltipan and might know where the family lived.

Sergio Hernandez Becarra, Mexico.

We are introduced to the project coordinator for Xaltipan. He tells us that after Sergio's family received the letter announcing our arrival everyone has been expecting us. Sergio and Maurilio were brought to town early this morning by truck to meet us. While we chat we are all served a breakfast of *tortillas* and beans. Sergio relaxes as he eats, however he still doesn't say much. We notice that during breakfast Sergio eats a large bowl of beans and about twenty *tortillas*, quite a bit for an eight year old boy who is less than four-feet tall and weighs only fifty pounds.

After breakfast the project coordinator tells us he would be happy to take us into the mountains in the truck so we can see where Sergio lives. Naturally everyone insists we sit in the front of the truck. Maurilio encourages Sergio to ride up front with us. After a few moments Sergio climbs inside onto my lap where he can look out the window. It is his first time ever riding in the cab of a truck. Maurilio and three other men hop in the back of the truck and off we go.

The dirt and gravel road winds through the mountains, clinging to the hillsides. The air is surprisingly clear. Usually the hills are blanketed with fog, or it is raining. The steep ridges are covered with pine trees. In the few valleys small coffee farms are interspersed with rows of corn, beans, and peppers. We pass a couple of scattered settlements, and the truck stops briefly to pick up a few people at each spot. After a ninety-minute ride, the truck is parked at a "village," two white-washed buildings on each side of a dirt plaza. Sergio's house is another forty-five-minute walk into the mountains.

At first I thought the people we picked up on the road just happened to be catching a ride, but as we leave the truck they all come along. They are all affiliated with the cooperativa. Ten of us hike up a long ridge. The trail is well-worn. We are amazed at the number of houses we pass, tucked under trees and behind rows of crops. Each little shanty has six, eight, or ten people living inside. We would probably be stunned at the total population of the area.

A group of neighborhood children is waiting for us outside of Sergio's house. The house has three different rooms. The main living room/bedroom has a tin roof and unpainted wood walls with small cracks between the joints of the wood. The second room is the kitchen, with a clay tile roof and even larger gaps and spaces between the board walls to ventilate the smoke from the fire. A smaller third room is being built of cement block. The floor in all three rooms is hard-packed dirt.

We are introduced to Sergio's mother, Rosa Becerra Osollo, who, like her son, is shy at first. Sergio has four brothers and one sister. His oldest brother left home at the age of sixteen to find work as an unskilled laborer in Mexico City. He is staying with an uncle. Without our sponsorship Sergio probably would have faced similar prospects. Still, even with school, Sergio's chance for a good, steady job in the area is slim.

Rosa shepherds a group of young girls to the kitchen to cook lunch. We sit in the main room on a wooden bench with a growing number of curious people from the neighborhood. The project coordinator tells us that the Xaltipan project started in 1986 and serves four Nahuatl Indian communities in the area. In those five years we are the first sponsors to come and visit a family! He shows us Sergio's case file and points out that Sergio is doing well with his school studies. He also shows us Sergio's medical reports. Sergio is listed as having fair health. The most common problems in the area are intestinal problems from poor sanitation and diet, and respiratory infections, including tuberculosis. The last page in the file is an itemized list of what Sergio's family has purchased with the extra twenty-five dollars we send each Christmas. This year they bought him three shirts, two pairs of pants, and a wool blanket.

It is amazing to see how the small amount of money we send makes such a difference not only to Sergio, but also his family and the community. A recently finished communal water system built by sponsor families brings water to within a hundred yards of the house. Cooperativa project coordinators also sponsor instruction on hygiene, nutrition, and health. Maurilio is presently building the family's first outhouse with material partially paid for by Christian Children's Fund. CCF calls these programs Family Helper Projects, because they require parental involvement through community work sessions.

After chatting for awhile, we excuse ourselves and check to see how things are going in the kitchen. The ceiling is very low. Being much taller than the women, I have to stoop to keep from hitting my head. A small wood fire is burning on a stone hearth built in the corner. Even with the ventilation from the holes in the walls and the cracks between the roof tiles, the room is smokey. Near the fire Yolanda, Sergio's older sister, is hand-grinding corn for *tortillas*. After grinding the corn, she pats the dough into patties and lays them out on a grill over the fire. Tass watches Yolanda and then tries her hand at *tortilla* making, which is more difficult than it looks. The dough keeps sticking to Tass's hands. Her *tortillas* have holes in them, and no matter how hard she tries to fill the holes the dough keeps sticking to her palms. In the time that Yolanda makes twenty *tortillas,* Tass makes two. Yolanda, Rosa, and the girls giggle and watch Tass discreetly, trying to hide their astonishment. They are not sure what to think about a woman who doesn't even know how to make a *tortilla*. When Tass jokes about the poor quality of her *tortillas*, the girls go into hysterics.

The cooperativa literature says seventy percent of the children in the area are seriously malnourished. The family almost never has milk, and only occasionally do they eat eggs or meat. They eat lots of *tortillas* and beans. Sergio is surprisingly small, obviously in part from his diet. Every two weeks the family gets a bag of soy protein as a part of our sponsorship. In our letter to

Tass learns to make corn *tortillas* by hand, Mexico.

the family we mentioned we are vegetarians. They would not need to kill a chicken on our arrival. So in our honor they purchased two tins of canned fish to go with the beans and *tortillas* for lunch.

After our meal we hike to Sergio's school. The building has two rooms, each with big open windows for light and ventilation, and a good tin roof. The rough wooden desks don't look very comfortable though. Sergio's class has ten boys and six girls. Most of them don't have shoes. The girls wear loose, colorful skirts and white blouses with cross-stitch embroidery. The boys have long brown pants and white or darker colored shirts. They all have big smiles.

We ask to see the coffee fields where Maurilio works. It is a forty-five-minute hike from the house each way. His fields are so far away because there is no available land any closer. Maurillo picks each coffee bean by hand as they individually ripen. He makes the equivalent of a dollar and a half a day. Slave labor.

After we hike back to the house we are asked the price of coffee in the U.S. The crowded room is stunned when we sadly tell them coffee sells from four to eight dollars or more a pound, depending on grade and quality. If the cooperativa had the financial resources to ship and sell good coffee to the U.S., without trade barriers, the farmers would make a liveable wage.

Simple, low-tech, grass-roots programs are so cost-effective. Unfortunately they are not as impressive for history books. Hence, government agencies and institutions like the World Bank push so-called trickle-down projects, where more of the funds and glory go to big banks and big business—where politicians can have their photographs taken cutting ribbons and dedicating big industrial projects.

Independent, non-profit agencies often have the best programs. To choose a charity we first reviewed a Wise Giving Guide from the National Information Bureau, which rates non-profit organizations. We found that Christian Children's Fund, one of the oldest and largest non-profit relief agencies in the world, has a very favorable rating. Less than twenty percent of each dollar is used in administration and fund-raising, among the lowest of any non-profit agencies. Eighty-one percent of the donation goes straight to the programs. We also like the Christian Children's Fund philosophy of encouraging respect for local customs and cultures. CCF's goal is to improve the lives of children and families around the world, including over 21,000 sponsored kids in the U.S.

The day passes much too quickly. Because we rode out in the truck, we need to go back when the driver is ready. If we had been on our bikes, we would have spent the night, maybe two. The option of cycling back out to Xaltipan would take two days, and that now seems anticlimactic. For now, one day has be be enough. We bid Sergio and the entire family farewell, hike back to the truck, and return to Cuetzalan to catch a series of buses heading west.

We get off our last bus in the city of Zitacuaro, Michoacan, and ride a few hours north into the mountains to Angangueo. From there we cycle higher into the pine forest to the tiny village of El Rosario, where we have arranged to meet our good friend, Janet Niichel. We first met Janet in Kathmandu, Nepal, during our world bicycle trip. Janet lives in southern California, where we get together every winter when Tass and I do slide shows in the area. We also meet each fall to mountain bike in Moab, Utah, and often meet for other adventures both in and out of the U.S.

We find Janet at a *Casa de Huespedes*, one of the two budget hotels in town. Janet is with her new boyfriend, Pat, whom we meet for the first time. We spend half the night talking, laughing, and telling stories. Still we are all up early the next morning, ready to see butterflies.

All monarch butterflies east of the Rocky Mountains in the U.S. and the Great Lakes region of southern Canada migrate each winter to this part of Mexico. The route takes many of them through Florida, directly south to western Cuba, south west across the Gulf of Mexico to the Yucatan, and west through central Mexico. Each November a mountainous area in Michoacan, seventy-five miles long and thirty-five miles wide, is inundated with Monarchs. They fill the air crossing mountain passes and traveling up valleys. Sometimes large groups of butterflies will create giant patterns in the sky. At other times they rise hundreds of feet into the air in enormous spiraling towers. By early December the patterns and towers disappear as the butterflies settle in, crowding together into stands of trees. Sometimes they shift positions once or twice to other trees. About nine monarch colonies form. Each group picks a spot around ten thousand feet above sea level, usually less than a mile from where the previous year's monarch group wintered.

Oddly enough, the sites they choose have very cool temperatures, averaging below fifty-five degrees. At that temperature monarchs are too cold to fly. Only on occasional warm, sunny days can they fly. Yet because the area normally doesn't freeze, they don't get too cold. The butterflies use the cool temperature to induce a torpid state, so they don't use up vital energy flying around. They rest. In the spring they will mate, and fly all the way back to the U.S. to lay their eggs. Then they will die.

The eggs hatch, but the monarchs that are born don't return to Mexico. They spend the summer in the U.S. After a few months they lay their eggs and die. The butterfly "grandchildren," which are born in late summer, are the ones that fly back to Mexico. So only every other generation of butterflies makes the trip.

How do they know how to find their way back? Theories abound. Perhaps they get their bearings off the sun. More likely they use the earth's magnetic fields. No one knows for sure, yet. Like most animal migrations, little of it is understood.

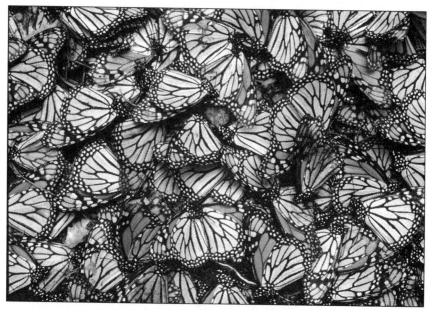

Dead monarch butterflies cover the ground at the
winter migration site, Michoacan, Mexico.

Monarchs will nest in pine and cedar, but they prefer the *oyamel* tree,
which has needlelike leaves. As we hike, the sun comes out briefly and soon
a number of butterflies flit in the air around us. When the sun disappears into
the clouds, the butterflies vanish. The trail winds up the steep hillside through
the forest. High above us we catch glimpses of an unusual golden brown in
the trees. As we get closer we see it is the monarch colony. Some of the trees
are completely covered, their branches drooping from the thick coating of
butterflies. Under the trees the ground is covered with dead butterflies. High
winds can blow the butterflies to the ground. Cold temperatures and rain can
also kill the outer layers of butterflies. One out of four can die in a severe
storm. The dead butterflies on the ground are so thick the ground crunches as
we walk over them. Yet all around us, thousands more practically suffocate
the trees, covering the trunks and every branch and leaf. It is amazing to think
how delicate each one is, and yet how strong, to have made such a journey.

Scientists discovered the monarch sites in 1975. Unfortunately, there is
concern that logging might disrupt the butterflies. If too much of the nearby
forest is cut, the climate of the entire region might be altered, affecting the
monarchs. Now that the area is being monitored, the monarchs have a much
better chance of being protected.

Janet and Pat join us for one last bus marathon to Puerto Vallarta on the Pacific coast. The city has long been a popular destination for the beach crowd. We have just a few days to relax at the ocean before going back to work. We go into total pamper mode. Leisurely breakfasts, reading at the beach, wonderful fish suppers at night.

I think of the couple we met in Costa Rica, traveling beach by beach up the coast. Then I think of all we have seen in the last three and a half months. I wouldn't trade our experiences for any beach paradise. The world is full of so many interesting places to see and things to do. I just want to keep moving.

Part V   1994

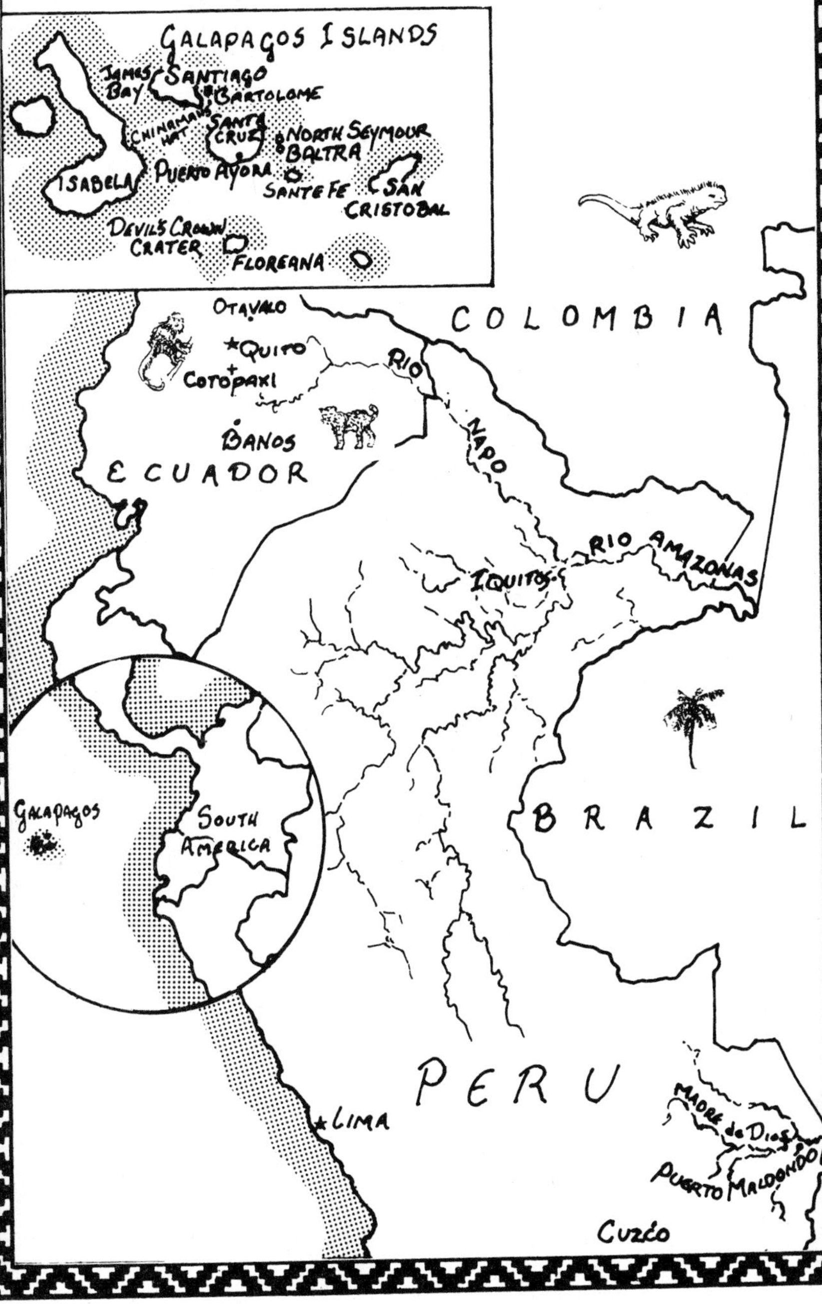

GALAPAGOS ISLANDS

James Bay
Santiago
Bartolome
Chinamans Hat
Santa Cruz
North Seymour
Baltra
Isabela
Puerto Ayora
Sante Fe
San Cristobal
Devils Crown Crater
Floreana

Otavalo
Quito
Cotopaxi
Banos
ECUADOR

COLOMBIA

RIO
NAPO

IQUITOS

RIO AMAZONAS

GALAPAGOS
SOUTH AMERICA

BRAZIL

PERU

LIMA

MADRE de Dios
PUERTO MALDONDO

Cuzco

14

Viva la Evolution!

In May 1994 we leave South Dakota and fly to Quito, Ecuador, high in the Andes mountains. At the South American Explorers Club we store most of the luggage we brought with us—mountain bikes, winter mountaineering equipment, and rainforest gear—and catch a plane going west, six hundred miles off the Pacific coast of Ecuador, to the Galapagos Islands.

The Galapagos Islands were probably first discovered by Inca sailors in the 1400s. The first Europeans visited the islands in 1535 when the King of Spain ordered the Bishop of Panama to sail to Peru. The Bishop was sent to investigate the ruthless brutality of the conquistador Francisco Pizarro and his men in conquering the Incas. The Bishop's ship traveled down the west coast of South America, but before it could reach Peru, a windless calm settled over the ocean. The boat drifted in the strong ocean currents, and was soon far from South America. Running out of fresh water, the crew spotted a group of islands, but despite lengthy searches they never found water. Later in his report to the King, the Bishop described the islands as barren and uninhabitable. He also mentioned in detail the abundant wildlife: sea lions, iguanas, and especially the giant tortoises. The Bishop named his discovery *Insulae de los Galopegos*, the Islands of the Tortoises.

Throughout the next two hundred years the western coast of South America bustled with Spanish ships. Boats from Spain carried supplies and payroll money for the army and a growing network of bureaucrats in South America, while boats with gold and treasure looted from the Incas sailed back to Spain.

In 1493 the Spanish Pope Alexander VI granted Spain most of the western hemisphere. The three other leading sea powers of the time, Great Britain, France and the Netherlands, viewed this so-called gift with disdain. While they did not declare war on Spanish interests and ships, all three encouraged private citizens to do just that. Buccaneers began patrolling the waters, sacking Spanish ships and stealing anything of value. Great Britain, France and the

Netherlands all labeled these marauding ships as patriots or privateers, while the Spanish viewed them as pirates. As time went on the buccaneers grew increasingly bold, not only attacking treasure ships, but sailing into ports to rob and burn towns. Soon the buccaneers were fighting not only the Spanish, but each other in their quest for loot.

After such battles the buccaneers generally high-tailed it out to sea to elude capture. They often came to the Galapagos to get water, which by now had been discovered on a few of the islands. They also filled their holds with huge Galapagos tortoises, which could live for months inside the ship without food or water, thus supplying the crew with a continuous supply of fresh meat.

By the early 1800s Spanish influence in the New World was declining. As South American countries started trading with Great Britain and France, everyone wanted to get rid of the buccaneers and make the waters safer for shipping. With the Industrial Revolution came a need for machine oil, which was not yet obtained from the ground, but processed from whales. The Pacific ocean off the South American coast filled with whaling ships, again coming to the Galapagos for water and turtles, which were stacked upside down in the ship's holds. Since each ship could take five hundred giant tortoises, the population of the tortoises throughout the islands was decimated. Three of the island subspecies became extinct. Sperm whales were also killed almost to the point of extinction, as were the Galapagos fur seals, whose pelts were the latest fashion in Europe.

At this same time a man was born in England whose name would later become synonymous with the Galapagos. After dropping out of medical school and briefly studying as a divinity student, Charles Darwin was unsure of the direction of his life. His father raged at Charles, "You care for nothing but shooting, dogs, and rat-catching, and you will be a disgrace to yourself and all your family." In 1831, at the age of twenty-two, Charles left England aboard the *HMS Beagle* on a five year exploration of South America. Charles' position was unpaid naturalist, and even then he was second choice for the job.

In 1835 the *HMS Beagle* dropped anchor for just five weeks in the Galapagos Islands. What Charles viewed in the Galapagos would forever alter his view of how life developed on our planet. Years later, looking back at his time on the islands, Darwin would call the Galapagos a "living laboratory of evolution." The confined habitats and small number of species living on each isolated island all worked to give Darwin a clear view of the adaptive process by which, according to his theory of evolution, one species becomes several quite different species.

During World War II my dad was stationed on Baltra Island in the Galapagos as a member of the 29th Bomber Squadron. The U.S. government built a huge runway and Air Force base to guard the approach to the Panama

Canal and monitor submarine activity in the South Pacific. Dad was stationed on tiny Baltra island for thirty-six months. "The Rock," he always called it. He was never allowed on any other islands.

The U.S. Air Force base is long gone, but we land on the same runway on Baltra, which now serves domestic flights. A small building, along with a large, open awning is the terminal. Everybody stands in line to pay an Ecuadorean government surcharge collected from all island visitors—$80 U.S. The Galapagos is not cheap.

Although this is my first trip in South America, Tass traveled through Columbia, Ecuador, and Peru during the winter of 1975-76 with her good friend Suzanne Martell. In 1977, after Suza traveled with us in Mexico and Guatemala, she returned to South America, and spent seven months on the Galapagos Islands. She lived with Franklin Angermeyer, whose family has lived on the island for years and is very well-known. Their relationship did not last, and Suza returned to the U.S., pregnant with Franklin's son.

We are eager to meet Franklin, who has a sailboat he charters out. To save money we book Franklin's entire boat—then find friends and other travelers to fill the five cabins and split the costs. Our group includes Janet Niichel, whom we have met for many adventures, including seeing the monarch butterflies in Mexico; Rich Henke and Rena Tishman, whom we often meet mountain biking in Moab; Ken Legler, an old friend of Janet's from Texas; and Terri and Georgina, two women travelers we just met in Quito. We'll spend each day hiking and exploring one island, then sleep on the boat, while the crew sails—if there is wind—or motors—if there is not, to arrive at the next island by morning.

Because of the increase in tourism to the islands, and the desire to preserve the natural beauty of the area, the Ecuadorian government wisely does not allow people to set foot on most of the islands without a government-certified guide, and even then tourists can visit only specific spots on each island.

Our guide, Juan, meets our group at the airport. He grew up in Guayacuil, but has been working as a naturalist in the Galapagos for years. He is instantly likeable. He explains Franklin is very busy preparing the boat and will meet with us later. We take a bus across tiny Baltra Island, then a ferry across the narrow channel to much larger Santa Cruz island, where we take another bus over gravel roads across the island to the town of Puerto Ayora.

At the docks we meet Franklin's partner, Sarah. She explains the boat is moored in another cove. Franklin is working on the engine and will meet us later. Sara takes us to meet Franklin's father, Gus. The Angermeyer family is firmly entrenched in Galapagos folklore. Gus and his three brothers moved to the Galapagos from Germany before World War II, long before the islands became a popular tourist destination.

Gus is totally eccentric. He lives in a large, igloo-like house made of black lava rock. The inside is filled with bones and unusual beach debris he has found over the decades. Tass, who loves bones and shells, is smitten by his wonderful collection of whale and dolphin bones and skulls. Gus is highly entertaining and rather madcap as he jumps around, showing us everything. When we pull out our camera to make photographs, which Suza had adamantly told us she wanted, Gus insists we can take his picture only if it is "not for publication!"

After our visit we take a small motorized *panga* boat out to the *Angelique*, the 96-foot sailboat that will be our home for the next week. As we move into our rooms, Franklin is still working somewhere deep inside the engine room. When we leave Puerto Ayora that evening, Vincent, the first mate, steers us toward our first destination, Floreana Island to the south. Finally just before bed we bump into Franklin on the deck. He abruptly says hello and then disappears back into the engine room.

In the morning we wake to find bottlenose dolphins piloting in front of our boat as we sail the last short distance to the island. Again Vincent is at the wheel. At a sheltered bay we drop anchor and pile into the *panga* to go to shore. Without a wharf or dock, we "wet" land on the shallow beach, quickly jumping out before the *panga* gets stuck. We splash through the surf, our camera gear stowed in waterproof bags. On shore the sandy beach is olive green from volcanic olivine crystals. A group of seals lie on the nearby rocks.

A baby sea lion sleeps soundly, undisturbed by our approach, Galapagos Islands, Ecuador.

It is so strange to walk slowly, as close as to within six feet of the seals, without disturbing them in any way. For some reason, nearly all the animals on the Galapagos Islands have no fear of humans. The islands are unlike any other place on earth.

We hike inland to a large saltwater lagoon. In the center of the shallow lake is a group of greater flamingos. Their pink color comes from the pink shrimp that makes up a large part of their diet. The birds are filter feeders. They stir up the water with their feet and their large, thick bills, then they sift through the agitated water using filter plates in their bills to sieve out shrimp and other nutrients.

On another beach rays swim underwater catching the surge on the incoming surf. We wade out into the water; the rays dart past our legs, sometimes just inches away.

We take the *panga* out to Devil's Crown crater for snorkeling. The crater is a mostly-submerged volcano. All that is left above water of the eroded rim is a few jagged chunks of rock. We are dropped off at one end of the crater and will be picked up at the other end. The current here is so strong we won't even need to swim, unless we want to stay in one place and watch something, or go back up current. We will just float along and watch the fish and the scenery until we reach the far side of the crater. Juan cautions us about hammerhead sharks. They are not considered too dangerous, yet he advises us to keep our distance.

Even though the Galapagos Islands are located on the equator, the water can be quite cold. The Humbolt current, pushed by trade winds, brings nutrient-rich water all the way from Antarctica. The water is only sixty-eight degrees Fahrenheit—we brought our wetsuits.

Six months of the year, December through June, the much warmer Panama current flows southwest toward the Galapagos from Central America. When these two currents meet at the Galapagos, one sixty-eight degrees, the other seventy-eight degrees, an upwelling of water occurs from the ocean floor, bringing even more nutrients to the surface.

Since that upwelling is occurring now, the water is cloudy, heavy with particulate matter. The sea is like a soup, the colors slightly muted. Still we have visibility to about thirty-five feet, and see numerous tropical fish: tangs, parrotfish, sargent majors. We also spot a few sea lions streaking through the water like rockets. They are probably feeding, as they take little interest in us and quickly disappear into the blue.

At the end of the day we all sit out on the forward deck, watching Floreana Island recede into the distance. We hear only a soft splashing of water as the *Angelique* makes her way across the ocean toward Santiago, the next island we will visit. Although everyone in our group has traveled extensively, none of us has much sailing experience. Rich, however, has ocean-kayaked in California, Baja, and Chile. He confides that his Klepper folding kayak has F and B, front and back, labeled on all the parts for putting it together—he can never remember which is the bow or stern. Despite the calm water of the ocean, most of us wear seasick patches, just in case.

Once we establish our lack of knowledge about sailing, we reminisce about other travels. We ask Rich, who travels more than any of us, about a recent mountaineering trip in Nepal. He tells us about the climb, adding an aside at the end that his group gave a "Yeti" award to a team member who made a big goof-up during the expedition.

"We could give a similar award for our group!" Tass declares immediately. "We could call it the Iguana Award!"

"At the end of each day we'll vote to see who gets the award!" Janet chimes in, ever the organizer.

"For today I nominate Juan!" Ken quickly adds. Juan left his coat inside a lava tube we explored, and didn't remember it until we were in the *panga*, just starting back to the *Angelique*.

Our whole group turns toward Juan and begins chanting, "Eee-guan-a! Eee-guan-a!" Juan tries in vain to talk his way out of it, but he is the unanimous choice.

After supper Franklin makes another momentary appearance. He is exasperated with the motor, which apparently isn't running at full power. Although the *Angelique* is a sailboat, the winds in the Galapagos are often calm for days on end, and a good motor is necessary to keep us on schedule when the winds die. After Franklin leaves, Ken muses aloud that, like Dracula, Franklin seems to appear only at night. Ken jokingly calls Franklin "The Count." I think he looks more like Frank Zappa with a wrench.

During the night our boat travels past the west coast of Santa Cruz Island to Santiago Island. In the morning we anchor near Chinaman's Hat, a small cone-shaped volcanic island that looks like a straw hat. We hike across the cracked lava formations and photograph marine iguanas. Darwin described the iguana as "a hideous looking creature of dirty black color, stupid, and sluggish in its movements." Marine iguanas are the only lizard that dives into the ocean to eat marine plants, moss, and algae. The male has a spine-like crest on top of its head which runs down its neck and back. Marine iguanas spend an enormous amount of time lying in the sun, warming back up after feeding in the ocean. Their body temperatures can drop an amazing twenty degrees after feeding in the chilly ocean water. Marine iguanas are exceptionally strong swimmers and can stay underwater five to ten minutes per dive, reaching depths of thirty-five feet. All four feet have a partial webbing between the toes, yet the iguana holds its legs motionless next to its body as it swims, propelling itself by making a serpentine motion with its entire body and tail. Perhaps the strangest adaptation is its ability to expel excess salt from

A marine iguana basks in the sun after diving in the ocean
for food, Galapagos Islands, Ecuador.

its body. The marine iguana brings the salt from its stomach up to a special
gland in its nostrils, then sneezes the salt right out its nose, which often crusts
up at the end of its nostrils or even across its face and the top of its head.

We sail west along the southern coast of Santiago Island, to Rabida Island. We have a wet landing on the dark red, volcanic beach and then walk
to a salt lagoon to view more flamingos, and snorkel from the *panga* in the
bay. I spot a huge sea turtle.

As we are drying off from snorkeling, Franklin makes an appearance on
deck. Ken is the first to ask the question we have all been jokingly discussing
for several days—Does the *Angelique* have a plank?

Franklin is somewhat taken aback by the question. He looks very stern.

"There is no plank" he answers as if the idea was absurd. "Why should we have a plank?"

The idea makes perfect sense to us. Walking the plank is something with which we could threaten one another. Somewhat disappointed, Ken asks hopefully, "Well, do you ever keelhaul people?"

Franklin gives him a look that implies if he did keelhaul people, Ken would be high on his list. Not to be discouraged, the Texan tries one last question.

"How about hanging people up on the yardarm?"

In the evening Juan is relieved not to be chosen for the Iguana Award. Janet, who has been dubbed by Ken as "The Contessa of Quicksand," gets the Iguana Award for sinking, in just two seconds, up to her knees in mud after misjudging a step while photographing flamingos.

In the morning we make a wet landing at James Bay on the west coast of Santiago Island, and walk down the rocky volcanic coast to a series of grottos, twenty to thirty feet deep and across. They are old lava tubes, the collapsed tops open to reveal the insides filled with beautiful turquoise water, and fur seals.

Fur seals are thought to have come to the Galapagos by following the cold Humbolt current, perhaps during an ice age. When the Ice Age ended, a small colony of fur seals was left behind. Fur seals have beautiful thick coats, and were almost completely wiped out when demands for their fur in

Tass swims with fur seals, Galapagos Islands, Ecuador.

fashionable clothing created a frenzy of fur seal hunting. Now they are protected against hunting, but still, life remains difficult for Galapagos fur seals, who have a double coat of insulation. They struggle to keep cool and out of the sun, and live mostly in underwater grottos and caves.

We quickly put on our masks, fins, and snorkels, and slip into the water with two fur seals. They playfully swim around us, then come up close to check us out with their large, expressive eyes.

But the best experience of all is on the east side of Santiago Island near Sullivan Bay. As we walk along the rough lava-bed coastline, fifteen sea lions follow along in the water. The sea lions continually pop their sleek heads out of the water, sniff at our scent, and then do somersaults and loops in the bay, enticing us to join them. Their body language says, "Come in and play!"

As we put on our masks and fins the sea lions congregate at the water's edge. They seem eager, almost impatient, for us to join them. We poke our heads underwater, and within seconds we are surrounded by sea lions. They swim toward us like torpedos, then do quick turns at the last second, rocketing past with streamers of water bubbles trailing in their wake. They must think we are so uncoordinated; we move and swim so slowly in comparison. They glide past at tremendous speeds with minimal effort. Often they swim upside down, in a lazy backstroke, yet if we reach out toward them they react with a lightning-quick change of direction to evade our touch. They rocket around us, above us, under us, like a game, coming close but never letting us touch them. They have sleek faces, big brown eyes, long whiskers, little laid-back ears. They almost grin at us in the water. Their bodies twist and contort together, like slithering eels doing looping backward somersaults, biting and nipping at each other, twisting and turning and circling back around toward us from a different direction. They play tag with each other as they swim in circles around us, then bullet straight at us, only to turn away at the last moment, and even jump out of the water over our heads.

As usual, Tass is the last one out of the water, and we all board the *panga*. Sea lions swim around the boat, poking their heads out of the water, watching us, enticing us to jump back in to play. As we motor back to the *Angelique* the sea lions give chase, surfing in the small wake the little dingy makes, occasionally leaping out of the water. When we show no sign of stopping, they finally give up following us, and head back to their island.

Once again Juan is greatly relieved not to get the Iguana Award. I get elected for losing my hat. Twice.

The Galapagos Island group includes thirteen major islands, six large islets, and fifty minor islets and rock formations, all formed as the Pacific plate creeps three inches per year eastward across a volcanic hot spot in the earth's mantle. The oldest of the islands was formed three to five million years ago,

Mayan ruins of Palenque, Chiapas, Mexico.

Temple of the Giant Jaguar,
Tikal, Guatemala.

Mayan *stela* with original red paint,
Copan, Honduras.

Woman in market, Zunil, Guatemala.

Yolanda, Sergio's sister, Mexico.

A Maya woman selling flowers,
Chichicastenango, Guatemala.

A woman from Otavalo, Ecuador.

In the Andes of Ecuador different villagers can be identified by the shape and color of their hats.

Kids in the market, Guatemala.

Hot chilies for sale, Ecuador.

A quiet market corner, Guatemala.

Highland vegetable market, Chichicastenango, Guatemala.

Dolls made of bread, Otavalo, Ecuador.

Murals painted on the walls of Daniel Ortega's house, Managua, Nicaragua.

A mask made of glass beads, Mexico.

A Maya woman weaving on a
backstrap loom, Guatemala.

Riding up into the Andes from the
Amazon Basin, Ecuador.

Bruce on Poas volcano, Costa Rica.

Cycling through the high and dry western Andes of Ecuador.

19,342-foot Cotopaxi volcano, Ecuador.

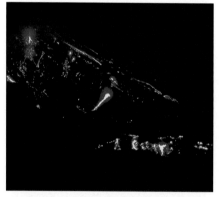

A night eruption on Arenal volcano,
Costa Rica.

Tass climbing up through an ice storm
in the middle of the night on
Cotopaxi volcano, Ecuador.

White-fronted capuchin, Manuel Antonio, Costa Rica.

Tass on a cloudforest trail,
Monteverde, Costa Rica.

Migrating monarch butterflies fill
the trees, Michoacan, Mexico.

A land iguana eating cactus,
Galapagos Islands, Ecuador

A dolphin pilots in front of our boat,
Galapagos Islands, Ecuador.

The Angelique anchored
near China Hat beach,
Galapagos Islands,
Ecuador.

Exploring the waterways on the Amazon river, Belen, Peru.

Klaus paddles us, one at a time, across the Rio Aguarico in the Amazon Basin of Ecuador.

A Cofan elder wears a macaw feather pierced through his nose, Ecuador.

Cuviers toucan, Amazon Basin.

A monk saki, Amazon Basin.

Tass cycling through Andean cloudforest into the Amazon Basin, Ecuador.

Rainforest leaf, Amazon Basin.

Many parts of the Amazon Basin receive over ten feet of rain per year.

Sunset over the Amazon Basin, Puerto Maldonado, Peru.

In the rainforest canopy, looking down at the tops of the smaller trees far below, ACEER, Peru.

Bruce, forty feet underwater, practicing the art of breath control, Baja, Mexico.

Paradise found, Cardonicito Bay, Isla Espiritu Santo, Baja, Mexico.

Our friends, Janet and Pat, kayaking into Ensenada Grande, Baja, Mexico.

Swimming with sea lions, Los Islotes, Baja, Mexico.

while the western islands of Espanola and Fernandina are less than one million years old. The Galapagos still hosts some of the world's most active volcanoes, with over fifty eruptions in the last two hundred years.

Because of the small amount of rain on the islands, the lava beds are mostly bare rock, devoid of much plant life. On the east coast of Santiago Island we walk across red aa (pronounced ah-ah) lava that is over three million years old. In many areas, splashed across this old red lava is black pahoehoe (pa-hoy-hoy) lava, or rope lava, which formed into beautiful and strange patterns while still hot, then coalesced into rock. We hike across giant spirals, patterns reminiscent of bundles of fabric and cloth, and convoluted patterns that look like brains or intestines!

At the start of our hike on Bartolome Island, Juan tells us that rats were introduced to all the islands via ships hundreds of years ago and have caused many problems. Today the government has programs to help get rid of the rats.

"There are no rats any longer on Bartolome Island!" he tells us firmly and seriously. Unbelievably, we take less than ten steps and come across a dead rat beside the trail.

"What is this?" I ask Juan, trying not to smirk.

Juan makes a little squeaking noise and throws his hands up into the air. He is stunned.

"A rat! I must report this!" Juan looks around wildly. "Perhaps a hawk was eating it and flew over and dropped it!" Juan says uncertainly. This starts us

Pahoehoe lava beds, Galapagos Islands, Ecuador.

all chuckling. The rat is flattened, nearly paper thin, like it was run over by a truck, which also doesn't make much sense. Finding the rat wouldn't be so funny if Juan hadn't just made a big deal out of declaring Bartolome rat-free. We are no longer listening to Juan's theories and protests. Instead, we all begin chanting, "Eee-guan-a! Eee-guan-a!"

We climb the highest volcano on the island. Along the way we pass spatter cones and cinder cones, along with a few lava tubes. We gaze across all the neighboring islands at the different colors of lava rock from the different eruptions: black, gray, orange, and red. Below us, standing like an enormous tower in the middle of Sullivan Bay, is Pinnacle Rock, a huge tuff cone of hardened volcanic ash.

We snorkel at the two beaches near Pinnacle Rock. Neither area has much of a reef, and we don't see any sea lions. But we do see a small gray body streak past us, wings flapping at its side like pectoral fins. A Galapagos penguin! We frantically chase after it, trying to make a photograph. The penguin is amazingly fast and extremely difficult to photograph. It rockets past a number of times before we finally think we have might have a good picture.

Through the rest of the day we laugh and joke about finding the rat on Bartolome Island. That evening we unanimously confirm Juan as today's winner of the Iguana Award. Later, as we are again recalling the incident, Juan shakes his head and tells us very seriously, "I think we should just stop talking about that rat!" When we all start laughing, Juan just shakes his head. But before long he smiles and laughs with us.

The next day we visit the large blue-footed booby colony on North Seymour Island. The name comes from the Spanish word bobo, which means foolish, given no doubt for the bird's unusual behavior and brightly colored feet. The courtship dance of the blue-footed booby is quite the ritual. Both birds drop their necks down low and then tilt their heads back up until their bills point straight into the sky, wings pulled back, whereupon they lift and present each foot forward in the air, back and forth from left to right, as if most pleased by the bright blue color of their feet.

After mating, both the male and the female collect sticks, as if they were going to build a nest. But when it is time to lay the eggs, the female doesn't use the sticks. She lays her eggs on the bare ground. The stick collecting is only a mating ritual to show the other bird each is serious about mating. Normally two eggs are laid, which hatch just a few days apart. Because of its advantage in strength and weight, the older chick usually muscles out its younger sibling, and gets all the food, until the younger chick dies. If the older chick is weak or has an illness, the younger chick will get the food and the older chick will die. Either way, only one chick survives.

When feeding, boobies dive at high speeds into the water to catch fish. To counter the impact of hitting the water they have shock absorber air sacs between their brains and their skulls. The blue-footed booby also has a long tail, which it uses as a rudder, enabling it to dive in very shallow water and immediately turn up toward the surface, without hitting the bottom.

The Galapagos birds that most profoundly affected Darwin's thinking were the finches. Thirteen species of finches are found on the islands, each with a different beak structure that specializes in gathering and eating a distinct food. The cactus finch has a long, pointed beak for feeding on cactus flowers. The large tree finch has a parrot-shaped bill for breaking twigs to eat insect larvae. The small ground finch sports a tiny sharp beak for removing ticks from tortoises and iguanas. The woodpecker and mangrove finches use a twig or a cactus spine as a beak extension to collect insects from holes they have burrowed. Darwin was convinced that all of these birds descended from a single species of finch parents, and that their differences were directly the result of a need to adapt to different environments for food. Darwin called this process adaptive radiation.

Likewise the giant tortoises on each island were divided by Darwin into fourteen different subspecies, each with a different-shaped shell allowing them to more easily get specific foods found only on their individual islands. Since there is little grass to eat on the island of Espanola, the saddle-back tortoises on Espanola have adapted a shell with an up-swept curve above the neck so they can reach their head high to eat leaves of tree branches and cactus buds.

Of the six hundred species of plants on the island, more than two hundred are endemic, found nowhere else in the world. Of all the land-based animals, reptiles and birds (excluding sea birds), over eighty percent are endemic. Even more amazing, many of these endemic species are found only on one island.

While Darwin's five weeks of observations on the Galapagos formed the base for his ideas about evolution, after he left the islands, twenty-four years passed before he published his monumental work, *The Origin of the Species*, outlining his theories of evolution.

"Are you ready?!" Franklin Angermeyer bellows across the boat. We are passing through the narrow channel between Baltra and Santa Cruz Islands. The sun is going down, and the channel ahead is crowded with small speedboats full of tourists on day trips from Puerto Aroyo.

The *Angelique*, however, is a ninety-six-foot, steel-hulled, Brigantine Schooner built in Holland before World War I. How we are going to maneuver through the slalom course of smaller boats ahead, can only be answered by our captain.

"That's how I like it!" Franklin roars, as much to himself as anyone else. Lanky and lean, he is full of explosive energy. We catch glimpses of his wild grin as he pops his head out of the wheel house window.

Franklin Angermeyer at the helm of the *Angelique*,
playing bongo drums and steering with his feet,
Galapagos Islands, Ecuador.

"Prepare for ramming speed!" he cries out as we near the boat of a captain for whom he has little respect, an upstart, one of the many newcomers who have moved to the islands in the last few years to work in the burgeoning tourist trade. Franklin lets out a maniacal chuckle, but his actions are all business as he deftly steers the *Angelique* through the tight squeeze.

In the last few days Franklin has fixed the engine, and we have had a little more time getting to know each other. We get a kick out of his wild antics, and appreciate him for the unique and unusual character that he is. He is definitely his own person.

For Franklin, growing up in the "enchanted islands" wasn't exactly idyllic. His father didn't believe in school, so his mother taught him to read and write and also put him to work. Scratching out a living on the barren lava beds was very difficult. Franklin left the islands to strike out on his own. At seventeen he ran a discotheque in Bogota, Columbia. But soon he returned to the Galapagos to get a boat and try his luck in the tourist trade.

The *Angelique* is his fifth boat. Franklin bought it in Puerto Rico and sailed through the Caribbean and the Panama Canal to the Galapagos. He spent his life savings the next few years rebuilding and remodeling the boat, converting it from a dance party boat with a capacity for ninety people, to a spacious yacht with private rooms and bath for twelve passengers and a crew of seven.

For our group, traveling on the *Angelique* with Franklin has been the perfect way to see the islands. Sara's cooking has been exceptional, and Juan has been a perfect guide, both knowledgeable and fun.

Of the two Plaza islands, only South Plaza has a site where tourists are allowed to visit. The island is covered with opuntia, prickly pear cactus. The cactus supports a large population of land iguanas, which wait patiently below the cactus for small cactus buds to fall off. The iguanas then roll the buds around for a few moments, to break off the larger spines. They swallow the buds, whole.

We walk along a high sea cliff, a great spot to watch gulls, shearwaters, and petrels expertly fly in the strong and constant trade winds. We spot a red-billed tropicbird, with a more than foot-long, streaming tail, like a banner in the wind.

Tass relaxing with sea lions, Galapagos Islands, Ecuador.

That evening Ken gets the Iguana Award for leaving the porthole in his room open, soaking his mattress. Juan is visibly relieved to have gotten through the day without another nomination.

Our last day we visit Santa Fe Island, and then repeatedly snorkel, first from the *panga* in an area teeming with sea lions, and then further out at a coral reef. We don't want the day to end. That evening, heading back to port at Puerto Ayora on Santa Cruz Island, we elect Juan, despite his best arguments, Iguana of the Week. Ken pulls out an award made of a piece of driftwood with an iguana drawn on it, and a little piece of dried up bone tied on with a piece of string. Ken solemnly presents it to Juan, who can only shake his head, smile, and laugh, as the rest of us chant, "Eee-guan-a! Eee-guan-a!"

15

The Avenue of Volcanoes

After ten days at sea level in the Galapagos, we are excited and breathless to be back in Quito, at 9,348 feet, the second-highest capital in the world after La Paz, Bolivia. We need to spend a few days in the city to acclimatize before moving higher into "the Avenue of the Volcanoes," a term coined in 1802 by a German explorer to describe the central valley of Ecuador.

At the Casa de Lisa we rendezvous with our friend Jim Hucks and his buddy John Leeland. They are in the communal room of the hotel playing a spirited game of poker with another traveler, using one-hundred-*sucres* notes. Although the bills are worth less than a nickel, they slam the notes down on each bet with great fanfare, as though they are one hundred dollars U.S. Real high rollers.

Jim and John have come down to climb 19,348-foot Cotopaxi Volcano with Tass and me. The next few days, while Jim and John explore the casinos and night life in Quito, Tass and I pack away our snorkeling and Galapagos gear, then organize the mountaineering equipment we left at the South American Explorers Club our first time in Quito.

I am plagued by a rumbling stomach and diarrhea and make three trips to a local clinic before finding I have an innocuous little parasite that doesn't require antibiotics and should go away by itself after a few days. Since we need to spend another day acclimatizing at the base of the volcano, I am hoping my stomach will be back to normal before we begin climbing the mountain.

Two taxis are required to get the four of us and all our gear to the bus station. We leave Quito on a two-hour bus trip to Latacunga, but we hardly get out of the capital before being stopped in an immense traffic jam. After sitting half an hour without moving, our driver edges up and over a few curbs, drives down a meridian, and somehow squeezes the bus through the congestion to the front of the snarled traffic!

A group of students has blocked the road to protest treatment of indigenous Indians, and the high price of gasoline, an interesting political mix. As our bus edges forward, a bonfire flares up in the road. While the drivers around us hesitate, our bus driver sees an opening and guns the motor. Our bus rockets forward and with a wild swerve scatters the mob of students, runs over part of the bonfire and then through a barricade. The students pelt our bus with rocks, but before they can do any damage we are out of range, roaring down the Pan American highway. Jim and John cheer wildly! Our adventure has begun!

The bus drops us off in the small town of Lasso, where we bargain for a small pickup to take us up into Cotopaxi National Park. We want to acclimatize by spending the night at 12,500 feet near a lake at the base of the volcano. Tomorrow we will hike up to the *refugio*, a climbers' hut at fifteen thousand feet, which will be our basecamp.

Tass and I ride in the front of the pickup, while Jim and John bundle up and climb into the back. After half an hour of twisting, climbing mountain road, we get to the entrance of the National Park and learn the park closes to vehicles every day at 3:00 p.m., three hours ago. The park guard can be neither cajoled nor bribed—we try both—into letting us go any further. We discuss camping at the entrance, but that would mean an extra twelve miles of hiking tomorrow. Our other choice is to return to Lasso where we can get another truck in the morning to take us up closer to the base of the volcano.

We ride back down to Lasso, which has no hotel. Another truck driver offers to let us sleep in a spare room at his house, if we promise to hire him to take us back up the mountain in the morning. We quickly agree.

The next morning we are happy to be traveling up to the volcano during daylight, as the landscape is one of the most unusual in all of South America. Called the *paramo* in Ecuador, or *altiplano* in Peru, this strange landscape exists only high on the windswept western slope of the Andes. As the truck climbs, the trees give way to fields of unusual stunted plants and shrubs that cling for survival above tree line. Due to moist clouds that frequently blow through the mountains at this elevation, the specialized plants of the *paramo* give the hills and meadows a tenacious carpet of green and gold grasses and plants. Now, in springtime, the *paramo* is covered with tiny colorful flowers that could easily be missed without a closer look.

The truck drops us off at fourteen thousand feet on the bare, windswept cinder flank of the volcano. We unload our backpacks and battle a fierce wind as we put on our expedition parkas, windpants, hats and gloves.

The *refugio* is only about one-thousand feet in elevation above us, yet it is a slow and labored climb. We all gasp for oxygen in the thin mountain air. We take our time hiking, and feel pretty good when we first arrive at fifteen thousand feet. The *refugio* is a two-story A-frame building with tables and a cooking area on the first floor and tiered bunks upstairs for twenty climbers. A dozen people mill about. A party of five Ecuadoreans has just come down from the summit and are climbing into their sleeping bags, totally exhausted. Assorted foreign climbers going up tomorrow with their guides are eating and packing.

We plan to spend tomorrow acclimatizing before attempting the summit. We will have a better chance of adjusting to the altitude if we hike one- or two-thousand feet up the mountain then come back down to sleep. This way we can also check out the lower sections of the glacier and leave a few wands to mark the trail.

Tass and I get headaches shortly after arriving at the hut, and by the time supper is finished we are also dizzy. Jim seems to be acclimatizing the best. John is doing okay, despite some stomach problems he picked up yesterday

Tass suffering from the effects of altitude sickness, Cotopaxi
Volcano, Ecuador.

in Quito. Flying in from a high elevation in Colorado has definitely given them an advantage.

Our first night in the hut seems to last forever. The poor acclimatization gives all of us weird, disjointed nightmares. My dreams leave me feeling like a rat trapped in a maze at the mercy of some twisted plot, a tormented prisoner, strapped in a straightjacket, forced to watch a broken projector showing the same mayhem over and over, time and again. Part of me realizes all the madness is only a dream, yet I can't seem to clear my head, which makes the nightmare worse. An eternity passes waiting for dawn.

At last a tiny glow of light shines through an upper window. Although I am exhausted, I get up. I cannot take another moment lying in such a miserable state. My head pounds as I rise. Surprisingly, after a few moments the nausea clears, my headache lessens, and I am able to force down some oatmeal. Tass and I stare at each other, slowly eating out of our cookpot, like two deranged escapees from a mental institution.

Two women from Tahoe, California, sit across from us. One of them has bronchitis and looks like death warmed over—pale face, sunken eyes, beads of perspiration on her upper lip. She stares dully into space. She arrived at the *refugio* yesterday, but she is hiking back down today. I don't know how she even got this far. Next to us is a Danish couple that arrived after us yesterday in the sleet and mist. The woman didn't have wind pants and was shivering from the cold. Now her husband is very sick, yet says he still wants to climb the volcano. I can't imagine that either of them has even the slightest chance of making it up the mountain, which is probably exactly what they are thinking of me.

We head out on reconnaissance up the volcano. At the top of the first snowfield, John and Tass find a place to relax in the sun out of the wind. Jim and I put on crampons and ice axes, then rope up and climb through a series of crevasses to check out our route onto the glacier. The day is stunning—deep blue sky, brilliant white snow, equally bright clouds hanging over the mountains around us. Heights are deceptive. Far down into the valley below the golden-hued *paramo* surrounding the volcano is itself more than twelve thousand feet above sea level. My sunglasses are not dark enough for the brilliant equatorial sunshine at this altitude. I squint continually to protect my eyes from hurting in the dazzling light. Jim and I work our way through the crevasses of snow and ice, occasionally leaving a wand for a marker. Finally, when the route ahead looks easier to find and negotiate we stop putting in wands and climb back down the glacier to the snowfield.

Jim and John brought snowboards to make a run down the snowfield to the hut. Tass and I watch enviously. With all the gear we brought to South America, we could not justify also bringing skis or snowboards for only a couple of runs on the volcano. So we glissade down, sliding squat over our boots, using our ice axes for balance, steering and brakes.

That evening we sit in the hut and discuss climbing strategies. Our plan is to start climbing at one o'clock in the morning, to cross the lower sections of the glacier at night, when the temperature is the coldest and the ice of the glacier most stable. Hopefully starting early will also help us to get back down before the hottest part of the day. On clear days the equatorial sun can create an incredible amount of radiant heat. On the lower slopes of the glacier the temperatures in the sunlight during mid-day can reach seventy degrees and more. Such temperatures not only melt the surface of the snow, but also create dangerous conditions by weakening ice bridges over crevices, greatly increasing the chance of accidents.

We have an even worse night of no sleep, but this time we console ourselves with the fact that we don't have to suffer all night long. At midnight we crawl, delirious, out of bed. I feel as miserable as I can ever remember. We get dressed and descend to the kitchen to choke down more oatmeal.

At one a.m. we leave the *refugio* and step out into the darkness. As Tass and I work our way through the rock scree up toward the snowfield our headlamps begin to flicker, a major cause for concern. We each have a spare set of batteries kept warm in an inside pocket, but even with backups, we worry that the first set of batteries is already losing power. We have five hours of hiking in the dark through glacial crevasses until sunrise. We are only fif-

Bruce scouting a route across the glacier on the
lower slopes of Cotopaxi Volcano, Ecuador.

teen minutes into our climb and are finding our choice of headlamps was rather poor.

Within thirty minutes my headlamp goes out completely. Tass's light is weak but still flickering, barely. We arrive at the snowfield and put on our crampons in the light of Jim and John's headlamps, saving our batteries.

Although there is no moon, the stars are incredibly bright. Even without lights we can see the basic outline of the snowfield above us. The headwall and start of the glacier is above that. With no other choice than simply giving up and returning to the *refugio*, we climb up the snowfield without lights, following Jim and John's silhouette. I can see reasonably well, but Tass has poor night vision and is very spooked. She questions how we can possibly make our way safely up the glacier without lights. I don't have an answer.

Half an hour later we arrive at the headwall of the glacier. Tass and I rope together, as do Jim and John. Although our ropes are 165 feet long, we don't want that much space between us. We each throw a fifty-foot coil of rope over our shoulders so we can hike about sixty feet apart. Besides crampons and ice axes we each carry a pair of jumars, mechanical ascenders which can be used to climb back up the rope if one of us should fall into a crevasse.

Beside us at the base of the glacier is the Danish couple and one of the women from Lake Tahoe, each with their own guide. As we prepare our gear, I can't help but notice how the guides for the other two parties rope up their clients. Obviously the clients don't have a clue about how any of the equipment works. They rely completely on their guides, who explain nothing, but simply tie them in. If anything happened to the guide, they would not have any idea how to rescue themselves, or him. They would be stranded on the mountain. Scary.

The guided groups left the *refugio* ahead of us, and again start up the glacier in front of us. Jim is agitated that we will have to follow them. He grumbles that they will slow us up, and probably be hard to pass. But I figure even though Jim and I scouted the bottom section of the glacier yesterday it won't hurt to tag behind the guided groups through the crevasses. At least we will have a fresh trail.

As we climb up a steep snow ramp onto the glacier, we don't have to worry about tailgating the other groups. They have all taken off like they are in a race. Their headlamps have already disappeared into the black void above us.

Ten minutes later a cloud of icy mist blows in, obscuring the stars above us and then everything else as well. Within minutes we are covered with ice. My glasses immediately ice over. I repeatedly scrape away the ice with my gloves and find myself wishing I had brought my big winter ski goggles, as well as a decent headlamp.

Jim and John are roped together, Jim leading. Tass and I, also roped together, follow behind, me leading. The plan is for me, with no headlamp, to follow close behind John using his light to see, while Tass brings up the rear with our remaining, marginal headlamp.

Tass is feeling ill, and is hiking at a slower pace. Roped to her, I am tethered at the slower speed, and Jim and John soon disappear into the mist. I repeatedly have to call out for John to wait; an exasperating situation for all of us. No one is able to go at a natural pace. Tass, with little light, expends extra energy flailing up the trail in the dark. I also fumble along. Despite my crampons my feet continually slide into old post hole footsteps.

The mist thickens, as does the ice covering our clothes. Now even Jim with his high-powered mountaineering headlamp is unsure where the trail goes. We are above the wands Jim and I set the previous day. We fumble around for half an hour. Jim stops to put fresh batteries in his light.

Lights appear above us as we sit in the snow. Three climbers stumble out of the mist, heading back down the mountain. In the blinding wind and sleet we can't tell who anyone is; they are only vague shadowy figures. We can only assume it is the Danish couple and their guide. The person in the middle moves with trepidation apparent even in the storm; obviously freaked by the steep descent and vertigo from the storm. I call out in encouragement for them to have a safe descent. We hear a mumbled reply as they are quickly swallowed by the mist and blowing snow.

We resume climbing and thirty minutes later again see lights coming toward us from above. Two bodies pass by, wordlessly, on their descent. Two more shadowy figures stop. They yell out and tell us of a protected spot ten minutes up the mountain where we can talk for a moment. When we get to a little sheltered place behind a large snowdrift, we find two men from Australia. They camped last night near the hut to save the six dollar hut fee, and were following the guide with the woman from Lake Tahoe. Spooked by the weather, the guide took his client back down. The Australians want to continue, but are not confident of going alone. They say if we are going to keep climbing, they want to join with us, or at least tag on behind.

Jim, John, Tass and I have a conference among ourselves. We feel reasonably confident we can continue the climb despite our malfunctioning lights. None of us shows any signs of frostbite, and we are relatively warm considering the wind and blowing snow. Unless the weather worsens we should be okay. But we are unsure about the Aussies. I note they are 'roped' together with what I think is an avalanche cord, which is much too thin to protect them if one of them falls.

"It's even worse," Jim replies, "They are using two sections of clothesline tied in the middle with a knot!"

No way are any of us going to rope up with these two and risk getting ourselves killed. We are also concerned about them climbing above us. However we are more than happy to let them follow us up the mountain.

Despite their lack of proper equipment, the two Aussies are incredibly strong. They soon tire of following behind Tass and me. At one point Tass stops for a brief rest and one of the Aussies derisively asks her if she really thinks she can make it to the top, which totally infuriates her. Before she can suitably retort, they pass us and jump in between us and Jim and John, cutting off the light we have been following. At the same time Tass's light goes out completely. We cross a three-foot-wide ice bridge with no light, the last straw.

We yell for Jim and John to stop. Another group discussion. Tass tells the Aussies, in no uncertain terms, that if they get between us and Jim and John and cut off our light, they have to give her their headlamp! To Tass's surprise they agree!

Now the volcano begins to get steep. We slip into mountaineering step— one step, two breaths, one step, two breaths. We try not to stop. We want to get a rhythm, but every thirty steps the will to keep going gives out and we are forced to stop and gasp, leaning on our ice axes, struggling for the energy to start up again. We don't really feel any better when we stop. We never get a feeling of rest no matter how long we dally, and each stop uses up a surprising amount of valuable time. We need to keep moving, no matter how slowly, or we will never make it to the summit.

Ever so slowly we creep up the mountain and out of the clouds of icy mist. The eastern sky lightens. The snow is covered with strange ice formations made by the blowing wind. Some of the formations are fist-sized. In another area they are the size of loaves of bread, crystallized into strange geometric patterns and flukes.

The sky continues to lighten; we put away our worthless headlamps. The heavens glow orange and red. As the sun comes up, we climb an endless ridge. Jim and John struggle up ahead of us, then sit exhausted in the snow. The Aussies have also passed them and are now out of sight. I have completely run out of energy. Tass is staggering below me. I collapse onto the snow. The thought of food makes me nauseous, but if we can force something down we might get some energy. I take off my pack and dig out some food and water as Tass struggles up to join me. We share a Powerbar and sip from my waterbottle. At least the view is grand. We are now well above the clouds churning down on the mountain and valley below. A few peaks to the west are sticking out of the clouds, but other volcanoes we hoped to see in the distance are hidden, embroiled in clouds and mist.

We struggle back to our feet. Jim and John have moved further up the ridge, but have now stopped again. From where we are it looks like they could be on the summit. An eternity seems to pass as we climb up to them, as if we are walking slow motion under water. Just as we reach them, we come over a small rise to see an enormous wall of rock and snow towering above us. A major part of the climb lies still before us. The Aussies are two small dots on the side of the mountain, halfway up the headwall.

For the first time I begin to question whether we will make it to the top. Tass is also stunned by the amount of climbing left, and expresses concern about whether we can summit. Jim and John have not moved. They have also hit the wall. Yet Jim is still determined to continue. He says he is going to cache his pack at the base of the headwall and continue to the summit with less weight. Jim's resolve inspires me, and I convince Tass also to leave her pack and keep going.

The headwall is very steep, yet in many ways much easier to climb. Like going up a ladder, we quickly see a definite altitude gain for our efforts, unlike the long ridge where we walked and walked and never seemed to make any progress. We traverse up the headwall close behind Jim and John. As we climb Tass suddenly begins to get energized. She repeatedly has to stop to keep from coming up too close behind me, which creates too much slack in the rope between us. Like our climbs of two different eighteen-thousand-foot peaks in Nepal during our world bike trip, now that we are above seventeen thousand feet, Tass is revitalized and has much more strength than I.

Now Jim begins to struggle. After leading all day at a slower speed than he would have liked, he has now dropped below even my pace. But I don't mind stopping to wait. I am totally exhausted, running on autopilot, volition mysteriously coming from somewhere in my brain. Everything is disjointed delirium. My body aches, my head is pounding, I just want to be on the top.

We climb through the steepest part of the headwall and meet the two Aussies, coming back down. Tass gives them back their headlamp and they tell us it is twenty minutes more to the top. I'm not sure I can keep this up for another twenty minutes. I just want to collapse in the snow.

The final ridge levels off. Because the slope doesn't look steep, I think I can cruise up the last distance. Instead I wobble, plod, stagger and stumble, barely moving, one painfully slow step at a time. Will I EVER get there?

Twenty steps left. An eternity of shuffling feet. Fifteen steps left. Another eternity. Ten steps more. I can see Jim and John, lying in the snow on the summit, which still feels so far away. Five more steps and at last I get a tiny surge of energy. I am almost there. Four, three, two, I let out a feeble shout. One more step.

I MADE IT! I turn and Tass is right behind me, looking energized and excited. WE ARE ALL ON TOP! I take a few breaths and then pull off my backpack to dig out our camera with a wide angle lens. I know if I don't immediately force myself to make some photos, I never will. The batteries for the camera are tucked away in the pocket of my fleece sweater, under my coat for warmth. I have to take off my gloves to put the batteries in, my fingers fumbling in the cold. I get the camera turned on just in time to get a photo of Jim throwing up from altitude sickness and collapsing back in the snow.

I force myself to stumble along the rim of the volcano, hoping to get photos of the crater. Cotopaxi is one of the highest active volcanoes in the world. But huge clouds of mist are rolling over the rim, completely filling the crater. The weather is extremely bleak and looks like it is going to get worse. I feel weaker and more exhausted than I ever expected. I stumble back along the crater rim to find that Jim and John have already started down the mountain. Tass is ready to go down as well. We didn't even get a picture of all of us together on the top.

The descent is a blur of stumbling exhaustion. I thought I would revitalize on descending to lower elevations, but I never get a second wind. Tass and I stop occasionally to make a few photos while Jim and John collapse in the snow and wait for us. We finally get off the glacier and take off our crampons to glissade down the last snowfield.

At the bottom of the snow line, we wobble down the loose scree of volcanic pumice to the *refugio*. We have been on the mountain for ten hours. It seems like much longer than that.

Jim Hucks throwing up from altitude sickness on the summit of
Cotopaxi Volcano, Ecuador.

We strip off the outer layers of our climbing gear and crawl into our sleeping bags for a nap. Exhausted as I am, I still can not sleep. After all of this I still haven't properly acclimatized, and I have a pounding headache. At mid-afternoon we force ourselves out of the sleeping bags, pack up our gear, eat a final, tasteless snack, and trudge back down the mountain to fourteen thousand feet to meet the truck driver who had dropped us off just three days ago.

Back in Quito, Jim and John leave on a bus to finish their two weeks in Ecuador exploring the Pacific coast. Tass and I pack our mountaineering gear into storage at the Explorers Club, and start getting ready for our mountain bike trip.

16

The Bird Man of Mindo

I relax in the Magic Bean, an outdoor cafe in Quito, Ecuador, eating breakfast and sipping coffee in the sunshine. I can sit all morning, even all day, in places like this, writing and reading, with food and dessert at close call. How wonderful to find a little quaint restaurant, a place to return to daily while in an area, a spot that gives a sense of familiarity in the constantly changing landscape of life on the road. Our second day at the Magic Bean the waiter greets us with a familiar smile. The third day I get an enthusiastic handshake and the waiter asks if I want the usual. I do—*huevos rancheros*, eggs and salsa on corn tortillas with beans, fresh squeezed orange juice, and coffee.

But as I sit and write after breakfast, the alarm on my wristwatch goes off. Nine o'clock. If we are going to get our expedition on the road, it is also time for me to get back to work. Our plan for the next stage of our journey is to mountain bike through the Andes north of Quito, to descend into the Amazon Basin, to mountain bike and travel by boat as we explore the world's largest rainforest, then to bicycle back up into the southern Andes to Quito.

At our hotel room we have all the gear we think we need spread out in organized disarray before us. The big question: Are we willing to carry all this stuff? As we put everything into color-coded stuff sacks, we realize we have way too much gear to fit in the bike panniers. We deliberately brought medium-sized panniers to force ourselves to keep our luggage light weight, relatively speaking. So, we now take everything apart, to rethink and repack. We go through each other's bags, making sure we can each justify the need for every single item. After much debate we sort out a sizeable pile of clothes and equipment, things we reluctantly can live without. Everything else is repacked. But again we have too much stuff. We are going to have to be ruthless.

Our camera gear, lenses, binoculars and huge bags of film are all sacrosanct. Also quickly deemed necessities are our small tent, sleeping pads,

168

sleeping bags, tool kit, first aid kit, cycling clothing, cold weather gear for the Andes, and rain gear for the Amazon. Our library of fieldguides, resource books and reading books are also necessities.

The one thing that takes up a ton of room that we suddenly decide we might live without is the cook kit and stove. Getting rid of the stove also means eliminating the extra fuel bottle, kitchen tools, spices and stuff sacks of oatmeal and other staple foods. On our world bicycle trip and again when cycling through Central America, we cooked our own food when camping, but also bought food from street vendors and ate in little cheap restaurants in towns, which gave us a chance to try the local foods.

Now we decide we will just get by on the local food, which we will supplement with bread, cheese, Powerbars and other foods that don't require cooking. We aren't too concerned about having to eat the same thing day after day. Both of us like rice and beans—we can eat them for months before reaching overdose, or so we tell ourselves. We figure it will also be easy to find cooked eggs and tortillas. Besides, the mountain bike part of our trip will be for only six weeks! We think the biggest sacrifice will be losing the luxury of making coffee early in the morning and not having hot drinks while reading at night.

Between bouts of packing and repacking, we ride our mountain bikes around town running errands. We spend numerous hours at the library of the South American Explorers Club. We have the itinerary for our Andes mountain bike route fairly set, but we are still unsure how best to explore the Amazon Basin. In the files of the Explorers Club trip reports we read numerous glowing accounts of Luis Garcia, an Ecuadorean rainforest guide. We visit his office, but Luis is in the *oriente*, the lowland rainforest of eastern Ecuador. We try to estimate the length of our bike route through the Andes and guess we will arrive in the Amazon Basin about the time Luis is taking a group out from the town of Coca. Yet we are hesitant to commit ourselves to signing on with the group; we don't want the pressure of having to reach Coca by a specific date.

We leave Quito on a quiet Sunday morning. Little traffic passes by on the narrow, bumpy streets, which makes our departure relaxed and stress-free. We are thrilled finally to have our bikes all loaded and to be heading out on a bike tour. Our first destination is northwest over Pinchachua volcano to the tropical forests near the town of Mindo on the western slopes of the Andes.

We take nearly four hours to ride out of the central valley of Ecuador and leave sight of the city, which fills the valley below. The seldom used, steep, switchbacked road up the back side of Pinchachua is paved with nasty sharp cobblestones. The climb up the volcano is tortuous, perhaps the roughest road we have ever ridden. Neither of us says anything out loud, but we are thinking similar thoughts. Such brutal riding on our first day is hard mentally, as we have not yet developed a rhythm of travel; nor have we warmed up physically. Snail touring on the Cobblestones from Hell. We can't help wonder how much of our route through the Andean backroads will be in similar condition. We remind ourselves this is just the first day. Don't panic. Relax and drop expectations, and get into the rhythm of bicycle travel. We can do this and have fun at the same time if we stop focusing on the jarring road and look up to enjoy the scenery.

At mid-afternoon we finally reach the summit and begin a spectacular descent down mist-filled canyons. The countryside is steep, rugged hills covered with tropical forest. The road down has the same jagged cobblestones, too jarring to get much speed going downhill. We think about our cameras shaking inside our vibrating handlebar bags, and squeeze the brakes harder to slow even more.

The sheer canyon walls are verdant, startling against the white clouds of mist rolling up and down the mountains. The narrow, winding roads have no guard rails. The edge of the road hangs precipitously from the canyon walls with enormous dropoffs into the valleys far below.

Our first stop is the town of Nono, a cluster of dilapidated buildings and a roadside restaurant. Inside the restaurant are three wooden tables with benches and a little kitchen with an open fire in back. Two old farmers are sitting at one of the tables eating rice. A few cases of Ecuadorean soda pop are stacked up against a dirty wall. A stooped, gray haired woman nonchalantly

Bruce riding on brutal cobblestone roads through the Andes, Ecuador.

looks up from behind a small glass-covered counter containing dusty boxes of old cookies and crackers.

"*Tienne arroz?*" Tass asks. Do you have rice?

"No" she replies, without explanation. Somewhat taken aback, we look again at the plates of rice the farmers are eating. Something is mixed in with the rice. Tass tries again.

"*Tienne arroz con huevos?*" Do you have rice with eggs?

"*Si*" she smiles and walks back into the kitchen to cook our meal.

Outside of Nono we cross a small pass and then start another spectacular descent into another steep, lush canyon. Despite more Cobblestones from Hell, the area is one of the most beautiful places in which we have ever ridden. The narrow road switchbacks down the steep mountainside with enormous drop-offs at every bend. We stop at the edge of the soft shoulder of the road to peer down landslide chutes, straight down the mountain to the bottom of the canyon far, far below. We continue to descend, the narrow road hugging the canyon walls, until we finally drop into the bottom of the gorge.

The road now follows the river through the lush growth. In many places the road has been flooded and washed out, covering the cobblestones with soft-packed dirt and gravel, creating a surface smooth enough to let the bikes pick up speed. We are soon rocketing down the canyon. The narrow road repeatedly twists and turns, preventing us from seeing more than one hundred feet ahead. Occasionally trucks come lumbering around the corners at the last second. Sometimes there is enough room for us to keep riding along the edge of the road—on one side our panniers scrap against the branches of the thick foliage overhanging the road; on the other side, we are just inches from the trucks. On narrower sections we pull to the side and stop as the trucks rumble past, belching smoke in low gear, drivers smiling and waving wildly, giving us the thumbs up sign.

We ride until the last bit of fading twilight, then find a little place to pull off the road and camp next to the river. We bathe in the ice cold river in the dark, surrounded by fireflies.

The next morning our downhill ride continues to the town of Tandayapa. The town has about ten buildings but no restaurant, only a little store selling crackers, sweets, and a few household items. No eggs, beans, rice, or bread. We sit on the stoop of an abandoned house and eat crackers, peanut butter, and cheese.

The road we take out of town is an even less-traveled track over the mountains. The killer climb is made more difficult by the large loose rocks covering the road. The canyon walls surrounding us are the steepest we have seen, almost completely vertical, and covered with lush cloudforest. But the mist covering the sharp ridges on the mountain tops does not billow over the

Bruce buying stale crackers and peanuts at a small *tienda*, Ecuador.

road to cool us down. Above, the sky is overcast, but despite the clouds the intense radiant heat of the equatorial sun builds like a pressure cooker. The humidity is nearly intolerable; we can hardly breathe.

With the loose stones covering the track, we both are absolutely maxed out riding. Our total concentration and energy is required just to keep up our momentum on the steep hill. We feel at the limit of what we can ride. Even with all the weight of our panniers, the rear tires often momentarily spin out on the loose rocks, requiring a burst of even more energy to keep from stalling and stopping.

Between gasps and grunts we discuss stopping to rest. But the trees beside the road have all been cut back, and there is no shade. We struggle on until, finally, we come to a cut into the hill that casts a thin band of shade along the edge of the road. We stop, flushed with hearts pounding, and drape our bodies over the handle bars. We are almost out of water. Despite the tropical growth around us, we haven't passed a single creek or stream along the road all morning. We didn't think getting water in a tropical cloudforest would be so difficult. On our world bicycle trip, Tass constantly monitored our water supply and fretted whenever the bottles were not full. Since she was always worrying about the water, and I paid little attention, we joked it was her job to do the worrying. I often pointed out that we had never been without water for more than a few hours. So what was the use of worrying? But

Tass never agreed. She claimed the reason we were never long without water was because she always insisted we fill all our bottles whenever possible!

Now we only have a little water left, and I notice Tass isn't drinking anything during our break. She insists on saving her water, just in case we don't find anything until we cross the pass and drop into the next valley. I continue to drink.

We resume riding, and soon I am out of water. Just when I am ready for another drink we hear the sound of water gurgling along the road. We climb off the bikes and walk up and down the road. The water is close, but we are unable to see it in the thick foliage. I bushwack through patches of huge leaves and climb down into a steep ravine before I can see the creek, further below me in a narrow, slippery crevasse. I unwind the inlet hose on our water filter and throw the line down into the crack. The hose just barely reaches. I pump enough water to fill all our water bottles. Resupplied with water, we cross the mountains and begin the long descent into Mindo.

For our trip Trek bicycle company sponsored us with two mountain bikes. The last few days Tass has been calling her new bike "Nina," a Spanish word of affection for a small girl. Now Tass is concerned I don't have a name for my bike. I come up with a couple of different possibilities, but Tass is quick to let me know she doesn't think much of them. After another half hour of jarring roads she suggests we call my bike Elvis. Because of my heavier weight and downhill speed on the cobblestones, Elvis is obviously "The King of Rock and Roll."

The last few miles into Mindo are the worst cobblestones, worn and shaped into huge nasty points. The pounding and jarring exhausts our arms and hands, as we are forced to constantly ride the brakes. The cobblestones make the rear wheels of our bikes feel squirrelly. We keep our rear tires at high pressure to guard against snakebite flats. Still we stop twice to check the tires; the way the rear wheels constantly drop off the cobblestones into the cracks makes our bikes feel like the rear tires are going flat, or all the spokes are loose. Yet everything is fine.

A rainstorm drenches us and turns the cobblestones to a slippery obstacle course. The last half mile we both slide out and crash on a turn. The panniers help to cushion our fall, but neither of us finds much humor in being wet and cold and going down on slimy, pointed rocks at the end of the day.

The rain lets up as we arrive in Mindo. At the edge of town we stop at a little *pension* hotel. Tass goes in to check it out while I hang out on the street with the bikes. A man on a motorcycle across the road smiles and waves, so I coast my bike over to talk with him. He is Vinicio Perez, a local guide and bird expert we heard about at the South American Explorers Club.

When Tass comes back out I introduce her to Vinicio, who suggests we get up at three a.m. tomorrow to hike to a lake in search of the Andean cock-of-the-rock, a rare and gorgeous bright orange bird we came to Mindo specifically hoping to see. But we are too exhausted to be so ambitious so quickly. Instead we make plans to meet Vinicio at five a.m. the next morning for a birding tour of the local valley. We'll go with Vinicio in search of the cock-of-the-rock the following day.

We stop at two more *pensiones* before checking into the Salon Norocci-dental on the town square, and get a room on the second floor with a balcony over the back courtyard. Another big storm rolls in as we put up clotheslines in our room and hang our gear out to dry. The hotel restaurant is the first place since Quito where we can get *frijoles*, beans, with our rice and eggs. The meal is wonderful; a true dining experience. Exhausted, we stumble to bed.

Five o'clock comes too soon. We crawl out of bed and meet Vinicio in the town square as the light of dawn grows in the eastern sky. For the first few minutes of our hike the light is too low to discern colors on the birds through our binoculars. We simply try to tell the species by the shapes of their silhou-ettes. Vinicio is enthusiastic about even the most mundane of birds. As we walk out of town even the common house wren excites him. We hardly have time to focus our binoculars on one bird before he is pointing out another bird in the opposite direction.

"Look! Look, over here!" Vinicio repeatedly exclaims in awe. "Oh! This bird is incredible!" In five hours of hiking we see thirty-eight different species, many with extraordinarily bright colors. I get a kick out of some of the bird names; my favorite of the morning is the tawny speckled pygmy tyrant. When the birds have all settled down in the heat of the day, we return to our hotel and eat mass quantities of beans, rice, and eggs. We are in caloric debt not only from our hike, but also from the lack of food the last few days cycling. I do some hand laundry, and we take a brief siesta before meeting Vinicio for more birding in the afternoon. As the sun goes down, we go to Vinicio's house for popcorn, and we study some of his bird books. His pictures of the Andean cock-of-the-rock interest us the most, and we hope to see one tomorrow!

We go to bed early, shortly after nine o'clock. Although I am exhausted, my mind races. Sleep is impossible. I can't shut off all the chatter in my brain. At eleven p.m. Tass yells at me for flailing around in our tiny bed every time I roll over. She accuses me of "cracking my knuckles in her ears," which some-how wakes her even though she is wearing ear plugs. She lies curled up un-der a thick blanket while I am so hot I can't even put my arms or legs under the single sheet on my side of the bed. I finally fall asleep after midnight. Our alarm goes off at 2:30 a.m.

We are supposed to meet Vinicio on the street outside the hotel at three a.m. Fifteen minutes before our rendezvous, it begins to rain. The tin roof on our hotel room magnifies the sound, making it seem as if there is a major downpour. Tass is convinced Vinicio will not show up in the storm. At three o'clock I check the street, which is empty. We relax a little more, and don't finish packing. Ten minutes later Vinicio arrives, totally unconcerned about the weather and ready to hike. We quickly double-bag our camera gear in plastic and finish getting ready. Another ten minutes go by until we head out the door. Now Vinicio is worried we will be late, and begins hiking at high speed. We fall in line behind him, talking little as we walk through the dark drizzle. Our tiny headlamps don't work much better here in the warm lowlands than they did up in the cold weather on Cotopaxi. Again, we use only one light at a time to conserve batteries. Since I have better night vision, Tass takes the light while I stumble behind in the semi-darkness as we race down the rutted track leading into the mountains. The hike is an obstacle course of muddy bogs, repeated small stream crossings, and loose rocks. Above us the clouds of mist occasionally clear to reveal a bright, starry sky. The moist, pungent odor of wet forest fills the air; lightning bugs flash in the grass alongside the trail.

Despite the cool mist Vinicio soon stops to take off his poncho, while I likewise remove my raincoat and strip down to my short-sleeve shirt. Tass, who is forever cold, happily keeps on her sweater and raincoat. We turn off the track, hike for twenty minutes down a side trail, turn onto another track and hike up a different trail, turn left, turn right, and soon find ourselves on a deeply rutted path surrounded by dense cloudforest. Vinicio checks his watch. He obviously thinks we are back on schedule because he slows down and we now hike at a more reasonable pace.

We ask him about his life. Vinicio grew up here in Mindo, and has eight brothers and six sisters. He has been a guide for fifteen years and has also guided climbs of volcanoes in the Andes, and guided in the *oriente*, the rainforests of eastern Ecuador. A very knowledgeable fellow.

"We climb now for thirty minutes. Very steep," Vinicio warns us at the base of a large ridge. The winding trail has high switchbacked steps cut into the dirt of the hillside, more like a ladder than stairs. We have to grab the trunks of small trees to pull ourselves up. The smaller-diameter trees all have a smooth, moss-free spot on the trunks, like a polished railing, where countless other hands have similarly grabbed hold during the climb.

We left our hotel with only a few *galletas*, little packets of locally-made crackers, for breakfast. Now we joke with Vinicio and ask him if he brought coffee and breakfast treats.

"An experienced guide would have a thermos of hot coffee for the poor *gringos*," we tease. We laugh as we list all the bird species we expect a good guide should point out as we relax and drink coffee. We tell Vinicio we also want to see monkeys.

"Of course we will see monkeys!" he replies. "They will bring the coffee!"

As we climb we occasionally come to small clearings and look back down into the valley to see the lights of Mindo twinkling through the darkness and mist. We cross the high ridge and descend a steep, eroded trail down a

Parrots and parakeets often mate for life, Ecuador.

slick ravine. Tass grabs a branch to lower herself down the trail. When she lets go of the end of the branch, covered with mud, it whips back and smacks me in the face, filling my mouth with dirt.

At the bottom we stop at a river to take off our shoes before crossing, and we hold each other's hands for balance. The water feels cool and refreshing on our feet. On the other side Vinicio tells us many trees ahead are covered in sharp spines.

"Be careful not to grab them if you slip," he warns. "The trail is steep and difficult."

The trail is actually so poorly established it is hardly recognizable. My headlamp, used briefly on the last descent, has again gone out. I slip and stumble behind Tass as we climb up the hill. Then the trail completely disappears where a large tree has fallen lengthwise across the path, bringing down an enormous tangled mass of vines and vegetation with it. We struggle up the chaotic mass of shattered moss-covered tree limbs and tangled vines. Everything is wet and covered with moss and extremely slick. We slip and slide, pushing and pulling each other up through the devastation and at last refind the faint trail. But we don't go far. Suddenly, on the incredibly steep hillside, Vinicio stops.

"This is the lake," he says quietly. At first we think he is kidding, getting back at us for our jokes about him bringing coffee. But he sits down in the mud on the steep hillside and takes off his pack. We stand beside him, un-

certain what to do. There is just enough light in the sky to see the surrounding hillside and valley. There is no water in sight, much less a pond or lake.
When Vinicio doesn't move we ask, uncertain, "Where is the lake?"

"Here," Vinicio answers matter-of-factly. "This is the lake."

He motions for us to sit down. Confused, we plop down in the mud beside him. He asks the time and I check my watch: 5:40 a.m. Satisfied, Vinicio
smiles and nods. "The lake will start in five or ten minutes."

Only now do we understand our mix-up. Vinicio had told us he would take
us to a lake, where we would see the cock-of-the-rock. We envisioned a small
pond, not on our maps, that was found up in the mountains. We had completely
forgotten that the clearing or area where the male cock-of-the-rock does its
dance is called a lekk, or "lake" as Vinicio pronounced with his Spanish accent.

Yet even with this misunderstanding, it is hard to believe that we are at
the lekk. There doesn't seem to be anything around us to make this particular
spot on the hillside special in any way. We can't believe that the shy and extremely difficult-to-spot cock-of-the-rock is going to fly in and do its odd little ceremony here before us.

As we sit and wait, the sky continues to lighten. A gigantic biting fly
buzzes noisily around our heads. Both Tass and I swat at it a few times, but
miss. It buzzes over toward Vinicio and circles his head a number of times.
He sits quietly watching the forest as if the fly is not even there. The fly continues to circle around him until, suddenly, Vinicio reaches out and grabs it
right out of the air. Without comment he holds the fly by the wings with one
hand, reaches into his backpack with the other, and pulls out a pump spray
bottle of insect repellent. Holding the fly at extremely close range he calmly
gives the annoying pest three hearty shots of repellent at point blank range,
and then, satisfied, tosses the fly over his shoulder to the ground. This singu-
lar act of revenge, played out so methodically—a payback to all the insects
that have been biting us the last few days—strikes us as extraordinarily funny.
We stuff our hands over our mouths to muffle our laughter and then resume
our quiet waiting.

"The lake starts," Vinicio quietly announces. A few moments later we
hear the first call on the hillside behind us. "Uuuuaaacccckkkkk!!" an undig-
nified squawk, like the sound of a chicken being strangled, echoes out over
the valley. The call is immediately answered by another cock-of-the-rock we
can't see in the foliage somewhere close directly below us on the hillside.

"Uuuuaaacccckkkkk!!" Moments later an excited cock-of-the-rock flies
through the dense foliage to sit, thirty feet away, unconcerned with us but
very upset by the calls of the other birds. More cock-of-the-rocks fly in, each
choosing a branch to best proclaim that this is HIS territory.

They are surprisingly robust birds, fifteen inches long, bright reddish-or-
ange with a beautiful crest of feathers crowning their heads. They strut and

ruffle their feathers as they attempt to impress and outdo one another with their beautiful plumage and vociferous proclamations of superiority. We are mesmerized by their ceremony. We try to make photos, but even when the birds are only fifteen feet away the thick foliage makes a clear photograph virtually impossible. Finally we simply sit and enjoy the show. The commotion lasts forty-five minutes, with, we think, ten different birds strutting their stuff.

There is a very brief lull in the noise. Vinicio turns and matter-of-factly states, "Lake finished." We look all around. The birds have suddenly disappeared. We sit on the side of the steep wall of rainforest and share our excitement with Vinicio, recalling the strange ritual that has been played out around us. Reluctantly, we get up and begin the long hike back to town.

We repeatedly stop to bird on the hike back, and are especially excited to see a beautiful mountain toucan and a racquet-tailed hummingbird. But no monkeys with coffee. The last few hours the birding degenerates with the heat of the day. We are also exhausted. Our necks ache from continually looking up into the trees, and only now do we realize the undersides of our exposed necks are covered in insect bites. It seems like we should be back to town, yet when we get to various overlooks there is still no town in sight. We feel like we have been walking forever.

"What happened to Mindo?" Vinicio jokes, as though the town has disappeared. We think he senses how tired we are and is just teasing us. But the next time he jokes, "Where is Mindo?" in a questioning tone, we realize he is as exhausted as we are, wondering if the hike is ever going to end. We finally return just before the afternoon rains. After lunch I sit on the railing of the second-floor balcony of our hotel, listen to the rain on the roof, and watch the swallows flirting through the air and swooping into the hotel courtyard below. I find the rain very relaxing; it feels wonderful to just BE. Somehow the rains help me to justify doing nothing but sit. I have so little of that in my life. I am forever driven to DO, to gauge the success of my days with what I see, what I accomplish. Now, because I am exhausted, I can rest contently, slow down, sit quietly, and just watch the world. The rains let up briefly and the flowering tree in the hotel courtyard fills with hummingbirds. I watch them from a distance without running for my binoculars or bird books. Above the hotel the clouds of mist move slowly across the mountains surrounding the town. I listen to the sound of the wet laundry flapping on the clothesline in the wind; the patter of the raindrops resumes on the tin roof. I sit in luxurious contentedness until the last light fades from the evening sky. Only when my stomach rumbles do I stir from my reverie, thinking about *frijoles*.

During supper we pore over maps and discuss our itinerary. Our next destination is Otavalo in north Ecuador. Normally there are three roads from Mindo to Otavalo, but the road we planned to take is closed due to a washed

Hiking with Vinicio Perez, the Bird Man of Mindo, Ecuador

out bridge. Talking with local truck drivers we learn another circuitous back road to Otavalo is in terrible condition. No one goes that way, and we are assured it is impassable by bicycle. We have heard those warnings before, and while we believe we could cross it on mountain bikes, it would probably be a prolonged epic. Since we are running on a tight schedule, we have to be choosy about our epics. If we are going to do a grueling ride, we would rather it be in another part of Ecuador. That leaves us with only one option, going back out on the same road we bicycled in, almost all the way back to Quito. Rather than using up valuable time retracing our path, we decide to take a bus back and resume bicycling in a new area north of Quito.

An Israeli who just checked into the hotel pulls up a seat at our table, and begins lamenting about his frightful bus ride coming to Mindo.

"Bus broke three times!" he exclaims in halting English, motioning wildly with his hands. "Once brakes all kaput! Driver fix brakes with wire!" he relates with astonishment. "And no line on tires!" After a moment we understand he refers to the lack of tread on the bald rubber. He shakes his head and shrugs. "Maybe why bus cheap...no spend money to fix!" We laugh along with him, even though we know the bus he describes is now parked outside the hotel—the bus we will ride tomorrow.

In the morning the bus driver informs everyone there is no battery on the bus, and he asks for volunteers to push the bus to get it started. Although the engine starts immediately, the driver spends the next half hour with his head under the hood trying to keep it running. I climb up on the roof to make sure our bicycles are tied down properly and then join Tass inside. The bus is nearly full when the driver puts down the hood and climbs in behind the wheel. He puts the bus into gear and the engine dies. A group of us jumps back out of the bus and give it another push. The engine starts again and the driver races the motor as we climb back aboard and take off into the mountains.

For the first few hours our driver is remarkably restrained. Then we realize this is because most of the road has been uphill. When we cross the last pass and begin our descent, the driver transforms from Doctor Jekyll into Mr. Hyde. The words of the Israeli echo in our minds as we think of the bailing wire around the brake cylinder. Tass is convinced the bus may simply fall apart from the excessive G-forces on the corners. I envision a front wheel coming off and the bus careening over the precipice and plunging into a bottomless canyon. We consider strapping on our bicycle helmets and discuss crash strategies, uncertain if we should remain inside or try to jump out a window if we go over a cliff.

We can't get off the bus fast enough when we arrive back on the Pan American highway. I climb on top to help get our bikes down and find Elvis hanging by a single rope, three-quarters off the side of the bus, with a big scratch in his top tube. We are lucky we didn't lose him on the wild corners.

17

Friends in Otavalo

After the cramped, wild bus ride it feels great to be back out on our bikes. We are thrilled to find that unlike much of the Pan American highway in Central America, here there is a wide shoulder, and surprisingly little traffic. After the slow pace of our mountain bike ride through the mountains to Mindo, it is fun to shift into big gears, draft off each other, and cruise along the tarred road. It is a relaxed and beautiful day, and by late afternoon we are riding the last few kilometers into Otavalo.

We stop at the first intersection into town to dig out a map of the city. A bus pulls up beside us and we hear a casual, "Hello, Bruce." The door of the bus is open, and inside is Rich, our friend from the Galapagos trip, sitting relaxed on top of the motor casing next to the driver. We had made plans to meet some of our friends here in Otavalo, and like us, Rich and Rena have just arrived. We rendezvous at the bus station and then the four of us check into the hotel Rocio. Since we are going to be in the area for a week, Tass and I splurge for an extra six thousand *sucres*, $2.60 U.S. per night, and get a "deluxe suite," a large room with a private bath. The next day we sleep in until eight o'clock, and then lie in bed and read.

Whenever we travel, Tass is in charge of researching illnesses to which we might be exposed, packing our first-aid kit, and knowing the correct antibiotics and medicines. Studying third-world illnesses is a rather grim business as far as I am concerned, but Tass finds a bizarre pleasure in learning about unpleasant diseases and infections, especially from the tropics.

Now Tass is studying *The Medical Guide for Third World Travelers*, by Dessery and Robin, and is constantly reading and quoting from the text. Despite my protests, she is compelled to share the gory details. "Ooooh! You want to hear something really gross?" Tass exclaims.

"Not really," I reply.

"Guinea worms are found in South America," Tass continues. "They en-

181

ter the body through contaminated water. The larvae burrow out of the stomach or intestines and migrate into body tissue. Most of the time there are no
symptoms until after about a year, when the female produces young and then
burrows toward the skin, usually in the legs or feet."

"Is there a reason I need to know this?" I ask. But Tass is just getting
started.

"When the worm reaches the surface a painful lesion develops, with a
three-inch diameter blister," she continues. "When it ruptures, the head of the
worm is often seen in the ulcer."

I groan and repeat that I don't want to hear any more. Tass changes the
subject by listing the names of a few drugs that can be taken to kill the worm.

"Listen to this," she adds with excitement once I have calmed down. "If
no drugs are available, a slow extraction taking many days is necessary. You
tie a thread onto the worms head, and gently wind it around a stick, a little
each day. It says patience is required to avoid breaking the worm, as they can
be two feet long!"

"How about you read your book and I'll read my book," I suggest. But
moments later she is at it again.

"This is interesting," Tass says. "It tells how to get a leech off your eye by
shining a flashlight close to the leech, which will move toward the light and
off the eye."

"Do I need to know this right now?" I protest again. Her incessant reading aloud and my growling stomach finally force me to get up and head out
to find breakfast.

That evening our friend Janet arrives with her fiance, Pat, who has joined
Janet since she was with us in the Galapagos. Janet launches into tales of their
last few weeks in Columbia: marathon bus rides, breathtaking scenery, torrential downpours.

Although the Inca culture is the most famous of the pre-Columbian civilizations in South America, many people are surprised to learn that the Inca
Empire existed for only one hundred years. The Inca people came from the
valley of Cuzco in Peru. In 1430 they were victorious in a battle with the
Chanka people, which started a rapid military expansion. As the Incas moved
north from Peru into Ecuador, they encountered the Canari people, who
fought valiantly for a number of years before being conquered by the Inca
leader Tupac Yupanqui. During this period the Inca leader had a son, Huayna
Capac, with a Canari princess, who grew up to inherit the Inca throne. When
he died in 1526, his empire stretched from central Chile in the south to southern Columbia in the north. Rather than leaving the empire to his eldest son
according to tradition, he divided the empire between his two sons. The rivalry between the two quickly lead to bloodshed as Huascar, the Inca of

Cuzco, went to war against Atahualpa, the Inca of Ecuador. Within a few years Atahualpa defeated his brother to become the leader of the empire. The Inca empire was badly weakened by the battles, and hardly ready to defend itself when Pizarro arrived in 1532 with his own plans to conquer the Incas.

Pizarro had the great advantage of surprise in fighting the Incas, who had never seen horses, let alone mounted calvary with steel armor, guns, or cannons. After only a few battles a meeting was arranged between Pizarro and Atahualpa to negotiate a possible settlement. When Atahualpa arrived, Pizarro ordered his men to ambush the Inca. Pizarro held Atahualpa for ransom, demanding enormous quantities of gold, silver, and jewels. When the ransom was paid Pizarro refused to release Atahualpa, and instead put him on trial and had him executed.

Atahualpa's general, Ruminahui, fought the Spanish for two years. It was a losing battle. Rather than surrender the Inca capital of Quito to the Spanish, Ruiminahui destroyed the city himself in retreat. He was later captured, tortured, and executed.

The Spanish rebuilt the capital of Quito, and Pizarro declared his brother, Gonzalo, the first governor. Gonzalo had a similar lust for gold, and sent his lieutenant, Francisco de Orellana, into the Amazon searching for a reputed city of gold. Orellana and his men never found such a city, and spent almost a year floating downriver to the Atlantic Ocean.

For the next few centuries Lima, Peru, was the administrative capital for the Spanish in the area. Ecuador remained a quiet province, with the Indians being forced to toil in the construction of churches and the development of banana plantations and cattle ranches. Indian uprising in the 18th century resulted in numerous casualties on both sides, yet little changed politically.

In 1809 a group of patriots attempted to break Ecuador free from Spanish rule. They overtook Quito and set up a new government, which lasted only twenty four days before they were defeated by troops loyal to Spain. In 1819 Simon Bolivar led the overthrow of Spanish troops in Venezuela, then marched to Columbia to liberate it from Spain. In 1820 the people of Guayaquil, Ecuador, with the backing of Bolivar, claimed independence from Spain. The ensuing battle lasted two years. Bolivar attempted to form a united government of Venezuela, Columbia and Ecuador. This new country lasted just eight years, and when it collapsed, Ecuador declared its own independence in 1830.

Since then the history of Ecuador has often been an open warfare between conservatives, mostly in Quito, and liberals and socialists, traditionally based in the coastal city of Guayaquil. The conservative President Moreno was shot and killed in 1875, while the liberal President Alfaro was killed and then burned by a mob in Quito in 1912. During the twentieth century Ecuador has had more periods of military rule than civilian rule. Since 1979 the country has again returned to a democratic government.

A girl from a small Andean village, Ecuador.

One afternoon I meet another foreigner walking down the street, and we go for a hike. Jonathan is a linguistic anthropologist from Texas who four years ago worked for six months in Otavalo. This is his first return visit to the area. As we hike he talks of all the changes.

"There is much more affluence!" he notes as a truckload of traditionally-dressed Otavalan Indians drives past on the narrow dirt road. "The Indians in this area have always been astute businesspeople, but now they seem to be getting much more respect from the rest of society." He also notes that many of the young men he knew who had short hair four years ago, now wear long pony tails in the traditional style of their Indian ancestors. "I think it is definitely a positive sign of pride and respect for their own cultural heritage. Many young people no longer follow the fashions of the *Latino* culture in the cities."

As we hike into the countryside, we pass numerous small rural homes. Jonathan calls out to the inhabitants in Quechea, "*Nanda manachi*," which translates literally as "Lend me the path." The locals all smile and wave at this foreigner who speaks their own native dialect, and reply "*Yali Pai!*" Go ahead!

Tass and I spend the next few days with our friends exploring the Otavalo area. Often we all head out together; sometimes just the two of us go alone. Due to the altitude and being on the equator, when the sky is clear, the sunlight is so dazzling and bright it is difficult to make photographs of the markets or people, the contrast between sunlight and shade being too extreme. Whenever the clouds move in and the light softens, we grab our cameras and head outside. Tass is thrilled to be photographing the women living in the area. She often sits for long periods of time with various women, chatting and laughing to put them at ease as she makes photographs.

The market in Otavalo is predominantly weavings, clothing, arts and crafts for tourists. Still, there remains a less visited animal market that starts earlier in the morning on the north edge of town. As the sky grows light people from all the surrounding villages bring in pigs, cattle, sheep, and horses to sell.

I like the pig market the best. The pigs are completely docile, until their owners attempt to move them. Then even the smallest pigs let out a continuous, piercing squeal. They are pulled and dragged on leashes through the market creating an enormous racket. The pigs lock all four legs in defiance. None of them moves even the slightest distance willingly. The larger pigs require teamwork to be moved. Three people will typically gather around the pig, two in the front holding the ears while the third lifts up on the tail and hoists the squealing, kicking pig across the market. Surprisingly, the moment the pig is released it instantly stops the piercing squealing and begins a contented grunting and sniffing about, no hard feelings, completely relaxed.

The prospective pig buyers walk between the leashed pigs, poking and prodding at them to determine the health of each animal. When the bargaining gets serious the buyers enlist help from others to grab the front and back legs and flip the wildly screaming and thrashing pigs onto their backs. While two or three people hold the pig down, the buyer jams a stick in the pigs mouth to pry it open. Using a piece of cloth or perhaps just a shirt sleeve, they grab the pig's tongue and pull it out to check the color and the health of the animal. All this time the pig is doing major squealing. Once this process is finished everyone lets go of the pig and it immediately jumps to its feet. Again within seconds the pig calms back down and, with no apparent hard feelings over its recent indignities, resumes sniffing and snorting along the ground, looking for scraps of food.

By nine a.m. the animal market is over, and we head to the town square to the clothing and textile markets. Despite all the beautiful weavings, carpets, sweaters and clothing for sale, we buy nothing. I had planned to get Elvis, who we now simply refer to as "The King," a few small woven sashes to decorate his handlebars, yet even that decision seems too overwhelming with so many choices of colors and designs. Neither of us is in the shopping mood. Instead we simply people watch and make photos. Perhaps we will get motivated for shopping later in the trip.

After the Sunday market our group again splits up. Rich and Rena head south to climb some volcanoes before returning to the U.S. Janet and Pat take a bus back to Quito. They want to bicycle in the mountains south of Quito and then travel by bus through Peru. We hope to meet them in two months in southern Peru.

18

Andes to the Amazon

After nearly a week in Otavalo the pull of the *oriente*, the Amazon Basin of eastern Ecuador, motivates us to pack our bicycles and resume riding. The week-long Festival of San Juan has started. In many of the mountain villages, we see groups of revelers striding up and down the narrow alleys wearing costumes and playing music. In the small town of El Quiche, we stop at the central plaza in front of a huge cathedral. Ten inebriated *gauchos*, each wearing natural wool chaps, colorful shirts, and bandanas, dance in a circle beside the church. They follow one another, stumbling along in a state of near stupefaction from drinking and endless marathon dancing. Like blitzed out dervishes on a bender, they swagger and sway, nearly falling over one another as they dance on and on. I cautiously pull out my camera and motion in a questioning manner to see if it is okay to make a few pictures. One of the dancers stumbles out of formation to wobble up to me, grinning all the while, and nods his assent.

But after a few minutes the dancer comes back to demand a photo of himself. I spend the next five minutes, surrounded by a crowd of stone-faced bystanders, trying to explain the need for film to be developed before I can produce any photographs.

"*Es necessito otra machina para photos,*" I ramble over and over, not making much headway. A group of six bright-eyed women joins the throng around me, each wearing a felt hat and bright-colored skirt and blouse—a collage of reds, pinks and greens. I desperately want to make photos of the women but I am not about to pull out my camera again with the unhappy *gaucho* swaying over me.

Finally one of the women in the crowd comprehends what I am trying to say, and explains to the gaucho my camera is not "*instantanea.*" I quickly nod in agreement, repeating the key words "*no instantanea!*" The *gaucho* and I spend the next few minutes laughing and slapping each other on the back

187

over our misunderstanding. Still, he eyes me oddly and keeps a firm grasp on my arm. The moment he lets go, I make a discreet exit and meet Tass back in the main plaza where she has been watching the festivities near our bicycles.

At night we quietly sneak off the road to camp in an untilled section of a corn field, and the next morning join the Trans-Ecuadorean road that will take us over the final Andean pass before we begin our descent into the Amazon Basin. At the base of the pass the road is surprisingly steep; we start out in our lowest gears. Our spirits are high regardless of our speed.

By mid-morning we have climbed into an even steeper canyon. A fierce, cold headwind blows, slowing us to a crawl. Further up the pass a gust of wind suddenly buffets us from the side. We swerve dramatically toward an abrupt drop-off at the edge of the road, and then nearly crash into one another as we overcorrect our steering and swerve back in the other direction. Another blast of wind forces us to drop an outside foot to the ground to keep from toppling over.

The truck drivers heading up the pass honk and wave at us enthusiastically, giving us the thumbs-up sign and flashing big smiles. They seem excited to see us up here. We are excited too. The view is stunning.

We enter yet another high valley above tree line and wonder if we are viewing the top of the pass above us. We caution each other about getting our hopes up only to find a false summit, yet it is tempting to think we could cross the pass within the next half hour. We stop in a little sunny spot sheltered from the wind. For a little celebration, I dig out two chocolate donuts I have been saving from a village bakery.

Back on the bikes and another fifteen minutes of riding reveals not the top of the pass but another climb up a long valley. We work our way up the valley to find yet another enormous climb above that. An hour later we come around a corner to find a giant wall of mountains. Now we begin serious climbing.

The headwind we have been battling all day turns bitter cold. Snow covers the tops of all the mountains around us. Still the road continues to climb. Again we stop to put on more clothes, plus gloves and wool hats under our helmets.

On the next corner we are hit by an arctic blast that just about knocks us off the bikes. Tass has to put her foot down twice to keep from going over. The cold mist turns to a driving sleet that stings our faces and freezes over my glasses. This is grim. The snow-covered mountains swirl in an icy fog and look so cold, bleak and barren that Tass momentarily loses confidence and begins to freak out, wondering if we are going to make it over the pass with the deteriorating weather. The wind is a relentless, howling nightmare. Banshee bicycling. The thought of stopping and trying to camp is even more frightening; we could get snowed in for days, and we are hardly equipped for a lengthy winter storm. I convince Tass that the best idea is just to get over the

Tass riding up through the mist into the Andes, Ecuador.

pass and drop down to a lower altitude as soon as possible. Our eyelashes freeze together. We can hardly see when we come around a corner and find a shrine to the Virgin Mary appearing out of the driving snow. As we pedal up to it, we see beyond the shrine that the highway plunges downhill back into the mist. We have made it! Papallacta pass, 13,330 feet!

How quickly our attitude changes! We are suddenly ecstatic, jumping up and down and giving each other hugs and pats on the back. We snap a few pictures and then, shivering but somehow also warmer inside, we push off into the wind, this time downhill, off the eastern side of the Andes.

Without the exertion of climbing, our body temperatures drop dramatically with the wind-chill of the descent. The icy road and fierce wind and sleet against our faces keeps our speed to a crawl. Now we have a new kind of torment—we want to drop quickly to a lower elevation and get out of the cold, but the wind chill is brutal whenever we let off the brakes. When we pick up any speed, the frigid air gives us ice cream headaches, numb hands and feet. We shiver violently as we slowly make our way down the pass.

After a few bone-chilling miles, we drop below the snow and sleet into a cold mist, and stop to get off the bikes and again shake some circulation into our feet and hands. We are so thrilled to be over the pass and out of the driving snowstorm that we are almost goofy with ecstasy, despite our nearly frostbitten extremities.

Cloudforest on the descent into the Amazon Basin, Ecuador.

We descend a few more miles and the mist clears. We pull over in the first spot of sunshine to try and soak up some warmth. More hugs and loud whoops of relief and joy. But five minutes later the sun goes back behind a cloud, so we continue our descent. We drop down a few more valleys until we come to a large lake where we stop to eat lunch as the sun pops back out. Despite the radiant warmth of the sun, both of us still have a deep chill that we just can't seem to shake. Another black cloud of mist rolls up the valley; by the time we finish eating, a cold rain starts to fall. We may be over the pass but we are still very high in the mountains, and hypothermia is still a major concern. We dig out our rain gear, put on our pannier covers, and head on down the highway.

The asphalt road that took us over the pass now turns into a rough, rocky road that twists and winds down the steep canyon. The rain continues long enough for us to get wet despite our rain gear, but when the sun comes back out it is amazing how quickly we dry off in the wind. Still, we just can't get warm.

The sheer walls of the canyon around us are covered with lush cloudforest. Small clouds of mist roll up and down the towering mountains, adding to the dramatic view. Sometimes we stop for photographs; other times we stop simply to stand beside the road and marvel at the cloudforest covering the canyon walls.

We descend through narrow, shaded valleys where the road is a muddy mess. Then we ride through wider, sunny canyons where the blazing equatorial sun has already dried the road so much that our bikes kick up clouds of dust. Occasional passing trucks cover us in dust; then we turn the corner, and drop into another shaded valley full of mud. In some areas we ride slowly to enjoy the scenery; in other sections we descend as fast as our bikes can go on the rough, rocky road. Finally we warm up.

As we continue to descend, we begin riding through valleys that have been cleared for cattle ranching. Along the road are little homesteads. Some barely could be called shacks; others have two stories with balconies and overhanging tin roofs. A few even have glass windows, but most simply have wooden shutters. Along the road men work in the fields putting up wire fencing. Others saunter beside the road, machetes dangling from their hands. All wear tall rubber boots. A few have baseball-style hats that say Chicago Bulls.

As we ride along, I think about the hardships of their lives. Clearing heavily forested land by hand, often on steep hillsides, raising dairy cattle—sloshing through the deforested landscape, covered with mud, corralling the cattle twice a day for milking—chopping wood for a fire each time you want to cook, hauling all the water by hand for washing, bathing and drinking. And raising big families.

As evening draws near it begins to rain, again. Although the rain is cold, we stay warm with the exertion of riding the rough downhills. We cycle past a number of beautiful waterfalls as the sky begins to darken. The canyon we are in has no place to camp on the steep muddy hillside. We press on to a junction in the road, where we have heard there is a little *pension*. But the *pension* is closed, and we don't like the vibes of a gas station/bar, the other building at the intersection. We are exhausted. The small town of Baeza is just a few kilometers up a nearby mountain. Riding up the steep road to town seems almost overwhelming, but we have little choice. We shift back into our lowest climbing gears and pedal up the road.

It is pitch dark when we arrive at the town, which has no working street lights. We ride around the village, peering into the blackness until we find a hotel, the *Hosteria El Nogal de Jumandy*, and then spend another ten minutes banging on doors before we finally locate the owner. Jorge is a squat, enthusiastic man with a scraggly beard and big thick hands; he gives us both a hearty handshake and a pat on the back.

The hotel is a two-story building on a hillside looking east. Our room, along with the dining room and a lounge area, has great windows that should offer spectacular views of the sunrise. The entire building smells of mold and mildew. The wooden floors sag and sway, creaking at the slightest pressure. Walking down the hall corridor to our room makes the entire building shake. No one could ever sneak up on anybody in a place like this.

We are both exhausted, yet our work is not finished. I put up a web of clotheslines, crisscrossing the rafters in our room so we can hang up all our wet gear, and another line on a porch for our tent, rainfly, and muddy pannier covers. I hand wash a batch of cycling shorts and other muddy clothes, and then pump all our water containers full with our water filter. Luckily we are the only guests in the hotel, so the building stops vibrating when we lie on our bed to read and study our maps.

As I look at the map, I realize my glasses are still spotted and smeared from riding in the rain. I give them a quick clean with my T-shirt, but when I put them back on they are still spotted. I try again, but they seem to get even worse. The more I clean them, the more smeared they become. I try using our camera lens cleaner, but it doesn't help at all. The coating on the plastic lenses has degenerated. The left lens is especially bad—it looks as if it has a thin coat of Vaseline smeared over it. I brought an extra pair of glasses to South America, but in the frantic elimination of weight and luggage, I left them in storage at the South American Explorers Club. Now all I have for backup are my prescription sunglasses, which I didn't wear today because of the dark and stormy skies. I can't bear the thought of a two-day bus ride back to Quito to get my extra glasses. Besides, I reason, I will probably wear my prescription sunglasses most of the time during the day anyway. In the evenings I'll just squint or put up with the marginal sight of my regular glasses. I can always hold my books extra close and read without my glasses. Or so I tell myself. We'll be back in Quito in a month; I can get my other glasses then.

We originally planned to continue riding down the Quijos/Papallacta river valley all the way to Lago Agrio. We heard at the South American Explorers Club that the road ahead is "the busiest in Ecuador," with truck traffic from the oil fields and boom towns that have sprung up in this part of the Amazon Basin during the last twenty years. Rather than avoiding the area, we plan to ride the road specifically because of the development. Since we are making a slide program about our trip, we want to photograph all aspects of the Amazon, including the realities of the oil fields and the timber and mining industries.

The last few days we have again and again been told that the road is narrow, muddy, and full of belching diesel trucks. Last night Jorge, the hotel proprietor, nearly had a heart attack when we told him our plans to cycle to Lago Agrio. He exclaimed the entire area was full of "*ladrones y narcoticos*"—robbers and drug traffickers.

Now all the horror stories are finally causing us to question our route. We don't want to give up the idea of riding to Lago Agrio altogether, but we begin to question our timing. Do we really want our first week in the Amazon Basin to be spent traveling through destruction, deforestation, and cultural upheaval? Perhaps we should take a different road into the Amazon via a more scenic route, give ourselves a chance to get a feel for the area, then if we still feel strongly about it, we can tackle the ride to Lago Agrio.

So rather than continuing northeast downhill, we leave Baeza and head south, along the length of the Andes up the Cosanga River valley. For the first hour the steep hillsides are heavily forested. In a number of places huge landslides have swept down the steep hills, covering sections of road, which have to be bulldozed free of trees and mud to remain passable. Some are short slides where the bank twenty feet above the road has simply collapsed. Others are immense long chutes starting a thousand feet above the road, where some high precipice has broken off and created a swath of destruction all the way down to the road and far below into the valley. Giant logs, stripped of foliage and branches, lay intertwined in the mud and ooze, piled high beside the road. Fresh tracks from bulldozers show in many places the road has just been cleared in the last few days. The older piles of debris have incredibly strong smells of fermentation—rotting vegetation oozes out onto the road from the piles of foliage and mud. We slow so the smelly water won't splash up on to our legs or panniers, and hold our breath as we pass by. In some areas the landslide debris is piled forty feet high. This is land slide season, and obviously it is a full-time job plowing out the debris to keep the road open. As we ride we think of the newspaper clips of buses being swept off the road,

The mountain roads need to be continually cleared of mud and debris
from frequent landslides, Ecuador.

and villages being destroyed by landslides. We didn't comprehend how frequently they occur, or how much of a terror landslides can be.

The valley widens and we begin to see more of the rampant deforestation that has come with cattle ranching. Despite the absence of trees in the valley, from a distance the hills look green and lush. But as we ride closer we see every one of the fields is covered with criss-crossed trails where cattle hooves have broken and scarred the land, leaving numerous areas of bare ground. Vast stretches of the road are covered with thick layers of black volcanic mud and sand that has washed down off the hillsides in the rains. Chronic erosion.

As we ride past the homesteads, I think of the people who live out here. In many ways I am looking back in time to what much of my own country was like one hundred and fifty years ago. U.S. history has romanticized the pioneers as hearty, good people who claimed the land and the country for the growing nation. Yet the Indians who lived on the land in a much simpler and holistic way viewed the settlers as destroyers of the land, people who killed off the buffalo for no reason and tilled the prairie soil, destroying the native grasslands. How ironic that many of us from the United States, descendants of those pioneers, view what is now happening in the rainforests of the world not through the eyes and standards of our pioneer ancestors, but more like the Indians, whose land our ancestors took and forever changed. For us, the cycle has come a full circle. When we look at all the homesteads, we see the loss of rainforest habitat, the loss of something unique and irreplaceable.

Like our own ancestors, the Ecuadoreans we meet homesteading don't view themselves as destructive. They feel they are colonists, working to tame and civilize their country, to bring it into the twenty-first century, to make something better for their families. They are extremely hard-working people, mostly shy and reserved, busy doing their chores and living out their own lives and dreams for the future; they are not particularly inquisitive about what we are doing here on bicycles.

At Cosanga we stop to eat lunch beside the road: PowerBars, peanuts, raisins and stale *galletas*, crackers we bought in a local tienda in the absence of bread or tortillas. They probably sat on the shelf for a few years before we bought them. Above us the road climbs up and over the *Cordillera de los Guacamayos*, Mountains of the Macaws, a small range that juts away from the Andes into the Amazon Basin that contains 12,241-foot Volcano Sumaco and two other high peaks. We cycle up the rough, rocky road back into the cooler breezes of undisturbed cloud forest until we round a corner and find a shrine to *Maria del la Camino*—the Virgin Mary of the Road, and the top of the pass. Hail Mary!

The clouds and mist are thick, cool, and refreshing. We pull out our maps and discuss how, if we are lucky, the clouds and mist might clear during our descent. Since we are on a mountainside, not in a valley, and we are now on the most eastern edge of the Andes, we might be able to see all the way out into the Amazon Basin. Hopefully, somewhere along the descent will be a vista with an unhindered view through the foliage to the east.

No sooner do we discuss all this than the mist rises, the clouds part as if on cue, and we can see a series of rainforest covered ridges dropping off like enormous descending steps all the way eastward into the lowlands. Suddenly, the Amazon Basin lies before us. The view is incredibly moving. We are so thankful we changed our route in Baeza! This is the way to enter the Amazon Basin! Nothing could be more beautiful than the stunning vista below us. Sitting here, we feel the fulfillment of three years of planning and saving for our journey. Our hard work is now paying off bigtime. We feel blessed and somewhat dream-like; torn between just sitting all afternoon and enjoying the view, yet anxious to resume our descent! We climb on the bikes with a final thankful nod to *Maria del la Camino* for the wonderful view, and head down the road.

The rugged, rocky road winds down the side of the sheer mountain wall. Clouds of mist roll in and out above us and below us as well. We repeatedly stop to enjoy the spectacular views, put on raincoats and rain covers when it rains, and then stop to take off our rain gear each time the hot, tropical sun pops back out of the clouds.

We drop down one ridge after another; for hours we descend through layers and layers of cloud forest, and then descend more. The road seems never ending. Repeatedly we look out in the distance, convinced that soon we will drop into a canyon that will force us, even if only for a short distance, to climb back up over a ridge before resuming downhill. But each time we get to the base of a ridge, another valley opens up below, and rather than a short climb we continue the uninterrupted downhill. In places the road is incredibly rough, with huge stones protruding out of the dirt. We slow to a crawl and bounce across. Our brake hands get cramps; our neck and back muscles ache—but what fun!

Heavy rains roll in. The road becomes a series of little rivers running under our wheels, and then larger rivers. The spray of water and mud from our tires soaks us from below as the rain soaks us from above. The sky turns even darker, and the pelting rain drops grow enormous. Soon sheets of rain cover us, as though someone was throwing buckets of water over us. We are still at a high enough elevation that the rain is quite cold. We come to a large tree overhanging the road and stop underneath to put on more clothes. We take turns holding our small, folding umbrella over one another as we frantically dig through our panniers to find our long underwear capilene tops to put on under our rain jackets.

More descending. The road turns from mud, rock, and gravel to a pseudo pavement—rough stones laid loose and unpacked and then covered with a layer of tar—like riding on corrugated tin. Still, the road is an improvement over what we have been riding.

The rain finally stops and the surface of the road smooths out to a bumpy and pock-marked highway. At last we can get off the brakes and let the bikes pick up speed. The descent is thrilling; blurring, rushing images of dense tropical foliage fill our peripheral vision.

More descending. Occasionally we pass homesteads, but much more often we ride down through virgin rainforest. What an incredible rush. Ever so slightly we feel the air warming. Wisps of steam begin rising off the warming pavement.

We stop at the village of Jondachi in hopes of finding food. We don't see any stores in the small group of houses that make up the village, but a lone wooden shack set off by itself below the other buildings has a small sign for a local soft drink nailed up on the outside wall—which means it is possibly a *tienda* selling crackers, tinned food, or maybe, if we are lucky, even more. Inside a single wooden table and bench is the only furniture in the front room. One tattered calendar, three years old, is the only decoration on the wall. An elderly *senora* comes out of a back room to stand, silently, looking at us.

"*Tenamos arroz y huevos?*" we ask tentatively. Do you have rice and eggs?

"*Si, hay*" she responds, smiling. Yes there is.

"*Y papas?*" I add, hoping for potatoes.

"*Si. Papas tambien*" she nods her head matter-of-factly, as though there could not be any doubt. She motions for us to sit down, then calls out the door to her son. We overhear her instructing him to run to see if any of the neighbors have eggs or potatoes to sell. He returns moments later with his hands full of food—we are in luck!

As our food is being cooked, we reminisce on other big mountain descents we have bicycled: from the Rocky Mountains down to the prairie; off high Indonesian volcanoes; over the Alps in New Zealand and also in Europe; and even through and over the Himalaya down onto the plains of India. But none of those rides can compare with our present descent from the Andes to the Amazon Basin. And it is still not over! Fortified with food, we eagerly climb back on the bikes to continue downward.

The descent goes on and on, the views continue to be spectacular. The vegetation around us grows more and more tropical. The air warms as we continue descending. The clouds part enough to let the sun color the evening sky. Distant ridges shimmer in hazy layers of tropical growth, each ridge topped by silhouettes of palms and moss-covered trees and vines. Birds call out, frogs croak, insects chirp, and still we coast down through the lush growth.

We stop again to enjoy a particularly stunning view and find that without the wind cooling us, the air is hot and muggy. However, when we resume our downward journey the rushing air again feels cool and fresh. Behind us the Andes are now a deep shade of purple, topped by clouds of gray mist.

Tass on the best bicycle descent of our lives, from the
Andes to the Amazon Basin, Ecuador.

Still we descend. The sun has long ago dropped behind the Andes in
the west, and now the light in the sky is also fading. We have been looking
for a camp site, but where the land has been cleared for cattle, the ground
is an uneven and muddy bog, with no hideaway places to pitch our tent.
We think the village of Archidona is about three miles down the road, so we
keep descending.

We ride by starlight; then the pavement comes to an end, making the outline of the road harder to see. Still we keep going. Exhilarated yet exhausted,
we ride into town and stop at the Hotel Regina, which is clean, quiet and
comfortable. It rains much of the night, but by morning the sky is clear. We
decide to take a rest day, as tomorrow is market day, which we would like to
see. We eat a relaxed and prolonged breakfast of eggs, rice, potatoes, and

bread—the starch diet—and then do some laundry. No sooner do we hang out our laundry, than it starts to sprinkle.

"*Mucho lluvia?*" Tass asks the senora. Will there be much rain? We wonder if we should take the laundry back down.

"*Bestante,*" she replies with a shrug. Enough.

We move our small batch of laundry from the roof clothesline and hang it under the eve of a shed. The *senora* leaves all her sheets hanging in the rain. It pours for four hours.

In the evening we return to a nearby restaurant for supper. A television in the corner shows Spanish sit-coms from Mexico and Brazil interspersed with reruns and a few current shows from the U.S. We wonder what the people here think of us; we are so unlike the North Americans they see on TV. We don't wear expensive clothes or shoes. Instead, we have loose baggy pants for the tropics and sandals—something none of the middle class locals would be caught dead wearing. We come from a rich country, yet we choose to dress like *campesinos* and ride bicycles!

The rains continue most of the night and off and on through the morning. We make numerous trips to the market and explore the town. Whenever the rains stop, the streets fill with people from the countryside in town for the Sunday market and church. When the fierce downpours let loose, everyone stands under the store awnings and overhanging roofs lining the sidewalks, staring at the rain and each other. No one does anything; everything seems to get put on hold, waiting for the rain to stop. Only one out of ten people carry an umbrella, and no one wears a rain coat or poncho, although the rain is quite cold. Amazingly, they all don't catch pneumonia. Everyone stands stoically, with hunched shoulders. We likewise stand around under the awnings and stare out at the crowds, trying to get a feel for their lives.

The Indians who live in this area are Quijos Indians. They are short with skinny legs—often bowlegged—wide hips, and chiseled faces with sharp jaw lines. When groups of Indians meet one another, they reach out like they are going to shake hands, yet instead of grasping each other's hands, they lightly and quickly touch their palms together. Even when one or two people come up to a group of six or eight, they will all touch palms with everyone else in the group, sometimes saying nothing, and then repeating the process when the group splits up and everyone leaves.

On one of my trips to the market, it begins to rain heavily. As I walk down the street, an Indian woman walking next to me begins eyeing my umbrella. She says something in Quechua and immediately jumps in beside me, sharing my umbrella. She is incredibly short and is wearing a colorful 1950s style dress that she probably bought used. Whenever we come to little streams of water over the sidewalk or road, she gives me an impish smile, and we jump in unison to keep us both under the umbrella. As we reach the market, she spots a banana plant in front of someone's house, breaks off a section of leaf, bends it back and folds it to make her own umbrella. She gives me a little wave and takes off on her own through the market.

The market runs along a gravel street that has turned into a small river from the rain. Twenty stalls line each side of the road/creek, each covered with a black plastic tarp held precariously by an assortment of bamboo poles and guy lines. Electrical cords run along the ground to equip the booths with blaring radios and a few lights. The electrical cords are completely submerged wherever the water gushes down the road.

Many of the stalls have used clothing from the U.S. Two used shirts sell for ten thousand *sucres*, about four dollars. Others have new 'counterfeit' clothing—cheap imitations of brand names in current fashion in the U.S. and Europe. Nearby piles of running shoes for sale are made to look like expensive brands back home. Other stalls sport brightly colored household products and decorations: wall ornaments, clocks, radios, plastic wallets and purses, plastic shoes, colorful flashlights, bright red batteries made in China, pirated cassettes, kitchen utensils, pots and pans, all stacked in huge, ornate piles under dripping tarps, all requiring the buyer to stand not only in the pouring rain but also in the creeks to shop.

At the far end of the street a crowd has gathered around two trucks, both full of fish packed in ice. The men are doing a booming business. I am surprised to find they are selling ocean fish, trucked all the way over the Andes from the Pacific coast. When I ask why they don't have river fish from the *oriente* for sale, the men say there are few fish in the rivers, which seems inconceivable. The last thing I expected people here would need is fish from the ocean. I wonder how many other surprises we will find in the Amazon Basin during our next two months.

19

In the Emerald Forest

The next day we leave town in a light rain. Our plan to ride to Coca has changed: the road is closed, buried under landslides. So we cycle to Misahualli on the banks of the Rio Napo, the largest river in the Ecuadorian Amazon. We want to spend a few days in Misahualli and visit Jatun Satcha, a small nature reserve nearby. By then we hope the road to Coca will be open so we can continue our mountain bike ride.

Misahualli is a quaint little town with a dozen shops, a few restaurants, and a couple of hotels. Many travelers who want a quick glimpse of life in the Amazon Basin bus down from Banos, spend a night or two in Misahualli, and then head back up into the Andes to visit the more traditional tourist destinations in the mountains. The few who are willing to brave heat, humidity, and insects use Misahualli as a staging area for boat trips downriver to Coca, or beyond.

In addition to mountain biking in the *oriente*, we also want to travel by boat on some of the rivers. In Quito we tried to set up a trip into the rainforest with Luis Garcia, a guide who was highly recommended in trip reports at the South American Explorers Club. We visited Luis's office in Quito, Emerald Forest Expeditions, but he was in the *oriente* and we did not meet. While cycling in the Andes we again called his office, still hoping to meet Luis in Coca, to join a group he was taking into the rainforest. But as the weeks passed, we realized we would never make it to Coca in time. Not knowing what our schedule would be, or where Luis would be next, we gave up hope of meeting him.

Now in Misahualli, we spend our first day hiking in the rainforest and photographing brown capuchin monkeys that live in a small protected area near the boat landing. As the sun goes down, we walk back to our hotel. When we pass through town, a man comes out of a shop and walks down the sidewalk beside us. His T-shirt says, "It is not too late to save the Amazon rainforest." We walk side by side in the same direction, and I keep thinking he

200

looks familiar. Suddenly it occurs to me that I saw pictures of him on the bulletin board in the office of Emerald Forest Expeditions.

"Excuse me," I smile. "Are you Luis Garcia?"

"Yes!" he replies somewhat startled as he reaches out to shake our hands. We explain that we are the bicyclists who wanted to go with him into the rainforest, but the dates had not worked. He smiles in recognition and says he heard about us not only through his office, but also through mutual friends who met us while we were cycling to Mindo.

"We are really disappointed that we didn't get to travel with you in the rainforest," Tass tells him sadly.

"You can still go with me!" Luis replies enthusiastically. "I am leaving tomorrow morning with a small group to travel down the Rio Napo for a week."

"Will you be coming back to Misahualli?" we quickly ask.

"No," he replies. "The trip will be finishing in Coca."

We sadly shake our heads and tell him we would love to go, but we have our bicycles with us. We can't leave our bicycles here unless we will be coming back to pick them up.

"No problem!" Luis laughs. "We'll take your bicycles in the canoes with us! In three days when we pass through Coca, we'll drop off the bikes, and at the end of the trip your bikes will be there waiting for you!"

We look at each other and quickly nod in agreement. This is too fortuitous a meeting and too great an opportunity to let slip away! We race back to our hotel to begin a major repacking of gear.

Everything to be left in Coca—our bikes, cycling clothes and gear, and cold weather clothes and gear—has to be organized so it can be dropped off quickly and stored safely. Everything we are storing and everything we are bringing with us must be double and even triple wrapped and bagged in plastic for the ride in the open canoe. We organize equipment late into the night.

Just before we go to bed, the rest of the group we are joining arrives at our hotel after their eleven-hour bus ride from Quito. The bus broke down twice, once with a flat tire and once when the rim on the brake drum exploded. Despite the prolonged ride and late hour, the group is upbeat. A good sign, no whiners. Everyone is enthusiastic and ready for adventure!

The next morning we eat breakfast and begin the process of getting to know each other. As all the crew members show up, we realize we are joining a formidable expedition. Luis, of course, is the lead guide and in charge of everything. His assistant guide is David (pronounced Daw-veed) Chongo, who is from the indigenous tribe Napo Runa, the Napo River People. David is the most exotic looking person we have seen so far in the Amazon—incredibly muscular and powerfully built, with sharp cheek-bones, a quick but shy smile, and long flowing hair tied back with a headband. He wears shorts but no shirt or shoes, and has a single, enormous jaguar tooth hung on a black cord around his neck—a real Tarzan of the Amazon. Also helping guide on this trip is Hazen Audel, a Native American from Flathead, Montana, who first came to the Amazon as an undergraduate student to study insects. Hazen lived in Misahualli for nearly a year, and became great friends with Luis and David. Hazen has just returned to Ecuador for a few months to help Luis guide. This will be his first trip. Three other crew members grew up in the Amazon: Anival, the pilot for the second canoe; Gary, our cook; and Chiri, a young boy who is the kitchen helper and general gofer.

In addition to Tass and me there are six other foreigners: two married couples, Robert and Noortje from Denmark, and Uri and Laura from Israel, and two men from the U.S., Tony and Bobby.

After a few hours everything is loaded into the giant canoes, and we set off downstream. The river is running high from recent storms. The water is a chocolate brown in sharp contrast to the lush green covering both sides of the river bank. The day is beautiful; the sky is bright blue with a few puffy, white thunderheads off in the distance. Our thirty-five-foot wooden canoe is a vibrant red with blue trim on the gunwales; the second canoe is bright yellow with blue trim. Both are piled high with gear. Everything we have is packed in stuff sacks lined with plastic, stored inside panniers double-lined with plastic, wrapped in huge mylar bags under a large tarp. As long as the boat doesn't tip over our things should remain dry!

After a few hours in the canoes we stop to take our first hike. Luis has studied with a number of traditional *shamans* and knows a great deal about the medicinal uses of plants. He stops repeatedly to explain the various healing properties of many plants, flowers, and vines. Luis is very patient and always waits for us to gather around him before he speaks, so no one misses what he is saying. As he makes small cuts to open different plants or slightly peels back bark to show us insects, he jokes and says he is only disturbing the plants "in the name of science."

Luis is part indigenous Indian and grew up in *la selva*, "the jungle." His father was a teacher, who moved to Quito when Luis was twelve. Luis was very shy and had a hard time adapting to life in the city. After finishing school Luis went to the University, but dropped out after a year to return to the *oriente*. Besides living as an apprentice with a *shaman*, he studied on his own and taught himself English by listening to rock music.

While Luis shows us things along the trail, David and Hazen scamper through the forest like a couple of kids starting their summer vacation. They dig with their hands through huge rotten logs, looking for insects, spiders, and snakes. While Tass and I and the rest of the foreigners repeatedly stop to slather ourselves with insect repellent, Luis, David, and Hazen refrain from using repellent. They also don't wear boots or shoes. David and Hazen even go shirtless. By the end of the hike, both their backs are covered with a mass

of welts from insect bites. I question Hazen about the bites, and he tells me
they will itch for only about a week. Then he gets used to it. He talks of being
at one with the rainforest, not struggling or fighting against the environment
but being a part of it, accepting the rainforest on its own terms. He will be
here for months, and apparently he considers being food for mosquitoes and
biting insects all a part of the experience. Interesting.

After our hike Luis performs a small ceremony to initiate us to the rainforest. Opening a small red achote berry, Luis dabs a finger into the soft pulp inside and puts a small red stripe on each of his cheeks. Then he jokingly begins
to put the red paste on each of us—substantially more than he put on himself.
Luis even writes "Hi Mom" across my forehead. We all get a chuckle out of
Luis's antics and take a few pictures of the "ceremony." But when we are finished the joke is on us. The paste is impossible to wash off! Water and soap
simply smear the red color all over our faces. Only then does Luis tell us that
some cosmetic companies use the paste as an ingredient in women's lipstick.

"Don't worry," he laughs, "The red will come off in a few weeks." But
with diligent scrubbing, everything but a rosy rouge color comes off after ten
minutes of washing. Luis tells us that by the next day it will all be gone.

As evening approaches we turn the canoes off the Rio Napo onto a small
tributary and go upriver for half an hour to our first camp. Luis has built two

Our guide, Luis Garcia, performs an initiation ceremony on Tass using the bright red
paste from the achote fruit, Rio Napo, Ecuador.

thatched huts on the land of a family that lives by the small river. One of the huts is quite large with a communal dining room and a number of little cubicles with cane walls and bunk beds. A covered ramp walkway connects the building to a second, smaller hut that serves as a kitchen. Luis pays the family for rent and also gives money to landowners of some of the trails we will hike along the upper Rio Napo, where recently there has been a dramatic increase in homesteads. By paying the landowners, Luis hopes to show people that it can be financially viable to leave sections of forest uncut.

As we unload our gear from the canoe, the kitchen crew unloads equipment and food from the other canoe, along with our bicycles, which are placed in the center of the camp—a position of honor. When different members of the crew have a few spare moments, they take turns riding our bikes on the trails around the camp. We show them how the gears work, and get as much enjoyment watching them ride our bikes as they do in riding them!

A rope swing hangs from a large branch overhanging the river, and we take turns swinging out over the water and dropping into the huge pool below. David has the best technique, with elaborate forward and backward somersaults. Tass, who has great muscle definition on her arms and back, makes a big impression with the crew as she swings out over the water. "*Muy fuerte!*" they continually say to her with admiration. Very Strong!

After supper we entertain ourselves by using flashlights to spot banana spiders and tarantulas in the thatching of the roof of our hut. David crawls up a support beam and uses a rubber thong and a little bit of coaxing to get a number of spiders to crawl onto the thong. David then climbs back down, one-handed, so we can have a closer look.

Despite David's nonchalant handling of the spiders, Luis tells us that banana spiders are very dangerous. While the tarantula has a sting much like a large wasp, the banana spiders are one of the most dangerous spiders in the world.

Later I go out with Hazen on a short night hike. We spot a number of tree frogs, ghost shrimp in a small pool, and I get a close-up encounter with a bizarre type of katydid when it jumps onto my neck and slowly crawls up across my face. The giant grasshopper has camouflage, making it appear as if covered with lichen and moss.

That night I start reading an Anne Rice vampire book I traded with another traveler in Otavalo. I normally don't read any horror genre, but thought it might be fun reading by candlelight, lying under mosquito netting in the Amazon Basin. Despite encounters with spiders and reading of vampires before bed, I sleep well. But the next morning half our group admits they had nightmares of spiders falling out of the thatched roofing onto them as they slept.

After breakfast we pull out a box with the largest tarantula David caught last night. As we admire the spider in the daylight, Luis talks about animals that can sense when people are afraid of them. Having been a paper carrier when I was young, I know first hand how dogs can sense fear and become even more aggressive if they know you are nervous. Luis believes that some insects and spiders also have this sense. He tells about people who have had fire ants crawl on them without biting them. Only when they got nervous about the ants, and the ants sensed it, did the ants bite.

"If you believe the tarantula won't bite you, you can let it crawl all over your body. It won't bite," says Luis. "But if you get nervous it can sense that, and then it may bite." Luis proceeds to demonstrate as the tarantula crawls over his arms and shoulders. He finishes by putting his hand down on the ground and letting the giant spider crawl down his arm and onto the ground.

I try to get the tarantula to crawl on me but it refuses to take any interest. No matter how I put my hands on the ground in front of it, the tarantula balks and will not get on me. I try to get it to crawl onto my foot. Still no luck. Luis tries to help. He quickly gets the tarantula to crawl up on his hand, and then places his hand on my shirt, encouraging the spider to crawl onto me. It takes just a few steps on my shirt and then leaps off onto the ground. We try again and again with similar results.

"Did you put on any insect repellent this morning?" Luis finally asks. I smeared repellent not only on my arms, but lightly spread it on my clothes as well. Now, when I WANT a tarantula to crawl on me, I am not having any luck.

"Well," Luis consoles me, "at least you know you have good insect repellent."

After much effort, I finally get the tarantula to crawl up my back and across my neck. It is a good exercise for me, and helps lessen my squeamishness around spiders.

We return down the tributary to the Rio Napo and stop mid-morning at the home of an indigenous family. Everyone relaxes in the shade, drinking *chicha*. Luis has told us that the woman who lives here is one of the few women who still does traditional pottery and sculpture, and that we can buy some of her wares. I would not think she gets many customers coming to her home, yet she seems to have little interest in showing us her work or making sales.

Everyone is wearing old tattered clothing. I look around the compound and through my "work ethic" eyes see plenty of jobs that could tidy up the homestead. But the people living here seem oblivious to any need to perform such chores. Instead, everything is *tranquilo*, tranquil, with *no problema aqui*, no problems here. Their plan for today, like most days, is to relax away the hours with small talk and drink.

After a few more rounds of *chicha* and amiable chatting with Luis and the crew, the woman's husband leads us to a large thatched hut on stilts where the pottery is made. Only after we have examined the wares for sale, and sat around a bit, does the woman come over. As a house gift David gives her a

Bruce gets up close and personal with a tarantula, Amazon
Basin, Ecuador.

bottle of very strong locally-made alcohol. Jungle juice. She immediately
cracks it open and takes an impressive swig. She passes the bottle around, encouraging everyone else to take a drink. It tastes like Everclear. I can take only
a small sip.

When everyone has been suitably relaxed, she gives us a pottery demonstration. Traditional pottery can be made only by the women. While she
works, she teaches her craft to a little girl, perhaps her granddaughter, who
climbs into her lap to watch the entire process. The woman occasionally spits
into the clay, which puts a part of her spirit into every piece she makes. She

works the clay into long strands to be coiled into pottery, and gives the little girl a small section of the clay to work as well, keeping her happily occupied. The old woman has a soft, gentle voice whenever she speaks to the girl, sometimes leaning over to whisper in her ear, at other times using hand motions to help direct her. The way they interact is very tender and touching.

After she has coiled the clay into the desired shape, she smooths the work with her hands and small curved scrapers. She uses a brush made from her own hair to paint on various glazes, natural dyes made mostly from minerals in the earth and rocks. Each piece takes about one week to make, including firing and glazing. We buy a few pieces and thank her for showing us how it is made. Again she seems very remote, uninterested in us, and uninterested in whether anyone makes a purchase. Perhaps she is just shy and unsure about how to take this fascination by foreigners with her work.

Out on the river in the late afternoon, Luis realizes we are not going to make it to the next planned camping area before dark. Instead, we will stop at the family home of two of our crew members, Anival and Chiri. Just before dark we land the canoes next to an eroded bank along a swift and tricky section of the river's current. As we unload our gear the crew members jokingly argue over who will get to unload our bikes. David wins and rides first one and then the other bike up the trail through palms and coffee trees to a small clearing with two stilt houses. The bikes are placed in the center of the courtyard, once again a spot of honor. After the remainder of the gear has been unloaded and supper started, the crew members take turns riding our bikes on the trails around the house. Anival and Chiri have not had much experience riding bikes, so rather than trying to pedal and steer at the same time, they take turns pushing each other, so they don't have to concentrate on two things at once.

David and Luis ask us what we are going to do with our bikes when we finish our trip. Our plan all along has been to sell them, as Ecuador charges very high taxes for excess luggage when flying out of the country. Luis and David immediately express interest in buying them and ask about the price. Tass and I have a brief conference. The bikes sell for six-hundred dollars retail in the U.S. In addition we outfitted them with a number of accessories, and we had to pay shipping to fly them to Ecuador. Plus bikes are worth much more in Ecuador because of the high import taxes on foreign products. Even after riding the bikes for two months, we could easily sell them in Quito for six-hundred dollars, probably more. We planned on using the money from the bikes to help pay for our travels in Peru.

But Luis and David gave us a big discount on their guiding fees when they learned we were making an educational slide program for schools. And they also already seem like good friends—we feel awkward charging them full price. We decide we will make a buddy deal, and sell the bikes to them for half price when we are finished riding.

After we eat our supper in the courtyard, we climb up the ladder to the small hut where the family lives. Inside is a cooking fire on a pile of dirt in the corner; in the other corner are three plastic garbage cans full of fermenting *chicha*. The mom scoops out a small bowl of the material, which is the consistency of bread dough, adds a splash of water and kneads the clumps of pulp by squeezing them in her fist and through her fingers. When it is the consistency of buttermilk, she hands me the bowl to take a drink. I take a small sip. It tastes like unsweetened yogurt, not bad at all. But I am a little leery of the cleanliness of the water that has been splashed into the mixture, and also the woman's unwashed hands kneading the uncooked, fermented brew. After one drink I politely pass the bowl along. Later Luis says he was surprised she even offered it to me. He tells us the Indians are leery of rejection. Rather than offer and risk being turned down—which is a real insult—they are usually more reserved and simply choose not to deal directly with foreigners.

Sitting around the fire, we chat with our hosts. Tass starts quite a commotion when she asks the age of the father. He thinks for a while before saying he is forty-eight. This begins a lengthy discussion as Chiri, the youngest son, says he is twenty. The father can not be forty-eight; his other sons are too old! He must be fifty-eight!

The mom chimes in and states that she is forty-two. But Anival thinks his brother, the oldest son who is not here, is thirty-eight! He tells his mother she has to be older. The discussion continues another half an hour. While the family tries to figure out everyone's age, we discuss their total lack of perception of time, of living without using a calendar.

"Time is not something they think about," Luis shrugs. "They have no reason to date things, because dates have no meaning to them."

Obviously they don't celebrate birthdays.

"What do they think about us being here?" we ask. We arrived unannounced and took over their yard and house with all our gear, set up our kitchen, and cooked by their standards an enormous feast.

"They like it that you have come!" Luis replies. "They are very interested in you, in what you do, in what you eat. Much of their lives centers around getting together with their neighbors, drinking *chicha*, and chatting. Your being here tonight gives them something they can talk about for weeks! They now have great stories they can share with all the people they know!"

As we talk we look around the house. There are no appliances, knick-knacks, hardly even kitchen utensils—just a few bowls and pans. A package of salt and another of sugar are the only things in the "pantry." We don't even see any rice. The main food is *chicha*, which is much like the mead drinks from the European Middle Ages—lightly alcoholic with a slight nutritional value but hardly adequate for proper nutrition.

Rosa, a young girl whose family we stayed with on the
banks of the Rio Napo, Ecuador.

The fire hearth looks like the valve cover head off a Volkswagon engine or
some equally unlikely piece of metal, with three pieces of rebar placed across
the top for a grate. A scraggly ratdog lies near the fire. A small pile of clothes
lies heaped in the corner—no drawer or even box to keep them organized.
Outside a few chickens run in the yard around a piece of corrugated tin and a
few scraps of wood. That is it. Tass and I have spent time with extremely poor
people, yet even we are amazed at how little the family has!

Uri, the Israeli, is totally blown away. "They live moment to moment.
They have nothing. We have so much stuff! It makes me question what I really need in life!"

Luis tells us there are many similar families in the area. The boys go to
Misahualli occasionally, the "big city." The girls don't get out much. Schools

are the biggest change in their lives. The last few years primary schools have opened up for many of the kids, but there are still very few secondary schools.

Marriages are still arranged, but now parents ask for their sons' and daughters' input. "Do you want to marry this boy?" If she says yes, parents go on as before and begin all the arranging. The families meet; however, the young couple is usually too embarrassed to say much to each other in front of their relatives. A second meeting of the families takes place, yet there is still a one- or two-year wait before the actual marriage ceremony. The families build the couple a hut, place them inside, give advice and gifts, and close the doors. The families continue the marriage party outside through the night while the newlywed couple stays inside. The average boy gets married between the age of fifteen and twenty; the average girl marries at fourteen or fifteen!

"Life here is much the same as in the past." Luis points to the *chicha* fermenting in the corner. "The *chicha* used to ferment in a hand-made ceramic jar. Now it is in a plastic container. However, most other things are the same." Outside I hear the brakes on our mountain bikes squealing and gales of laughter from Chiri and the other riders out in the dark courtyard. I wonder what kind of changes the next generation will see in the Amazon Basin?

A big storm erupts in the night. I get up at four o'clock and throw a raincoat over our mosquito net to stop the water dripping through the roof thatching on to our bed. At five o'clock the wind and rain increases, blowing rain in horizontally through the side of the hut. I guess it is time to get up. Because of the rain, we eat breakfast in the family's kitchen, where Luis heats up bread in a big skillet over the fire. Jungle toast. The rains continue as we pack up and carry loads through the mud to the canoes. Our whole group chips in money for a gift of thanks to the family. Tass takes it to the father, who repeatedly shakes her hand in gratitude. The mother is close to tears.

We have a cold, wet canoe ride to Coca. We have read when it rains in the Amazon some travelers just wear a swimsuit and pack away all their clothes to keep dry. But here in the upper Amazon the temperature is much too cold. We wear rain pants, our big rubber boots, long sleeve shirts and rain jackets with hoods pulled up snug.

In Coca, Luis stops to get special permits to travel further downriver. From here all foreigners must be accompanied by a guide or have a permit from the military in Quito, or work for an oil company! We unload our bikes and extra gear and carry them to the Hotel Auca for storage until we get back.

As we travel further downriver, scattered rain showers roll in and out all afternoon. At least the rain is warmer, although we still have to wear our coats. We have a relaxing, contemplative day, sitting in the canoe watching the river bank pass by and staring at the water. Even though our canoe is thirty-five feet long and over four feet wide, it sways and tips unsteadily from the various river currents. In many places we pass whirlpools; in other places

the water boils up from currents made by sand bars, stones, or logs buried under the surface.

Although the Rio Napo is over a quarter mile wide in this region, the river
is quite shallow if we leave the main current. David stays ever watchful at the
front of the boat, directing Anival, who stands in back next to the engine piloting our boat. We get a chuckle out of the signals that both David and Luis
use to keep us in deep water. They seldom give a yell or call. Instead, they do
brief, vague arm or hand movements that to us, the uninitiated, seem completely baffling. Yet Anival picks up the cues immediately, and turns first one
way and then the other, or slows dramatically, or lifts the propeller all the way
out of the water just at the last second as we scrape over a submerged log.

When the river is especially low, David uses a pole to dip into the river,
checking the water depth as we slowly cruise through the shallows. We joke

David Chongo, with a jaguar tooth necklace, our rainforest
guide, Amazon Basin, Ecuador.

that if we were in the U.S., the pole would have exact markings to calibrate the depth, and the lookout would call out the precise water levels. But here the lookout says nothing, and it is up to the driver, way at the back of the boat, to tell approximately how deep the pole goes into the river.

Despite the look-out, and the incredible memory that David, Luis, and Anival seem to have of the countless bends and curves of the river, we suddenly find ourselves smack dab in the middle of the huge river, stuck in the sand. Five of us jump out of the canoe into the ankle deep water and begin pushing first one direction and then the next, trying to get back into deeper water. No luck. While Luis, David, and Anival discuss what to do next, Hazen walks down river away from the boat, searching for deep water. He looks so strange, standing 100 yards away from the boat, out in the middle of the enormous river, with the water only to his ankles. He looks as if he is walking on water.

With no deep channels in sight, we push the boat back upstream toward the right hand river bank, which is over a quarter mile away. Pushing the canoe is hard work, but it feels great to get up off the hard wooden boat seat and stand in the cool water getting some exercise.

Late in the afternoon we turn off the Rio Napo and head north, upstream on the Rio Panayacu, a small tributary. The water is much darker, the color of black tea as compared to the creamy milk chocolate of the larger Rio Napo. The smaller river is only about thirty or forty feet wide and very slow moving. It twists and winds through the thick vegetation of flooded forest. The air is full of the cries of birds that flit above us from tree to tree. The evening light has a soft, warm glow, and the water gives crystal clear reflections of the dense foliage hanging over the river's edge. The light is too low for making photographs from the moving boat, so we sit back, relax, and enjoy the stunning scenery. As I lean over the side of the boat a sudden shape breaks the surface of the water ahead of us, then disappears to leave only a ripple of tiny waves spreading out from the center of the river.

"Dolphin!" I yelp excitedly. David, who is now at the motor and who also spotted the dolphin, instantly kills the engine. We drift along quietly, all of us peering expectantly up the river. Nothing. Luis begins looking all around us, so I do the same. The river is almost black from all the decaying vegetation; it is impossible to look into the water and see the dolphin swimming underwater—visibility is less than a foot. Suddenly the dolphin surfaces behind us. This time I can see a light pinkish hue on the dolphin's back when it takes a breath. Living so long in the murky water, pink river dolphins have lost most of their sight and rely on echo location to navigate through the water. Since they can't see, they don't jump into the air like ocean dolphins. Although we sit quietly, waiting, the dolphin does not make another appearance.

We resume traveling upriver and soon come to the entrance of Laguna Panacocha, the small lake with a camp where we will spend the next three nights. The lake is beautiful, calm and clear with wonderful reflections, surrounded by flooded forest. We see another dolphin as we cross the lake; then we turn into a small cove where an observation tower has been built in a one hundred and fifty foot ceibo tree. A path made from four-foot in diameter, wooden cross sections from a tree, laid into the ground like stepping stones, runs from the dock into camp. The path takes us through a small clearing to the lodge and sleeping huts, all surrounded by huge trees and primary forest. The setting is delightful. Each hut is built on stilts with a covered front porch with wooden chairs; inside is a small bedroom and private bath with running water. Mosquito nets cover all the beds, yet there are few mosquitoes, as the nearby rivers are all blackwater and inhospitable to mosquito larva due to the excessive tannin in the plants. To keep things quiet and peaceful, the camp has no generator; we use candles to read, which adds to the cozy charm of the thatched huts. We may have found rainforest paradise!

I set my alarm early to get photos of the sunrise from up in the ceibo tree, but the next morning the sound of heavy rain on the thatching means there will be no views. We stay in bed, drifting in and out of sleep, warm, dry, and cozy under our mosquito net, listening to the relaxing and hypnotic sound of the rain. The soothing rhythm repeatedly lulls us back to sleep.

At seven o'clock we get up for a pre-breakfast walk. I forget to shake out my rubber boot before putting it on and feel a distinct lump under my foot. I quickly pull off the boot and turn it upside down. After three good shakes, a baby tarantula about two inches long falls out, somewhat dazed, to lie momentarily rolled up in defense and terror in the middle of the floor. After a few seconds it uncurls its legs and zips across the floor and out of the hut through a crack in the wall.

After breakfast we load into a canoe to head further up the tributary on a day trip. The rain clears as we take off, but resumes before we have gone more than a mile. Soon it is raining as hard as I've ever seen rain. We are in the pouring rain, surrounded by water. There is no dry land, just flooded forest, dripping trees and leaves; water everywhere. At first we take turns making a few quick photos, while the other holds our umbrella. Within moments water is dripping straight through the fabric of our small portable umbrella. The lens on my camera completely fogs up inside the glass. We panic and scramble to bury our big cameras in layers of plastic bags, but it is impossible to do so without also getting moisture in the bags. So much water is running down the sleeves of our rain coats that even with our backs hunched over under the umbrella we can't dry our hands enough to open a pocket and take out our point and shoot cameras from under our rain coats. We chastise ourselves for not bringing the underwater camera we used in the Galapagos!

The birds have all disappeared. We have no hope of seeing animals or monkeys. The heavy rain pounds on all the leaves and vegetation with an almost deafening roar. The entire forest seems like it is under a waterfall.

As we travel up the Rio Panayacu, the rain begins to slow, and finally stops. Before long the sun comes out, partially, and Tass is able to get her camera back out. Mine remains fogged. We motor along very slowly for another hour and then go on a four-hour hike, half of which is in substantial rain.

Being out in the rainforest with Luis is wonderful. He is the ultimate sensitive guide. He knows interesting and unique facts about so many plants. He is always enthusiastic; digging roots and tubers with his machete for us to sample, encouraging us to taste "lemon" ants, pointing out many things we might otherwise miss. David and Hazen also add a tremendous zest to our expedition. At an enormous tree covered with vines, David and Hazen climb hand over hand in the pouring rain up and down the vines in amazing feats of jungle gymnastics. Like Luis they are sharp-eyed in spotting animals and birds, and simply great fun to be with on a rainforest expedition.

Although we have only an hour or two without rain, by the end of the day we have spotted fifteen new species of birds including hoatzins, banded aracaris, orange-winged parrots, white-breasted toucans, guans and chachalacas. Even more impressive we sight FIVE species of monkeys: saddleback marmosets; white-faced marmosets; wooley monkeys; spider monkeys; and a group of red howler monkeys, including a female with a baby clinging to her back as she jumps from limb to limb. We also see a three-toed sloth.

In the evening we all sit around the tables in the dining hut, studying bird, animal, and insect fieldguides by candlelight. We share with one another interesting items we read, and help each other identify what we saw during the day.

After supper Uri, Hazen, and I go on a night hike. They look for bait for fishing tomorrow while I make photographs of insects and lizards. The coating on the lenses of my glasses which began degenerating in Baeza is now completely ruined. My glasses are completely unusable, so I wear my prescription sunglasses even on the night hike, which strains my eyes and gives me a light headache. As we hike, I feel isolated and cut off from everything around me.

After the hike Hazen and I stay up late talking about the rainforest. I am amazed that he grew up in a northern, mountainous climate. He has spent only one year in the rainforest, yet it seems like he has lived here his entire life. Around him I feel like a real novice. I am almost paranoid about mosquitoes and sandflies—one or two bites and I instantly cover myself in repellent. I wear a big raincoat whenever it rains, and lug around a fanny pack and daypack full of camera gear that all must be double- and even triple-bagged in plastic. My equipment forces me to behave as though I am afraid of water.

Hazen seldom wears a shirt, much less a rain coat. Nothing seems to faze him. All he carries is a machete to dig through rotten logs in search of spiders and snakes. He is incredibly mobile, always climbing up and down tree roots and vines, exploring every nook and cranny. He seems totally at one with the rainforest environment.

Hazen tells me he first came to Ecuador at the encouragement of a friend who also studied insects. Although his friend enjoyed his work and what he was doing, Hazen said he was never totally comfortable in the rainforest, despite two years of studying here. One night they both drank *haiawasca*, a powerful drug distilled from a rainforest vine, in a traditional ceremony with a shaman. The shaman warned them to stay in the hut and not go out into the rainforest during their trance. During the ordeal Hazen felt his spirit bond with the rainforest. But his friend had the opposite reaction; he ran into the forest in terror, and was not found until the next morning. The experience totally changed his friend's personality, and he was unable to continue his work. His friend returned home to the U.S., but it did not help.

"He has never been the same," Hazen solemnly shakes his head. "I believe he lost his soul that night in the rainforest. I don't think he will ever recover unless he returns to the rainforest to get it back. There are very powerful energies here. It is not something to take lightly."

The next morning we paddle in small dugout canoes to fish. I catch a red-bellied piranha almost immediately; it is one of the most dangerous piranhas—a meat eater that hunts in packs. Red-bellied piranhas are only moderately good to eat, not much meat and too many bones. But I keep it anyway, as much for the novelty as anything else. The teeth are amazingly sharp and pointed. After cleaning it, I cut off the head; Tass keeps the lower jaw to take home and put on our mantel.

In the afternoon Tass and I paddle by ourselves in the little dug-out canoe through the flooded forest. In the dry season Laguna Panacocha is a distinct lake. But now in the rainy season it is surrounded by an even larger body of water, as much as thirty feet deep. Only the tops of small hills remain above the high water level. In the flooded forest, the smaller trees are completely submerged in the water; medium-sized trees have just their tops protruding above the water's surface. Larger trees stick out of the water, their lower branches spread out under water or just at the surface. Paddling through the flooded forest in a dugout canoe is both magical and extremely odd. We paddle right into the center of trees, pulling the branches apart to make a pathway for the canoe, ducking under some branches, rocking our canoe over others that are just below the surface. The bromiliades and epiphytes that cover many of the upper branches are right at eye level.

The birding is excellent as we quietly float through the branches of the trees! We drift through numerous trees full of raucous, two-foot long hoatzins.

A red-bellied piranha which we caught and ate, Amazon Basin, Ecuador.

They are incredibly ungainly and always look like they are losing their balance on their perch. They bluster and flap their wings as they teeter on the smaller branches at the end of the tree limbs. The hoatzin is considered the most prehistoric of all birds, and is the only bird to have a claw on the 'elbow' joint of its wing. The hoatzin builds its nest over water; if threatened, the baby hoatzin will jump into the water. When the danger passes the baby hoatzin uses the wing claw to help it climb back up the tree into the nest.

Small plants that don't even need soil to grow float on the water's surface. I scoop up handfuls of the tiny plants, floating along by themselves. They each have small tentacles hanging down into the water like roots, catching nutrients. In places where there is little current, the plants tangle together to form a thick coating across the water, sometimes creating floating islands, where larger plants can take hold and grow.

As we paddle, the gray rain clouds break apart and we are treated to a wonderful display of reflections on the water. In some areas it is hard to see where the trees and foliage end and the reflections begin. Everything blends together in a intricate pattern of lush growth.

The only thing to disturb our wonderment is the leaking of our dugout canoe. Every five minutes I have to bail water, and still we sit in two inches of water most of the afternoon. Finally we spot a small island to take a break from sitting in the water of the canoe. On shore we find a huge nest of leaf cutter ants. Only darkness and the thought of getting lost in the maze of growth and channels makes us turn back toward camp.

The next morning the water level is three feet higher than the previous day, an astounding increase considering the enormous volume of water covering this area. Even though there have been no heavy rains in the area by Amazon standards, Laguna Panacocha and the Rio Panayacu have risen due to a rise in the Rio Napo, into which they flow. The radio reports the Rio Napo is flooding because of torrential rains in the eastern Andes. The high water of the Rio Napo is not allowing the water from our area to drain out at a normal flow. Even though the Rio Napo is almost an hour downriver by motorized canoe, the Rio Panayacu is so flat that the rise in the Rio Napo has caused a back log of water all the way upriver to our lake!

We pack up and leave in the pouring rain. As we travel down the Rio Panayacu, the water level everywhere is much higher than when we came in. Long before we reach the Rio Napo, we are amazed to see the black water of the Rio Panayacu turn chocolate brown from the backwater off the Napo. The overflowing Rio Napo is forcing the lower section of the Rio Panayacu to run backwards!

When we enter the Rio Napo we are confronted by a vast sea of destruction. Logs, branches, and debris float in enormous, tangled piles throughout the river. The mist, fog, and drizzling rain all add to an other-worldly feeling of desolation and ruin; as if the end of the earth has come in a wall of muddy water. Enormous trees float past, others lie momentarily stuck in the mud and sand, their branches reaching out to embrace the river, or to catch other debris and logs or even unwary canoes in their grasp. We are forced onto smaller though equally swollen branches of the Rio Napo to avoid large rapids and standing waves in the main channel.

Our big canoes are only moderately stable, and could sink if tipped. None of our gear has been tied in, and only a few life jackets are on board. An accident would be a major disaster! On a side channel we pass a bridge whose pilings have caught so many trees and branches I am amazed the bridge has not buckled under the strain—the web of logs and debris has spread out from each piling to block nearly half the swollen river. There must be tons of pressure from the rushing water pushing against the mountain of logs on the bridge. Only one small area is open for our canoes to pass through.

Moments after we pass under the bridge, the propeller on the canoe full of gear and luggage jams from debris in the water. Anival has to lift the motor out of the water to clean out the prop. The canoe immediately loses all its forward momentum and begins to drift backward, picking up speed toward the log jam. Anival continues to struggle to free the prop. Luis calls out in concern and David stops the motor on our boat, but there is little we can do but watch Anival frantically clear the prop. It is amazing how quickly the canoe is swept by the current toward the tangled pile of logs. At the last second Anival drops the motor back into place. He jerks on the starting rope of the engine. Nothing happens. He pulls the rope again. The motor roars back to life. For a few seconds the canoe simply stays in one place, just ahead of the crush of water and logs under the bridge, and then the engine builds momentum and the canoe heads back upstream.

As we get closer to Coca we see many homesteads and farms along the river with field after field of destroyed crops. Luckily most of the homes are built on stilts and have not been swept away. But the crops of corn, yucca, bananas and coffee now lie ruined under water. Luis says the water in this area has been this high only twice in the last fifty years.

After seven hours we arrive back in Coca, cold and soaked. Since there are no daytime buses—it is usually too hot for long distance travel during the day—most of our group is catching the evening bus back to Quito. As is often the case, after such an intense experience with a group of people, the ending seems both abrupt and sad.

Later in the evening after a shower and supper, I find Luis in a little tavern. He has just made a series of phone calls to his office in Quito. He and the crew have to leave tomorrow and travel further up the raging river, resupply in only one day, and then meet a group from Denmark to take into the rainforest. Being a guide is exhausting work. We drink a few beers, and Luis is finally able to relax, briefly. We reminisce about our trip, and Luis talks about the life of a jungle guide. He speaks with deep emotion about the rainforest— what he has spent his life learning about, and sharing with others.

"I want people to know there is a very special place in Ecuador!" he tells me reverently, speaking of the *oriente*. "If they know about it perhaps they can help save it!" On his T-shirt is written Luis's deepest belief, his life's cause. I hope, for all of us, that the words are true: "It is not too late to save the Amazon Rainforest!"

20

The Price of Oil

Our first morning in Coca is spent doing laundry, reading, and napping. In the afternoon I sit on the porch of our hotel room writing in my journal. In the courtyard I hear kids having fun playing and screaming. Tass comes in and tells me the noise is not kids, but parrots in the trees! I have to look for myself to believe it. The parrots have obviously heard kids playing in the courtyard and are now mimicking the laughter and sounds of kids on the swings.

We try to call Christine, our travel agent in Quito, who told us to constantly reconfirm our flights to Peru next month or they might get cancelled. But the phone company building is closed. A sign says all the phone lines are down in the *oriente* due to the storm, despite a second sign which claims the phones are all hooked up via satellite. Go figure.

Coca is an oil boom town. The streets are dirt—filled with mud in the rainy season and choked with dust in the dry season. Pools and streams of waste water overflow from the roadside ditches; wooden planks laid in the mud provide tenuous walkways to ramshackle shops lining the streets. Exorbitant prices are the norm, as everyone tries to stake a claim and cash in on the oil boom economy. The people have an energetic, almost intoxicated attitude.

In my late teens and early twenties, I often worked three-to-five-month stints in the oil fields of eastern Wyoming to raise quick cash for adventures. I have been a roustabout, roughneck, truck driver, and oil rig deck hand. I remember those times of work as hard but exciting—making big money to fulfill dreams and launch myself into other projects. I financed a five-month trip to Africa, two winters in Central America, and a year ski-bumming in Jackson Hole by working in the oil and coal fields.

During those intense work sprees, I made numerous friends. My co-workers were often rugged characters, rough and rowdy, but likeable. Like me, all had dreams of making money, then returning to their homes or moving on somewhere else, anything but staying and working in the oil fields. By my third or fourth time working in the area, it was sad to see so many of my co-workers still there, years later, working at jobs they constantly complained about, living in an area they didn't like. Despite the big paychecks, most seemed unable to save money. Every Friday was payday, but by the following Thursday most were broke, caught in a vicious cycle of work and spend, always bewildered where the money went. Even though it was financially successful for me, I stopped going back. Despite the money, the oilfields lost their adventurous appeal.

By our second day in Coca, I am filled with the same feelings I had when I stopped working in the Wyoming oil fields. I feel a sadness in Coca; the frailty and tenuousness of people's lives is overwhelming. That such a bleak and depressing town could be viewed as the Promised Land by so many people shows what humans are willing to overlook in the quest for economic livelihood, and to what end companies will go in the search for oil. Yet it is not just the people of Ecuador that have created the town. Coca is booming because of the lifestyles of people in the U.S., and other prosperous countries, who are responsible for the bulk of the world's need for oil.

We made the decision to cycle through the *oriente* oil fields because we want to see everything that is happening in the rainforest—the beauty as well as the destruction. Like it or not, there are many boom towns like Coca, not just in the Amazon, but in rainforests everywhere, and also in mountains, deserts, and even the Wyoming prairie. It is the price of oil.

Our plan is to ride to Lago Agrio near the Columbian border. As usual, we are not going the most direct route, but doing a loop to the northeast first. Since we have heard only horror stories about this area, we are on alert as we ride out of town. But most drivers simply honk and wave and give us plenty of room. They seem to get a kick out of the two *loco gringos*, crazy foreigners, on bikes. Tass continues to create shock and amazement when the truck drivers pass and realize she is a woman.

The soft tar on the road and the oil sprayed on the gravel sections have strong, nauseating petroleum fumes. By noon the tar on the road begins to melt from the heat. Our tires make loud sucking noises from the sticky goo. When we look behind us we can see the tracks of our tire treads imprinted in the road. We stop for a break and our kickstands sink into the tar so quickly it is impossible to let go of the bikes without them tipping over. Even our shoes leave footprints in the tar, as we dig snacks out of our panniers.

By afternoon we are delirious from the heat. It hasn't rained in two days: no storms to cool down the temperature. At least the sky is mostly cloudy—when the sun pops out we broil. Despite constantly slathering on sun block, our skin is frying. We feel like we are in the early stages of heat exhaustion.

Tracks from our bicycle tires imprinted in the melting tar
of an Amazon Basin road, Ecuador.

When we plotted our route, we knew we would be on roads built by oil companies, as those are the only roads in this part of the Amazon. Because the roads were built mostly during the oil boom of the 1970's, only twenty years ago, we thought many of the back roads would be swaths cut through primary rainforest. But the rainforest along the roads disappeared long ago. Already all the land has been cleared, often completely deforested, to make room for colonists—cattle ranches, coffee plantations, and little homestead shacks dot the countryside.

All the roads have oil pipelines beside them. We stop at a few oil drilling rigs beside the road. The workers are very friendly and we take pictures of them standing next to the bikes. We are surrounded by large petroleum storage tanks, processing plants and pumping stations. It amazes me that all of these towns, all of these roads, all of the homesteading has occurred because of the oil boom.

Yet everywhere we see signs proclaiming *Esta finca se vende,* "This farm for sale." After the rainforest has been cleared, most farmers find the underlying soil is actually very poor for growing crops or grazing cattle. Many homesteaders want to sell out to unsuspecting buyers, and move on. Equally sad is the pollution from the oil and mining companies. A 1989 report by the government states that in Ecuador alone oil companies **daily** discharge 4.3 mil-

Oil pipelines line the roads built by oil companies into the Amazon Basin, Ecuador.

lion gallons of untreated toxic waste into pits, almost all of which quickly leaches into the ground water and rivers. And this same scenario is occurring in other countries throughout the Amazon Basin.

Our map shows that nine miles before the town of Shushufindi we should cross the equator. When we get to what we believe is the spot, there is no sign. We stop along a stretch of road and take a few self portraits, thinking we are on, or at least very near, the equator.

By the time we ride into Shushufindi, we are baked with sweat, dust, oil and dirt. Like Coca, Shushufindi is a bustling oil boom town. Huge, mufflerless diesel trucks rumble the dusty streets, belching clouds of smelly, black smoke. Piles of refuse and litter lie strewn about, blowing in the hot wind. All the local buses are flatbed trucks with no sides, simply a series of benches in rows one behind the other like church pews, a flat roof for shade with a luggage rack and room for extra passengers on top. Even when the buses are not full, many people ride on top where it is cooler with the breeze, and a little less dusty. The sides of the bench seats offer the only bit of color in the town; all are painted with picturesque motifs of tropical islands, birds, and lush foliage.

The first hotel we stop at has cell-like rooms with no windows and nasty-looking beds. Guaranteed fleas. I go back outside where Tass waits with the bikes; she says a number of people walking past have told her we should stay elsewhere. No kidding. We are directed out of town to a second hotel, which is cleaner but somewhat pricey. When we tell the owner we are going to look around for another, cheaper hotel she is stunned. She shakes her finger at us and says all the other hotels in town are very dangerous.

Still we head back into town and find a hotel on main street owned by a great family. We get a clean room—with a shower. Tass takes the first shower and comes out a new woman. "That was the most wonderful shower of my entire life!" she announces, flopping in exhaustion on the bed. As I shower, Tass digs out our other two maps of Ecuador and finds that on both of them Shushufindi is located south, not north, of the equator. We didn't cross the equator after all, but we should tomorrow.

The next day we continue north. At first there is moderate traffic, oil field trucks full of drillers and roughnecks, but no buses. There are no more towns at the end of the road we are now on, only pipelines and oil rigs, pipelines and pumping stations, pipelines and oil tanks, and more pipelines. The road ahead dead-ends at the Rio Auguarico. There is no bridge or ferry for vehicles, only a motorized wooden canoe that we have heard is sometimes available to take passengers and, we hope, bicycles across.

Since there are no towns ahead, we thought the traffic would diminish as we ride northward, but surprisingly it increases. Dump truck after dump truck roars past on the gravel road. Obviously some oil company is building yet another road further north. Four days have now passed since the last rain and the intense tropical sun has baked the gravel road bone dry. Each truck stirs up enormous clouds of dust that cover us in a thick silt.

We start the day rather lethargic, and only get more and more tired as the sun beats down on us and the trucks roar past. Even when we pass small areas with uncut forest, we seldom stop to pull out the binoculars to look for birds or animals. The rainforest as seen from an oil pipeline road is hardly inspiring. Perhaps the harsh, blaring light from the sun is also to blame; the bright light reduces everything to simple black and white silhouettes when we look up. Even though we are exhausted, the weather is too hot and muggy to stop for long. Only the slight breeze from riding gives us any reprieve from the heat.

My arms ache, my back aches, my neck aches. My butt is sore and raw from chafing against the seat. We are dirty, sweaty and grimy, engulfed in suffocating clouds of dust.

At the Rio Auguarico we find two young men who will take us across the large river in their canoe. They ask if we carry guns for protection. We reply no. They shake their heads and tell us many bad people are in this area. The countryside is extremely dangerous. Very reassuring.

We ride only a few miles before we are convinced, according to two of our maps, that we must be crossing the equator. Again we hope for a sign, something to mark the spot for a photo, but there is nothing. Obviously the

Although no signs give the exact location, we think we are on the equator,
Amazon Basin, Ecuador.

exact location of the equator is not a major concern for the people living here.
Still we are sure that somewhere very close is that romantic and almost mystical line. Regardless of not knowing exactly where it is, we are inspired to be
crossing the equator in the Amazon Basin—on bicycles!!

The oil field traffic lessens north of the Rio Aguarico. Suddenly we realize all the truck traffic on the previous road actually made us feel safe. Now
we go long stretches without seeing any vehicles. We feel isolated and vulnerable. The few people who drive past squint and look oddly at us. They seldom wave or smile. We don't like the vibes in this area.

We eat lunch at the little town of Dureno. We are starting to get tired of
scrambled eggs and rice two or three times a day. We realize that leaving our
stove behind to save weight was a major mistake. This is a terrible country for
vegetarians or anyone who wants good food. Except for the Chinese restaurants, which thankfully are found in all the larger towns, no one cooks with
any vegetables, and there is surprisingly little fruit for sale in the markets. No
wonder there are no Ecuadorean restaurants in the U.S.; there is no
Ecuadorean cuisine! The only typical dish is *cuy*, roasted guinea pig—which
looks like a little broiled wiener dog on a stick—hardly a meal destined to become a rage outside Ecuador.

After lunch we sit, delirious, unable to move due to heat and exhaustion. We guzzle down numerous *agua minerales*, soda waters and juices, and slump with our backs to the wall, dozing in a stupor of haze and humidity. When we finally force ourselves back up and out into the broiling sunshine, it is easy to make the decision to take a side trip, away from the oil and development.

21

Cofans

We have heard there is a Cofan Indian village nearby, and that it is possible for foreigners to sometimes stay with families in the village. The village is not on our maps, and our directions are rather vague. The first difficulty is to find the turnoff from the main gravel road to Lago Agrio.

When we reach the prescribed number of kilometers along the road, there is no intersection. We ride further and still no road. Finally we stop at a homestead to ask directions, and are told the "road" to Cofan Dureno is a few kilometers back the way we have come. We ride back and this time, about where the road should be, we spot a small footpath going into the forest. We ride down the path. The trail is great singletrack riding in the shade of overhanging trees. Unfortunately it doesn't last long, and we come out on the bank of the Rio Aguarico. The second difficulty.

One of our guidebooks says travelers can sometimes get canoe rides across the river; if you stand on the river bank yelling and whistling, someone will usually come and get you after a few hours. We take one look at the river and question the advice. The river seems much too wide for anyone to hear us on the other side. Still I shout and call across the river, just in case. After five minutes, I abandon the idea and sit down next to Tass to wait.

Half an hour later a short woman wearing a red T-shirt, skirt, and no shoes appears out of the forest beside us. She tells us in Spanish that she is a Cofan and is also trying to get a canoe ride across the river. When I ask if she has been waiting long she replies "*algun tiempo,*" which translates as awhile, but probably means a real long time, as all the people here have the patience of Job when waiting for a bus or boat. I yell out again, which causes her to smile with enthusiasm. She seems very impressed with the loudness of my voice. We sit by the bank of the river, scanning the opposite shore. Every few minutes I give out a loud yell. After a time the woman disappears. Another hour, still no canoe.

We hear the far-off squeak of bus brakes on the main road. A few minutes later a young boy shows up, dressed in a bright red shirt, nice jeans, and tennis shoes. Klaus introduces himself with a smile, and asks in Spanish if we want to visit the Cofan village. We say yes. He asks if we would like to stay in his house.

Klaus disappears and a few minutes later reappears paddling a tiny dugout canoe he obviously had hidden somewhere nearby. He has changed from his town clothes, which he has wrapped in a plastic bag, and is now wearing shorts and no shoes.

Tass and I look at the canoe and then at one another, and back again at the canoe. It is questionable whether it is big enough to take one of us across the river, not to mention the bikes and luggage. Klaus tells us he will take the luggage of one bicycle at a time, and will ferry it to a rocky island, which we will portage with the bikes and gear. We laugh when he informs us that what we thought was the far bank of the river, is only an island. Yelling across the river for a canoe ride was someone's idea of a joke. No wonder the Cofan woman smiled at me when I yelled out, not because I have a loud voice, but because she probably thought I was nuts.

Klaus takes off with Tass's luggage, poling and then paddling his way to the island. Tass goes next, with her bicycle, one side of the handlebars hanging over the canoe into the water while she huddles, as small as possible, in the front of the boat. Her every movement causes a major wobble in the tippy craft.

My turn. Like Tass, first all my luggage goes across without me. As I watch Klaus paddle the little canoe, I remember that all the film we have shot since leaving Quito is in one of my rear panniers. I envision him tipping and the pannier sinking into the river with a month of irreplaceable photos. But Klaus makes it to the island, where Tass helps him unload the gear. He returns for me. By the time we load the King into the tiny canoe there is hardly any room for me. I squat in the remaining space, trying to sit as low as possible and keep my center of gravity on the bottom of the boat with my handlebar camera bag cradled in my lap. The gunwale is riding extremely low in the water, only a few inches above the surface. With each tip of the boat water splashes in and soaks my butt, which is resting on a couple of sticks placed in the bottom of the boat. One end of the King's handlebars drags deep in the water and so does the saddle whenever the boat tips slightly.

The island is a huge rockpile, built up from the ever-changing course of the immense river, much too rough to ride, and exhausting to walk. The sun is out full force, reflecting off the white rocks. There is no shade. We bake as we carry our bicycles and gear across. On the other side Klaus appears in the boat. He points to a canoe on the far shore coming toward us and tells us it is much bigger. Reinforcements are on the way!

Klaus's father, Rovang, is paddling the large, dugout canoe. How he knew to come out and get us is anyone's guess. Like Klaus, he has an en-

Klaus, a young Cofan Indian, takes Bruce and his bike across the
Aguarico in a dugout canoe, Amazon Basin, Ecuador.

dearing smile and warmth. He is an easy man to trust. We load Tass with her
bicycle and gear into the canoe and she is off. I stand on the bank watching
Rovang paddle out into the current. The canoe is quickly swept away downstream. Rovang keeps a steady rhythm paddling across; once they are through
the area of fast current, he turns the boat upstream and paddles back even
with us on the far shore, five hundred yards away.

The Rovang returns to ferry me across to the shore, which is yet another island! We carry everything across the second island to the last narrow channel—with the strongest current yet. This time Rovang takes our luggage, while
Klaus ferries each of us separately with the bikes.

On the final shore the entire family turns out to carry our luggage. A troop
of children, all younger than Klaus, each grab a pannier and carry it, slung
over their shoulders or balanced on their heads, heading down a jungle path.
We race to get our bikes out of Klaus's canoe and up the steep river bank so
we can keep up with all our gear disappearing down the trail. Klaus asks if he
can ride Tass's smaller bike. We wonder if he knows how. We show him how
the gears work, and he quickly jumps on and takes off without a problem.

The village is spread out over a large, cleared area, with each house having plenty of space from its neighbors. Rovang's family lives in a typical Co-
fan-style hut. The house has a thatched roof and is built on stilts high enough
to keep everyone above the low-flying sandflies. The floor and walls are

made from the outer sheath of a palm tree, peeled and pounded out flat into one- or two-foot wide sections. A log with notched steps is propped from the ground up to the door and serves as a ladder/gang plank to enter the house.

Inside, three rooms are divided by walls made from palm matting: a communal area/living room that will also serve as our bedroom; a kitchen that is also the sleeping area for the mother and father; and another living room-kitchen-bedroom for one of the sons and his wife.

The family has obviously had foreign visitors in the past. No one crowds around to stare at our every move. Instead they go about their own business, which is wonderful for us, as it gives us a more realistic idea of what their lives might be like.

In the evening guests come over to visit, so we pull out postcards and photos from home. On our world bicycle trip we took postcards from South Dakota, including a photograph of Mount Rushmore with Ben Black Elk standing below, wearing traditional Lakota clothing and beadwork, and an eagle feather headdress. When we showed it to indigenous people, they never noticed or asked about the giant rock carving of the Presidents. Instead their eyes always went straight to Ben Black Elk standing below. So on this trip we brought close-ups of traditionally dressed Sioux Indians. Now everyone asks numerous questions about the beadwork and especially about the feathered headdresses.

"Ooooohhh," Rovang says approvingly as we show him each photograph. The Cofans are also famous for the feather "crowns" they wear, made of brightly colored macaw and parrot feathers.

"Aaaahhh," Rovang intones in fascination as Tass explains that the Sioux use eagle feathers, and describes eagles and how high they can fly.

The photos of our families also cause much discussion. Rovang is impressed by my dad's gray hair and asks his age. Everyone is amazed to learn my dad is seventy-three. Unlike the family we stayed with on the Rio Napo, Rovang knows his exact age and the date he was born. He is forty-four, and his wife is thirty-nine. She is younger than we are and, incredibly, has nine children!

That night Rovang recommends we set up our tent in their living room. We hardly need any encouraging. The air is filled with mosquitoes, and since nightfall we keep seeing giant jungle cockroaches scurrying through the holes in the palm walls and floors. A bug-proof sleeping area sounds appealing. The family goes to bed a little before ten o'clock. I lay in our tent and write in my journal for an hour. Only after I turn off my headlamp and lie down to sleep do I hear Klaus come in; he has finally worn himself out riding Tass's mountain bike up and down all the trails through the village.

We may be out in the rainforest, but the village is not quiet at night: barking dogs, crying kids, and roosters so eager for dawn they begin crowing hours before sunrise. In addition, every time anyone gets up in the night to go outside to the bathroom, their footsteps shake the entire floor of the house.

The next morning we relax and hang around the house reading, writing, and contemplating life in the village. Although the house is built on stilts to get above the sandflies, and we have been slathering ourselves with repellent, we are acquiring an alarming collection of no-see-um bites, especially on our feet and ankles. Suddenly, something much larger bites my foot, sending a sharp pain up my leg. I give out a yelp, and tell Tass I just got a nasty sting.

"Great!" she replies ecstatically. Ms. First Aid jumps up and immediately digs for our medical kit. "Now we can try out our snake and bug bite extractor!" For the last two months Tass has periodically pulled the extractor out of our first aid kit, wishing she could use it! The extractor looks like a giant yellow syringe, complete with special adapters for hard-to-reach bites between the fingers and toes. Tass puts the extractor on my foot and enthusiastically pushes the plunger. The suction immediately pulls up an impressive welt of skin into the tube, and blood oozes out of the bite.

"Cool!" Tass is quite entertained. Maybe it is just her enthusiasm, but I feel an instant relief from the bite.

Between hikes to explore the village, we sit in the house and watch family members work on handicrafts. Rovang is making a wooden comb, methodically whittling out each of the teeth, one by one, from a piece of bamboo. He carefully shaves each individual tooth down smooth to the perfect size, until, after half a day's work, he has twenty teeth, enough to weave together to make the comb.

The mother makes necklaces and bracelets from seeds, feathers, and even the iridescent shells of a bright green beetle. The oldest son carves out traditional knives from wood while the daughter-in-law strings together bracelets. Each is fascinating to watch.

Klaus continues to ride Tass's bike most of the day, while his older friends ride mine. Each time a different friend wants to ride my bike, Klaus politely comes and checks to make sure it is okay. Meanwhile the younger kids in the family occupy themselves playing with sardine cans, the razor sharp lids half pried off and hanging bent in the air. The kids put sticks in the cans and push them around like cars. The adults are unconcerned by the sharp metal on the toys. Tass wryly notes at home she doesn't merely throw the sharp lids away but carefully puts them back into the can before tucking the whole thing in the garbage.

One of the little boys is about eight years old and slightly chubby, by Amazon standards. Everyone in the family calls him Gordito, "little fatty," a loving nickname. We get a kick out of their interactions. Everything is relaxed and casual.

Rovang carves out each individual tooth to make a traditional comb,
Amazon Basin, Ecuador.

As we are sitting out on the porch watching the kids play, an older man walks past with a foot-long, bright red macaw feather pierced through his nose and sticking out to one side. Tass, never one to mince words, runs inside to ask Rovang, "Who is the guy with the feather in his nose?" He is Rovang's father, one of the village elders. Tass rushes out of the house to talk with him and within minutes has him posing for pictures. She notes he has a tiny flag of Canada pinned to his hat, a gift from a traveler through the village a year ago. Tass digs through our gear and finds a pin from South Dakota, which he happily hooks on his hat.

Throughout the day we discuss things we observe about the family, and note that they also spend considerable time discussing us. Although they speak to one another in the Cofan dialect, they occasionally use various Spanish words that give hints about what they are discussing. We are always referred to as the "*bicycletas*", or "*gringos,*" and we often hear the names of towns on our itinerary listed during their conversations with neighbors. We laugh and imagine what they must be saying.

"Can you believe it, they take pictures of everything!"

"They sleep in their tent in the middle of our living room!"

Tass watches as the mother dyes some cloth. One of the plants she uses for a dye looks like sliced carrots. Curious, Tass asks if it is a carrot. The whole family erupts in laughter.

"The gringa doesn't know carrots!"

Sitting in the house, watching the family make handicrafts, it would be easy to think that life for the villagers is tranquil and easy. Like many indigenous people, the Cofan are trying to balance a lifestyle between two very different worlds. They are being courted by oil and timber companies who want to buy their land. Others want to plant large coffee and banana plantations on Cofan land. Before the arrival of the Spanish, there were tens of thousands of Cofan Indians. Today there are only five Cofan villages in all of Ecuador, and less than six hundred Cofan Indians. The village we are in recently split, with one group of families moving downriver, away from the encroachment by oil companies, loggers and homesteaders. The group that left wants to be more isolated, to preserve the unique Cofan lifestyle and to live in a completely traditional manner.

When Rovang talks of his people, he says the word Cofan with a reverence. He believes the Cofan are special and have value because they are unique; he wants others to respect and appreciate his people. He does not want the Cofani spirit to be lost. Yet the pull of the outside world is strong. Rovang is interested in the larger world; that is why he opens his home to foreigners. He also wants the income house guests will bring. He dreams of buying a new gun, a thirty-foot canoe with a motor, and a motorcycle to get to town.

We would be arrogant to judge the choices the villagers must make as "right" or "wrong." It is their lives, their culture, their choices. We can only hope they are allowed to make the decisions on their own terms, without pressure.

We leave the village, this time in a larger, motorized canoe. The rain pours down on us as we ferry back across the river, but the sun comes out as we once again mount our bikes.

22

A Return to Oil Madness

The gravel road to Lago Agrio has no shade. The humidity is suffocating. We battle heat exhaustion on every climb, as we bike over the hilly countryside. On the downhills we get a minor reprieve; the hot wind is preferable to no wind at all, and the rush of air offers a momentary relief from the oppressive, oven-like temperature.

Everyone we see on the road stares suspiciously at us. We have been warned about smugglers, drug runners, and bandits, but why is everyone else so dour, sour, and grumpy? Even when I call out an enthusiastic *"Buenos dias,"* Good day, to people along the road, I get only reluctant and forced greetings in return, or just icy silence and blank stares.

Hardly surprising, the dogs along the road are uniformly vicious. Tass has had it with evil dogs, and loudly yells "Shut Up!" as they chase our bikes, snapping, barking, and growling. I joke that she should at least yell at the dogs in Spanish so they know what she is saying, but she only glowers at me. We carry rocks, which we hurl at the worst offenders to keep from being bitten.

The road is dirty and dusty, and we are covered by sweat and road grime. Our ankles are swollen from the heat and insect bites and itch terribly. We are having some fun now. Tass expresses alarm that she has sacrificed many things to save the money to come here, to do this. What in the world were we thinking when we planned this route? Right now both of us would sell our bikes very cheaply.

On the outskirt of Lago Agrio is a vast industrial park with fields of huge petroleum tanks, oil pipelines, and fenced yards full of oil derricks, drilling equipment, and rusting scrap metal. It is hard to imagine that at one time this was all lush rainforest. Through how much more of this do we want to bicycle?

As we enter town we are surprised to find paved streets and sidewalks, and no graffitti-covered oil pipeline running through the middle of town. The pipelines go around the town—at least someone had a little civic pride when they laid out the town.

We are dirt- and grime-encrusted, but we are more hungry than dirty, so showers must wait until after we eat. We ride past a few uninteresting restaurants and pick a sidewalk cafe that looks like it should be on a beach: brightly colored aqua umbrellas shade bamboo tables and chairs with floral prints. We do a quick clean-up in the bathroom, collapse into luxurious comfort in the padded chairs, and order mass quantities of food and drink. We've been living the last few days on rice, canned tuna, and Powerbars. We eat all the food in front of us and then order more.

Don't even think of trying to steal this toilet,
Lago Agrio, Ecuador.

After a few hours of eating and lounging, we leave the shade of the umbrellas in search of a place to stay. The hotels in our price range all have dark, moldy-smelling rooms with poor ventilation. Real heat boxes. We visit seven hotels, all equally grim. Finally, in desperation, we book into the Hotel Willigran. We simply can not handle any more searching. Still, as we struggle to get the bikes up the stairs and into the room, we begin to second-guess ourselves. But once the bikes are upstairs, we talk ourselves back into taking the room—where else can we go?

As we unpack we realize the wooden floor in our room has been recently oiled. Actually, over oiled. The room is so dark, we still don't realize how bad it is until we take off our shoes to walk to the shower, and can feel the oil covering the bottoms of our feet. We immediately check our luggage. The oil has already soaked up into the bottoms of the panniers we set on the floor.

We complain to the manager, who is unsympathetic. Why would oil all over the floor be any problem? Naturally, no other rooms are available. We shuffle all our luggage onto plastic bags and wear our sandals to go to the bathroom. The smell of the varnish fumes slowly builds in the listless air. We seem to be inundated with oil: surrounded by oil drilling, oil pipelines, oil sprayed onto the gravel roads, now even an oily, smelly room! People here take their petrochemicals seriously.

Although our room has screens on three sides, they all face into hallways with minimal airflow. If we put down the curtains, it is suffocating. With the curtains up, we feel like we are in a fish bowl. After a few hours the smell of oil is overpowered by the growing smell of sewer gas from our bathroom. The toilet doesn't have a seat. Because of leaking water, much of the bathroom floor is covered with a puddle of water. Yet there is little water pressure when we take quick late night showers to cool ourselves down. We hold our breath from the smell, and keep our sandals on, leaving little oily footprints with each step across the bathroom puddles.

Could things get any worse, we wonder?

The twin beds are worse. Broken, swaying, and smelly, the beds conjure undesirable images of thousands of people who have used them in the past. The sheets on beds throughout Ecuador don't fit; they are always too small, so after even the slightest tossing and turning, of which we do plenty, the bottom sheets come loose. We awake in the night, hot and sweaty, sheets in a pile on one side of the bed, and find ourselves lying on the awful stained mattresses. We don't even want to think about what might be living in each mattress.

The room is relatively quiet, until eleven p.m., when the hotel manager strikes up a loud discussion with a friend. Even with our earplugs we hear their voices reverberate up and down the hallways until after one a.m. In the dark I can hear Tass tossing and turning in her squeaky bed, frantically scratching at all her insect bites. It is easy to lose control and sink into a frenzy of scratching during the long, sleepless hours of the tropical night. And scratching never stops the itching, but only makes it worse.

At three a.m. a bus prepares to leave on the street out front. The barker announcing the bus's departure yells over and over that the bus is ready to go. Why can't he just shutup and leave! Half an hour after the bus departs, another crier yells for a different bus departure. Because of the daytime heat, many of the long distance buses travel only at night. The third bus of the night arrives shortly after four a.m., and the driver finds someone parked in his spot. The bus driver simply lies on his enormous foghorn for ten minutes, until finally someone moves the offending car.

Fifteen minutes later the hotel night manager walks up and down the hallways, whistling loudly. The noises drive us crazy. Yet we wonder if the other guests even notice. Most of the people here were raised in tiny crowded homes with large families, crowing roosters in the yards, blaring radios in the houses, and noisy, mufflerless trucks and buses roaring up and down the streets. I think many of the people have been bombarded by noise so much that they seem nervous when it is quiet. The noise seems almost comforting to the people, and certainly not anything to complain about.

Our whistling hotel manager comes back and turns on all the hallway lights. Even with the curtains closed our room is totally illuminated. It is five a.m. From the noise on the street, I would guess the whole city is outside our door. We crawl, delirious, out of bed and head downstairs to the street.

Unlike us, Lago Agrio is wide awake. Like a big stirred up ant pile, everyone works to grab a slice of the boom-town pie. From the chicklet gum sellers, to store owners, to construction workers, everyone on the street rushes about, hard at work. We stand swaying on the sidewalk, and suddenly reach our oil town saturation point.

"Of all the places we could be in the world, how have we ended up here?" Tass asks me in a daze. I have no answer. I look at all the people up and down the street. Lago Agrio is their life, their existence. Most will probably never leave; they will die here. We, however, have a choice!

"We don't have to stay here," I reply, as much to myself as to Tass. "We can leave any time we want!" We have both joked about how crazy our route has become, but now I am serious. "In fact," I add with growing excitement, "let's leave right now!"

We run back up the stairs to the oil room and pull out our map. We are a long way from anyplace sane. Tass smirks and points at the Columbia border, just a few miles to the north.

"What the heck," she jokes, "let's cross the border into Columbia and get photos of guerrillas. Kids love gorillas!" Tass laughs, making a pun over the confusion elementary school students often have between gorillas, primates living in Africa, and guerrillas, revolutionary soldiers. The real joke, that now

Local buses in the Amazon Basin have open sides to allow plenty of
ventilation, Lago Agrio, Ecuador.

doesn't seem so funny, is that the route we have planned is equally crazy. We
were going to ride west out of Lago Agrio along the trans-Ecuadorian
pipeline—the road with the most truck traffic of any highway in Ecuador—
back into the Andes.

Strangely, our ultimate goal is to travel east, downriver where the Rio
Napo, the largest river in Ecuador, meets the Rio Amazonas near Iquitos,
Peru. Because of border disputes, including a recent war, no travel is allowed
between Ecuador and Peru along the entire Amazon frontier. To get to the
confluence downriver, we have to go west, back into the Andes to fly to the
Pacific coast of Peru, and then fly back into the Amazon Basin on the Peruvian side of the border. We want to spend our last month in the Amazon Basin
traveling by boat—where there are no pipelines and no roads—and hiking on
forest trails.

"Let's buy a bus ticket to Baeza to get back to some cloudforests," I suggest impulsively. "We can bike south along the Andean foothills before riding
back up over the Andes at Banos." Tass doesn't need convincing. We make a
beeline to the bus station. The bus to Baeza leaves in just forty-five minutes.
We race back to our room, pack up everything, and have our bikes and gear
loaded onto the bus with fifteen minutes to spare. We are outta here!

Sitting, waiting inside the bus, Tass talks about the upcoming ride. "I'm
looking forward to this. I haven't had a really good fright for awhile," she

laughs, referring to the kamikaze bus drivers. "Maybe fear will help me forget about the itching on my ankles."

The road out of town is flat, monotonous, hot, and dusty. In addition to countless trucks roaring up and down the highway, the gravel is deep and loose and full of large stones. Brutal riding conditions. We don't regret for a moment our decision not to bike.

I sit, exhausted, staring out the window. With each hour we ride, I feel more fatigued. As the bus begins climbing out of the lowlands, I realize I am running a fever. When we reach Baeza we decide, since we have already cycled this section of road, we will catch another bus to Tena, and resume cycling in new territory.

That night in our hotel my fever breaks three times, each with a major sweat leaving me drenched. Tass eagerly gets out her *Medical Guide for Third World Travelers*, turns to the Quick Reference for Common Causes of a Fever, and proceeds to terrify me with all the possible illnesses I might have.

"Do you have fatigue, sore throat, or a non-productive cough?" she asks, reading from the book.

"No cough," I reply. "Why, what would that be?"

"Typhoid fever," she says, and goes to the next section: Fever Without a Cough.

"Do you have shaking chills that come and go periodically, occasionally with diarrhea?"

"No diarrhea," I shake my head.

"Okay, that would be malaria." She skims past schistosomiasis and intestinal bacterial infections, which have bloody diarrhea, and tries again.

"Do you have a severe headache or neck stiffness?"

"No headache, thankfully."

"Well, then it's not meningitis. If meningitis is suspected, don't take antibiotics," Tass adds matter-of-factly.

I thank Tass for that last tip, and then point out that it could be something a little less extreme. "Don't they have plain flu listed in that book?"

"Well," Tass responds hesitantly, "do you have chills, fatigue, sore throat, with or without cold symptoms?"

"Yes," I respond tentatively, wondering what it might be.

"That could be just plain flu," Tass admits, then smiles and adds, "Or it could be viral upper respiratory syndrome, strep throat, viral sore throat, tonsillitis, or mononucleosis!"

23

Back to the Andes

The road south of Tena winds along the base of the Andes mountains. The next few days could be some of our hardest cycling. We will be climbing back up into the Andes, yet still be riding in the hot and humid climate of the Amazon Basin. We won't have any reprieve from the heat until we are much higher up in the mountains.

Both of us have upset stomachs—and deadly farts. Even under the best of conditions, it can be difficult to pass gas while riding a bicycle. It doesn't come naturally. We have to lift up off the saddle and stop pedaling to relax enough to make it work. Now the difficulty is compounded as we never know when a little diarrhea will leak out, making a nasty mess in our biking shorts that must be washed out by hand. Yet if we hold in the gas, we get painful stomach cramps. So we do very hesitant baby farts, slowly eking it out to make sure everything is safe and dry.

At the village of Santa Clara, composed of four houses next to the road, we stop for cold mineral water and some bakery snacks. Neither of us has much appetite because of the oppressive heat. We chat for a few minutes with the *tienda* owner, and I ask about the road ahead. As we resume riding, I tell Tass I am uncertain over his comment about the road.

"I couldn't tell if he was saying it was seven kilometers until the start of the hill, or that the hill was seven kilometers to the top."

"Or maybe he has seven children!" Tass jibes. She thinks my understanding of Spanish is still a little slow. Apparently she is right, for the climb begins right outside of town, and the hill is much longer than seven kilometers. Naturally we are cycling up the hill in the hottest part of the day. The air is still and so stifling we can hardly breath. As we climb, my heart pounds in my chest, and I feel a throbbing, tingling dizziness. Although we have been drinking as much water as possible, we both feel dehydrated. Neither of us has peed all day, and now we don't even have enough moisture left in our bodies to sweat. Instead we get waves of cold chills and goosebumps as we ride.

The road snakes up a high ridge; cleared land and cultivated farms intersperse patches of uncut tropical forest. Occasionally trucks and buses rumble up behind us, honking continually, in part to warn us they are approaching, but mostly because they hope we will give up this madness and wave them down to climb on board as paying customers! But we wave them around, and they roll past, belching out clouds of thick black diesel smoke. A few heads poke out the windows, staring at us in disbelief. We don't believe we are out here either!

The climb continues. Most of the trees are cut back away from the road, but every so often there is a small patch of shade where we can stop to give our tingling, heat exhausted bodies a rest. Just when we start to wonder if we can keep riding, we round a corner to find a small *tienda* beside the road, complete with fresh spring water coming out of a bamboo trough under the shade of a tree. We scoop the cold water onto our arms, splash our chests and backs, and soak our bandanas before laying them over our heads. The woman in the store folds her arms on the open window sill and lies her head lazily on her arms, watching us.

"*Mucho calor!*" Tass says in exhaustion. Very hot.

"*No mucho,*" the woman replies, unimpressed. Not very hot.

I want to say, "Get out of the shade and ride this loaded bike up the hill, and then see if you think it is such a pleasant temperature!" But I don't. Instead I fall back to our standard explanation of our adjustment to the heat.

"*Nosotros viva in Estados Unitos cerca Canada. Mucho fria,*" I say. We live in the U.S. near Canada. It is very cold.

"*Oh,*" she replies, now with sympathy. "*Muy Norte.*" Very far north. She shakes her head and makes a tsk-tsk noise through her teeth. "*No la gusta fria.*" I don't like the cold.

"*Mucho nueva tambien!*" Tass gets very dramatic. Lots of snow as well! "*Es necessita mucho ropas!*" You need to wear many clothes! The woman continues shaking her head and making tsk-tsk noises in amazement. Our discussion of freezing cold weather makes us feel a little better. Tass braves the subject of what lies ahead up the road. The woman tells us we are almost to the top of the pass.

As we continue riding, a thick bank of clouds rolls in, giving us a reprieve from the sun. Before long a huge, dark thunderhead forms, and we ride right into it. A shrine to Maria de Camino appears out of the mist. Hail Mary!, Guardian of the Highway. Despite the black clouds the rain misses us as we ride through rolling hills.

We are exhausted, but still we ride on. We ring our bike bells at each other, trying to give one another a morale boost, to take our minds off the repetition of

relentless pedaling. At times like this we are too tired to enjoy the scenery. All
we can think about is getting our sore bottoms off the saddles, taking our aching
and exhausted arms off the shaking, bouncing handlebars, and sitting up to ease
the stiffness and pain that burn like red-hot coals on our necks and backs. All
we want is to arrive at our destination—to be there, not here.

The road becomes an endless series of rolling hills. We climb each hill in
our little chainring, then sit up and coast in exhaustion back down the other
side. And do it again, and again, and again, and again.

"You have to promise you won't tell any friends at home about this," Tass
intones seriously. I look over at her, trying to figure what she is talking about.

"Imagine," she continues, "what everyone would think if they knew we
have become coasters!"

Tass is a fierce competitor in mountain bike racing and especially loves
downhill races. I am famous for some spectacular downhill crashes, always at
high speed. Usually when I crash, I am still pedaling, trying to go even faster.
Now, neither of us has the energy to pedal; neither of us is interested in speed.
We are coasters on the back side of each hill. Somehow this is funny enough
to keep us laughing the rest of the way to Puyo.

The road, which was running south along the length of the Andes, now
turns west up into the mountains. The next morning we are stopped at a military checkpoint. Guards with machine guns solemnly direct us to an office

Bruce riding back into the Andes from the Amazon Basin, Ecuador.

where our passports are inspected. An officer hands us forms to fill out. We fill in the top section, but then there are a couple of questions in Spanish we don't understand. In Spanish we ask the officer what they mean. He begins yelling angrily, repeating the words we don't know, as if by shouting the words at us we are somehow going to understand. Not knowing what else to do, we write down meaningless words and numbers, simply filling in all the spaces, and hand the forms back to him. He seems satisfied with the results. Obviously he doesn't read English.

Another guard with a machine gun asks about our bikes. He points to the bell on my handlebars, and asks me what it is. I find this rather ironic. Across Ecuador kids instantly recognize our bicycle bells, and often ring them without asking. But this guy, who is entrusted with a machine gun, doesn't know a bicycle bell when he sees one.

Another group of guards gathers around our mountain bikes and pushes all the buttons on our shifters, which is hard on the derailleurs when the bikes are stopped. But we are not about to tell them to leave the bikes alone. When we are cleared to leave, we grind our gears as we pedal away, trying to get the derailleurs shifted properly and straightened back out.

We climb into the Andes on a dirt-and-gravel road, up a narrow canyon filled with cloudforest, and at last the temperature cools down. The canyon walls are very steep; trees and vegetation hang in the air above us over the road. I think of all the landslides we have seen, and I wonder about the precarious trees and loose earth dangling above our heads.

It begins to rain. At this elevation many storms are intense yet brief. We pull out our single portable umbrella and take a break to eat lunch. When the rain shows no sign of letting up, we continue eating. Finally, when we are stuffed, the rain stops and we head out. Two minutes later it begins raining again. This time we keep riding; within minutes we are soaking wet.

The rain brings clouds of mist that roll up and down the canyon walls, dramatically adding to the beauty of the ride. In places the one-lane road is so narrow that when buses pass we have to stop and huddle against the moss and ferns along the dripping canyon walls, our feet in streams of water running down the inner edge of the road. Where there is no room to stop or stand on the inside of the road, we sometimes have no choice but to stop on the outside edge of the road, beside perilous dropoffs, and let the trucks and buses pass on the inside, hoping they won't knock us off the cliffs. In many of these places tire tracks in the mud run right to the very edge of the cliffs, showing how close some vehicles have come to the dropoffs. Even a slight landslide would plunge the bus or truck hundreds of feet to the river. We are nervous riding our bicycles close to the edges; imagine the weight of fully loaded buses in the same spot!

Streams continually cross the road, and waterfalls spray mist onto us as we ride past. In one place a thirty-foot overhanging waterfall pours water right into the middle of the road. A few buses slow down for a free wash as they pass under the waterfall.

At a long tunnel we wait for a vehicle to follow; the inside of the tunnel is too dark to see without lights. A truck comes up and the driver kindly waves us in front of him so we can ride ahead in the light of his headlights. The curving tunnel is a singlelane, full of dripping water. The truck headlights cast our shadows out before us, obscuring rocks on the road. We ride into darkness at a slight uphill grade, trying to ride as fast as we can so we don't hold up the truck behind us. At the other side we sprint out of the way and wave to let the truck pass; the driver honks enthusiastically as he roars up the hill.

In the town of Banos we get our first hot shower in almost a month. Banos, which is Spanish for bath, is famous for its hot springs. People come from all over Ecuador, and all over the world, to enjoy the hot baths. Over the years the tourist industry has grown until today there are over fifty hotels in the small community. Hotels and restaurants catering to *gringos* crowd up and down the narrow streets. We stay a few days in a hotel recommended by friends with the unusual name *Plantas y Blanca*, Plants and White.

While in Banos we eat breakfast each morning at a little restaurant on the roof of our hotel. The ceiling is a bright-white canvas tarp, and the walls are glass. We religiously order number two off the menu: two pancakes with fruit and yogurt, with butter and fresh cane syrup. I also have a *banano con leche*, banana blended with milk drink, and we both have coffee with hot milk on the side. Our breakfast is a small ritual that give us tremendous satisfaction after all the rice and greasy eggs we have been eating.

For lunch we are daring and daily try a different restaurant, but each afternoon we go to Cafe Cultura to read and have hot chocolate and scones. A little kitten there always sleeps in Tass's lap. The "in" restaurants change every few years despite the recommendations of guide books. The easiest way to tell which is the latest *gringo* hangout is to simply walk up and down the street and see where the crowds are. This year Cafe Hood seems to be the favorite supper spot. Travelers can be like lemmings. Despite many who claim they want to get away from it all, most travelers seem to gravitate together whenever possible. Each evening we happily join the crowd; we've had plenty of time by ourselves.

It rains every day we are in Banos, but we don't care. Between non-stop eating we take steam baths on the top floor of our hotel. Carlos, the manager, places us inside wooden boxes with just our heads sticking out, then fills the box with steam, scented with fresh eucalyptus leaves. Next we do cold water towel treatments, wrapped up like mummies, with Carlos making sure we are always comfortable. We go back into the steam box, return to the cold water dip, then head for more steam in a box. We finish with a cold, high-pressure, pulsating spray from a hose. Very refreshing!

The weather is cold and raining when we ride out of Banos. We are sad to leave; we could spend weeks here. We hoped to get views of Tungurahua volcano, but all the mountains are covered with clouds. We recall the words of a Belgian writer who traveled in South America in the 1920s: "Anyone who doesn't like clouds has no business coming to Ecuador."

Although we never see the tops of the peaks around Banos, the lower flanks of the mountains are spectacular in the mist, especially when the sun momentarily breaks through to bathe everything in dazzling light. The mist adds to the magnitude of the canyon walls, the cultivated fields hanging from steep precipitous hillsides, the depth of the valleys and immensity of the mountain walls.

As we continue to climb, a few buses pass by with travelers we met during our stay in Banos. We hear shouts and greetings and see white *gringo* arms waving at us out bus windows. Up, up, into the Andes we climb. We are both in good health and the riding seems easy on the smoothly-tarred road.

The mountains become drier as we climb, and the countryside reminds us of the area around Solola, Guatemala: small family farms, mud brick houses with thatched roofs, fields of corn. Rows of giant agave cactus divide the fields and line the hiking trails into the mountains.

We stop in the small weaving community of Salasaca. Today is a big market day in nearby Ambato, so Salasaca is quiet. Only one stall selling weavings is set up in the dusty main square. Inside, three women sit chatting. One of them spins wool. They jump up and give us a sales pitch, each pointing to various weavings, trying to convince us to buy something. We look and smile, and give our standard excuse when we aren't in a shopping mood.

"No quiermos mas pesado!" we joke and point at the bulging panniers on our bikes. We don't want any more weight! *"Bestante cosas!"* We have enough stuff already!

This tactic leaves even the quickest salesperson speechless. They laugh and agree. *"Si, mucho cosas!"* Yes, you have many things!

We dig some food out of our panniers to make lunch. Gusts of wind blow clouds of dust over us, and the women insist we eat out of the wind in the back of their stall. One of the women clears out a pile of weavings to make room on a woven mat. We make peanut butter sandwiches while they go back to work, spinning, chatting, and laughing.

When we finish eating we go over and sit with them. We end up spending the entire afternoon hanging out and chatting. They are real characters. Ignasia Chango is the most outgoing, a real jokester, with the happiest, carefree laugh. Carmen Jimanez, is older and more dignified, yet also funny and quick. Jauna Jimenez is a bit more shy. Tass immediately bonds with the

Carmen Jimanez, Salasaca, Ecuador.

women, and makes wonderful photographs as she chats and laughs to keep them relaxed and at ease with the camera. Before long Tass has our postcards out and shows the women pictures from South Dakota. Naturally, the American Indian photos are a big hit. In fact, Carmen likes one of the photos so much she hides it, hoping Tass will not notice. But Tass is on to all the tricks, and counts the postcards when she goes to put them away. Still it takes awhile to get the guilty Carmen to confess and hand over the goods. She blushes and chuckles through the whole process, and we all laugh hysterically when she reveals where she hid the postcard under her hat.

   Although we had not planned on buying anything, we have such a wonderful afternoon that, when it is time to go, we decide we must buy something from each woman. We try to keep it simple. We start out with a small weaving from Ignasia. Carmen has a medium sized weaving that could make a wall hanging or a table cover. But the only item Juana is selling that interests us is a large geometric weaving, thick enough for a throw rug. Rolled up, it is the size of a sleeping bag. We still have to cycle over numerous Andean passes, yet regardless of all common sense, we buy it.

We arrive in Ambato just before dark. The city is still vibrant from all the crowds here for market day. We ride down streets teeming with Indians from all the surrounding villages, all wearing their own colorful wardrobes. Everyone is in the last frantic stages of the market, either trying to make final sales, or packing quickly to catch buses or trucks to their villages. We wind through the activity to find a downtown hotel, quickly stash our bikes, and head back onto the streets to enjoy the last few minutes of light before finding supper.

The next morning we spend some time in the main market, making photographs. Tass spots a couple of traffic cops walking down the street. She makes a quick photo. Although she uses a telephoto lens, one of them spots her. He comes up, shaking his head and says *"Propaganda—prohibito photos."* It is typical right-wing military paranoia. What does he think, that she is going to sell the photo to Peru? We make a quick exit to a side street and Tass grins, wags her finger back and forth at me, and utters our often-used Gus Angermeyer quote from the Galapagos. "Not for publication!"

We stop in a little bakery to buy a snack. I point at a pastry, and ask the clerk if it has pineapple inside.

"No Pina," she shakes her head.

Tass asks if a nearby sweet roll has chocolate.

"No," the woman informs her. Surprised, Tass asks again.

"No. No chocolate," the woman says again.

Regardless, we each order a pastry. We go outside and sit on a bench to eat. Mine is pineapple and Tass's is chocolate. Go figure. Tass shakes her head and points to another traffic cop walking down the street. "I think I'll go take a picture of that policeman!" she jokes.

We spend much of the afternoon sitting on a park bench in the sun, watching people walk past. Tass makes photos while I write in my journal.

My right shoe came apart while in the Amazon basin, and I used duct tape to put it back together; the front of the shoe is wrapped in silver tape. Sitting on the bench, it is humorous to watch people walk by, and see their reactions when they notice my taped shoe. In Latin America it is safe to generalize in saying that shoes are a real big deal. All eyes go straight to my foot. Some try to slyly look at my shoe out of the corner of an eye; others simply stare as they pass, eyes riveted in horror at the tape. No one can figure out if I am just very poor, which doesn't make sense, or whether I am a simpleton, unaware of my social blunder. It goes against everything they expect of me— a wealthy *gringo*—with faulty shoes!

An Indian woman with two little girls walks past. She wears a sporty green felt hat and skirt, a white blouse, a thick orange shawl, and layers of glass-bead necklaces. She has two young girls with her, both rather disheveled. The oldest, who is about four, has uncombed hair pulled into a loose ponytail. She is crying and is snot-nosed from her tears. She wears red plastic shoes and carries a box of gum. Her mother, who looks angry and upset, is insisting that the young girl go and sell the gum in the park. The mother mocks the little girl's tears and walks off to the other side of the park to sit, knitting on a bench.

The little girl with the gum staggers off in the opposite direction, crying profusely. She wobbles up to a man sitting at a nearby bench, crying and telling him her sad story. He responds instantly and she makes her first sale. She runs across the park to her mother, and hands her the money. Now, somewhat emboldened, she approaches a woman, who also buys from her. We also buy gum, and Tass makes some photographs. After a few minutes the girl moves on in search of more customers.

Her mother continues to work on the other side of the park. The smaller daughter, maybe three years old, languishes behind with her mother for a time, and then when her mother doesn't give her any attention, becomes bored and begins wandering in the park. She heads toward the center statue and occupies herself by throwing kernels of dried corn onto the sidewalk, and getting on her hands and knees to lick them back up with her tongue.

After half an hour the gum seller has run out of customers, and comes back over by us, to see if we will buy more. We do. Her younger sister comes over to join us. She wears an orange skirt and a dirty, bright yellow sweater. She is also snot-nosed with uncombed black hair sticking out from her green hat. A couple of ragamuffins, as my dad would say.

Another young girl, with clean jeans and an apron, also sells us gum. She is eight. She looks almost Tibetan. But she is not selling nearly as much as the little ragamuffin. The older you get, the harder it is to sell; you lose the cuteness factor.

We stop for an afternoon snack in a hip little sidewalk cafe. Inside schoolgirls huddle together crowded on benches, laughing and chatting, while a large screen TV pumps out the latest rock videos from the U.S. and Europe, many quite risque. What must the uniform-clad schoolgirls think of the scantily clothed, gyrating bodies, the fast-paced action, the wealth and opulence of everything on the screen? At home I enjoy music videos, but seeing them here, blasting out in front of young kids, they seems vulgar and distorted. Sitting here, I feel embarrassed by my culture.

That evening in a little neighborhood *panaderia* we get "the best cup of coffee in Ecuador," according to Tass, who is known for grand pronouncements in rating food. She lavishly praises the proprietor for the quality brew,

A young girl sells gum to earn money for her
family, Ambato, Ecuador.

and insists we return in the morning for breakfast on our way out of town.

We arrive early, Tass eager for more good coffee, but find the coffee machine is not on. The owner sadly informs us he is unable to use the coffee machine today, and only has instant coffee. As we order breakfast, he notes that Tass is obviously disappointed. A few moments later he returns triumphantly to tell Tass it is possible to have one cup of coffee from the machine. But Tass's excitement is short lived. She watches in horror as the proprietor returns to the machine, puts a cup under the spigot, fills it with the cold dregs of last night's coffee, puts it in a microwave, and serves it to her.

"You like the coffee so much," Tass later quips to me, pretending to be the owner, "we **saved** this cup just for you."

We want to spend our last week in Ecuador doing a mountain bike tour through the western Andes. We ride up the southern end of the central valley of Ecuador, the Avenue of Volcanoes. But like our previous time in the valley climbing Cotopaxi volcano, all the volcanoes are covered with clouds. We begin to wonder if we will ever get a view of all the mountains.

We rejoin the Pan American highway. In this part of Ecuador the Pan American can be a one-, two- or four-lane highway, depending on the disposition and fearlessness of the drivers. When there is no oncoming traffic, many of the trucks and buses prefer to drive right down the center of the road, making the highway dangerous when oncoming traffic does appear, but remarkably relaxing for us, as most traffic is in the middle of the road when it passes, giving us plenty of room to spare. Still, it is not our favorite place to ride, and we are glad when we reach the turnoff to Saquisili. We arrive an hour later and check into the Salon Pinchachia, a little two-story family hotel with fairly clean rooms.

Ever since ruining my glasses in the Amazon Basin, I have wanted to return to Quito to get my spare glasses. Now that we are only a few hours away by bus, we can't resist heading to Quito for a few quick errands. We leave our bikes and hitch a ride back to the Pan American highway and flag down a bus to the capitol. The bus is a typical, crazy, high-speed ride, and we feel much more vulnerable than on our bikes. The driver passes other vehicles and trucks even in the midst of oncoming traffic. He simply flashes his lights, honks the horn, and stakes his position in the middle of the road. Luckily everyone else gets out of his way.

The Thursday market at Saquisili is one of the largest markets in Ecuador, spread out over eight different plazas along with all the streets in between. Only one small section has items marketed for *gringos;* everything else is for locals. There are huge animal markets with chickens, pigs, cows, goats, and sheep for sale. In another area all kinds of fruit and vegetables are sold individually and in bulk for stores and restaurants; other booths have clothing, both new and used, shoes, hats, household items, kitchen utensils, farm equipment, weaving supplies, wool, dyes, and more.

Vendors walk up and down the street selling everything imaginable. One fellow has one arm covered with elastic cords for sale; in the other arm he carries plastic sacks of mothballs—a unique sales combo. Many sell brooms. One man carries three shiny new office chairs, complete with rollers and adjustable backs, all wrapped in plastic. Actually, I need a new office chair...

We see three-foot wide bowls, made from truck tires, and smaller bowls as little as two or three inches wide, all made from car tires. An old woman pounds out scrap metal to make hand scythes and uses a hack saw to cut little teeth into the blade of the scythe. She sits on the ground with her legs bent so her feet and toes form a vise to hold the tool she is making. She also makes scissors, by hand!

Tailors work on sewing machines run by foot treadles and do a booming business patching tattered clothing. Nearby is watch-repair alley with a row of workers hunched over tiny portable tables, an array of tiny watch parts spread before them, their tables precariously balanced along the edge of the jostling, crowded alleyway. Music pulses from pirate tape vendors, highly amplified to maximum distortion. One woman sits just inches from the front of a screeching speaker, nursing a little girl, selling corn, and seemingly oblivous to all the commotion.

We eat breakfast at *Senora* Rosalita's in the middle of the vegetable market, hemmed in by *campesinos* selling produce bagged in fifty-pound sacks. *Senora* Rosalita is a heavy set woman with a bright-colored apron and a wonderful smile. She has one wooden table big enough for three people, or perhaps four, if you are close friends. She sells steaming hot milk, hard-boiled eggs and bread. We buy milk, and she hands us a jar of cheap instant coffee and a jar of sugar to take off the bite. As we eat and take in the surroundings, she calls out to people who pass by, her regulars. Many people stop and wolf down their food, eager to get back to their wares lest they miss a big sale.

Food vendors symmetrically stack tomatoes, potatoes and oranges into tiny piles, precariously balancing one on top of another. Women shuck corn and pea pods. Others sell onions or garlic. We see giant cabbages twice basketball size and twenty-pound balls of cane sugar beautifully wrapped in brown, dried palm fronds.

Everywhere are food stalls using every conceivable animal body part made into soups, sauces, and goulashes. Pigs baked whole, splayed out in giant pans, with apples in their mouths. Rows of *cuy*, guinea pig, grilled over barbecues, skewered on sticks with the head still in place and teeth barred in a ghoulish grin, like little baked dachshunds. And for dessert there are brightly colored whipped creams, served like ice cream in cones, with so many preservatives the cream doesn't melt in the intense equatorial sun.

I wonder how any of the people make any money. All around, others sell the exact same thing, all at pitifully low prices. Everyone sells to people who have as little money as they have. We listen to them haggle over tiny sums of money. In the few larger transactions, the buyers wave handfuls of *sucres* in front of the seller's face and under the nose. Some buyers even try to put the money in the seller's hands or pockets, to secure the deal at the lower price.

One part of the transaction is always certain: *"No tenemous cambio,"* I don't have any change, the vendors always say. No matter what the price, how big or how small, nobody has change. This is especially amazing since

Using her hands and feet as a vice, a woman makes scythes,
knives and even scissors, Saquisili, Ecuador.

the largest bill printed in Ecuador is ten thousand *sucres*, less than five U.S.
dollars. Equally impossible is getting change for a five thousand *sucres* note,
or a one thousand sucres note, less than fifty cents in U.S. dollars.

After nearly eight hours we are marketed out. We return to our hotel, eat
a lunch of eggs, rice, and beans, and pack our bags. Our next destination is
Zumbahua, a remote mountain village with an even more traditional market.
We head out of town on a back road, a dusty, washboard-filled track lined
with giant agave cactus. Although our map shows a single road, the valley is
full of intersecting dirt roads. At each intersection we take the road that looks
most traveled. Before long we have serious doubts about whether we are still
on the right road. Finally we spot someone walking along the dusty trail.

"Que camino ala Pujili?" we ask hopefully. Is this the road to Pujili?

"Directo!" the moustachioed man shouts triumphantly, and points down
the road. Straight ahead! We ride on, reassured. Less than a minute later we
arrive at a three way intersection, with none of the roads continuing straight
ahead. The right hand road appears to be more traveled, but it is hard to tell.
We go right. The hot tropical sun, intensified by the altitude, beats down un-
relentingly. Occasionally we climb ridges that enable us to see out across the
broad central Ecuadorean valley. There are numerous small roads on all the
surrounding hills. We figure even if we are not on the regular road, we will
still end up there, or near there, eventually.

We arrive in Pujili exhausted, and would check into a hotel, if there was one. We spend an hour chasing down rumors of where we might rent a room. No luck. We are too tired to ride far, but have no choice except to head out of town to find a place to camp.

The road winds up into the mountains in a series of switchbacks. Despite the steep angle of the hills, the countryside is densely packed with houses, each on a tiny plot of land. Exhausted, we ride and ride without seeing anywhere to camp. As it grows dark, we reassure one another that we will find something. We eyeball a few abandoned mud-walled huts, some simply crumbling walls without roofs, but none will completely hide our tent from the road.

Finally we stop where someone has leveled out a place on the hillside to build a house. We scan the area and then wait a few minutes for it to grow even darker. We don't want to draw any attention to ourselves. We are too tired to deal with a crowd of locals should our camp be detected. We just want to relax quietly. The immense central valley of Ecuador lies below us. Off in the distance the soft light of alpenglow illuminates the summit of Cotopaxi, poking up through the clouds. Down in the enormous valley lights begin to appear in the windows of countless little thatched huts.

Only now do we begin setting up camp. We talk in soft voices, mindful of a house just below us over the hill. We place our tent between two huge agave cactus so that it is barely visible to uphill traffic. We duck and sit quietly every time a vehicle comes up the road.

Total darkness. We take quick sponge baths outside the tent. Just as I finish, a woman and two kids suddenly come over the hill from below. It is too dark for her to see me clearly. I huddle naked next to the tent, trying to quickly dry myself off, then jump inside.

"Que alli?" She cries, startled. Who is there? What can I reply to calm her down? Anything I say is going to sound strange.

"I'm a gringo," I reply in Spanish. "We are bicycling; it grew dark so we camped. Is it okay if we camp here?" I quickly add.

The woman is uncertain how to react to this unusual story. She yells at the kids to go back and get her husband, and says something about ladrones. She thinks I might be a robber. Tass quickly gets out of the tent to calm her, while I get on some clothes. No sooner do I get dressed than the husband arrives. Everything is explained and we soon are all laughing together, recalling how we surprised one another in the dark. They become very concerned that we will be warm.

"Mucho fria aqui!" they tell us over and over. Very cold here! They also ask, "Tiene luz?" Do you have lights? They offer to go find a key and have us sleep in a nearby building that is abandoned, but we already have our tent up and don't want to move. We graciously decline their offer. After more small talk and much handshaking, they all go off to bed.

We lie in our tent and read by headlamp. Every fifteen minutes a vehicle comes up the road. When the vehicles draw near, we turn off our lights to stop our tent from glowing in the dark, and lie quietly listening for the vehicles to pass. Later we lie in the dark and listen to the sounds of the countryside. The neighborhood dogs yap incessantly. Every once in a while when they stop for a few seconds, we can hear a low rumbling noise, which sounds like steady traffic on a far-away interstate. But there is no such road. After a few minutes we realize we are hearing the cumulative noise from thousands of dogs barking far down in the valley. The noise lasts all night long.

We get up before six a.m. and quickly break camp before we draw any crowds. The kids from the house below walk shyly past on their way to school. We cycle up into the mist for an hour before stopping to eat breakfast: bread, peanut butter, crackers, and Tang. Now that we have stopped, the wind is freezing. We put on tights, pile coats, hats, and gloves, and sit eating by the side of the road, watching the mist rising up from the valley below. A station wagon taxi full of *gringos* passes by; everyone waves frantically as if we are long lost friends.

We continue riding up the endless switchbacks. At each turn we look back down at the road we have ascended, which snakes like a ribbon back into the mist. We ride above treeline into the *paramo*, the high windswept western slope of the Andes. Strange stunted plants and golden clumps of grass are interspersed between tiny flowers. This area seldom gets rain; all the moisture comes from the thick clouds of mist that blow across the high, exposed ridges. As we ride we point out unusual sights to each other and shorten the name *paramo* to *mo*. We ride through *mo* mist; visibility drops to barely twenty-five feet. We occasionally pass *mo* homes; *mo* dogs chase after us through the *mo* mist. We see *mo* sheep. We are *mo* cyclists.

The wind is fierce as we crest the first of the high passes onto a barren, grassy mesa. The tufts of golden grass flutter and wave, tossed by gusts of wind. Each field seems alive, churning with patterns from the force of the howling wind.

Occasionally we spot groups of shepherds huddled behind huge tussocks of grass, trying to escape the wind. They are all quite shy. We see people a few turns ahead on the road, but by the time we arrive at the turn, they are gone, hiding somewhere, crouched behind the long tufts of grass. We sneak glimpses of arms and tops of heads and caps behind the grass. Only when we are a few hundred yards down the road do the people stand back up to stare and watch us ride away.

Tass has been dropping behind on the climbs. I slow to let her catch up. She isn't feeling well, and doesn't have her usual strength. Regardless, she doesn't stop, but keeps pedaling at her own rhythm. I ride beside her.

"Where's Mary?" I joke, referring to the inevitable shrine on the top of the pass, wondering when the climb will end.

"Where is the latte cart?" Tass responds without smiling.

We cross the pass and find ourselves on the rim of an immense, desolate valley. The view reminds us of Ladakh, a part of northern India on the Tibetan plateau, a stark, surreal landscape, a patchwork of fields in shades of brown and gray. The countryside is so barren it is beautiful in a haunting way. The howling wind forces us to quickly drop over the summit. Unfortunately, the wind only gets worse as we descend into the canyon below. Luckily, the wind is now mostly at our backs, but when the road switches back we are hit first from one side, then the other, then head on. The stronger gusts bring us to a complete stop. We drop one foot to balance the bikes, tuck our heads, and hold onto the handlebars with all our might to keep from being blown over. The wind whips up huge clouds of dust that fill our eyes and sting our faces and hands. We feel like we are being sandblasted.

As we continue to descend, the violent blasts of wind become less frequent. Surprisingly, between each gust the air is remarkably calm. We relax and sit up to enjoy the spectacular scenery. Small thatched houses now dot the steep mountain walls, each surrounded by a quiltwork of tiny fields, like a mosaic painted onto the landscape.

Occasionally we ride through groups of houses clustered along the road, but there are no stores. The people are still extremely shy, almost as if frightened by us. We don't take any photographs of the people and are careful even about photographing the countryside if people are nearby.

A French couple in a rented four-wheel drive vehicle waves us down. Holding a map, the man asks for directions. They have no idea where they are.

"Aren't you afraid of the people?" the man asks in disbelief as he eyes our bicycles. He pulled up at the last farmhouse to photograph a little boy, and the whole family threw rocks at him. We are hardly surprised. The people here seem totally spooked.

We descend for an hour until we finally reach the bottom of the immense, barren valley. Ahead of us is yet another pass. The gravel road switchbacks up the hillside into a monstrous headwind. We are both blown off the road, twice. Once Tass's bike is lifted off the ground when it is blown over. Clouds of stinging sand from the barren fields blow across our faces, hands and legs like sandpaper. Grit fills our eyes, ears, and noses.

"Where's Mary?" we question again. We had been told this second pass was not very high, but halfway up we realize that is obviously wrong. We still can't see the top. I am exhausted. I can't imagine how Tass, who is becoming sicker and sicker, is able to keep going. She is now running a fever, and her face is completely white. She is the Zombie Cyclist. If a truck or a bus would come along, I would flag it down for a lift, but there is no traffic. So we keep riding.

At the top of the pass we can see the small town of Zumbahua down in the bottom of a deep valley. We pull off on the side of a hill to try to find a place out of the roaring wind to eat a snack and get some energy. Though the last six miles are downhill, the road looks especially rough and rocky. It will probably take at least another half an hour to get there.

Zumbahua is built on a hillside near the bottom of the barren, windswept canyon. The uneven dirt streets are covered with large, rough stones. Remnants of torn plastic bags blow about in the wind and pile up into heaps in every corner. Zumbahua is the dirtiest town we have seen in all of Ecuador.

Tass, who is sinking into delirium, stays with the bikes while I search for a room. The first hotel is above a *tienda* selling typical supplies: sodas, crackers, bread, and sweets. The back room is full of propane bottles, and it smells like they have some serious leaks. As I climb the back stairs to the hotel, I imagine the entire building exploding. A young girl shows me a dirty room; the bathroom has a pile of leaking kerosene containers stacked in a corner. I decline on the room.

The next place is simply two spare rooms above a local restaurant. As I walk through a dark passageway to the stairs, I pass the kitchen, where half a cow is being butchered on a large wooden table. Mounds of meat and various body parts are heaped in bloody piles. I can barely see the steps, and stumble up the stairs to a small room. Enormous waves of heat waft up through the cracks in the floor from the kitchen below. Apparently the room is right over the stove. Again I decline.

On the street I meet Jorge, a ten-year-old boy, and his smaller brother, Jugo. To our surprise, they inform us there is another hotel in town. They guide me to their family's hotel, a paradise of quiet cleanliness. As we check in Tass shakes from chills; her face is white and pale. In our room she lies down on the bed and I cover her with both our sleeping bags to break her fever.

While Tass sleeps I help Jugo and Jorge fix a flat tire on their bicycle. I ask whose bike it is.

"*Es para nosotros juntamente,*" Jorge answers. It is for both of us together. "*Somos pobre.*" We are very poor.

Although the hotel has lights, there is no electricity in town at the moment. As it grows dark I light a candle and put on my headlamp to write. Later in the evening as I am reading, I hear feet running down the hallway and then frantic pounding on our door.

"*Aye luz! Aye luz!*" Alfonso, the father, yells out triumphantly. There is light! There is light!

With Tass sleeping, I really don't want to turn the lights on, plus I am comfortable lying where I am, reading by candlelight. But our host is not about to give up.

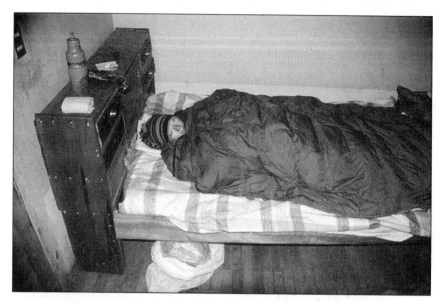

Tass sweats out a fever, with everything she needs close at hand:
tylenol and toilet paper, a headlamp to find the dark communal bathroom,
and plastic bags for throwing up, Zumbahua, Ecuador.

"Luz! Luz! Aye luz!" He continues to yell until I get up, turn on the light and thank him for coming upstairs to tell me. Tass wakes up from all the commotion and says she feels strong enough to go out and eat some plain rice. After her simple supper, she wobbles back to our hotel and again I tuck her under our sleeping bags.

At six a.m. a terrible screeching noise fills our hotel as a market loud-speaker on the hotel roof is turned up to full third-world volume. An annoying series of announcements, crackling, and screechy music begins. Despite the abrupt wake up, Tass feels a little better.

We head out early to the animal market and watch groups of *campesinos* walk in from the mountains with loads on the backs of llamas. The llamas have a slow and easy camel-like gait. They lumber into the village and stand calmly as they are unloaded and then tied together in out-of-the-way corners. They have large, droopy eyes with long lashes and big fuzzy ears, which they sometimes hold back flat against their heads, like rabbits.

As usual, the pig market is good for a few chuckles. Pigs NEVER want to go where their owners want them to move. Even if it is just a few feet, an incredible tug-of-war always ensues. Screeching, wailing as if being flailed alive, the pigs scream out at the slightest pull of their leashes.

We walk through the "fast food" section of the market. The main meal being served is goat-head soup. Everybody sells it—huge pots full of goat skulls, each one split in half, lengthwise. Each bowl comes with one single eye staring up out of the broth, half a jaw—the row of teeth floating in the broth with a ghoulish grin—and half the brains. The brains can be scooped out with a spoon, but it takes fingers to pluck the eyeball out of its socket. After being picked clean, the skulls are thrown to the ground where packs of dogs fight over each prize.

Zumbahua is full of dogs. Packs of vile, mangy mongrels scrounge, skulking in doorways and cowering under tables, desperately searching for food. The villagers constantly kick and shoo them out of shops and away from food stalls. But the dogs are incredibly persistent. In seconds they return, quivering, searching for food. They prowl through the village with one eye watching for kicks from pedestrians, the other eye watching for attacks from other dogs, and both eyes looking for food. The dogs fight over food scraps, they fight over territorial rights, they fight over females in heat. There always seems to be one or two of the females being chased through town by a group of uninvited suitors, each biting and snapping at the others as they hound their love interest up and down the squalid streets, hoping to make even more dogs.

We leave the sheep-head soup alley and walk over to the fish market, which smells even worse. The fish are all fried whole and then brought up from the coast. Hardly fresh. Six inches long including head and tail, they appear to be nothing but skin and bones.

Occasional gusts of wind blow huge clouds of dust through the market and into everyones eyes, ears, and food. Piles of litter swirl about with every gust. Despite the bleakness of the town, or perhaps because of it, Tass shoots numerous rolls of film. She is feeling much better, and is able to eat a hard-boiled egg and some bread. By late morning we are ready to continue biking to our final destination, Laguna Quilotoa volcanic crater.

More wind and dust out on the road. Looking at the barren dusty fields and the small ramshackle huts, at the dirty, poorly dressed people trying to scratch out a living in this high-altitude desert, we wonder how they face each day. Tass says she would be overwhelmed with despair living here. The people have limited education and a total lack of resources. What chance do they have of a better life?

Nearly everyone we meet asks us for *"un regalo,"* a gift, *"un pluma,"* a pen, or simply money. Obviously previous tourists have passed through giving things away. Now, like playing the lottery, the locals all ask for money from the tourists, hoping somehow they will have a lucky break. From little toddlers who can hardly walk to hunchbacked old men and women, the area is a countryside of beggars. Farmers working high on hillsides yell down for

Goat head soup, Zumbahua, Ecuador.

"un regalo!" as we pass by below. The continual barrage is exhausting. Everyone we meet wants a gift.

The road to Quilotoa crater degenerates into a prolonged series of sand traps. With the weight on our bicycles, it is impossible to float and ride through the sand. We sink into it. Even in our lowest gears, we grind to a stop. Pushing the bikes is difficult as the front wheels refuse to track straight and plane sideways into the sand. We have to push on the saddle, with no weight on the handlebars for the bikes to go straight.

At the South American Explorers Club we were told this section of road was fairly level. In Zumbahua we were told there was just a little climb up to the volcano. Despite this information we climb to 12,300 feet—higher than any of the passes we crossed the previous day!

A headwind continues to batter us; by the time we reach the summit of the crater, the wind has reached gale force. Below us, the walls of the immense crater drop down into a stunning, deep blue lake over a mile wide. Clouds cover the mountains all around us, yet the crater itself is bathed in sunshine. We planned to camp along the crater rim, but after scouting around the area for an hour, we find little in the way of good campsites. The wind is so strong, it would be a miserable night in the tent.

Two young boys have been tagging along with us since our arrival at the crater, insisting that the area is too dangerous to camp, as a crazy old man who lives nearby might bother us in the night. They recommend we stay with their family. We give in and follow them back to a nearby village where a sign proclaims "Cabanas Quilotoa, Umberto Latacunga Proprietor."

Umberto and the entire family rush to clean out a building which appears to be a stable when not housing guests. The building is well made out of cement blocks with a tile roof instead of thatching. Inside the roof is so low I have to duck under the rafters, yet there is plenty of space to easily set up our tent on the packed dirt floor. The wind continues to howl and buffet the building. In the evening we lie in the tent, huddled under our sleeping bags reading. Even with the rain fly on the tent for extra warmth, the light of our candle in the tent dances from the howling wind, coming through cracks in the building and the tent fabric.

In the morning the mountains around us are still covered in dark clouds. We leave our bike luggage in the cabana and ride our unloaded mountain bikes back to the crater to enjoy some narrow, single-track trail riding around the crater rim. The path is exhilarating as it winds across the top of dramatic cliffs and steep hillsides dropping into the crater. The exposure is like riding the Poison Spider portal loop in Moab—with hurricane-force winds.

We return to our *cabana* for a breakfast of coffee and eggs. Umberto tells us he and his brother have *tipica*, typical, paintings for sale. We ask to see the paintings and also the area where he works. He takes us to his house, a tiny, dark, one-room cinder block building. There is no furniture. The bed is simply a pile of reed mats on the dirt floor. In the corner, divided from the rest of the house by a wall of clear plastic, is his studio. A single window, less than a foot square, offers marginal light for him to work. On his small, homemade desk is a collection of fifteen film cans full of different colored paints—the artist's palette.

The oil paintings are done on leather animal skins stretched out on wood frames, showing snow-covered volcanoes with villages, farmers, and llamas on the lower slopes. Although they are quite simple, we find them very beautiful and touching. Perhaps we are moved by them because of our time with the family, or because we have seen the dreary place where the artist lives and works. All of the pictures have a bright blue sky, small puffy white clouds and a bright shining sun. Everything looks so happy and idyllic; the people are all smiling. Is this what Umberto sees when he looks around his home in the mountains?

We buy two of the paintings, pack up, and get out to the road in time to flag down the first of a series of four buses to take us back to Quito. Our last week of mountain biking is finished. On the bus I look out the window. I am filled with a tremendous euphoria for having cycled through these desolate mountains; I feel incredibly alive and ready for more adventure.

I watch a falcon flying against the fierce wind. The bird flies alongside the bus for nearly half a mile, at the same speed as our loaded bus, which at the moment is chugging slowly up a hill. The falcon flies just a foot or two off the ground, trying to stay as low as possible and out of the gale. Struggling into the wind, using bushes, trees, and houses as windblocks, wings flapping rapidly, the beautiful bird is hardly moving forward, yet it doesn't give up.

24

On The Amazon

Back in Quito we get a top floor room in the Hostel Florencia, take a long shower, and have a wonderful fish dinner at a little sidewalk cafe where we can watch the bustle of vendors, tourists, and locals. Tass feels better and eats her first real meal in a week.

For the next three days we do another big gear shuffle to prepare for the final month-long stage of our trip. I give The King and Nina a thorough cleaning and tuneup. Tass uses touchup paint to cover the scratches from the last six weeks of travel. We ride the bikes, one last time, to the office of Emerald Forest Expeditions. Nina and The King will spend the remainder of their days being ridden in the Amazon Basin by our guide friends, Luis and David! We also donate extra tires, pumps, parts, and a repair kit.

We eat at the Magic Bean, do laundry, send FAXes to research stations we plan to visit in Peru, call my parents and Tass's mom, call our housesitter and secretary, eat at the Magic Bean, pick up and exchange gear stored at the South American Explorers Club, buy chocolate cake at the Oro Verde bakery, send postcards, eat at the Magic Bean, and pack bags late each evening. Near midnight, the last evening before our flight out of Ecuador, we collapse, finished, with everything checked off our list. We are ready to resume traveling.

At five a.m. the beeping of my wrist watch alarm wakes me from a deep sleep. Moments later I hear Tass's backup alarm going off. In twenty minutes we are standing on the sidewalk in front of our hotel, waving down a taxi. We have just two bags each: a medium-sized backpack and a small fanny pack for camera equipment. No bicycles. No mountaineering equipment. No snorkeling gear. Not even a tent! All we have with us is rain gear, rubber jungle boots, flip-flop thongs, an extra change of clothing, an assortment of books and cameras, and eighty rolls of film. We haven't traveled this light since our first trip to Central America twenty years ago.

Our first flight is to Guayaquil, Ecuador. We quickly grab seats on the left side of the plane to get good views of Cotopaxi and Chimbarazo volcanoes as we fly over the Andes. After landing at the Guayaquil airport, we strike up a conversation with an American couple in their late fifties who have even less luggage than we. They work in Quito for a Christian Radio station and are going to Peru for a vacation. Last year they went to Nicaragua.

"Our kids say we travel like gypsies!" they laugh. They have turned the table on the stereotype of hard-working corporate parents with free-spirited, vagabonding kids. In this case the children are pursuing lucrative, high-pressure careers, wondering—and worrying—if mom and dad will ever settle down. Like us, they are flying on to Lima, and they give us hints on getting from the Lima airport to downtown cheaply.

"Cross the street outside the airport and you can get a taxi to town much cheaper than the taxis outside the terminal!" they advise. In Lima we do as they suggested. When our taxi takes off, we spot them waiting for a city bus—an even cheaper, although time-consuming way into town.

Our taxi driver's name is Miguel Rommel. "I am the Peruvian Desert Fox!" he tells us triumphantly. He takes us downtown to a cheap hotel. Miguel is so friendly, we make plans for him to drive us back to the airport tomorrow on our connecting flight to Iquitos.

Lima is a vivacious city with a much different feel than Quito. The narrow streets are lined with two-story colonial houses, many with ornate hanging balconies overlooking the noisy, congested streets. The sidewalks are bursting with vendors selling snacks, roasted peanuts, camomile tea, and fruit salads. The local specialty is the *chorrizo*, a large, sugar-coated pastry. Delicious. Others sell clothes, shoes, batteries, kitchen utensils, handbags and small appliances.

A man walks past with a plastic bowl full of cake batter. Vigorously he stirs the mixture with a wire whip; a hands-on advertisement for the hundred other mixing whips for sale, hanging from his arms. A man selling women's handbags has fifty purses strung over his shoulders and arms, and stands asleep on his feet leaning against a building. With the sidewalk full of vendors, mobs of pedestrians spill out onto the street, where everyone dodges the swarms of taxis—most of which are Volkswagen Beetles.

"Old Volkswagens don't die; they go to Peru!" Tass marvels as a dozen Beetles pass by us in a row. A few are shiny, but most show serious wear: patches of rust, dented fenders, broken mirrors, windows that don't open or don't close, broken door handles, loose, ripped and broken seats. Some have whole sections of the car body missing, leaving engines and wheels sticking out uncovered, all offering much cheaper rates than the shiny yellow taxis that also cruise past.

At city bus stops, the crowds of people fill the streets. The swarm is so tight the passengers can hardly get off the bus, and unloading takes forever.

The loaded buses crawl through the crowds, trying to resume the routes. We give such jammed-packed areas a wide berth; it is the perfect place to be pickpocketed. Many people have told us horror stories about Peru in general, and Lima in particular.

"Don't trust anyone! They will pick your pockets, slash your bags, drug you, and even steal your glasses!" Despite the dire warnings to leave our cameras locked in our hotel room, we carry our cameras in hand, with the shoulder strap wrapped around our wrists. We keep a close eye on the crowds, and each other, and have a great time exploring and photographing Lima.

Actually it is amazing that there are any robberies at all, given the ubiquitous presence of armed police throughout the capital city. At the main plaza, police with Uzis and riot masks stand around armored personnel carriers. Nearby are tanks with rubber tires for cruising on city streets, armor-plated paddy wagons, and trucks with water cannons and large, iron barricade-breakers covering the front end. Private security guards stand in front of all the banks and jewelry stores. Even department stores, clothing stores, hotels, and restaurants have guards posted everywhere. Peru has been plagued by a small, violent group of leftwing terrorists who call themselves the *Sendero Luminoso*, the Shining Path, with a political philosophy modeled, oddly enough, on the discredited madman Mao Tse Tsung, who in the last decade has been reviled even in his homeland of China.

The next morning we call the airport to confirm our evening flight to Iquitos and learn we are not even listed on the computer. We have been bumped. We spend half a day at Americana Airlines and at last get a seat on another flight into Iquitos. The next morning at the airport, we again meet the couple who work with the Christian Radio. We ask how they liked Lima.

"Everyone was so friendly and kind! We rode the bus all the way to our hotel for just sixty cents," they proudly tell us. "The hotel employees said no one has ever come to the hotel from the airport before on a public bus!" Now they are off to Cuzco.

We board the plane for Iquitos and have a spectacular flight over the twenty thousand-foot peaks of the Cordierra Blanca. The Andes form a huge natural barrier running north and south off into the horizon. On the eastern side of the range, immense clouds covering the Amazon Basin push up against the entire length of the mountains. As we begin our descent the plane drops into the enormous sea of clouds and mist. We lose all visibility and don't emerge from the clouds until we are only a few hundred feet above the ground.

A mixture of clouds, mist, and smoke fills the air. The landscape below us looks hazy and surreal. For just a moment we see rainforest, and then wide tracts of cleared land. We fly over a few huge smoldering piles of burning wood, but most of the land has been cleared long ago and is now dotted with cattle.

The heat and humidity hits us like a blast furnace as we step off the plane. We carry our backpacks to the small airport terminal and catch a ride the six miles to town on a motocar, a three-wheeled motorcycle taxi. The breeze in the open vehicle is refreshingly cool on our already sweating bodies. A canvas awning shades us from the sun, and we have a great view of the countryside. The road is filled with other motocars, all buzzing like worker bees, a few single motorscooters, and a couple of cars and trucks. As we get closer to town, the traffic increases. Our driver races through the streets, vying for position with swarms of other motocars, passing and repassing each other as one or the other is forced to slow for traffic or pedestrians.

All the vehicles in town are shipped here, upriver, on barges or large oceangoing ships. Other than the six mile road to the airport, and one other thirty mile stretch of road heading south, there are no highways in this entire area of northeastern Peru. The only way to reach the city of Iquitos is by plane or boat.

We check into a hotel and head out for our first view of the Rio Amazonas, the Amazon River. At this time of year, the river is only a couple of miles wide as it passes near the city. Ever changing in its course, the river has in the last few years been moving away from Iquitos, leaving a desolate series of enormous mud flats and sand bars across the former flood plain. Hardly majestic from this view along the bank, the river looks more like an immense

Amazon river, Iquitos, Peru.

series of receding lakes, surrounded by muddy tidal flats. It is hard to imagine that in some areas the level of the river water can vary as much as forty feet between the highwater and low water seasons.

We visit the nearby town of Belen, where the streets are even more congested. Every square inch of space in the market area is taken by vendors selling all varieties of fish—piranha, catfish, bass, pirarucu—and countless others we don't know. Our motocar inches along at slower than walking speed through the congestion. We are in no hurry; we sit back, relax, and view the market from the shade of the awning. Often the road is so narrow, I am certain the rear wheels are going to hit a pile of vegetables laid out in a neat row on a tarp, but the driver always manages to maneuver past. The vendors never seem the least concerned; they hardly watch us pass.

We drop down a hill toward the river and the paved and cobblestoned streets turn to dirt. Belen has been called the Venice of the Amazon because during the high water, half the town is flooded under eight to twelve feet of water. All the houses on the lowland spit along the river are built on especially high stilts. Now it is the dry season, and the Venice of the Amazon looks more like the mud and refuse capitol. Piles of garbage lie heaped in mounds. Ponds and little creeks of sewage draw thousands of flies. Although not as scenic, it is still fascinating to visit at this time of year. The dirt road turns to mud as we ride closer to the river. When it is not possible to ride any further, we pay our driver and walk.

All of the homes are on enormous stilts. Some have closed-in lower levels around the stilts; these rooms are simply used half the year and then abandoned when the water rises. Water marks on the buildings are ten feet high. The owners of the houses on open stilts hang hammocks and store boats under the houses during the dry season. Rickety stairs or simply logs with notched steps lead to the upper floors. Some of the houses have porches, also built on stilts, but most are so open that a porch is hardly needed. None of the houses has glass windows or even screens or mosquito netting. Only a few have shutters. Privacy is less a concern than adequate ventilation; the first priority is to make sure that any and all breezes blow through the house.

The stilt houses are the middle-class homes of Belen, for the people who own a spot of land, even if it floods yearly. The poorer people live even closer to the river, lower on the mud banks, and build their homes on huge balsa log rafts. When the water rises the houses float to become houseboats half the year. During the dry season the rafts lie sadly marooned in the mud. Logs and wooden plank have been laid in the mud for pathways to the houses. Other people live in small boats anchored in the water along the muddy banks. Sanitation facilities are nonexistent; in the dry season there is no flow of water to wash the city clean. The poor people use the river for their drinking, bathing, and toilet.

A man paddles by in a canoe loaded with household goods—a floating store traveling from boat to boat and house to house—he yells out to advertise items for sale. Although a large metal floating dock has been built nearby in Iquitos, it is almost deserted. The vast majority of commerce comes into the city via the mud banks of Belen. Men and women of all ages hire themselves out as human pack mules and carry products from the boats along the mud banks up through the maze of congested alleys to the cobblestone streets on higher ground, where the products are loaded into carts, motocars and trucks, and distributed throughout the city.

We came to this area to spend a week at one of the more famous ecotourist lodges/research stations in the Peruvian Amazon. The lodge is near the confluence of the Amazon with the Rio Napo, the river on which we traveled earlier, further upstream in Ecuador with Luis Garcia. There are three sites here we will visit. The Explorama Lodge is the main complex where we will spend a few nights before traveling to the more remote Explornapo camp, and then on to ACEER, the Amazon Center for Environmental Education and Research, which has a small lodge and a one hundred-foot high, half-mile long suspended walkway through the rainforest canopy.

Explorama Lodge was started in the 1960s by two anthropologists, and today has quite a diverse clientele. Scientists and researchers stay at the camp, along with wealthy Europeans and North Americans on whirlwind ten-day tours of South America. These folks fly into Iquitos and boat up to the camp to spend a night in the world's largest rainforest, and then they leave the next morning. Most other tourists come for two to five days.

Together with International Expeditions, all the sites host an environmental program where school kids and their families from the U.S. come for a week-long rainforest experience. Since we are creating a slide program for schools, and are former environmental education instructors, we think it will be interesting to visit the site with a school group.

The group we will join meets the next morning. Since there are about forty of us, we are divided into smaller family groups. Our group has eleven members. Ellen, a single mother with her four kids, Becky, Sarah, Adam and Mary, along with her nephew, Hays, make up the largest part of our group. Another single parent, David, has come with his only daughter, Rebecca. Ben, a young teenager, is traveling alone. Tass and I round out the group. Our leader is a local guide named Reny, and the assistant leader is Bob Wolff, a spider expert from Illinois.

We have a three-hour boat ride on the Amazon to Explorama Lodge, a series of buildings connected by a thatch-covered walkway on stilts. All the buildings are also thatched and on stilts. The main gathering area is a large dining room with a high roof on poles and no walls, only screens to keep out the insects. Each guest room has bunk beds and half-walls, the top half being

Early morning mist on the Amazon River, Peru.

open without screening. Only curtains can be pulled for privacy. Kerosene lights provide the only light at night. No generator, no noise. The outhouses are simple pit toilets but there is running water in the shower house. The lodge is rustic and very quaint.

Our first afternoon there is a craft fair at the lodge. Thirty local villagers come to demonstrate traditional basket weaving, pottery making, wood carving, roof thatching and more. We are most interested in the blowgun demonstration, and make a beeline to check it out before the rest of the group comes through.

Three men work on blowguns in various stages of construction. They show us how the blowgun is made, a slow and painstaking process using the simplest of tools. A knife or machete is used to carve out a channel in two long sections of palm wood. Then the two halves are glued together with a thick black resin, creating the inner barrel of the blowgun. The two pieces are wrapped with a palm frond "tape," further sealing everything together. A mouthpiece of wood is fit onto one end, and then a long straight stick, also made of palm wood is rubbed back and forth like a ramrod inside the barrel along with fine river sand to further smooth and polish the passage for the dart. A good blowgun takes three or four weeks to make.

The oldest of the men, Pariso, has only half his teeth, but a wonderful impish smile. He grabs a finished blowgun, pulls out a thin wooden dart, puts a wisp of cotton around one end like a Q-tip, and pops it into the gun. A quick puff of air sends the dart one hundred feet, to stick quivering in the wooden wall of the nearby shower house. Using one of the camp shower houses for a target strikes me as funny. I make a charade about someone showering and getting hit in the rear with a dart. Pariso lets out an amazingly loud laugh. With a hearty chuckle he repeats my charade for his friends, who likewise think this is quite hilarious.

Tass and I take turns using the blowgun. We both hit the shower house, but our darts wobble through the air at an obviously slower speed. Pariso's darts fly so fast, we can hardly see them. His blowgun is much finer than the ones being constructed. Even though it is over six feet long, and would be a major hassle to carry, I ask if he would sell it. We bargain awhile, and take turns shooting it a few times. The blowgun is a beautiful piece of work. I really like it.

By the end of the afternoon, we have settled on a price, forty *soles*, about eighteen dollars U.S., a good deal as much smaller, touristy blowguns were selling for twelve to fifteen dollars in the oriente of Ecuador. As a part of the deal, Pariso includes a quiver made of palm fronds, which is full of darts, a woven bag with cotton fletching and a piece of piranha jaw to etch the ends of the darts. I ask him to include a few darts tipped with deadly *coari* poison from tree frogs. He asks why, and in a moment of inspiration I remember all the vicious dogs in Ecuador that wanted to bite us. I tell him I need them for *perros malo*, bad dogs. This brings yet another hearty laugh, and Pariso repeatedly slaps his thigh and repeats my response in Spanish to his friends. He gives me six poison darts, which I very carefully wrap and put in the bottom of my backpack.

When Explorama was built in the 1960s, the surrounding area was isolated and not developed. Since then the relentless tide of homesteaders into the area, along with an increase in the population of villagers and indigenous people, plus an increase in tourism, has contributed to a dramatic environmental change. Explorama has made admirable efforts to work with the changing reality of the area by working to integrate and support the local people and economies. The cultural fairs help keep local crafts alive and also offer alternative incomes to area residents.

Explorama has also adopted a small rural school. Visitors are encouraged to bring paper, pens and other supplies to donate to the school. Like most schools along the river, it is running with no amenities. Because of the impossibility of getting and keeping qualified teachers, many village schools get student teachers who come to teach during their summer vacations, sometimes donating their time until they get certification, and then they move on to better-paying jobs at schools in less remote areas.

A few years ago a doctor from the U.S. visited Explorama and was astounded by the lack of local health care. Within a year she gave up her practice in the U.S. and moved to Peru to start a clinic, which is also partially sponsored by Explorama and the guests who visit. We go to the small clinic, and are given a tour by the doctor.

"I am sure all of you are travelling with first aid kits that have much better supplies than anything people here have in their homes. In their houses they have no medicine cabinet, no bandaids, no aspirin, nothing!"

A large sign on the wall lists prices for various treatments:

First office visit—no charge
Tooth extraction—four *soles* ($1.80 U.S.)
Regular birth—seven *soles* ($3.15 U.S.)
C-section—thirty *soles* ($13.50 U.S.)

The doctor notes that many people have poor diets, and most of the local people don't eat vegetables. Her own attempts to plant a garden have also failed. "The soil is too poor," she tells us. "There is nothing to use for fertilizer." Likewise there is no garden at the lodge; all the vegetables we eat are shipped into Iquitos. Amazingly, almost none of the food we have been eating can be grown locally. Nearby on the bank of the Amazon is a small store with a sugar cane mill where cane is pressed and distilled into a strong jungle alcohol. The man who owns the mill is called Poloco.

"No one knows why," explains Reny, our guide, when he introduces us. "He is not Polish." Poloco says nothing, but stands smiling sheepishly. "He is white," continues Reny, referring to Poloco's Spanish ancestry and talking as though Poloco was not even in the same room. "Poloco has a big house. It shows that if you want, you can work hard and have a big house even in the jungle." Reny thinks for a moment and then continues. "Other people living here don't care about big houses. They don't want to work hard all the time. They just want to have a small house, and they are happy."

I think Reny views guiding with similar low-key aspirations. He has a sharp eye, and helps spot numerous birds and monkeys, but he also passes by many things that we stop to examine, and doesn't share much information, even when asked. Perhaps he is simply shy.

Our assistant guide, Bob Wolff, is both personable and full of information. Bob has spent time in rainforests throughout Central America, but this is his first visit to Peru. Still, Bob quickly becomes our unofficial leader. Bob wears Bermuda style shorts, a nice dress shirt, gray dress socks, and tennis shoes. Standing on a rainforest trail he looks so "normal" it makes him eccentric. His business card says Doctor Spider, and has a picture of a tarantula. Bob has a wide knowledge not only of insects, but of other fields and disciplines; we stay close to him whenever possible.

Even with the increase in human population near the main lodge, we still spot numerous birds and see troupes of saddle backed tamarins, a small monkey, passing through the trees. Pairs of scarlet macaws and blue and gold macaws live in the trees around camp and even in the roof thatching of the main lodge. In the morning a huge tapir walks slowly through camp and down the thatched and stilted wooden walkway running between buildings.

The enjoyable part of being with a young school group is watching the transformation of the kids' comments from "Yuk!" and "Gross!" to "Wow!" and "Cool!" Bob is priceless, especially on our night hikes. He does a wonderful job helping the kids to find spiders in the dark by catching the reflection of their eye shine with flashlights. Everyone is constantly calling, "Hey Bob! Come look at this!" and proudly pointing to what they have found. Adam sums up the respect and awe of the students, and cracks up the adults,

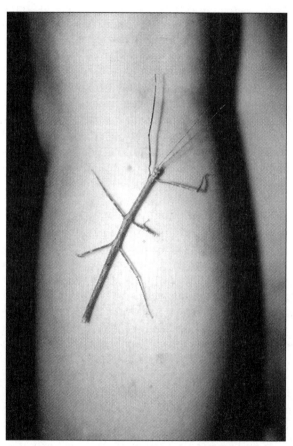

A walking stick slowly crawls up Tass's leg,
Amazon Basin, Peru.

when he finally asks in utter astonishment, "Bob, how do you know about all these bugs?"

After two nights at Explorama, we take a boat further down the Amazon and then turn up the Rio Napo. Tass and I ride on the front deck of the boat. A type of bass, we think, occasionally leaps out of the water, sometimes four feet high with ten-foot long jumps. One jumps and hits the boat with a loud BONK! head first, and then plops back into the water. We wonder if it knocked itself out. A few minutes later another fish jumps all the way into our boat, and then another does the same. We pick them up and toss them back into the river.

We spend the day exploring the area by boat and also do some short hikes. In the evening we stay at the more remote and primitive Explornapo camp. We have a delightful evening chatting with three researchers. One of them is Rosa Gentry, the Peruvian wife of the famous and highly respected rainforest biologist, Al Gentry. Al was tragically killed last fall in an airplane crash. Rosa still wears her wedding ring; she and her co-worker Sally talk about Al as if he were still alive. We listen to wonderful stories of their adventures working in the rainforest.

Later in the evening Bob joins us, and the discussion turns to strange rainforest illnesses. Rosa tells us when Al heard a friend and colleague had contracted Bubonic plague, his response had been, "Not fair!" Al prided himself in having experienced many strange tropical diseases. Being left out on a rare and unique disease was disappointing—or so he joked. Bob is also fascinated by tropical diseases and has a particular interest in botflies.

"Have you read the chapter "Jerry's Maggot" in the book *Tropical Nature?*" Bob asks. We have all read the book; still Bob relishes in reminding us of the details. Botflies learned long ago that they are too slow and noisy to land and deposit their eggs in the skin of a suitable host, whether that be a monkey, a bird, or a human. So some botflies glue their eggs onto the root hairs of plants growing near the openings of rodent burrows. When the rodent passes through, its body heat hatches the egg, which deposits the larva onto the animal. The larva then wiggles through the animals fur and burrows into the skin.

One type of botfly has a different tactic. It captures female mosquitoes carrying eggs. Without harming the mosquito it glues its own eggs onto the mosquito eggs. The botfly has learned to do this with only a specific type of mosquito that is a very quiet flier, which gives better odds that the mosquito will land on animals without being noticed and swatted. When the mosquito bites its victim, the body heat of the victim again causes the botfly eggs to hatch. The tiny botfly larvae fall off the mosquito onto the new host, where they immediately burrow into the skin, leaving the mosquito free to fly away.

Once the tiny botfly larvae burrows into the skin, it is not easy to get them back out. The larvae are the thickness of a hair, and have two hooks that hold them inside their burrow in living flesh. If you grab and pull the "head" end of the larva sticking out of its hole in your skin, it simply digs deeper the hooks on the other end. Pull too hard and the botfly larva will break, leaving a part of the larva in the burrow, which can quickly become infected. Leave the botfly alone, and it will develop at its leisure, eating the flesh around its hole for sustenance. Botfly larvae secrete antibiotics that stop competing fungi and bacteria from ruining its own food supply. Thus the botfly poses no danger to the host, except for possible psychological trauma!

The botfly larvae breathe air through a respiratory spiracle, which is like a little snorkel poking up through the skin. Immersing the body part in water will cause the larva to thrash wildly in its burrow because its air supply is cut off. The larva is often killed by plugging the hole with milkweed sap, but then it must be surgically removed to stop infection. Many of the local people have large scars where botflies were not removed, but were left to fester untreated.

Two other methods also work to get rid of botflies. Raw meat can be placed tightly over the wound, cutting off the air supply and forcing the larva to burrow up into the meat, trying to reach air. After a few days the meat is removed, along with the botfly.

But it is a second, more interactive method that interests Bob. This entails carefully catching the respiratory spiracle of the botfly larva and winding it around a toothpick-sized stick. The stick is slowly twisted over the course of a few days, and similar to the removal of a Guinea worm, the botfly is carefully wound up and winched out of its burrow. Bob confides he is hoping to be bitten by a botfly, so he can experience the process. "Just like reeling in a fish!" he says with relish.

The next day we hike to the ACEER center, a part of the 250,000-acre Amazon Biosphere Reserve. The reserve, set up as a non-profit organization, hopefully will someday expand to one million acres. The center has sleeping huts and rooms for research and lab work, but we are most excited to get up into the canopy walkway.

The walkway is made of two steel cables holding an aluminum ladder laid flat with wood planks on top for a walking surface. More cables are strung above for a railing, along with nylon ropes and nylon mesh sides for added safety. The pathway starts from the top of a small, two-story hut and climbs at a gentle angle, gaining forty feet of elevation in the two hundred-foot span to the first tree. Another small platform circles the tree trunk, and the next section of walkway leads up thirty feet higher to a second tree. The walkway continues to take us up in gradual stages, culminating at a height of 118 feet with about fourteen different observation platforms. After half a mile it descends back to the ground.

We zigzag up through the walkway. With a brief stop to bird at each platform, it takes about an hour to do a relatively fast first exploration. Once the initial reconnaissance is finished, we know which trees have fruit and where birds and monkeys might be feeding. Now we head back up to go over the whole system again, this time more slowly and thoroughly.

The differences in temperature and light along the walkway are amazing. We start in the shade of the forest floor, where the air is still and muggy and there is very low light for photography. As we climb into the sub-canopy, there is a slight breeze, and a few more patches of sunlight, but in the shade the air is still relatively cool. The air gets hotter and hotter ascending into the canopy. We sweat profusely, even when sitting still on the platforms watching for birds and animals. Swarms of tiny wasps and flies torment us. They don't sting or bite, but incessantly fly in our ears and around our faces and get tangled in our hair. They constantly get trapped behind my glasses and fly in

Canopy walkway, ACEER camp, Rio Napo, Peru.

maddening circles between my lenses and my eyes. In the few places the walkway spans between the highest of the emergent trees above the rest of the canopy, the temperature is absolutely sweltering in the sun.

Many of the platforms along the walkway are connected to the largest emergent trees, huge old giants with inner branches thicker than the trunks of normal-sized trees. The branches are all fully loaded with bromeliades, vines, and mosses that grow in the boughs of the tree. The ecosystem up here is completely separate and distinct from what is on the ground. Specialized species of plants, animals, reptiles, and even insects live their entire lives without ever venturing down to the ground. The weight of all this growth on the huge branches is enormous; older branches often break from the stress. A single trunk bromeliade can hold gallons of heavy water; the thick moss covering the branches is like a giant sponge coating, also full of water.

In the late afternoon it begins to cool down—a better time for seeing birds and animals. Bob, Tass, and I stay on one of the highest platforms near a flowering clusia tree and watch the sunset over the rainforest. The colors of the sky are so beautiful, we don't descend the walkway until it is completely dark.

The next morning we get up early to return to the walkway to experience the pre-dawn light. The sky is cloudy; pockets of mist hang between many of the trees and add to the wonderful, mystical feel of the morning. Although the clouds block the actual sunrise, the sky fills with the radiant colors of dawn— yellow, pink and even purple hues glow through the clouds and mist. The multilayered tops of the trees, with the mist hanging in between, look like mysterious, floating islands on an enchanted sea.

I watch the sunrise with Rosa and Sally while Tass heads with her camera and telephoto lens to the flowering clusia tree. As the colors of dawn fade, I join Tass at the platform over the tree, which is full of bright yellow-orange flowers, with flashes of iridescence from the colorful birds that flit from blossom to blossom feeding on nectar. We see opal-crowned tanagers, opal-rumped tanagers, short-billed honeycreepers, green honeycreepers, purple honeycreepers, gold and green tanagers, black-headed parrots, white-necked jocobins and more.

We could stay up in the walkway for days. We talk Reny into letting us go up one more time after breakfast; then our group itinerary forces us to move on to the next activity. We leave the Rio Napo camp and boat back to the Amazon.

In the evening as we boat up the Amazon, back to the main Explorama camp, thousands of raucous parakeets fly overhead. We hear each group before we see them and quickly scan the sky. Suddenly they appear over the trees, wheeling and turning with rapid wingbeats, flying low and fast. Most small groups contain an even number of birds—parrots and parakeets mate for life. As the sky grows darker, the number and size of the flocks increase dramatically—one group after another in an excited frenzy of wingbeats, squawking continually as if saying, "Let's go this way! Let's go that way!" The flocks rapidly swerve left and right as they race across the sky and disappear into little dots. Yet a few more moments pass until their voices also fade into the distance.

We pass the nesting island of the birds. Huge mist nets have been set up to catch parakeets for the thriving pet market. Captured birds will spend the rest of their lives separated from their mates in a tiny cage. Some will be sold as pets in Peru. Of the birds that are exported, only one in ten survives the trauma of being shipped to other countries.

In the middle of the Amazon Basin, a place we have wanted to visit for years, we have a relationship meltdown. The timing could not be worse! We simply want to enjoy our surroundings, but issues keep coming up that require our attention and energy.

Just prior to our arrival at Explorama, Tass lamented she is, "feeling tired of talking about Bruce and Tass!" Because we make our living giving slide programs, other travelers sometimes ask lots of questions about our business and lifestyle. Too often the conversation shifts around to us. To make matters worse, Tass believes that whatever the question, we both answer the same way, like identical twins.

"I don't know how two people who consider themselves such individualists could end up in a relationship where there is no individuality!" Tass shakes her head. We work and play together twenty-four hours a day, 365 days a year. Suddenly that does not seem so beneficial.

"We have nothing that we don't do together. We have lost ourselves in this relationship!" She questions if there is any longer a separate Tass without Bruce, or separate Bruce without Tass.

For Tass, feeling lost in the relationship is compounded by feelings of being cut off from family and friends, not only here in South America, but also sometimes when we are on slide tours in the U.S. She occasionally wonders if she is slowly drifting out of the lives of our friends—out of sight, out of mind. Our gypsy lifestyle means we are home only twelve weeks this year.

These issues are compounded by other problems. Since our arrival at Explorama, we have found ourselves stuck in camp management mode. Our five years working at Storm Mountain, the camp and environmental center, taught us to evaluate every aspect of running a camp. Now we seem compelled to remark to one another on the things at Explorama we would change if we were managing the facility. None of the issues is so big we would complain to the staff. Instead, we just continually make comments to each other. Neither of us likes being so nitpicky, yet we can't seem to stop critiquing everything. We sound like the South Dakota Critics, and we are driving each other crazy.

Perhaps we just need a little break from each other. We eat at different tables, to have a little space, and talk with other people. We try to avoid talking about us and our business, and we are deliberately vague about our profession.

None of this goes without being noticed by our group. Bob makes a comment about us "trying to get away from each" other at dinner. And eleven-year-old Mary expresses surprise when she learns that Tass and I are married. "I thought you were just friends," she says. After years of having people remark positively on our relationship—how loving we are with each other, how we are the ideal couple—we feel a shock to realize everyone now has a very different view of us.

We remind ourselves that all relationships go in cycles. Even soulmates have times when they just don't want to be around each other. Now we struggle to keep the vision of our relationship, our belief in a future together. We realize this is a critical time, because words spoken in anger and frustration can destroy trust and years of commitment.

We have had three or four similar crisis periods over our twenty years together. We have weathered such storms only through tremendous effort and work, with exhausting discussions requiring the highest priority of energy and commitment. As usual, I am the eternal optimist. I believe we can fix and repair any problem; we can mold ourselves into whatever we want to be. We may not always control life's events, but we can control how we will react to those events.

At Explorama, by popular demand, Bob leads another spider-intensive night hike. He shows us different kinds of webs and talks about the anatomy of spiders, such as the way the mouths work when spiders eat. He points out the palpus organs, little feelers next to the mouth. As he is showing us the body parts of a spider, he mentions which is the copulatory organ.

There is a slight pause in the conversation. Ben, a young teenage student, asks, "What is a copulatory organ?"

The adults chuckle.

"It's like a penis," I reply.

"Oh!" Ben retorts matter-of-factly, trying to save face in front of the group. "Why didn't you just say so!" Again there is a brief silence. The three boys scatter away from the light into the darkness, giggling hysterically over this new word. But halfway through the hike, the boys mix copulatory with olfactory, the organs for smelling, and now giggle at that word. By the end of the hike olfactory has been mixed up with oropendula, the name of a beautiful bird.

The following night we go to a mist net set up to catch bats. The bat's echo location, which enables them to find the tiniest insects to eat, is surprisingly not able to detect the fine thread of the loosely woven net. At the first net we find a short-tailed fruit bat. Using a single thick glove to protect against a bite, Reny carefully untangles the little bat. Once it is free he gently holds each wing so we can have a closer look. The wing skin has a soft, delicate feel and is so thin we can almost see through the wing when a flashlight is held behind it. All the veins are perfectly silhouetted. The little bat is hopelessly ugly, yet somehow cute, and totally defenseless. Everyone is concerned that the bat be handled with the utmost care. When we are finished, Reny gently tosses him back into the air to fly off into the darkness.

Later we return to find another short-tailed bat. This one is severely tangled. Bob and I hold the net while Reny works to untangle the little fellow. Finally Reny has to cut the net to get the bat free. Traumatized, the poor little bat is scared silly. When Reny holds him up, the bat's tiny penis sticks straight out in the air.

"Look out for his oropendula!" the boys yell. "He's going to pee!" A little squirt shoots out, narrowly missing us. The boys go off in convulsions, once again giggling in search of darkness.

Later in the evening we hear cries of "Bob, Bob! Come quick!" We run out to have a look ourselves. The three boys are excited but also a bit unnerved in the eerie glow of kerosene lanterns and dark shadows near the outhouse. They shudder as they take us inside to examine a tailless whip scorpion, a spooky-looking carnivorous arachnid. The body is five inches long, with even longer legs and antenna, and two large pincers, each with a row of nasty barbs that can inflict a gash on a finger, or hold an insect prey in a vise-like death grip, allowing the whip scorpion to leisurely enjoy its meal.

The next morning I walk slowly down the trail, thinking about the rainforest. I am finally feeling much more at home in the jungle. It seems more familiar. Even when I am hot and uncomfortable, I feel at ease. I don't fight it. The heat, the hot rubber boots, the mud all seem more bearable.

That afternoon our group visits a traditional Yaguna Indian village. Indians living near the lodge have set up the village so tourists from the lodge can see their traditional dress and barter for crafts in exchange for T-shirts, household items, flashlights, and fishhooks. The village is set up in a clearing. In the center is a large, thatched communal building with a twenty-foot roof, surrounded by small lean-tos and shelters, each with a few Indians selling handicrafts: beaded necklaces, woven baskets, balsa wood carvings, wooden bowls, darts and blowguns.

Everyone in our group is a bit shy. Most of the students huddle together, shuffling from one display to the next, surrounded by semi-naked, painted Indians. For Tass and me it feels too weird to just pull out the camera and start making photos. Instead Tass sits down with some women and watches them work while I head off by myself into the central building.

The inside of the building is dark. My eyes take a few moments to adjust to the light. Two logs lie across the dirt floor. Two men sit on the logs, chatting. They acknowledge my presence with slight nods. I smile and sit down beside them. From their conversation, and from the direction of their gaze, I gather they are discussing a few holes in the very top of the roof. As I listen to them speaking in their native dialect, I imagine their conversation goes something like this:

"I suppose one of us should climb up and fix the roof."

"Yeah, that hole is getting bigger."

"On second thought, the only time we are in this building is when the crazy white people come over. I really don't care if this place leaks or not!"

"Good point! The last time I climbed this roof I nearly fell and broke my neck! Let's not worry about the roof!"

"I agree. It is too hot to fix the roof anyway. Maybe we'll fix it next month."

"Yeah, maybe we'll do it next month!" As they talk I look up at the roof and nod my head as they do. Sure is a long way up there all right. I can't see much hurry to fix it either.

I get up and place my camera in the corner, facing the three of us. I set the self timer and nonchalantly walk back over and sit down. I laugh and point at the camera, which is now beeping and flashing a red light. The men also look at the camera and laugh, probably thinking, "These crazy *gringos* and all their gadgets, what is this *loco* fellow up to now?"

The camera beeps speed up and we all chuckle at the flashing light as the shutter snaps our picture. Now we really laugh. They are probably thinking, "This guy is really goofy!"

I am thinking, "These guys are really great!"

With the camera no longer beeping, they soon lose interest, and turn their attention once again to the roof. Finally they get up to head out into the sunshine. I follow. Most of our group is still shopping. Tass is busy chatting with the women. She beams me a smile. My two acquaintances pull out blowguns and begin target practicing.

I spend the rest of the time getting blowgun lessons. We shoot at a little carved, wooden tapir sitting on top of a post. Although their blowguns are nearly six feet long, they don't hold one arm out along the length of the shaft to steady it. They hold both hands close to their faces around the wooden mouth piece, with the full length of the gun hanging suspended in the air. Despite this seemingly impossible grasp of the gun, they have excellent aim. The force they get on the darts is amazing. Tass joins me, but our darts wobble and drift as they head for the target. We have a wonderful afternoon.

Some might say the traditional village idea is all contrived and set up—a Drugstore Indian encounter. But if it were not for the craft and cultural day at the lodge and the bartering exchange at the traditional village, most of these people would abandon the customs and crafts of their heritage. Many of the

Traditionally dressed Yaguna Indians practice using their blowguns, Amazon Basin, Peru.

settlers coming into the area have little respect for the Indians, who are often encouraged to abandon everything from their "primitive" past. Tourists showing interest in the uniqueness of the Indian heritage may help the native people keep respect for their own culture in a changing world.

During the little free time we have together in the evenings, we rehash our personal issues. Still, nothing seems to get resolved. Because of our tight schedule, we have little choice but to simply keep trying to find a resolution to our problems in between all our other activities. We still have fun, and can even joke and laugh with each other, but there is an undercurrent of tension in our relationship that is very stressful for both of us.

25

A Festival in the Andes

Our next destination in the Amazon Basin is the Rio Tambopata in south-eastern Peru, a remote area known for its wildlife. Although less than seven hundred miles south-east of Iquitos, it is in a completely different watershed. The Tambopata drains into the Madre de Dios, which empties into the Madiera, which doesn't join the Amazon until halfway through Brazil. To reach the Tambopata by boat would take a four-thousand-mile river trip. Our plan is to fly.

Naturally no direct flights are available. First we must fly back to Lima on the Pacific coast, then to Cuzco high in the Andes, then to Puerto Maldonado in the Amazon Basin where we will take a boat up the Rio Tambopata. Since we must go through Cuzco anyway, our plan is to take a short break in the mountains, to let our itchy bug bites heal before returning to the rainforest.

After getting bumped on our flight into Iquitos, we reconfirmed our return flight to Lima when we arrived in Iquitos ten days ago. Two days ago an employee from Explorama reconfirmed our flight again. Now we reconfirm one more time when we arrive by boat back in Iquitos. Each time we are told our flight will leave at seven p.m.

The day of the flight we go to the airport two hours early. At the Americana Airlines counter we are surprised to see they are already checking luggage through. Our luggage is carry-on, but we must go through the line anyway to check our ticket. After checking in, we saunter over to the gate, thinking we have ninety minutes before our flight. Within a few moments we are called to board the plane. The minute we find our seats the plane takes off—more than an hour ahead of the time listed on our ticket! Through all the reconfirmations, and even just now at the ticket counter, no one told us the flight time had been changed!

We arrive in Lima late at night. Although we are earlier than we expected, Rommel, the Peruvian Fox taxi driver, is already at the airport to meet us as planned. He drives us straight to our hotel, then returns to pick us up five hours later at four a.m. for our flight to Cuzco.

From the airport in Cuzco we catch a taxi downtown. Along the way our taxi driver tells us of a big festival in Qoya, a small town in the Rio Urubamba valley an hour away. He drops us off at a hotel. We feel like collapsing into bed, but his words keep echoing in our minds. *"Festival grande! Mucho danza tipica!"* Big Festival with lots of traditional dancing! Oddly, no one else we meet in town seems aware of any festival, neither at our hotel, nor at the little restaurant where we eat breakfast, nor even at a tourist office we visit. Despite our exhaustion, we make a typical Bruce and Tass pack-it-all-in decision. We jump on a small *collectivo* bus going into the mountains toward Qoya.

The seats in the tiny white van have been bunched together and extra wooden benches installed to allow a maximum number of passengers. Luckily today is a slow day, so only eight of us are on board as we head out of town. Still, my knees jam into the seat in front of us. The road is in terrible condition. Road crews have dug huge holes in the road, presumably to patch sometime in the near future. The day is hot. The men on the road crews all wear long pants, shirts, and sweaters despite the radiant heat of the tropical sun. A few wear balaclavas. Other groups, similarly dressed, stoke wood fires under large drums of melting tar. Waves of heat dance by the fires. The sun beats down.

The countryside is a dusty, golden brown: the dry season. Everything looks parched in the shimmering haze. Barren fields are framed in dry, windblown terraces that climb up the sides of the mountains. We cross a desolate pass and drop down a switchbacked canyon to the town of Pisac along the Rio Urubamba. We are surrounded by snowcapped mountains. This would be a grand road for bicycle touring!

Our bus comes to a stop along the main highway where a narrow, dusty road leads to the small town of Quyo. A small group of locals gets off with us. We chat with a young man from Pisac as we walk the short distance to the town. He tells us the festival will begin today, once Mass is finished in the large, colonial church. The festival will last three days.

The cathedral is packed with Indians in brightly-colored costumes standing shoulder to shoulder, listening to the soft voice of a priest whose words barely reach the crowd in the back of the building. As the service ends, we exit quickly and position ourselves outside for photo opportunities. An enormous crowd of brightly-costumed dancers begins to stream out, each group entering into formation with its own small band of horns, drums, and flutes. The musicians strike up a lively beat and the dancers begin their routines as they slowly make their way toward the street. Once a space clears, the next group comes out of the church in completely different costumes and masks, and lines up in formation with its own band playing a different tune. Within minutes there are more dancers than audience. Still more and more dancers swarm out of the church. Each group joins the parade around the town square, dancing merrily to the accompanying music, twirling and swaying to the beat.

Although there are few spectators, crowd control is rigidly enforced by animal dancers, whose masks are made from real animal skins—deer head masks complete with antlers, goat heads, cow heads, sheep heads—all with human eyes looking out where animal eyes once gazed. The animal dancers all carry long thin branches which they use like whips to ruthlessly smack anyone who steps into the street.

Still more dancers emerge from the church! Many of the groups represent people from Peru and other parts of South America: dancers with masks showing puckered lips are whistling Argentines; another with flashy, glittering blue and white cowboy costumes are Bolivians. My favorites are gauchos with long, crooked noses carrying bottles of beer. They repeatedly do a drunken swagger, throw back their heads, tip the bottles to their grinning mouths, do another funny sideways step, then all together toast the clear blue sky.

Another group has masks with stern faces and crooked noses. They carry a black book which they sternly tap with a small whip. We ask who the dancers represent.

"*Catolica!*" everyone laughs in reply. Strict Catholics thumping their Bibles! Obviously everyone has a good sense of humor, since the dancers just came out of the church and the celebration commemorates the Ascension of

Dancers dressed as Inca warriors in front of the cathedral, Quyo, Peru.

Masked dancer, Quyo, Peru.

the Virgin Mary into heaven. As with many highland festivals, the celebration is a curious blend of traditional Spanish Catholicism, Inca and pre-Inca beliefs and customs, and more recently, Liberation theology.

Each group of dancers does little jigs and performances for us whenever we point our cameras in their direction. Everyone is friendly and helps explain what the various costumes represent. Perhaps most amazing of all, we see only one other small group of foreigners at the festival. They show up for less than half an hour, and then leave. We are near Cuzco, the most heavily touristed city in all of Peru, and yet no other travelers are around!

A group of female dancers dressed in white lace comes out of the church. They are the first group that does not have caricature masks. The expression on their faces is of angelic contentment. Behind, a crowd of men carries litters with ornate statues of the Virgin Mary dressed in the frilly, doll-like clothes of Spanish Catholic tradition, common throughout Latin America.

As the procession with the Virgin Mary leaves the front of the church, the first group of dancers has circled the town plaza. The lead group takes a place in the center of the plaza and continues to dance. As each successive group finishes circling the plaza, it also takes a place in the center, until all the dancers are lined up in a colorful, twirling kaleidoscope of a Grand Finale, with each group still dancing to its own music.

When finished, most of the dancers leave the plaza to feast in the homes of the villagers. Only the dancers representing the Incas and the pigs stay to chase each other around the square. Brandishing spears, the Inca warriors chase the pigs, who roughly jostle and bump into the spectators as they run high speed through the crowd. When the Incas catch the pigs they whack them with their spears and throw the pigs over the length of the spears, which are carried on each end by an Inca warrior. The pigs lie on their stomachs over the spears, as if dead, and are carried to the plaza and thrown in a pile, which soon grows quite high and must be suffocating for the bottom pigs.

Once all the pigs are on the pile, they suddenly come back to life. Now the pigs all jump up, pull whips out of their belts, and begin chasing the Inca warriors. The pigs are no more gentle with the whips than the Incas had been with the spears. The pigs whip the warriors with gusto; sometimes three or four pigs gang up and pummel a poor Inca. The crowd stays well clear of each battle, not wanting to get caught in the fray as the pigs drag the warriors across the courtyard, and pile them in a heap.

Through the afternoon different groups of dancers return to the courtyard to perform. We watch until late in the afternoon when finally the last dancers disappear. The celebration will begin again later in the evening, but will not feature the lavish costumes. Most of the celebrations in the following two days will occur in small groups meeting in private homes. Exhausted from standing all day in the hot sun, we head back to Cuzco.

The next day we visit a number of cathedrals in town, but we find the decorations inside oppressive. I am overwhelmed by the fascination with misery in Spanish Catholicism. Christ is always portrayed in the paintings and statues as suffering in agony, covered with blood. Relentlessly dying. Like a rivalry, each altar strives to depict the most horrific, abused, and trampled soul. The imagery seems so unnatural, so removed from Christ's life, what Christ was about. What happened to the teaching and healing, the compelling messages, the joyous parties—turning water to wine? Where is Christ as friend, mentor, and role model?

Our bad mood continues outside the church, where we have a big argument over the same issues we began struggling with at Explorama. Now we sit on a park bench, first one, then the other pouring out grievances and frustrations. Afterward we sit for an hour, saying nothing, too depressed to even move. The fact that we are again not getting along seems overwhelming. We both feel trapped in our own rigid schedule. Suddenly neither of us wants to be in Cuzco, or even in South America.

We stew awhile longer, and then begin to feel stupid. We are ruining our day, our week, and if we don't get it together, we will ruin the rest of our trip, not to mention our relationship. Neither of us wants to go off on our own. We just want to get along, like we normally do.

We resume talking and finally begin to get to the heart of the matter. In the last month, I have taken as many photographs as Tass, which she now admits has been bothering her more than she realizes. On our world bike trip Tass carried our main camera, along with three lenses, and made most of the photographs. I had a small point and shoot camera, and only occasionally used the larger camera—mostly at temples and ruins. On our Central America bike trip we knew ahead of time we were going to make a slide program for our business, so both of us carried cameras and lenses. Still I shot much less film than Tass. Now that has changed.

Tass says she doesn't want to discourage me, if I really want to get into photography, yet she feels it was one thing she did that I didn't. The last few weeks she has felt like she has lost all uniqueness in the relationship. I have writing, which I alone do, while she has nothing that I don't also do. She has lost her individuality.

I reassure her that I am sensitive to the loss of identity issue. I think we each need a comfortable image of our own uniqueness in the relationship, of what we contribute, without feeling any competition or pressure to perform and live up to expectations. I jokingly remind her that not many of my Central America photographs made it into our slide programs. I guess I have been making more photos, trying to insure that I get something of quality.

The individuality issues runs deeper than just photography. We talk of ways to encourage each other in separate endeavors within the parameters of our relationship, to ensure that we don't smother each other. We both have very strong personalities. We give each other reassuring hugs, feeling sorry that so much anger has been vented. Yet, we are glad that everything has been vocalized. Although painful, by dragging all the issues raised into the open, we have made it possible to address the problems together, and to work to make changes. As we walk back to our hotel, we feel like we have weathered a storm. We feel like a team again.

The next morning we discover the La Yunta Cafe, which has the most wonderful pancakes—fruit covered with chocolate syrup. After breakfast Tass heads out to make photos, while I spend the morning eating and catching up on my journal. Vendor after vendor stops by, trying to sell me postcards, sweets, clothes, sweaters, shirts. If I look up or show the slightest interest, they hang over me, chattering, for five minutes.

For the twentieth time, a voice asks me if I want to buy something. *"No, gracias,"* I give my usual reply, without even looking to see what is for sale.

"Okay!" a small voice replies in English, "maybe next year!"

I chuckle and look up. A ten-year old boy stands before me smiling, his hair neatly parted and combed. He wears a beautiful handmade Peruvian sweater. I look in his basket for something to buy. He is selling pottery. I pick out two small bird whistles: a toucan and a parrot. He wants four *soles*, about two dollars U.S. I bargain him down to three *soles*, but when I get out my change purse, I have only two *soles* in small change. The rest of my money is in larger bills. Neither he nor I can face the hassle of trying to find change for the bills. He asks for my pen in lieu of money. I give it to him. Luckily I have another one in my pocket so I can keep writing.

As the boy moves on, two people come in and stand quietly by the door. Beggars often come to the restaurants for food. Like regulars, they stand meekly in a corner until a waiter spots them. The waiter ducks into the kitchen and returns with a small bag of food. We find it very touching: a voluntary and direct welfare system.

We visit the Inca ruins of Sacsayhuaman. The only thing left of the once impenetrable fortress are the large foundation stones that were too big for the Spanish to loot for the construction of their buildings and churches. Incredibly, as recently as the 1930s stones were still being taken from the site!

We walk up to single stones weighing hundreds of tons. The stones have been chiseled and carved to fit perfectly together, forming immense towering walls four hundred feet long. The buildings must have been beautiful on the high ridge, looking out over the Andes. The stonework is amazing; imagine the hours it took to carve the giant stones by hand! The intricate joints between the stones are so tight, it is impossible to slip a thin knife between the cracks.

On the highest hill in the ruins is a sacred circular structure, located over what the Incas believed to be a positive energy site. A number of Peruvian students sit in corners between the rocks, studying in the shade. It is interesting that so many people would choose to come here to think and work.

Many of the locals we meet, as well as other travelers, can't believe we are not going to Macchu Pichu during our time in the mountains. Tass hiked the Inca trail to Macchu Pichu in 1975 with her friend Suza, and has great pictures of the ruins. I would love to see the ruins, but we have heard as many as one thousand people a day visit the site in August. I would rather save the experience for another trip, perhaps another time of year, when everything is green and there are fewer tourists. We hike the Inca trail in the opposite direction, taking the short way back to town.

Llamas often have ears pierced with
colorful ribbons, Peru.

Tass heads for Cafeteria Haylliy which has, according to Tass, the best Lemon meringue pie of the trip. I head to a small park to sit on a bench in the sun to think and write.

A little boy with a small cardboard box of candy, cigarettes, and crackers comes up and quietly sits next to me, watching me write. Finally I put down my notebook and buy some lemon drops from him.

"*Que pais usted viva, amigo?*" He asks. What country are you from, my friend?

"*Estatos Unitos,*" I reply. The United States. His face lights up in wonder.

"*La gusta! Mucho hente para Estatos Unitos comprar para me.*" That's great, many people from the United States buy things from me. I ask him if he works all day long.

"Si, se vende total la dia!" he replies. Yes, I work all day long. He is seven or eight years old. He stands for a moment and says, *"Hasta Luego, amigo,"* Goodbye, my friend, and heads off down the park.

It is a simple encounter, yet it touches me deeply. How is it that I am born with such financial opportunities and blessings, and he is born into such hardship. I sometimes wonder if I should just write out every last one of my travelers checks and give it all away.

If I had enough courage that is what I would do. Instead I write lamentations in my journal. Yet I don't feel guilty as much as I feel humbled. Am I really doing enough with all the opportunities I have been given? Am I living to my potential?

Tass stops by for a moment, just to tell me she loves me. A tourist van drives past. In the back seat a foreigner takes a photograph of a church from the moving vehicle, through the dirty window, looking directly into the sun. Tass shakes her head in amusement.

"Wouldn't it be fun to see some of the bad photographs people take? We could have a big party and guests could bring ten of their worst slides!" We laugh at the thought. Tass gives me another kiss and heads down the street.

Later we stop at a photography store to buy extra rolls of Fuji film. The store takes credit cards but doesn't have an imprint machine. The clerk simply sets our credit card on the counter, lays the form over the card, and rubs a coin over the whole thing to make an imprint. Why not?

That evening we go on a date to celebrate making up with each other and eat at a little sidewalk cafe named Emperador Pizzeria Restaurant Turisiticoa. The menu has hilarious English translations for the meals:

Gordon Blue
Steak at the Toaster
Spaguetti at the Batter
Mustard of Cracker (Chicken)
Chicken at the Pineapple "Hawaiian Style"
Fried Chicken with Chinese
Ravicle Cream of Milk and Ham
Salad of Cheff

We toast our time in Cuzco. Tomorrow we leave for the rainforest of southeast Peru. One last chance to catch chagis disease, botfly or malaria!

26

Jaguar

Our flight out of Cuzco is terrifying. The plane can't seem to get off the ground in the high, thin air. Down the runway we go, faster and faster, the wings of the plane vibrating and shaking; still we never lift off. Finally at the very end of the long runway we rise into the air.

However, we fly along, barely off the ground. Steep mountains loom around us. Tass digs her fingers into my leg; she is totally gripped. I try to reassure her, and myself as well.

The plane makes a hard-banked left turn. Out the windows, the view is steep terraced hillsides. No sky. The tip of the wing looks like it will hit the mountain. I glance around the plane. Half the passengers appear as nervous as we. The others are oblivious, reading and chatting, unaware their lives could end at any moment.

The plane shudders again and manages to climb enough to miss the first mountain, but another higher mountain fills the right side window. This is definitely an exciting flight. The pilot manages to keep the plane climbing, and slowly we rise above the mountains below. Andean peaks, twenty-two and twenty-three thousand feet high, covered with snow and ice and surrounded by clouds, fill the horizon.

Crossing the Andes and dropping into the Amazon Basin we see huge, unbroken clouds of mist and haze settled up against the entire eastern side of the mountain range. We enter into the clouds, and see nothing but mist for most of the remainder of our flight. Just before we land we drop below the clouds and can see a huge expanse of rainforest, then cleared land and homesteads pop into view, as well as swarms of tiny dots. Cattle.

Stepping off the plane feels like stepping into a sauna. A large yellow sign warns of yellow fever. A guard checks the medical records of all the passengers. Anyone without the proper vaccination certification is ushered into a small room. Inside a nurse dispenses shots, nearby lies a pile of syringes and a little ice cooler full of serum. The passengers in the room all try to talk their way out of the vaccination, but the guard nearby ignores all protests. We already have our vaccinations, so thankfully we bypass the airport clinic.

While everyone else stands in the stifling building waiting for their luggage, we head for the door. All of our luggage is on our backs. We hire a three-wheeled *motocar* and head into town.

Puerto Maldonado is incredibly spread out with wide streets, some even paved, but nobody uses them. The town is quiet and sleepy. We check into the Hotel Wilson and are given a clean room that even has a seat on the toilet. What luxury!

In the evening we head out for a snack. The temperature has cooled down, and we are amazed at the transformation on the streets. The town is full of motorscooters and bicycles. The sidewalks bustle with pedestrians. We pass store after store that we had assumed were out of business. Now all are open and doing a thriving business.

Cities throughout Ecuador and Peru have sidewalks full of unmarked holes. Puerto Maldonado, however, is in a category of its own, with holes everywhere—many a foot or more square and one or two feet deep! Holes for water and sewer connections, holes for electrical connections, holes for phone lines. Some have broken lids, others never had covers. Many are half full of litter, others have ponds of scummy water. Tass is certain she is going to fall into one. Despite her amazing athletic prowess on bikes and skis, and at rock climbing, she can be klutzy when walking, often stumbling and stubbing her toes. Plus, she has terrible night vision.

After an ice cream snack we return to our room and lie on the bed under the ceiling fan. The temperature is still too hot to be under a sheet. Restless, we talk about our trip. This is our last adventure; in two weeks we will be home. We think about lying on our couch, eating popcorn and catching up on the latest videos. Despite the work of travel, Tass feels out of shape. She is excited to get back into an exercise routine of mountain biking and working out in the gym. I am also looking forward to mountain biking—without the weight of panniers—and especially to rock climbing!

The next morning we treat ourselves to breakfast at the fanciest hotel in town: eggs, bread, marmalade, coffee, and a huge papaya juice. The total for both of us is eight *soles*, about four dollars. I give the clerk a ten *sol* note. She doesn't have change in the cash register, so she digs in her purse. Still no change. She asks two other employees sitting at another table if they have change. They don't. We are in the nicest hotel in town, with a lush garden and a fancy restaurant, and yet there is not even the equivalent of one dollar in the till, and no one working here has a dollar in his or her pocket.

Yesterday afternoon we talked with a woman from the Explorer's Inn, the lodge/research station where we will be staying this week. She thought we would be the only ones going in the boat upriver. Last night we saw her at the hotel and she said five more people would be in the boat. Now when we arrive at the mud bank where the boat will pick us up, we find seven other people.

Tourism has grown rapidly in this area. Our three-year-old guide book to Peru claims this area is not for inexperienced travelers and is on the fringe of the rainforest *"gringo* trail." Trip reports at the South American Explorers Club listed only a few options for guides into Rio Tambopata or nearby Manu National Park.

But in Cuzco we found the streets lined with agencies offering trips into Manu National Park. Many people have told us that just this summer there has been a dramatic increase in people offering guided trips. But many of the agencies are unauthorized to take people into the National Parks. We hear rumors of one hundred people camping on a *cocha* beach in Manu near breeding areas of giant river otters, which is disastrous as the otters are very shy and could quickly be driven away. The boom in tourism is so explosive that no one knows what is going to happen next. Obviously without some rules, everything will turn into a wild jungle free-for-all. Everyone is concerned, yet uncertain how many guides there should be, or how many people should be allowed in which areas.

The history of the lodge where we will be staying shows the rapid transformation. The owner, Max Gunther, bought the land years ago with the idea of starting a hunting lodge for wealthy Europeans and North Americans. After a few years Max realized the area could not support big game hunting. He began catering to researchers studying the rainforest. As the reputation of Explorer's Inn grew, tourists also began visiting the lodge.

Max is now older and works out of his office in Lima. A few months ago he removed the manager of the lodge and apparently turned the business over to his wife, Mirtha, who meets us at the boat. She is Peruvian and has spent most of her life in the city. Although she is nice, she seems out of her element. She is accompanied by her accountant.

We also meet our fellow passengers. They are all Europeans: a group of friends from Spain and Italy and a couple from Denmark. Another woman stands near the boat wearing a huge, black leather motorcycle jacket. She has high-water cotton bellbottom pants, a loose cotton shirt with tons of beads, and a couple of wooden flutes strung around her neck. I don't have anything against black leather jackets, but they are not exactly functional rainforest attire. I wonder what a person would be thinking to not only bring, but then wear, such a jacket in the tropical heat. As she boards our boat, Mirtha introduces her as our guide. Our guide is wearing a leather motorcycle jacket.

Okay, I tell myself, mindful of the South Dakota Critic syndrome, give her a chance. Since all the guides are supposedly doing research projects, I decide to break the ice and ask about her field of study.

"I haven't decided yet," she replies, and drops the conversation.

We board the boat for the five-hour ride up the Rio Tambopata to Explorer's Inn. As the boat heads up the river, Tass and I whisper together, wondering if we have made a big mistake coming to the lodge. We console each other, thankful we have to stay with our guide only for two orientation hikes. Then, we are free to hike the trails on our own for the remainder of our stay.

As we head upriver it becomes apparent our guide is not good at spotting animals, or is simply not interested. She doesn't even have binoculars. Mirtha is preoccupied in a conversation with her accountant. The other passengers are very excited; this is their first time in the rainforest. We point out things to them along the river: turtles on logs, oropendolas in the trees, blue and yellow macaws flying overhead. The river is low, with huge sand and mud banks. In one area we pass through fifty-foot high canyons where the water has cut through the red clay soil.

We spot two scarlet macaws flying overhead. When they land in the top of an overhanging tree, we motion for the boat driver to slow down so the other passengers can see the birds. He accidently kills the engine. With the motor stopped, we realize the air is filled with the sounds of a huge flock of parrots. Tass and I scan the trees but can't spot them. Suddenly we notice movement on a clay bank. It is a *colpa*, a lick where birds come to eat the clay soil, possibly to get minerals to help digest acidic rainforest fruits and seeds. Now we insist the boat driver pull over to the river bank, where Tass and I jump out of the boat and scramble up a small hill to get a better view.

The clay bank is covered with two hundred cobalt winged parrots. Because of the time of day and the angle of the light, they are hard to see clearly, but it is amazing to watch nonetheless. The noise of their chattering fills the air. After a few minutes the other passengers, who stand close to the boat, get back aboard. We stall, and Tass moves closer for photographs. At last, very reluctantly, we return to the boat. We could have watched the parrots for hours.

The guide didn't get out of the boat, so I assume she has seen the *colpa* plenty of times. I ask if other species of parrots flock here. She shrugs her shoulders indifferently and says, "I don't know. I've never seen this before."

After four hours on the boat, we arrive at the camp. A palm wood walkway leads through the rainforest to the lodge. Six thatched dorm areas built three feet off the ground flank a large, two-story lodge housing the kitchen, dining area, and meeting areas. The setting is wonderful. We are given a glass of fresh fruit juice and then shown to our rooms. Each screened-in room has its own private bathroom with shower and flush toilets, but no seats. The rooms are spacious, the bed comfortable and firm. The lodging looks great.

We have just a few minutes to change into our jungle clothes and rubber boots for our first hike. Our guide shows up, no longer wearing the black leather jacket, and is slightly more personable than she was on the boat. She

Canoeing on the Rio Tambopata, Amazon Basin, Peru.

shares some basic info on plants and rainforest ecology, but not much. We tag along at the back of the group and do our own thing.

In the evening we go out looking for caiman. A different guide, a woman from England, is very knowledgeable and fun. But we spot only one little caiman, a foot long, which one of the boat operators picks up out of the water so we can all have a closer look. We gently examine the little fellow and then put him back in the water. Only a few years ago it was common to see adult caiman all along this river. Now, even at night with powerful flashlights to scan the river bank for crocodile eye shine, it is very difficult to find caiman. The crocodiles along this entire section of river have all been hunted and shot.

At five a.m. a knock on the door is our wake-up call. Breakfast is half an hour later and by six a.m. we are out on the trail for a half-day outing to Cococha, an oxbow lake formed when the river changed its course and left a curved, isolated lake, surrounded by rainforest.

After three hours of hiking, we arrive at the *cocha*. On the bank is one regular canoe, and two canoes that have been lashed together with boards to create a single, double-hulled canoe. All six of us pile into the double-hulled canoe for a tour of the oxbow lake.

As we set off, I spot a group of giant river otters on the far shore, five hundred yards away. They are very rare and also very shy. We don't want to spook them. Even though we are far away, we stop paddling and just sit still and watch.

They have also spotted us. Through our binoculars we watch them periscope, lifting their heads and the fronts of their bodies high out of the water to look our way. We see six of them, the entire family that lives at the lake. Sometimes they swim like dolphins; we can see their backs rise out of the water each time they take a breath. Other times they swim more like a beaver or muskrat, with their heads held continuously above the water as they look around. We watch them swim until they disappear into the haze at the far side of the lake. We give them plenty of room, and dip our paddles into the water to set off in the opposite direction.

Hoatzins nest all along the bushes and trees on the lake, making loud indignant squawks as we draw near, then thrashing loudly through the trees as they move from perch to perch. They are two feet long and the most ungainly of birds. Their awkwardness is heightened by their penchant for roosting in thick brush and insisting on flying, rather than hopping, from branch to branch. With each little movement, they create an enormous racket as they thrash their wings through the foliage trying to lift off, accompanied by hoots, honks, gurgles, and growls.

Groups of macaws fly over the lake, almost always in pairs or in groups with even numbers. Like parrots, macaws mate for life and seem to enjoy squawking at each other throughout their relationship. Tass thinks they simply enjoy hearing the sounds of their own cries echoing through the forest.

On the hike back, we spot a troupe of saddleback tamarins high in the canopy. Our group spreads out along the trail to watch the small monkeys racing through the trees. Our *Neotropical Rainforest Mammals* field guide describes tamarins and marmosets as having "heads decorated with a variety of ear tufts, tassels, ruffs, manes, mustaches, or mantles of long hair." The largest, the black-chested mustached tamarin, weighs only one-and-a-half pounds and is the size of a large squirrel. They have claws instead of nails on their fingers and toes, so they can climb trees like squirrels, hopping right across the bark, or like monkeys, from branch to branch. The males carry the young on their backs; we watch out for little hitch-hiker humps.

After five minutes, Tass is startled to notice, just twenty feet from us, a lone tamarin, lying as relaxed as you please, with its stomach on a branch and its legs dangling in the air, watching us. Even after I slowly walk up to join Tass for a closer view, the tamarin lies calmly on the branch, observing us. Then reluctantly, it moves on.

Each hour we hike gets hotter and more humid. Now is the heat of the day, and we have been out seven hours. Everyone is soaked in a combination of sweat and mosquito repellent. Tass and I are tired. The rest of the group walks like zombies, stumbling along in single file, staring at the feet of the person ahead, trying to avoid roots and obstacles on the trail.

We return to the lodge, happy we have put in our two orientation hikes and can now set our own itinerary. Another researcher/guide, T'ai Roulston, has agreed to take us to one of his favorite birding areas. T'ai was born in the U.S. and has traveled extensively, including a bicycle trip across Africa. We hit it off immediately. After the heat of mid-day, we canoe a short way up the Rio Tambopata and hike for half an hour to a series of small ponds. T'ai leads us to a perfect spot with a good view of the shoreline and the trees overhanging the clearing. Just a week ago T'ai was at this same spot, sitting quietly, when he spotted movement on the far bank. A full-grown jaguar came ever so slowly out of the forest and cautiously made its way down to the pond. Unaware that T'ai was less than one hundred yards away on the opposite bank, the big cat crouched at the water's edge and drank. It was the first sighting of a jaguar in the area in three years!

Unfortunately, the chance of spotting the jaguar again so soon is almost nonexistent. Jaguars cover enormous ranges; the big cat is long gone from this area. We don't expect anything quite so dramatic and are happy to sit, bird, and chat very quietly. Tass is in good humor, and keeps us chuckling. As we look out over the lake, macaws keep flying over the forest canopy behind us, against the sun. We are unable to identify them as they show absolutely no color, only a silhouette against the bright sky. As the third such group passes by, Tass excitedly whispers, "New species!" We scramble with our binoculars to take a look, but see only yet another macaw silhouette.

"Black macaws," she chuckles.

We spot what we think is a small toucan flying deep through the trees. But it turns out to be an oropendola. A few minutes later we make the same mistake.

"New species!" Tass chortles. "Toucan oropendola."

At supper we meet some of the fulltime researchers who stay at the lodge and work in the area. T'ai is asked to relate his jaguar sighting. Some scientists who have spent years in the rainforest have seen only tracks of the big cats. At the urging of others, Fernando Cornejo, a Peruvian botanist, shyly acknowledges he has seen five jaguars! Three times he has seen a jaguar sleeping on a tree limb in Manu National Park, about three days north by boat. The other two jaguars were in northeastern Peru.

Identifying things in the rainforest can require tremendous patience, determination, and luck. Hiking the next morning we hear a loud bird call that sounds like a seal barking, with hiccups. Even though the bird calls unremittingly, we can't pinpoint it. We crane our necks and squint our eyes looking up into the trees, all to no avail. We listen intensely, trying to discern which tree the bird is in. For the longest time we think the sound is coming from the top of a huge palm, but no matter which direction we look, we spot nothing. We scan a giant cycropia, but still no bird. For the umpteenth time, I force my way through the underbrush to get another angle on the forest canopy and finally spot something way up on the top of the largest emergent tree in the area. To get the view, I look up through a series of openings in the subcanopy foliage, the main canopy foliage, and then through the leaves on the emergent tree itself. All I see are a few tail feathers and two legs sticking down. The bird looks guan-sized, about two feet tall, but I don't think it is a guan.

Now that I have finally spotted it, and know where it is, I force my way back through the brush to meet up with Tass. We spend the next ten minutes trying to find another spot with a better view through the forest canopy, but can't even relocate the high branch of the tree, much less the bird squawking away on the branch. We have to walk nearly one hundred yards and look from a completely different angle before we can once again spot the top of the tree and, yes, we think we see the bird. It is on a nest, or maybe we are seeing some kind of termite nest close by in the line of vision. No, it is a bird nest, we think. Our only hope is to try to identify the unusual voice later.

The air is still, the humidity stifling. Simply breathing requires work and effort. I think I spot a tayra, an animal slightly larger that a weasel, walking down the trunk of a tree. All I glimpse is the hindquarters and a bushy tail. We sit quietly, watching to see if we can catch another sighting.

When we are occupied, searching for something, or watching something, we momentarily forget about the heat and discomfort. If an animal or colorful bird appears, we click into stealth mode. But between these sightings, it is easy to get lethargic as the heat drains the energy out of our bodies. As the morning wears on, we begin to feel like mules with our cameras over our shoulders on tripods, binoculars around our necks, fanny packs full of gear around our waists, and daypacks with fieldguides, raincoats, water bottles, food, hats, sunscreen, and insect repellent.

We spot movement, but it is a nondescript warbler or wren in the underbrush. We no longer have the energy to get out the binos for these ho-hum sightings. It is close to the heat of the day, and we need something more exotic to catch our interest! We hike back to the lodge on auto-pilot, too delirious to think, just watching our footing and wiping the dripping sweat from our eyes so if something BIG appears, we will at least see it.

From one to three o'clock the heat is nearly intolerable. We hang out in the lodge library, studying field guides. We find an orientation booklet with big letters: PLEASE LEAVE ON BOAT. Inside are pages of information explaining all the sites from Puerto Maldonado upriver to Explorer's Inn—none of which was shared with us or any of the other boat passengers. The little library is full of displays, posters, and pamphlets explaining the area, none of which are being utilized. Everything is covered with dust.

A study of this area lists five types of forest in the region: Subtropical Wet Forest, Very Wet Subtropical Forest, Subtropical Rainforest, Mountainous Subtropical Rainforest, and Low Mountain Subtropical Rainforest.

A Peruvian Ministry of Agriculture report on the Madre de Dios area states 215,000 hectares (one hectare equals 2.47 acres) of land were cleared in this region in 1983. By 1990 the figure doubled to 400,000 hectares, of which nearly eighty percent has already been abandoned! The rest of the cleared land is listed as having very low productivity. The report says the migrant population arrives in the area with the intention of getting rich quickly. Everyone starts out with traditional activities such as agriculture, logging, raising livestock, or extracting alluvial gold. When the expected wealth does not materialize, the population moves on to other forested areas to begin the same cycle. The people are "developing" the land using extractive methods which cannot be maintained long-term. These activities all have alarming consequences on the environment, and ultimately ruin any hope for a quality standard of living.

According to the report, nearby Alto Huallaga had phenomenal bird habitat but, "has been completely degraded by the cultivation of coca." Cocaine is ruining lives and creating problems all over the world and is also destroying vast tracts of rainforest.

The next morning we leave extra early and hike non-stop back to Cococha, the oxbow lake. We have permission to use the small canoe. T'ai has warned us the canoe has a bad leak, so we take the largest bailing bucket and two handmade wooden paddles hidden under a nearby tree. The lake is half-covered with mist, quiet and still. The early morning light reflects a golden hue off the mist. Everything looks surreal. The water is as smooth as a mirror.

Tass has out the telephoto lens, and her camera is on a tripod at the front of the boat. I paddle and steer at the back.

"Do you think the bump in the water ahead is a log?" Tass asks quietly.

"Yes," I reply. Ever so slightly, the log begins to move.

"It's a caiman!" we whisper-shout at the same time in excitement. I paddle slowly, just enough to keep our momentum. The caiman swims lazily ahead, unconcerned, yet when I try to speed up, the caiman also increases its speed, keeping the same distance between us. I stop paddling, and we slow back down. The caiman also slows down. Only the very top of its head is above water, about one foot long with bulbous eyes sticking up like two periscopes. A spectacled caiman. We guess the total length of the crocodilian at about five feet.

We find it rather humorous to be watching a caiman in such a leaky canoe—our own Cococcha Titanic. Every ten minutes I have to bail out four inches of water from the bottom of the canoe. Our camera gear is perched

precariously on a shaky wooden bench in the middle of the canoe, surrounded by water, both inside and outside the canoe.

The morning light is perfect for photographing hoatzins on the far shore.
Tass keeps her tripod at the front while I paddle for the best camera angles.
We work as a good team and manage to drift slowly up close to a number of
the birds. Sometimes five or six of the large birds crowd onto one thin, sag-
ging branch. They squawk and flop over each other indignantly, using their
wings to vie for position. Crests erect, the hoatzins crane their necks to stare
at us, feathers flushed and puffed up. They regard us with disdain. We regard
them with mirth.

In the canoe, on the water without shade, the sun is especially hot. We
have long ago shed our heavy rubber boots, shirts, and pants. I paddle in my

Bruce bails water from our leaking canoe,
Cocacocha, Rio Tambopata, Peru.

underwear. We keep an eye out for river otters, which we don't spot, but we see numerous turtles sunning on logs. Macaws and parrots fly overhead. We paddle all over the cocha until our arms are exhausted from the weight of the heavy, waterlogged wooden paddles. As it grows closer to mid-day, we are forced off the water by the intense radiant heat of the sun. We beach the canoe and retreat into the shade of the trail.

The book *Tropical Nature* talks about having a bowel movement when hiking in the rainforest, and then returning after a few hours or a day later to see what has happened. I deliberately did not use the toilet in our hut this morning, just so I could go in the woods. I walk a few steps off the path, clear away a spot of dead leaves and do my business. I'll check on the results later.

Another forced march back to camp in the stifling heat. We are beginning to feel familiar with the area and with many of the sounds, sights, and smells of the rainforest. We no longer complain much about the heat or fight against it. It still saps us of energy, but that is okay. It is all a part of the experience. At camp we take showers to try to cool off, then lie naked on top of our beds, reading and talking.

"You really have to put in time to become familiar with the rainforest environment," Tass muses. "Each day we see a few things, and now after five or six weeks, I look back and am amazed at all the things we have experienced." The rainforest reveals itself slowly.

We drowse in and out of sleep, read for awhile, then snooze a little more. At four o'clock I get motivated enough to get up and do some writing. I head over to the lodge and drink a couple cups of hot coffee to get a sweat going, and to get some caffeine in my body. A few other people shuffle in and out, totally lethargic. HOT!!

At supper Tass kicks me under the table and makes a flicking motion with her eyes. I look over and see one of the woman guides methodically picking parsley out of her potato and beet salad. The vegetables have been cut lengthwise, like french fries. Cleaning all sides of a long, slippery vegetable is no easy or quick undertaking. She cleans off not just the larger pieces of parsley, but even uses her fingernails to pick away at the tiniest segments, which are then set on her plate and arranged and rearranged repeatedly into specific piles with her knife and fork.

Tass watches for a few minutes and then leans over to whisper, "I don't think she has both oars in the *cocha*."

Another guide comes in from upriver and tells us mining horror stories. She saw five or six new dredges, each eating up large sections of the river bank. She also saw an increase in miners working sluices, and gold panners using mercury. One man had a ball of mercury as big as her fist, and was swishing it around in the pan with the gold and water. When he finished he put the mixture into an old piece of shirt and then squeezed out all the water and muck. He opened it back up, picked out all the loose pieces of mercury he could from the cloth, then threw all the rest in the water. We have read that all the fish for sale at the Puerto Maldonado market have dangerously high levels of mercury poisoning. No wonder.

Later in the evening as we are studying fieldguides, Tass looks up as two men come in the door. She kicks me under the table.

"I think those two guys are somebody," she whispers discreetly and nods her head toward the door.

"I think we are all *somebody*," I jokingly reply and glance at the men.

"You know what I mean," Tass whispers in exasperation. "Somebody special."

"How can you tell?" I question, humoring her.

"Something about the way they are dressed, the way they move and look around." She shrugs her shoulders.

They are dressed in normal rainforest attire. Nothing special looking to me. However now that Tass has pointed them out, they do appear to be different from most of the tourists in the room. They appear to belong in the rainforest, as it they are very comfortable here. They walk through the room and disappear into the back. Fifteen minutes later they return and sit at the table next to us. Tass strikes up a conversation, and it quickly becomes obvious both are serious birders.

"I'm Victor Emmanuel," the man says after a few moments as he extends his hand. "I have a nature touring company," he adds, unnecessarily. We have long known of him. Victor is a famous birder, nearly on par with Roger Tory Peterson in birder expertise, practically a birder deity. We shake hands.

"We feel like we know you," Tass replies. "We have been getting your trip newsletters for fifteen years." Tass can't help but chuckle and add, "We have never taken one of your trips, but we always read where you go to find out the hot spots. Then, we go by ourselves."

Victor's friend laughs heartily and extends his hand.

"My name is Barry Zimmer." In mock seriousness he adds, "I thought we got all the people like you off our mailing list long ago."

Despite our jokes, we offer appropriate reverence. We are terrified of saying something dumb. Barry explains that they have been at a large *colpa* for eight days, scouting out a site for a trip next year. Barry leads numerous trips each year, not only in South America, but to Central America, Africa, and even Antarctica. Being good enough to lead a Victor Emmanuel tour for one continent indicates a hot birder. Even more impressive, Barry leads high quality clientele to such diverse regions with entirely different species.

Victor and Barry are stunned to learn we are so close, yet not going to the *colpa* up the river. But the only way we have of getting to the *colpa* is by hiring a boat from Explorer's Inn, which means we must also hire a guide from the inn. We also have to pay for a boat driver. Since the trip takes a full day each way, the gas for the canoe is terribly expensive. The cost for the trip would be as much as our entire week at Explorer's Inn. And we would get only two hours at the *colpa*. We don't want to go unless we can stay a few days. Perhaps another trip.

The next morning we get up at 4:30 a.m. so we can be out on Cocococha for sunrise. A great potoo, a nocturnal bird related to owls and nightjars but with an enormous mouth, calls out with gusto, sounding surprisingly like a howler monkey. One of our bird books describes the voice as a *"loud, guttural, snoring, GWAWWWRRRR or WOWWWRRRR."*

We shovel down a quick breakfast and head out on the trail at high speed. The hike to the lake takes just over an hour, if we walk fast and absolutely don't stop to look at anything. The sky has a beautiful pink hue as we arrive. We set off once again in the Cocococha Titanic. Instantly we spot a caiman, but this time it immediately drops below the surface, out of sight. The morning haze thickens and obscures the sunrise. The light is poor for our plan of photographing panoramas and reflections on the water, so we turn our attention to bats.

A number of bat colonies live on dead logs and palm trees hanging over the water. We canoe slowly and stealthily up to the logs to see the bats, hanging on the sides of the trunks. They are long-nosed bats, with little furry brown bodies and squat heads. They blend in remarkably with the bark on the tree. They just look like little spots. Even as we draw near, they are hard to make out unless we look very closely. When our canoe is only a few feet from their perch, they explode into a whirling flock of shadows as they take to the air.

Without saying so, both of us are also hoping for another glimpse of the rare, giant river otters. Despite our vigilant surveillance they are nowhere to be seen. With the heat of the day approaching we are ready to get off the lake and out of the sun. As we start down the trail, I check the place where I went to the bathroom two days ago. I don't see the spot, so I walk back to the main trail and try another place. After a few minutes, I realize the first spot I looked was correct after all. I go back and look again.

The reason I don't see any feces is because there is nothing left. When I look carefully, I can see the spot where I used my boot to scrape aside some loose leaves to clear a piece of ground. I bend down even closer. There is absolutely no trace; not a single little spot is left. The ground has literally been picked clean. Dung beetles have carried everything away. I grab a twig and poke the ground, and notice there is a tiny soft area. The area moves. I use the stick to break the surface and find a nest of little maggots, wiggling in the moist earth.

During the heat of the day, I go with T'ai to Laguna Chica to test-ride a canoe he tried to repair with plumber's putty, the only thing available at the camp. T'ai takes the only seat in the back of the boat, while I kneel up front. The good news is that all of the holes he patched have stopped leaking. The bad news—water gushes into the boat from a number of holes he didn't see. The water in the boat is soon too deep for me to sit, so I prop myself up on the bow. The flimsy aluminium boat has no strength or rigidity; the weight of our bodies on each end slightly buckles the craft. The center of the boat bows up out of the water enough for an air pocket to form, stopping the little geysers leaking in the middle of the boat. Now the ends begin leaking. We don't bother to bail the red, murky water out of the boat; instead we turn the canoe around and quickly paddle back to the dock before we sink.

Early the next morning we awake with smiles to a chorus of red howler monkeys. Their booming growls and hoots continually crack us up. Today is our last day at Explorer's Inn and our last day in the rainforest. We decide to do a seven-hour hike to Katicocha. We head out on the Big Tree trail and then hike down the Haleconia Trail. The vegetation is completely different from other parts of the reserve. We hike through bottom land covered in palms that can survive being underwater all through the rainy season. This would be a good area for tree frogs! The trail is seldom used. In many places huge trees have fallen across the trail. We have to bushwhack through the wreckage of broken branches and tangled masses of limbs, vines, and other smaller trees that have been uprooted. At such areas it is surprisingly easy to lose the trail if we are not careful and alert.

As we hike further, we come to an area with huge towering trees. Many of the trees have enormous buttress roots, like giant stabilizing fins that extend out to support and balance the weight of the tree. Some of the buttresses go into the ground; others form into giant roots that spread out from the tree across the top of the ground. Even fifty feet from the tree some of the roots are still a foot in diameter, like enormous cables lying tangled on the forest floor. I follow one root, winding into the forest—it goes on and on and on, snaking around one tree and then another. One hundred feet. Two hundred feet. The root slowly shrinks in diameter. At two hundred and fifty feet from the tree the tendril is still five inches thick. The tendril ultimately joins a tangle of other roots, and either fuses with them or sinks into the ground, it is impossible to tell.

The above-ground root systems emphasize the poor quality of the soil. We walk past trees that have been uprooted and blown over. All the roots grew along the surface. Even the largest trees have no tap root, nothing that burrows deep into the soil. No nutrients are found there. All the roots run out along the ground in an effort to anchor the tree and remain in the thin zone of soil where they can absorb nutrients and minerals. A foot or two deeper, and the soil has no life.

We stop at a few more trees to make photos, and then come across an enormous kapok tree. The buttresses on the tree are so big we decide to take a self portrait, standing together, surrounded by the giant roots. We chat as we set up the tripod, amazed by the vast size of the tree. We make a few photos and then change lenses and do a few more. I walk partially around the tree, trying to photograph the huge limbs of the tree, spanning out over the upper forest canopy.

I walk back and join Tass, who is busy photographing haleconia flowers. I decide to walk around the tree in the opposite direction, for a few more photos.

On the back of the tree two eight-foot high roots branch out from the trunk like giant fins. I walk between the buttresses, which tower on each side

We stop for a self portrait at the base of an enormous
kapok tree, Rio Tambopata, Peru.

over my head and come together as they meet the trunk of the tree. I drop on one knee, wedge my body close to the tree trunk, and shoot a wide angle of the roots around me and the tree above me.

Click, whhrrrr. It is the last picture on my roll of film, the camera begins to automatically rewind. I stand up and reach for a fresh roll of film from my waist pack. As I reach down to click open the back of the camera, I hear an odd thump in the tree roots.

I sense something.

Startled, I look up as a huge black shadow explodes towards me out of the tree. I hear a loud scream. Then I realize I am the one who is screaming.

The scream erupts out of me. It explodes from my chest. Later Tass will tell me it is the most primal scream she has ever heard—a first man scream. For a moment she can't believe it is me. Terrible premonitions fill her mind. She wonders if I have been bitten by a bushmaster, one of the most deadly snakes in the world. Perhaps I am already dead.

For me, everything becomes surreal and flows in slow motion. I realize the shadow coming at me through the air is a **jaguar!** I am stunned, baffled by how the cat could be coming out of the tree! Nothing makes sense. Jaguars are so rare that I had never even hoped to catch a glimpse of one. Now it seems I have cornered one! While my mind struggles to accept the reality before me, another part of me watches with an intent, yet detached interest, as if I wait, with curiosity, for the end of a movie.

"Don't worry where the jaguar came from!" the voice in my head commands. *"Pay attention! Don't miss watching the last few seconds of your life!"* The jaguar is all teeth and claws. I am totally convinced I am going to die.

But the jaguar does not touch me. It passes over my head—so close, so very close. I turn and watch it land, fifteen feet away. I am taken by the jaguar's incredible power and beauty as its feet touch the ground, with hardly a sound, and it leaps away. The image of its long tail hanging in space—is forever branded in my mind.

As the jaguar vanishes into the forest, I question whether I really saw it at all. But then my body shakes so hard that I can barely stand. My breath is gone, as if punched out of me. I know the jaguar was real. The jaguar passed over me, and I am still alive.

Everything continues to flow in slow motion. I listen to Tass's panicked screams. I can hear the terror in her voice as she calls out to me. But I am still frozen in place. My lungs have no air. I can not speak.

As Tass runs around the tree toward me I am finally able to stammer, "I'm okay!" And then Tass is beside me.

"A jaguar!" I blurt out, "was in my face!" What I say hardly makes sense to me, and much less to her.

She spins around, screaming, "Where, where?" But the jaguar is long gone. Still I can hardly speak.

Again Tass yells, "Are you all right?" because she can feel my terror. Full of hysteria and adrenaline, I begin babbling, and show her where I was standing when the shadow exploded toward me, and how I thought the jaguar was going to rip off my head. I recount how, when it didn't, I turned to see the jaguar still in the air. Though only a moment, it seemed like forever. Then the cat disappeared into the forest, and I am still alive!

But as I tell the story it makes no sense. Hadn't I just photographed the side of the tree where the jaguar appeared? How could I have not seen it? For a moment I am uncertain from which direction it jumped. Then we notice a depression in one of the buttresses. Carefully I lift up Tass for a peek. Inside is a perfect hide-a-way for a napping jaguar.

The jaguar had been there all the time, listening to us chat and joke and take photographs on the other side of the tree. And then I had come even closer, to within a few feet of where it hid. Still the jaguar did not move until my camera began to rewind, until perhaps the strange, whirring noise finally spooked it.

As we talk, I grow more and more euphoric. I feel like I have been given a gift. Neither of us cares that we don't have a picture of the jaguar. We are

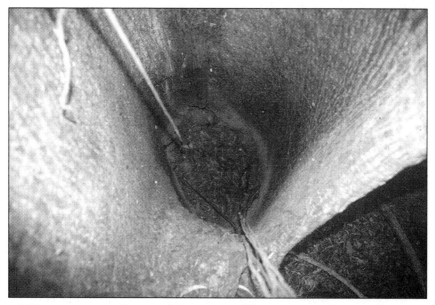

A hide-a-way down in the roots of the kapok tree, the perfect place for a napping jaguar, Rio Tambopata, Peru.

simply thrilled I am still alive. The experience was an adrenalized, mystical encounter. I stand staring at the area, going over the encounter again and again. I realize I am reluctant to leave the tree. I want to keep replaying what happened in those few, quick seconds, so vividly imprinted in my consciousness. We make some photos of the base of the tree and joke around, trying to release the lingering anxiety and emotions.

Finally we pack up our gear and begin the four-hour hike back to camp. The air is thick with the smell of the rainforest and full of the sounds of insects and birds. The sweat drips down our backs as we hike through the womblike heat and humidity. Tomorrow we will boat down the Rio Tambopata to Puerto Maldonado to begin the series of flights that will take us back to Quito and then home.

I feel ecstatic and incredibly alive. I am still somewhat in shock that I am walking down the trail, that I am not lying dead, bleeding on the jungle floor.

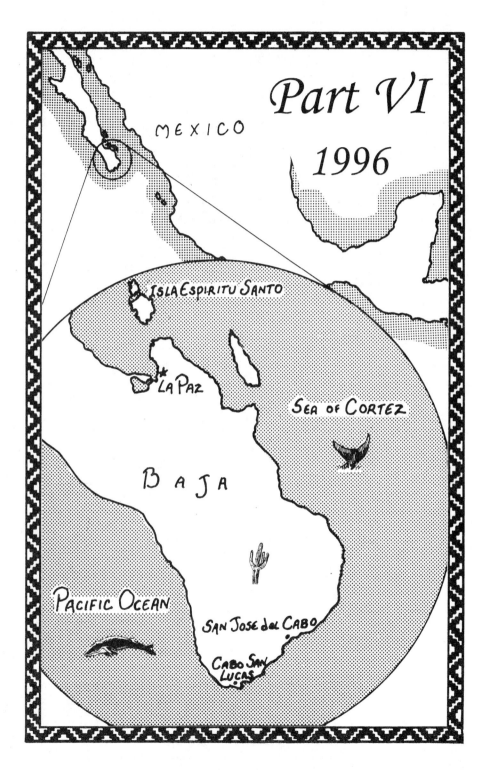

27

Baja Bob and the Whales

In 1994 during our winter slide show tour, we meet Bob mountain biking in California. We stop at a scenic overlook together, and as we chat, we discover we have mutual friends. Bob invites us to his house for supper.

Bob spends part of each winter monitoring and studying whales in Baja, Mexico. He regales us with great stories. Because we give educational programs in schools, Bob extends an invitation to meet in Baja "sometime."

We return to California the following year, and meet Bob one night for Thai food. He again invites us to Baja. This time we make tentative plans to meet a year later.

"Chances are I'll be there in early February," he says, flipping the pages of his calendar back and forth. He doesn't set an exact date. Bob isn't sure about his schedule. We mark out ten days on our calendar, and during the next year talk with Bob only briefly.

"Bring a tent and camping gear for sleeping on the beach. We never know where we'll be next," Bob says over the phone. "We follow the whales."

In the second phone call he suggests we bring one of our slide programs. "You could do a few evening programs at an upscale hotel in exchange for lodging. Bring some nice clothes." The only other information Bob gives us is the name of a restaurant where we are to rendezvous, and the name of a waitress he knows.

We land in San Jose del Cabo and arrive at the restaurant in the evening. The waitress tells us Bob isn't expected until the following night. She doesn't know the directions to the villa where Bob is staying, but says it is somewhere down the coast.

The next morning we eat *huevos ahogados*, poached eggs, which are interestingly translated as "drowned eggs" on the street-side cafe menu. We decide to spend the day snorkeling and trying out the underwater camera gear we have brought, which we have never used. We borrowed a underwater housing which fits over an A2 camera body. A friend has also loaned us a much smaller underwater Nikonos. To be safe, we test everything first in the fresh water of a sidewalk fountain, then jump on a bus to the beach.

After a day of snorkeling, we hitch a ride back to town with a retired couple from the U.S. When they discover we flew here and simply walked down the street to find a hotel they are stunned.

"You came down here without a hotel reservation?" They shake their heads in amazement. "Aren't you the adventuresome couple!" We smile and laugh. In town we develop the print film we shot underwater at a one hour photo lab. Everything looks great from both cameras. Now all we need is to find Bob, who does not show up that evening.

The next morning we are able to send Bob a radio phone message. Since we don't know how long it might take until he gets the message, we pack up for another day of snorkeling. The moment we step out of the hotel onto the sidewalk, a large brown van screeches to a stop in the street before us. Instantly the passenger door flies open and there is Bob, behind the wheel.

"Taxi?" he asks with a deadpan nonchalance.

"What are they at?" Bob asks without taking his eyes off the ocean horizon. I glance at my wrist watch, which is in stop-watch mode.

"Four-ten," I reply, and quickly look back to the ocean. Four minutes and ten seconds.

The pod of humpback whales we are tracking has been surfacing every six to eight minutes for the last three-and-a-half hours. They are traveling at four knots and have made a large arc out in the Pacific. Now they head back east, toward the Baja coast.

We each scan our own section of ocean. We also take occasional quick peeks into one another's territory, just to be sure no one screws up and misses a sighting. Staring out into the endless ocean looking for a spout or flukes is an exhaustive strain on the eyes. We never know when the whales will change breathing patterns or directions, and come up someplace completely unexpected. Or simply disappear.

"Five-forty-five. Getting ready to come up," I announce.

Bob stands up and glances around, then alters our direction slightly, using a stretch of shoreline eight miles away as a bearing. For the last hour the whales have been swimming straight toward that far landmark.

My neck and shoulders ache from days of being hammered and pounded by the thrashing of our small zodiac in the rough chop of the windblown ocean. I drop my chin to my chest for a moment to ease the strain in my neck, and stare at my lap.

"See any whales down there?" Tass jibes.

I jerk my head up, but she has already turned her head back to scan her own territory, and is thereby beyond reproach.

"Seven-twenty," I reply, trying to change the subject.

We start guessing where they might come up, trying to figure how two passing marlin fishing boats will effect the whales' direction.

"They may not be able to hear us," Bob explains. Our small four-cycle Honda motor is much quieter and less polluting than conventional two-cycle outboard motors.

"They may come up right next to us. Or under us!" he adds, with a trace of concern.

Suddenly the water breaks forty feet off our starboard side. The humpbacks' white pectoral fins are clearly visible just below the surface: a shimmering flash of white with beautiful light green highlights. The four whales take a breath.

We veer in a little closer.

The colors of the pectoral fins flash again, slightly ahead of us now. Bob gently increases our speed. The juvenile breaks the surface again, exhales, breathes back in, and drops below the surface. No tail—a good sign.

When humpbacks want to dive deep, they compress their hinged ribs, squeezing and compacting their enormous lungs, radically changing the buoyancy of their bodies. By lifting their two-ton tails out of the water they

Following and monitoring humpback whales, Baja, Mexico.

point their noses downward, and basically drop into the ocean. The humpback's dive is not propelled by swimming downward, but by using its vast weight and sudden change in buoyancy to rapidly sink in the water. When it approaches the desired depth, the whale simply spreads out its huge pectoral fins like wings and levels off far below the surface.

Again the whales all take a breath. But this time all four lift their tails and sink out of sight.

Finding whales is not always easy. Most days include hours of scanning the ocean with no whales in sight. One particularly uneventful day we spend the entire morning searching fruitlessly, and by mid-afternoon we are tired and grumpy. The ocean is remarkably still and calm with no wind. The sun beats down on us until finally we simply begin nodding off. We stretch out lazily and nap on the pontoons.

After half an hour we slip into the water for a wake up dive. Bob shows us how to enter the water quietly without splashing or slapping the surface, which any nearby whales might interpret as a sign of aggression. We drop into an immense blue void, the clearest water we have seen so far on our trip. Shafts of sunlight stream all around us and down into the depths below. For a second we experience vertigo, as if we are hanging, suspended in space.

Bob swims down to about fifty feet, descending amazingly fast, following the beams of sunlight down. I try to dive down to him, but at about thirty-five feet I lose my nerve. Bob hangs calmly in the void of blue below me, signaling me to keep coming. But the last fifteen feet seem impossibly far. I didn't clear my mask properly as I descended, and now my head throbs as the mask pushes into my face from the pressure. My lungs feel like my last breath was minutes, not just seconds ago.

I bail and head for the surface, which looks like a cloud of shimmering mercury a long way away. Instead of slowly rising back to the surface, I kick like mad, using up even more oxygen. I break the surface, gasping for air. But after only a few breaths, I begin chastising myself for failing to reach Bob. Why didn't I just relax and hold my breath another ten seconds? What is the big deal? I have snorkeled down to forty feet in the Caribbean. Perhaps I am just a little out of practice.

I try again, but do even worse. Psyched out, I decide not to press the issue and instead circle lazily, twenty feet deep, listening for whales. Finally I climb back into the boat, just as Bob begins another deep dive. We watch over the side of the boat as Bob slowly recedes and fades out of sight, sinking deep into the ocean.

More than a minute goes by until we see Bob again, breaking the surface. He immediately grabs the boat, sputtering, and quickly pulls himself aboard.

"I was about thirty feet down, taking a crap, and a huge marlin swam past and scared the hell out of me!" Bob exclaims. He glances over his shoulder as if the marlin might jump in the boat. "What does a person have to do to get some privacy around here!" he yells, looking down into the ocean below.

We are stunned that Bob would hold his breath and dive thirty feet to go to the bathroom. He notices the surprise on our faces, and explains that marlins are very territorial, and could easily rip a person wide open with just one slash of their spear-like noses.

We listen politely and then ask about the "taking a crap" part of the story. Bob doesn't understand our amazement.

"Where else are you going to go when you are out swimming around in the middle of the ocean?"

Bob can free-dive to one hundred and twenty feet. He can dive to sixty feet and stay at that level for sixty seconds. At seventy feet he can stay down for fifty seconds, eighty feet for forty seconds, ninety feet for thirty seconds, one hundred feet for twenty seconds, one hundred and ten feet for ten seconds, and at one hundred and twenty feet he basically dives straight down and comes back up.

When he was first learning to snorkel, Bob did not worry about diving deep, but focused on being relaxed and calm, especially when coming back up. He found that taking a huge breath before each dive is not as important as some might think. The air already in your blood is what is important. To learn about proper breathing, Bob worked with a number of people, including opera instructors, ventriloquists, and synchronized swimming coaches. He believes snorkeling is not about learning to hold the breath, but learning breath control.

In the evening I stand in the shower, check my watch, and don't take another breath for sixty seconds. When I do breathe again I try to stay relaxed and calm. Thirty seconds later I stop breathing again for another minute. It doesn't seem that difficult in the shower.

We spend days following the whales in the Zodiac and have plenty of close encounters on the surface. But today is the day for which we have been waiting: the water is crystal clear, and Bob has his underwater video camera ready for action.

We bob miles from shore, straddling the rubber pontoon on our Zodiac; each of us has one leg in the boat and the other in the water—masks on, snorkels in our mouths—watching a pod of enormous adult humpbacks coming toward us. The whales snort and exhale loudly as they leisurely break the surface, one hundred feet away. No tails. They are heading straight toward a point just thirty feet to our right. Hearts racing, we wait for the sign from Bob to quietly slip into the water.

No one is sure why whales breach, yet everyone agrees it is spectacular to see! Baja, Mexico.

Full of adrenaline, yet trying to remain calm so we won't use up excess oxygen, we swim underwater so our fins don't splash on the surface, and head as fast as possible in the direction of the whales. Surrounded by an immense blue void, shafts of sunlight stream past us down into the blue-black water below. We look from side to side as we swim, not sure where the whales might suddenly materialize, hoping they don't dive deep and pass by unseen in the darkness far below.

Then we see something. At first it looks like the billowing sails of a ghost ship, coming out of the mist. With giant graceful arcs the shimmering sails take form in the undulating light. They are the white, barnacle-encrusted pectoral fins of the whales. Seconds later their darker bodies take form out of the blue water—two giant locomotives, just at the edge of visibility. Ethereal whales. They are diving and quickly disappear into the void below.

I sense movement and look up to one side. I need another breath but now there are two more whales, even closer beside me, but moving away quickly—if only I had spotted them a few moments earlier; they must have passed less than twenty feet behind me! My lungs scream for air as I hang suspended thirty feet down, making photos. As the second group of whales fades into the void, I bolt for the surface, heedless of Bob's instructions about calmly coming up for air. As I near the surface, I notice the whales are turning and coming back into view. But now all I can think of is air.

My head breaks the surface, and I gasp for two quick breaths. Neither Tass nor Bob is in sight. I remember Bob's warning to always check on the unanchored Zodiac, to make sure a sudden wind or current isn't moving it away. I spot it and instantly dive again, fearful the whales will have disappeared. As I descend, my lungs and brain are already screaming for air. Instead, I kick like crazy and swim toward the hazy image of the whales. They seem to hang suspended in space, lolling around. As I swim toward them, they slowly come back into focus. The juvenile hangs under its mother's belly, playfully rubbing against her pectoral fin.

I desperately want to dive closer, but I even more desperately need air. As I head for the surface, the two whales begin to swim off to my side. Their huge pectoral fins move as if in slow motion, yet they quickly disappear from sight.

For ten minutes I continue to play a game of hide-and-seek, with the whales always swimming just beyond my vision and then circling back lazily, taunting me to swim harder and harder to catch up.

After numerous long dives, I break the surface, gasping for air. Between ocean swells I see Tass, smiling and waving, a hundred feet away. She disappears back under the water. I also take another breath and dive again. Perhaps the whales will turn toward me one more time.

Back home, on the phone, I tell Bob I am writing a story about our adventure with the whales.

"Leave me out of it!" he moans painfully. "Change my name to Bob or something. And don't go telling everyone exactly where the whales are either!" he adds.

"Last month I was working in another area and there were people all over the whales. Two and three boats at a time. Remind people they need to use common sense if they spot a whale. Give the whale plenty of room! Whales deserve their own place on the planet as much as you or I!"

Okay, Bob!

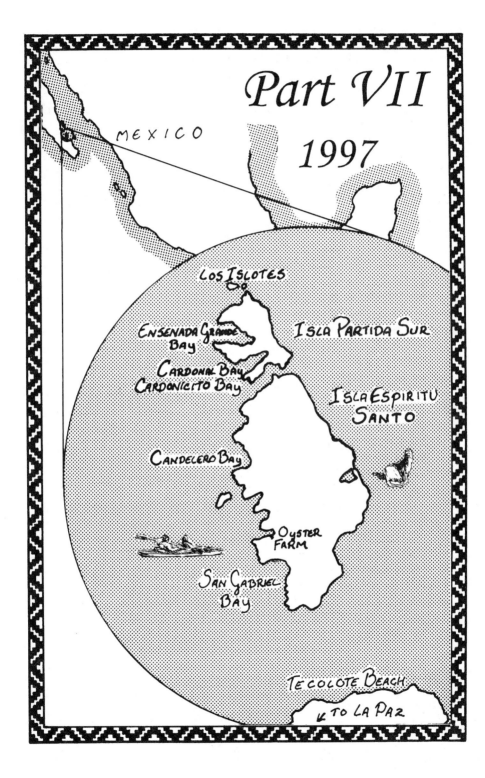

Part VII
1997

MEXICO

LOS ISLOTES

ENSENADA GRANDE
Bay

ISLA PARTIDA SUR

CARDONAL BAY
CARDONICITO BAY

ISLA ESPIRITU
SANTO

CANDELERO BAY

OYSTER
FARM

SAN GABRIEL
BAY

TECOLOTE BEACH

TO LA PAZ

28

Isla Espiritu Santo

In February we take a break from our slide show tour, store our van at the Sacramento airport, and take a night flight to Los Angeles. We arrive after midnight and have just a few hours until our flight to Baja early in the morning—just enough time to pick up a kayak.

The first two taxis we try to wave down are already full. A limousine driver walks up and asks where we are going. He is at the end of his shift, ready to go home, and our destination is along the way.

"Company policy prohibits me from soliciting rides," he tells us with a smile. "However, if you were to ask for a lift and suggest a price, I might accept the offer, at a cheaper rate than the taxis!"

"How much is a taxi to Manhattan Beach?" I ask.

"About twenty to twenty-five dollars," he replies.

"Okay, will you give us a ride for fifteen dollars?" I say.

"Let's go!" he smiles and opens the door for us. This is our first limousine ride—an auspicious way to start our trip! Unfortunately our friends Rich and Rena are sleeping and don't see us arrive at their front door in grand style! We wake them up, and Rich leads us out to his garage, where he hands us two large bags containing their collapsible folding Klepper kayak. We go through more piles of kayak gear, and Rich lends us a few other miscellaneous items we might need, like paddles. We stay up late talking. Rich and Rena, who traveled with us in the Galapagos and who we met again in the Andes, have arrived home just today from a two-month journey in India. At four a.m. Rich gives us a ride back to the airport with the kayak.

We fly to La Paz, Baja, where we are to meet our friends Janet and Pat. They were married last year, and for a honeymoon kayaked forty days on the Sea of Cortez. Near the end of their journey they spent three days on Isla Espiritu Santo, which became their favorite spot of the trip. Our plan now is to spend two weeks kayaking and exploring the island.

"We don't have a schedule!" Pat jokes. "And we are going to stick to it!"

He and Janet arrive a day late in La Paz. The extra day has been a welcome break for Tass and me, a chance to organize gear, hang out at La Terreza, a wonderful sidewalk cafe with large, comfortable wooden chairs, eat fresh fish fried in garlic, and watch the sunset colors through the silhouette of palm trees lining the sidewalk along the bay.

The next morning we pile as much of our luggage into Janet and Pat's already overloaded van as possible, strap the kayak and extra bags onto the roof, and drive the short distance to Tecolote Beach. Although Espiritu Santo is only four miles off the Baja coast, fast changing weather and major tidal currents can make the crossing a bit of an adventure. The weather has been unsettled the last four days; winds in the bay have created large, breaking waves. Our plan is to get our boats loaded and ready, and the moment the weather clears, which most likely will be tomorrow at dawn, we will take off.

I have assembled Rich's Kleeper kayak only twice: the first time five years ago; the second time two years ago. One bag contains about twenty-five wooden parts to assemble into the frame. The other bag contains the canvas hull. By squinting and closely examining each wooden part, I can just make out a faded F or B marking: Front and Back. Rich believes the terms bow and stern are too confusing. Amazingly, within an hour I get the boat together. We carry it to the water's edge and begin loading up.

Unlike backpacking or bike touring, where baggage weight is a crucial issue, kayak touring is more like car camping. We bring all sorts of luxuries: camp chairs, lantern, coffee press; Tass brings two large stuff sacks of books. Plus we have two weeks' worth of food, along with twenty gallons of drinking water in one and two-gallon mylar bags. Figuring how to efficiently pack the inside of the boat and then solidly tie everything else onto the top of the hull takes until mid-afternoon. As we pack, the clouds disperse and the winds die down.

We talk with Ramon, the owner of a restaurant on the beach. Although it is late in the day, he advises us to leave now. The tide is right, and lately the winds have been worse in the morning. We tell him our itinerary. If the weather is too severe for a kayak crossing on the day we are to return from the island, he will come across in a boat and pick us up to insure we don't get stranded and miss our flight home. A great back-up.

The wind continues to die as we shove off. The water calms surprisingly quickly. Since it will be dark in less than three hours, we set a strong, steady pace paddling. Major new muscle usage. The afternoon light is warm and pleasant. The water is so smooth we can almost see reflections on the surface. In two hours we are on the southern end of Isla Espiritu Santo, Holy Spirit Island.

Tass paddling in the front of our two-person folding kayak,
Isla Espiritu Santo, Baja, Mexico.

The first Indians began settling in Baja from California ten thousand years ago. Archeological evidence suggests things were relatively peaceful until the arrival of the Spanish. In 1532, the conquistador Cortes sent two ships to explore the western coast of Mexico looking for trade routes, gold, and pearls. Both ships disappeared. In 1534 Cortez sent out another two ships. The crew on one ship mutinied and sailed into a large bay in southern Baja, where most of them were killed by Indians. The few survivors escaped with a number of beautiful black pearls. The pearls were later shown to Cortez, who was impressed enough to lead an expedition to the bay himself, this time with soldiers and horses. He founded a colony named Santa Cruz, and stayed a year before returning to the mainland. The remaining colonists suffered two years with food and water shortages and attacks by Indians before they also returned to the "mainland" (at the time it was believed that Baja was an island).

Sixty years later another colony was established in the bay, this time named La Paz, The Peace, because the Indians were now friendly. The town was abandoned after the stockade and most of the buildings were destroyed by fire. In the early 1600s settlers again returned in search of pearls, using Indian divers who reportedly suffered great headaches diving so deep, quitting only when blood ran from their ears. After fifty years the Indians revolted. One story claims the revolt was crushed when a Spanish admiral invited the Indian leaders to supper and shot them with a cannon! More revolts followed.

A Mission was started, but most of the Indians soon died from diseases brought by the conquerors. The Mission was abandoned. In 1811 another settlement was established, and La Paz grew slowly to become the capital of Baja California Sur, the southern half of the peninsula. By the early 1900s pearls had become so rare that an oyster farm was built on Espiritu Santo. In 1940 disease killed the oysters, and the farm was abandoned. Today no permanent houses exist on the island.

That doesn't mean, however, that no one else is here. Because of its beauty and close proximity to La Paz, Espiritu Santo receives a steady stream of visitors. Large commercial fishing boats ply the channel and bays around the coast and the island, along with smaller *panga* boats owned by individuals and families who fish with hand nets, sometimes staying in fish camps and temporary shelters on the island.

Tourist sport fishing and diving boats also frequent the waters. A few commercial groups also run kayak trips on the island, mostly bringing their clients across the main channel in powerboats, then letting everyone kayak a day or two along the island bays before motoring back to La Paz.

The next morning the sea is rough. We shrug our shoulders and decide just to stay where we are camped on the southern most beach. The total distance we are going to kayak could easily be done in five days. We have two weeks, which will ensure plenty of time for snorkeling, hiking, and also relaxing, with a number of days when we don't have to move camp.

Espiritu Santo is a desert of cactus and barren rock surrounded by beautiful bays along the western coast, with numerous small sandy beaches. Tass and I hike up the largest hill near our beach. By Baja standards this year has been a wet winter, and the desert is now in bloom. Most of the plants and shrubs are flowering, and the ground is covered with a carpet of tiny flowers. Many of the cacti have huge, beautiful blossoms. On top of the mountain we have a sweeping view of the southern end of the island. We can see the next two bays along the west coast; the water is a beautiful, rich turquoise blue. Espiritu Santo actually is two islands divided by a narrow channel, with a number of smaller islets. Our plan is to circumnavigate the whole group in a clockwise direction.

The next day is clear and beautiful, so we kayak and explore the first bay around the western coast. While kayaking to the second bay, we spot small Pacific manta rays, about three or four feet across, which occasionally leap completely out of the water. They also swim lazily, not far from us, just below the surface, with the tips of their wings poking above into the air. This habit of hanging out near the surface on calm, sunny days has unfortunately cost many of the rays their lives, as they are easily speared by fisherman. Later we meet three men who have been harpooning rays. They get four large fillets

Enormous cliffs show layers of sandstone and volcanic rock,
Isla Espiritu Santo, Baja, Mexico.

from each ray and sell the meat to Japanese buyers. We also pass large shrimp boats. One has "House of the Rising Sun" and other rock classics blasting over a surprisingly distortion-free PA system which we can hear from a mile away. At the second bay, out of range of the music, we snorkel for an hour before setting up camp.

The following morning is Tass's forty-fifth birthday. I make a leisurely breakfast of pancakes, fresh papaya, and coffee. We kayak a few hours and stop again to snorkel in a small cove. Later we spot a fish camp and paddle over to buy fresh fish. At El Candelero beach we poach the fish and have couscous with spicy Thai green curry and vegetables. Janet produces a lemon birthday cake with a single, fat, red candle perched on top, and we sing "Happy Birthday" to Tass.

The next day we paddle across the narrow channel to the northern section of the island, Isla Partida Sur. We paddle against a strong headwind into El Cardonal, a two-mile deep bay with two beaches at the end. The first beach has a long, shallow approach. The tide is going out, and we are afraid our kayaks might be stranded in the mud if we get too close, so we anchor them knee deep in the still, calm water and walk the last few hundred yards through the tidal flats to the beach to eat lunch and take a hike to admire the cactus.

When we return to the bay, the tide has receded enough that our boats are now in ankle-deep water, too shallow for us to paddle. We walk the boats a few hundred yards to deeper water, and then paddle to the second beach to camp, away from the mangroves and mosquitoes.

Fierce winds blow all night, but the weather is calm by morning. Still the sea is very rough, with six-foot swells in the main channel. We tentatively paddle out into the fray, just to get a little experience in rougher water. Although the swells seem large, they are not breaking, and we paddle straight into them. However, we are unable to go around the point on the north end of the island due to the waves. Even the *pangas* and larger boats are not going around the point.

We camp at Ensenada Grande. A few shrimp boats and yachts are anchored out in the deep water of the bay, but we have the small beach on the north side of the bay all to ourselves. Two couples come ashore in dinghies, just to look around for a few minutes. Both are on multi-year sailing trips. The second couple has a somoyed, which with its thick, long white fur is not exactly a dog fit for the tropics, or for a sailboat. It has a doggie harness so it can't fall overboard. They give the dog tranquilizers during long crossings in rough seas so it doesn't get scared or seasick, which we find touching and hysterical.

We have great snorkeling in the protected water along the cliffs of the bay. Everywhere we see little underwater canyons and caves in the rock. We spot a panamic green moray eel, and Guinea fowl puffers in both their black and white polka-dot stage and their bright yellow stage.

The next morning during breakfast a hummingbird flies around camp for nearly fifteen minutes. With a buzz it zips up to Pat, who is wearing a flower print shirt, and checks him out at very close range before flying over to investigate our kayaks, then our tents, then us again.

As we eat, the waves on the ocean subside. We jump in our kayaks and paddle for Los Islotes, a group of small islands on the northern edge of Isla Partida. Our route takes us along beautiful, tall sea cliffs with caves and a few arches. We pass a small islet, a fantastically sculpted rock formation just a few hundred yards long, jutting out of the ocean. The top is completely covered with nesting sea birds.

Further along is Los Islotes, where even larger rock formations protrud out of the ocean. The islands are a nature sanctuary, with blue-footed boobies, frigate birds, pelicans, and gulls. The small rocky point between the islands is covered with sea lions. A few large bulls lie onshore, and a few more patrol the water next to the rocks.

Since Los Islotes is a nature reserve, it is illegal to set foot on the islands or to anchor a boat within seventy-five feet of shore. Three dive boats are anchored the proscribed distance from the island, near the sea lion colony. We ask permission to tie our kayaks to one of the boats, and change into our wetsuits. The water is a chilly fifty-eight degrees. Even with wetsuits, we can stay in only about thirty minutes per dive. Although we can't swim up to the sea lion colony,

Sea lions sleeping on the rocks, Los Islotes, Baja, Mexico.

the sea lions can swim out to investigate us, which they do immediately.

Underwater the sea lions are unbelievably fast and fluid. They twist and turn their bodies in all directions. Just when we think they are really spinning fast, they increase their speed and rocket off in a different direction and out of sight. Seconds later they come zooming back into view, heading straight at us, and only at the last second do they turn and avoid a high-impact collision.

After five minutes, many of the juvenile males swim at us rather aggressively, with mouths open, exposing large yellow teeth. Snapper sea lions. It is obvious they also play rough with each other; most have numerous nicks and cuts, probably from sparring and play-fighting.

We swim in circles, trying to keep an eye on the feisty young male sea lions. Suddenly out of the corner of our eyes we spot one of the big bulls patrolling past. No playful antics for this big bruiser. He is all business as he solemnly glides between us and shore, checking out any competition for his territory. His body language says, "Cross this line and you'll be crab food, buddy!" We head the other direction.

On our second dive, we spot a bull with a huge gash across the back of his neck, an ugly gaping wound. At the end of the dive a younger sea lion bites Tass on the knee, not hard enough to draw blood, but hard enough to rip her wetsuit and leave a nasty bruise. I decide I have had enough. But Tass is still gung-ho for a third dive. After warming up, she slips back into the ocean for another round with the snappers.

Following our adventure with the sea lions, Tass keeps terrorizing me with her sea lion imitation—she repeatedly comes at me unexpectedly, mouth open wide and teeth barred, inches from my face—when I jump back in surprise she breaks out laughing!

I am easy to sneak up on. A week ago, on my very first dive on the island, my right ear plugged. My second time snorkeling my left ear plugged. Annoyingly, they have stayed plugged.

"This is the quietest and most peaceful island I have ever been on!" I joke to Tass. I can hear the others talk only if I am close. The sound of my own body fills my ears. I hear each breath loudly, and the sound of my throat when I swallow. When I talk I hear the vibration of my voice in my bones and muscles. Very strange.

We stay a couple of days at Ensenada Grande, enjoying our camp just a few feet above the high-tide line. I love the smell of the sea. Although we take salt water baths, our bodies feel neither crusty nor itchy. Actually our skin feels kind of good and well-cleaned. Tass looks beautiful with her hair all bleached out and skin so tan. We are Beach Boy and Ocean Girl.

Perhaps it is the relaxed pace of our journey, with plenty of time for sitting and thinking; perhaps it is the island itself, Isla Espiritu Santo, Holy Spirit Island, that is conducive to contemplation. For whatever reason, I find myself

Sea lions play fighting with Tass (her hand is on the left), Los Islotes, Baja, Mexico.

often introspectively sitting on the beach looking out at the turquoise water or up on the cliffs covered with cactus.

Who am I? Who do I want to be? What do I want to be doing in five years? In twenty years?

I think about my work, my writing, the slide programs we do. I seem destined to be capturing and sharing moments in time. I love my life, but sometimes I wonder if my life has an adequate spiritual quest, or am I just caught up in the day to day adventure of travel, the excitement of discovery and exploration?

"If you are going to do something, do it right!" my dad constantly told me while I was growing up. I think my own guiding statement might be, "If you are going to do something, do it to the extreme!" Right or wrong, my inclination in life has been to become totally obsessed by whatever I am doing.

I take a break from my contemplation to snorkel in the bay. The reef environment is incredibly diverse and fascinating. The shimmering sunlight breaks into myriad patterns as it passes through the rippling waves above. I am surrounded by purple sea fans, orange sea fans, brown, red, and orange coral. Territorial neon-blue-speckled damsel fish dart towards me, while bright red hawkfish hide out in the branches of coral, and schools of yellow stripped sergeant majors swim past. Below me slow-moving, box-shaped balloon fish, covered with thick spikes, glide by, and regal coronet fish—three feet long yet only as big around as my wrist with a snout the thickness of my thumb—swim stately along. Guinea fowl puffers, black with tiny white dots, use just their tiny dorsal fins to motor around like sideways helicopters.

I feel so incredibly fortunate to be here! I wonder if God gets the kind of joy and pleasure from creation that I do in times like this; does God also marvel at the diversity of life, the colors and patterns of nature? Suddenly it occurs to me that perhaps God is viewing and enjoying creation through me, at this moment, through my excitement and delight. Is that why life is evolving, so God can continue to create, and then share the process with what has been created?

And is that why **we** create things, why people become artists, writers, musicians, builders, inventors and engineers—to share that same joy, fascination, and wonderment in making something new? Or why we teach: to share knowledge, to share in the wonder of the world around us?

In the afternoon the wind dies, and suddenly the beach is filled with sandflies. We pack up and paddle by ourselves an hour southward to El Cardonal bay. Pat and Janet will join us later in the evening. The bays along the western side of the island have been so beautiful that we have changed our route plans. Instead of circumnavigating the island and paddling back along the east coast, which is mostly sea cliffs, we are going to return along the western side. That way we can revisit a few of our favorite bays, and also see a few we didn't explore.

We practice various paddling strokes and also take time to sit quietly and just glide and float, checking out the rock formations on the sea cliffs, the pelicans on shore, a large osprey nest in a Cordon cactus, and the fish swimming in the crystal clear water under our kayak. No one else is in El Cardonal bay; both beaches are deserted.

The next day we hike across the island to look out east over the Sea of Cortez. Later we paddle to Cardonicito. The beach is very small; our campsite is only a few inches above the high tide line. As we eat supper we constantly monitor the rhythmic advance of the tide. Because the beach is so shallow,

More types of cactus are found in Baja than almost any other place in the world, Isla Espiritu Santo, Mexico.

when the ocean rises just a few inches, the water comes fifteen feet closer. The sound of the surge with each rush of water is like a rainmaker. Very hypnotic.

According to our tide charts, high tide tonight is at 10:45 p.m. As we lie in bed in the tent, the sound of rushing water repeatedly causes us to worry that the tent is about to be immersed. Periodically we stop reading to peer out the tent with our headlamps, making sure the water is not at the tent door. Camping on the edge. High tide passes. The waves reach just a few feet from our tent. No more worries until tomorrow's high tide late in the morning. And tomorrow night we will go through the whole process again!

Our trip is nearing its finish, time to get back to the southern end of Espiritu Santo. We wake up to strong winds out of the southwest. Headwinds. As we eat breakfast we look down the bay to the ocean with our binoculars. Sailboats pass, sails down, relying on their motors to move to another anchorage, rocking and rolling wildly in the waves. As we pack up, the winds remain high. I climb a hill for a photograph of the bay and camp, while Janet gives Tass a neck message. At noon the waves finally begin to die down. We still have ample time for the eight-mile paddle ahead of us.

Janet and Pat kayak with us out of the bay and then head east through Los Partida channel to explore a sea cave on the northeastern side of Espiritu Santo. They will stay here a few more days, then return to the mainland and do another two-week kayak trip further north before returning home. We say goodbye, then paddle westward across the channel, occasionally glancing over our shoulders and watching our friends paddle off in the other direction. Although we are sad to part, it is a good confidence builder for us to be alone.

The waves continue to calm as we paddle. Still I can barely talk Tass into taking a quick lunch break. She is in full Destination Mode. She wants to paddle hard and fast to San Gabriel bay before the weather changes. We see a large school of dolphins, half a mile away, but they don't come any closer. Just before we get to San Gabriel, the wind suddenly picks up, just enough to give us a little scare, along with a hard workout at the end.

We are alone on San Gabriel beach: no moon, just the brightest stars imaginable. The milky way runs across the sky. Orion, Gemini, Canus Major look down at us, camped in the sand, gentle waves lapping nearby on the shore. My left ear has unplugged. Sound is wonderful.

The next morning the sky is filled with big clouds. The wind blows fiercely. Today we are supposed to cross the channel back to the mainland. We console ourselves that the weather seems to change every four hours. Surely it will continue in that pattern. But the clouds above look like nothing we have seen so far on our trip. We smell rain. Moments later a rainbow appears off to the west. Through our binoculars we scan the ocean, which is covered in whitecaps. Not a single boat has passed up or down the coast.

Two hours later the sky clears, but the winds continue; the sea is extremely rough. Giant clouds quickly reform in the west, and soon the entire sky is overcast. The wind continues, now extremely warm and muggy. A few boats go by, pitching violently, throwing huge sprays of foam over the bows.

"Most kayak accidents occur when people are trying to meet schedules and go out when they should just stay on the beach." Janet's parting words of advice ring in our ears. We remember our first kayak trip, five years ago, when Janet, Tass, and I spent a week paddling around the islands of Bajia de Los Angeles, further north on the Sea of Cortez. At the end of the trip the weather turned bad. We waited a day for better conditions, but the weather stayed nasty. We ran low on water and time, so we paddled back to the mainland in extremely rough seas. The journey was an epic. Despite being blown off course by the wind and currents, we made it across. The next day a group of kayakers with much more experience came to visit us. They were camped on the mainland beach waiting for the weather to clear before crossing to the islands. Hearing that we made the crossing in such conditions, they wanted to meet us, thinking we must be very good kayakers. We laughed, somewhat lamely, and explained it was just the opposite. Apparently we didn't have enough sense to know any better. Through sheer luck, we made it across without capsizing and getting blown out to sea.

Now we hope to use a bit more caution. We have no choice but to stay put. Our campsite is protected from the wind; we decide to read behind our tent where the sun is warm. But we are both restless. We really want to cross under our own power. Just five minutes pass and Tass picks up the binoculars to again scan the ocean.

"Just checking the wind," she explains.

"How does it look?" I ask.

"Hard to say. The wind may be lying down slightly. The whitecaps don't look quite so big. Still, I suppose it is better to err on the side of caution."

I nod in agreement and go back to my book. Minutes later, I pick up the binoculars.

"I definitely think the sea is calming a little." Still, the waves are as large as anything we have paddled, and the roughest part of the crossing is out of sight around a far point. Again we agree it is just too rough. Regardless, we are still unable to relax and read. Within five minutes Tass is again looking through the binoculars.

"I think the whitecaps are smaller," she reports. Since we can't seem to relax and read, we decide to pack up the tent and paddle out to the edge of the bay for a closer look at the ocean. If things look good, we will paddle to the far point to check out the channel back to the mainland. "We can always come back and camp here if things look bad," we reassure each other, not wanting to do anything foolish.

The weather looks the same as we paddle across the bay, the waves slightly larger than we expected. But as we get out along the coast, the waves become big, round, rolling swells that lift the kayak as they pass. Exciting, but not threatening. We continue paddling to the point.

The view of the ocean is hard to read low in a kayak. The waves ahead appear nothing worse than what we have already done. Still, starting across the channel is a big commitment. We have both seen how quickly the weather can change. We sit in the Kleeper for fifteen minutes, bobbing up and down, watching the ocean, trying to decide what to do.

"Lets go for it!" we both say at last, and begin paddling. Now it is serious business. We work to find a steady rhythm that carries us at top speed, yet at a pace we can maintain for two hours. We concentrate on pulling the paddle back with one hand while pushing it forward with the other, keeping our shoulders dropped and relaxed, our waists tilted slightly forward, turning the trunks of our bodies to give power to each stroke.

Occasionally big waves break over the boat, interrupting our cadence and almost bringing us to a stop. Other waves drop off in front of us, allowing the kayak to surf down the back sides, giving us little boosts of speed.

"Is that the ferry?" Tass asks with a sudden panic in her voice. Off in the distance I see an enormous ship coming out of La Paz bay. The channel we are crossing is a shipping lane for a daily ferry to the western coast of Mexico. The responsibility of avoiding collisions rests solely on the kayaker. Ships are too big to stop or to steer around small boats. Chances are the crew would never even see a kayak in the water. It is up to the kayaker to keep a safe distance, and the axiom is: Never ever try to outpaddle or outrun a ship.

As the ship comes out of the bay it turns toward us, into the channel. Tass flips out. She is convinced we are sitting ducks. But I think the angle of the ship sets a course that will make the ferry pass behind us through the channel. I try to reason with Tass, but I can tell she is not convinced, and she is getting more and more panicked.

"Remember in elementary school when we had to take Iowa tests?" I finally ask. "There was a section called Spatial Relations. I always got a 100% in Spatial Relations. Not 90%, not 95%, but 100%! Trust me, the ship is not coming straight at us. Even if we just sit here the ship will miss us by five hundred yards, maybe a bit more!"

Still, neither of us wants to remain here like a sitting duck in the shipping lane. We keep paddling, and Tass relaxes slightly. True to my word, the ferry passes behind us with plenty of room to spare. Still, Tass refuses to let up our pace. She won't let me stop to eat a Powerbar, or let me take time to pump out the water we are sitting in, water that leaked through our spray skirts during a number of dunkings by larger breaking waves. We keep paddling even as we near the mainland. Tass is unstoppable, and does not slow down or miss a paddle stroke. Only when the front of the kayak gently comes to rest on the sand of Tecolote beach, does she put down her paddle and relax.

Glossary

cabana—small bamboo or reed-walled hut with a thatched roof

campesino—peasant or farmer

Casa de Huespedes—cheap hotel or boarding house

cenote—cavern or well holding water in limestone rock

chicha—alcoholic drink often made from fermented corn

chicle—gum from a tree

cocha—an oxbow lake formed when a river changes its course and leaves a curved, isolated lake

colpa—an exposed riverbank where birds come to eat the clay soil, probably to help digestion of acidic rainforest plants

comedor—restaurant

confradia—traditional Mayan social and religious body which oversees village activity

contras—Nicaraguan guerillas sponsored by the U.S. both openly and covertly during the Reagan administration

cordillera—mountain range

cordobas—Nicaraguan currency

empanadas—vegetable or meat pies

finca—farm, ranch or plantation

frijoles—beans

gauchos—cowboy

gringo—foreigner (female—*gringa*)

hospadaje—cheap hotel or boarding house

huipils—handmade blouse, usually with colorful embroidery

isla—island

jugoria—a shop selling fresh fruit drinks

Latino—of Hispanic or Latin culture

matadores—bull fighters

milpa—maize, corn

mercado—market

mestizo—people of mixed Spanish and Indian ancestory

motocar—three-wheeled motorcycle taxi

oriente—the lowland rainforest of eastern Ecuador

palapa—small building with thatched roof, sometimes built on poles
without walls

panaderia—bakery

paleta—fruit juice popsicles

panga—small wooden boat

Quetzal—Guatemalan currency equal to $1 U.S.; bird in the trogon family
with two-foot long tail feathers

paramo—high altitude grass and shrubland with specialized plant life to
withstand extreme ultra-violtet radiation near the equator

pension—cheap hotel or boarding house

peso—Mexican currency

refugio—climbers hut or shelter in high mountains

shaman—traditional medicine man, healer or medium

senora—title of respect for a married woman

serape—shawl or blanket

si—yes

stela—carved statue (plural—*stelae*)

sucre—Ecuadorean currency, in 1981 30 *sucres* equal $1 U.S., in 1992
1230 *sucres* equal $1 U.S, in 1994 2300 *sucres* equal $1 U.S.

sol—Peruvian currency (plural—*soles*), in 1994 just over two *soles*
equal $1 U.S.

tienda—small restaurant

tortas—round cake

zocalo—town square or park

IMAGES OF THE WORLD

Slide Presentations and Assembly Programs

Programs are available for elementary and middle schools, high schools and colleges. We also have adult presentations for workshops, seminars, teacher in-service training, civic and community events.

* **World Bicycle Tour** A multi-cultural, two-year bicycle trip around the world. Interesting customs and traditions along with humor and adventure make this four-continent tour our most popular program. Students are challenged and inspired to pursue their own dreams.

* **Volcanoes of the World** Smoking volcanoes, lava, eruptions—this program is continually updated with new travels. From the Ring of Fire to the Sahara Desert, see how volcanic activity has shaped the earth.

* **Rainforests and Mayan Ruins** Bicycling through Central America to see cloud forests, rain forests, nesting sea turtles and the winter migration of monarch butterflies. We visit magnificent Mayan pyramids, colorful highland markets and stay with descendants of Aztecs in Mexico.

* **Africa** Tracking lions on foot, bicycling across the Kalahari Desert, visiting isolated Himba villages while four-wheeling northern Namibia—we see African wildlife, and experience African culture, up close and personal.

For information, please contact:

Images of the World
P.O. Box 2103
Rapid City, South Dakota 57709-2103

www.imagesoftheworld.com

Books from
IMAGES OF THE WORLD

The Road of Dreams $14.95
    A Two-Year Bicycling and Hiking Adventure
    Around the World
Andes to the Amazon $15.95
    Seven Journeys in Mexico, Central and
    South America

Shipping (first book) $3.00
    (each additional book) $1.00

Please send check or money order to:

IMAGES OF THE WORLD
P.O. Box 2103
Rapid City, South Dakota 57709-2103

Visit our web site at www.imagesoftheworld.com

4⁰⁰

Gen 082314 TØ